Harré and his Critics

Harré and his Critics

Essays in honour of Rom Harré with his commentary on them

Edited by Roy Bhaskar

Basil Blackwell

Copyright © Basil Blackwell 1990

First published 1990

Basil Blackwell Ltd
108 Cowley Road, Oxford, OX4 1JF, UK

Basil Blackwell, Inc.
3 Cambridge Center
Cambridge, Massachusetts 02142, USA

British Library Cataloguing in Publication Data

A CIP catalogue recorded for this book is available from the British Library.

Library of Congress Cataloging in Publication Data

Harré and his critics: essays in honour of Rom Harré with his commentary on
    them/edited by Roy Bhaskar.
        p.   cm.
    Includes bibliographical references.
    ISBN 0-631-15868-5
    1. Science – Philosophy.   2. Social psychology –
Philosophy.   3. Realism.   4. Harré, Rom.   I. Harré, Rom.   II. Bhaskar, Roy,
1944–
Q175.H3274   1990
501 – dc20   89-29755
                                                                                CIP

Typeset in 10 on 12 pt Garamond by Best-set Typesetter Ltd
Printed in Great Britain

Contents

vi *Contents*

Acknowledgements

My first debt is to Hettie Harré who was in, together with Philip Carpenter of Basil Blackwell and me, on the instigation of this project at a secret meeting in the Cowley Road. She was to prove an invaluable source of information and ideas. My second debt is to Rom himself who agreed to write a commentary on the papers initially presented to him on his sixtieth birthday in December 1987. My next debt is to the contributors for the punctuality of their papers and their salience for Rom's thought. I would also like to acknowledge and apologize to a large number of people who would have liked to have contributed to this *Festschrift* but whom we were – for reasons of space – unable to invite. This is itself testimony to the affection and esteem with which Rom is held in the academic world. I would also like to thank Philip Carpenter for his constant editorial encouragement and continuous support throughout the project. Thanks are also due to Andrew McNeillie of Basil Blackwell for expertly shepherding this book through the production process, to Ruth Kimber and (initially) Sonia Argyle for copy-editing, to William Outhwaite for reading the original drafts of the papers, to Sue Kelly for much appreciated secretarial assistance and to Hilary Wainwright for her encouragement.

Roy Bhaskar, Linacre College,
Oxford, January 1990

The editor and publishers wish to thank the following for permission to use copyright material: American Psychology Association for figure 9.1 from P. M. Bentler and G. Speckart, 'Models of attitude-behavior relations', *Psychology Review*, 86 (1979), 455. Copyright © 1979 by American Psychology Association; The Guildford Press for figure 9.2 from R. Buck, *The Communication of Emotion*, 1984; Penguin Books Ltd. for figure 3 from Michael Argyle, *The Psychology of Interpersonal Behaviour*, Fourth Edition, figure 5.1. Copyright © 1967, 1972, 1978, 1983 by Michael Argyle.

Introduction: Realism and Human Being

Roy Bhaskar

I

Rom Harré was born in Apiti, New Zealand, on 18 December 1927. At the age of twenty-five Rom resigned from his post teaching Applied Mathematics and Physics at King's College, Auckland and in October 1953 he and Hettie Harré set forth for Oxford. They spent a year en route in Lahore, where Rom taught Applied Mathematics at Government College, University of Punjab, and arrived in Oxford in October 1954. Rom's University Supervisor was John Austin and his College Tutor was Peter Strawson. In June 1956 he obtained his B. Phil. in Philosophy. He then spent a year as a Research Fellow in Birmingham University and three years as a Lecturer at Leicester, before returning to Oxford, on Friedrich Waismann's death, as University Lecturer in Philosophy of Science – a position he still holds. He was a founder member of Linacre College in 1962. Since 1974 he has regularly taught a summer course at SUNY, Binghamton, where he is Adjunct Professor of Social and Behavioral Sciences. Rom has spent a part of each vacation since the late 1960s writing at Casa Harré in Alicante, Spain.

Rom has been a prolific writer, a dedicated and inspiring teacher and a tireless and resourceful peripatetic lecturer over the years. Since his *Brief Introduction to Symbolic Logic*[1] he has authored, co-authored, edited or co-edited well over forty books. Of most importance in this corpus are probably the strand defending and developing a realist approach to science – stretching from *Theories and Things*[2] through *The Principles of Scientific Thinking* (henceforth PST)[3] and, with E. H. Madden, *Causal Powers* (henceforth CP)[4] to *Varieties of Realism* (henceforth VR)[5] – and the strand explicating the philosophical foundations and presuppositions of (social) psychology – from, with P. F. Secord, *The Explanation of Social Behaviour* (henceforth ESB)[6] to the trilogy: *Social Being* (henceforth SB),[7] *Personal Being* (henceforth PB)[8] and *Physical Being*.[9] But Rom has also written on such subjects as nicknames,[10] soccer violence[11] and primate behaviour.[12]

If there is a common factor present in all Rom's work it must be his passion for knowledge and, in particular, scientific knowledge; and more generally his enthusiasm for that grand *conversation* which, on his view, constitutes the stuff of social life. Rom is one of the world's collective workers and many of the contributors to this *Festschrift* have collaborated with him on one or more joint projects. The essays collected in this volume were all originally presented to him at a party at Linacre College, Oxford, generously hosted by Basil Blackwell, on the occasion of his sixtieth birthday. They testify to the breadth and depth of Rom's interests. Most have been revised somewhat for publication. We are fortunate to be able to include in this volume Rom's own commentary on them, a commentary that represents a short, book-length resumé of the current state of his own philosophical thought.

The essays presented to Rom fall naturally into three groups. Those by Marjorie Grene, Peter Manicas, John Lucas, Jerry Aronson and Roy Harris take up themes relevant to Rom's espousal of what he characterizes in his commentary, 'Exploring the Human Umwelt' (henceforth EHU), as a strong policy and a weak or qualified convergent realism (see pp. 297, 320 below). These essays comprise Part I of this book. The essays in Part II – by John Roche, Robert Weingard and Michael Redhead – broach topics in the philosophy of physics. The remainder of the essays – by Michael Argyle, Tony Crowle, Paul Secord, Jean-Pierre de Waele, John Shotter, Charles Smith, Jose Luis Rodriguez Lopez, Uffe Jensen, David Taylor and Vernon Reynolds – all raise issues in the philosophy of the human, or more generally life, sciences. All the essays, save for those by Weingard, Redhead and de Waele, will be accessible to the interested general lay reader as well as to the specialist. Those three should be skipped by the uninitiated, at least at a first reading, and will not be discussed further in this introduction.[13]

I now want to describe briefly, with the exceptions already mentioned, the contents of Parts I–III of this book, before contextualizing the latest phase of Rom Harré's thought as presented in his concluding commentary.

II

In VR Rom Harré distinguishes three ontological realms, defining a scientific methodology appropriate to each. There is Realm 1, the realm of objects of direct, common sense-experience; Realm 2, the realm of objects of possible, technologically aided, sense-experience; and Realm 3, the realm of objects beyond all possible experience (see VR, pp. 72–5 and passim). The chapters by Marjorie Grene and Peter Manicas each raise matters germane to Harré's account of Realm 1. Grene contrasts Gibsonian direct perception, which both she and Harré favour, to the more classical, indirect representationalist account offered by philosophical psychologists like Gregory. On the traditional view perception is mediated by sensation or sense-data and constitutes in a sense a hypothesis about the world. On the Gibsonian ecological account perception is an immediate activity of the organism in its niche, environment or (to use the term Rom Harré appropriates from von Uexkull (p. 301)) 'Umwelt'. Peter Manicas, following a hermeneutically sensitive reconstruction of William James' thought, raises the question of why Harré thinks he needs the non-corrigible veridical perception apparently afforded by Gibsonian theory as an epistemic base for knowledge (pp. 35–6). For Manicas one can have direct access to objects with only historically shifting and judgementally corrigible conceptions of them, ontological realism plus epistemological relativism, science without a 'base'.[14]

John Lucas embarks on a rich investigation of the concepts of reason and reality, together with others of their kin, and their contrasts – as, in his words, a prolegomenon to their varieties. He argues that 'reality is thing-like not in being non-personal, but in not being confined to any one particular person, and therefore being the same for all persons, and in this sense omni-personal and universal' (p. 44). Thus 'the real shape of an object [such as a penny] is not the shape that is not apparent to anyone, but what is invariant as between all apparent shapes' (p. 44). Of course, it does not follow from this that the real shape is not the shape which it possesses and would [continue to] possess, even if there were no one to know it, and *a fortiori* no appearances. In his response to Lucas, Harré takes up Lucas's point, saying that 'science is a set of techniques, both cognitive and practical, for arriving at beliefs about what is invariant for all views' – but he then goes on to make the unfortunate – because idealist – slide: 'but there is nothing which is independent of any view' (p. 307).

Jerry Aronson's paper consists in an argument for extending the policy realism which Harré defends in VR, on which it is rational to mount searches for the referents of (plausibly) hypothesized entities, to a form of convergent realism, on which the successive members of a theory family converge or approximate closer to the truth. Aronson points out that the correlation of predictive success and material adequacy can be experimentally confirmed for Realm 1 (as in the case of the car mechanic who systematically isolates, gradually homing in on, the fault) and contends that overall convergent realism can be justified – provided only we accept a principle of epistemic invariance (p. 54). This says that the epistemological situation remains the same irrespective of which (anyway historically variable) realm the entities concerned are in. In effect, Aronson's principle claims that how the world is not affected by the contingency of whether we happen to be in a position to observe it or not.

Roy Harris sets up and attacks a thesis that he dubs 'surrogationalism'. This consists in the idea that words have a meaning by 'standing for' entities, etc. and that these entities are given independently of those words (p. 64). Harris sees this thesis as central to the self-image of science as the 'accommodation of language to the causal structures of the world' (p. 85) and as extending from Plato to contemporary realism. In his reply to Harris, Harré makes it clear that he rejects the second tenet of surrogationalism: 'entities are never given' – though they may exist – 'independently of words, concepts, procedures and practices' (p. 321). He also usefully distinguishes two species of essentialism. One, linguistic essentialism, that there is something which a word *really* means, he rejects. The other, material essentialism, that each kind of material being has a constituent structure causally responsible for its manifest properties, he accepts – at least for 'some restricted domains such as inorganic chemistry' (p. 323). This allows Harré to reconcile the historical continuity of use of words like 'copper' and 'poliomyelitis' with discontinuity in (and discovery of) our knowledge of structure.

John Roche furnishes a fascinating catalogue of unclarified concepts, distinctions, gambits and techniques from nineteenth- and twentieth-century physics. Of particular importance on Roche's list to Harré is the distinction between descriptive or representational and auxiliary mathematics, or rather uses of mathematics, in physics. In the representational as distinct from the auxiliary use of mathematics every concept employed in the physical analysis of a natural phenomenon has a physical meaning. For both Roche and Harré confusion of these modes of reasoning is a source of much philosophical error in physics or its meta-theory.

Moving on to philosophical controversies in the domain of the human sciences, Michael Argyle considers the contribution of cognitive social posychology to the analysis of social interaction. He examines a number of models, ranging from stimulus–response behaviouristics to the 'coordinated interaction model' (CIM), which Argyle regards as 'very much in line' with Harré's ethogenics and symbolic interactionism, 'except that it is supported by detailed empirical research and makes a number of specific predictions concerning practical problems' (p. 148). For Argyle all his models have applications, but it is CIM that he thinks most useful for analysing characteristically social or other-oriented behaviour. This is to be seen 'like two people cooperating to produce a joint outcome'. 'Building a house, sawing a tree, dancing and sexual intercourse are models for social behaviour in general' (p. 149).

Tony Crowle starts by reminding us that in ESB Harré and Secord urged us to take agents' own accounts seriously. In an ingenious paper, Crowle argues that one type of informant's report which, at least when uttered by deviants, is routinely dismissed as evasive or misleading, namely 'I don't know why I did it' [IDKWIDI], 'may well be true and therefore ... should be taken seriously' (p. 154). Positing a total attack and a total defence variable, such that when the former is greater than the latter the individual is, so to say, 'primed' for deviance (p. 160), Crowle shows that if saying why an agent did what s/he did implies assigning weights to a large number of variables then 'there are many possible different patterns that lead to the conclusion that the doer cannot in truth say why he did what he did' (p. 163); and that 'at least some of the persons who offer reasons why they did what they did (particularly those who offer different reasons at different times) ought to be saying IDKWIDI, but instead are [merely] offering a story that seems appropriate to them in their circumstances' (p. 163).

In a wide-ranging survey, Paul Secord considers the gradual shift from 'subject' to 'person' perspectives and their current uneasy mix in social psychological research. On the subject paradigm, people are treated as passive outcomes of antecedent forces – as, in effect, in Garfinkel's words, 'judgemental dopes'. On the person paradigm, they are viewed as intentional, self-initiating and self-monitoring, imaginative agents, who are morally responsible for their actions. Reviewing the Milgram and dissonance experimental research, Secord comes to the conclusion that 'in designing experiments, it is best to assume that participants will behave like persons unless they are explicitly prevented from doing so' (p. 176). Secord identifies the *social constitution* of action as a central unifying idea in recent critiques of orthodox positivistic social psychology. But he warns that social psychologists, like psychologists in general, have typically focused on the individual and 'inner' at the expense of the social and 'outer' facets of human life. This is a critique of individualism which Harré trenchantly takes up in section III of his commentary.

John Shotter explores the apparent tension between the 'tendencies to naturalism occasioned by [Harré's] realist stance' and 'the anti-naturalistic tendencies occasioned by his [recent "social constructionist"] concern ... with the intricate workings of moral orders in the structuring of people's social activities' (p. 206). Adopting Vygotsky and Wittgenstein as his mentors, like the later Harré from the time of at least PB (1983) on, Shotter argues that an ontology apposite for social life is much fuzzier, more open-ended, less determinate, more negotiated and morally charged than the Harré of ESB – with his emphasis on individuals as powerful particulars and action as in accordance with (virtually) fully specifiable rules – would allow. It seems that there has been a definite shift (or, as Smith might say, 'drift' (p. 225)) in Harré's thought here.

As Rom Harré puts it in EHU:

> The conceptual framework developed by Shotter, Secord, myself and others was, so to say, crying out to be applied . . . It seemed to me that there were, in principle, three ways in which one lived as a human being. One had a *social mode of being* defined through one's relations to others in all sorts of joint activities. Then one had a *personal mode of being* defined through one's relation to oneself, through which one existed for oneself as an individual. Finally one had a *physical or material mode of being* defined by one's relationship, as embodied, to the material world and to others as embodied beings. *(p. 353 below)*

These three modes of being identify, of course, the subject-matter of Harré's metapsychological trilogy. Harré recapitulates the central theme of SB in his commentary in the following terms:

> It seems to me that every human action has to be considered as having two aspects. There is its contribution to the moral career of the actor (and, in strongly collectivist societies, that of his or her relevant group). This is the expressive aspect. But there is also its contribution to the maintenance of life itself. This is the practical aspect. There is a dialectic, but not of the sort Marx supposed. The dialectic is between the sometimes contradictory demands that the expressive and practical orders place on historically situated actors. *(p. 354)*

Charles Smith and Jose Luis Rodriguez Lopez are both concerned with the relations between the practical and the expressive orders. Smith argues, anticipating the results of his important study,[15] that auctions 'are processes not only of exchange, but also means for managing ambiguity by establishing social meanings and values' (p. 226). But although the pursuit of respect, honour and reputation, which Harré sees as the key to the expressive order, play a role in auctions, they are in themselves relatively secondary, being for the most part 'means to . . . other ends', especially the 'definition of the situation'. For it is in situations of ambiguity and uncertainty, especially over value, that auctions flourish. Rodriguez shows how when, for example, under regimes of Taylorism and Fordism, the importance of the expressive order in the work-place is denied, parallel unofficial structures tend to emerge. He analyses the process of collective bargaining in the Spanish Telephone Company in dramaturgical terms and considers how strikes, for instance, can be understood as pressing claims for honour and dignity and wider social ends as well as financial gain and material security. Finally, he looks at changes in the work ethic in the

Spanish telephone industry (*espíritu telefónico*) following recent declines in the authority of the Church, Army and the family, the ideological pillars of Francoism.

In a sensitive paper, Uffe Jensen argues that Dennet's fashionable theory that we create ourselves by writing or telling our self-history (or auto-biography) cannot sustain the distinction between the writing self who is a victim of self-deception and the one who is not. Jensen contends that Harré's more elaborate theory, pivoting on the transcendental unity of consciousness and agency as well as autobiography and on the phe-nomenon of psychological symbiosis, also fails on this count. However, implicit in symbiosis is a moral principle – of interpersonal responsibility – which can be articulated and lived in our lives more or less adequately and fully. Jensen concludes that 'all selves, i.e. all beings who have appropriated the principles of point-of-view, agency and *interpersonal responsibility* and who in symbiotic processes have been supplied with necessary social capacities, are real' (p. 270). But some selves are more real, i.e. less self-deceived, than others.

The final two chapters of Part III move on to the domain of our physical or material mode of (social) being. In a striking essay, David Taylor shows how certain sicknesses, real and somatic in their effect but 'of the imagination' in their aetiology, must be seen as aspects of a defence mechanism 'which from one perspective we call hysteria but from another perspective we understand as belief, and from another, as magic' (p. 274). The stunned stupor and frenzy shown in battle hysteria are responses to events in which the traditional textbook responses of flight and fight are unavailable. Taylor suggests a biological and evolutionary value for the mechanism (pp. 280–1) and poignantly documents some of its contem-porary human effects. Vernon Reynolds explores the extent to which we are like and unlike our primate ancestors and the extent to which the 'anthropomorphic model of man' (ESB, chapter 5) can be used to make sense of their behaviour. Reynolds concludes that 'however we differ from apes in our use of language and tradition, and our cultural self-construction, we probably have more in common with them than we care to admit. And if, one day, monkeys start to study us, they may well have less difficulty than we do in acknowledging the extent of our common kinship' (pp. 293–4).

III

I now want very briefly to contextualize Part IV of this book. In three works of the early–mid-seventies there is no doubt that Rom Harré, with his collaborators, helped to break the mould of orthodox philosophy of science and social psychology. These works were PST, CP and ESB.

What was Harré's 'Copernican Revolution' in the philosophy of science? It was 'to see the traditional view that the deductive system of laws is the heart of a theory, and an associated picture of the mechanisms and permanent objects are but a heuristic device, turned upside down. It is to see the model as essential and the achievement of the deductive system among the laws as a desirable heuristic device' (PST p. 2; cf. also ibid., pp. 15, 46–7). Others – Popper, Kuhn, Lakatos and Feyerabend, most notably – had critiqued the *monistic* theory of scientific development explicit or implicit in the orthodox schema. Harré, together with Scriven, Polanyi, Toulmin, Hanson and Hesse, played a key role in undermining the associated *deductivist* theory of scientific structure. This theory was rooted firmly in the Humean theory of causal laws, and *Causal Powers* was a brilliant invective against it. But the Humean theory of causal laws formed the lynchpin for a whole galaxy of theories – from the Popper–Hempel theory of explanation and Nagel's theory of reduction to inductivist and fallibilist criteria of (dis)confirmation and rationality – and problems too – from the problem of induction and the paradoxes of confirmation to the problem of subjective conditionals and that of distinguishing a necessary from a merely accidental sequence of events.[16] Harré's was, I think, the decisive voice in undermining the idea of the *sufficiency* of Humean, Popperian, Hempelian criteria. What I tried to do in *A Realist Theory of Science* was to complete the attack by undermining the idea of their *necessity* as well – a point Harré had questioned, but not systematically thematized.[17]

Now Harré's Copernican Revolution – his inversion of the standard relationship between deductive skeleton and animating model – could be given a Kantian or a Copernican interpretation. In so far as the emphasis was on the model being imposed on the phenomena by man, it veered in a Kantian direction; in so far as the emphasis was on the model putatively designating something real, the mechanism generating the phenomena, it veered in a Copernican direction. Formally, these two positions can be reconciled in the idea of scientific progress occurring by means of a dialectic in which plausible models are subsequently (directly or indirectly) empirically checked out for the reality of their designata,[18] which then become the phenomena to be explained, and so on. Moreover, it is easy to show that, without a Copernican explication, the Kantian move was vulnerable to empiricist counter-attack.[19] Be that as it may, I think that Harré's work remains poised, on a knife-edge, between transcendental idealism and transcendental realism, pulled now by the parsimony of the former (Kant, Wittgenstein, Bohr), tempted then by the permissiveness of the latter. I cannot defend my suspicion here; but it is worth remarking that, if it is right, this may be not only a source of weakness, but of strength.

It gives Harré's work a kind of concrete rootedness in the phenomena of the day,[20] which a realism of greater metaphysical consistency might well lack.[21]

'For scientific purposes, treat people as if they were human beings,' enjoined ESB (p. 84). This was the basis of what Harré and Secord called 'the open souls doctrine': 'in order to treat people as if they were human beings it must be possible to accept their commentaries upon their actions as authentic, though revisable, reports of phenomena, subject to empirical criticism' (ESB, p. 101). Social science, including psychology, must incorporate what I subsequently called a 'contingently critical hermeneutics'[22] or what Giddens referred to as a 'double hermeneutic'.[23] Human beings are not, of course, the only social phenomena; and the existence of unacknowledged conditions, unintended consequences, unconscious motivation and tacit skills all place limits on what social actors may know about what they do in or in virtue of their activity.[24] But *The Explanation of Social Behaviour* did as much as any one book to make human scientists aware that hermeneutics is a necessary, if not a sufficient, condition for any knowledge of the human world, and thus, at a remove, for any human knowledge at all.

IV

The way in which Harré himself exploited the possibilities opened up by the breakthroughs of the seventies is best seen in VR, SB and PB. These systematic books form the background to EHU. In EHU Harré is at his most Kantian: Gibson, Bohr, Wittgenstein, Vygotsky, von Uexkull, Fleck form the parameters of the work. There are echoes too of the thought of two other philosophers much influenced by Kant: Gaston Bachelard and Jürgen Habermas. For Harré, 'before the proposition is the "scientific act", a purposeful intervention in a natural system, guided by theory and assessed by reference to criteria of practical success or failure' (p. 303). Moreover, 'the current properties of the world, the "total" world, which ground the dispositions we ascribe as affordances, can never become available to us independently of the apparatus that we have the ingenuity and the technical skills to construct. "The limitations of my equipment are the limits of my world"' (p. 302). For Bachelard, in science 'above the subject, beyond the immediate object ... is the project'.[25] 'Science *realises* its objects without ever finding them already in existence'.[26] 'The true scientific phenomenology is essentially a phenomeno-technics. It instructs itself by what is constructs.... Science raises up a world no longer by a magical force immanent in reality, but rather by a rational force immanent to the mind'.[27] 'Experimental conditions are the same as preconditions of experimentation'.[28] The affinity between Harré and Habermas is even clearer. Harré's duality between the expressive and the practical orders (reaffirmed at p. 354 below) finds its counterpart in Habermas's duality between lifeworld and system.[29] Harré's dictum that 'so far as anyone has ever been able to ascertain there are only two human realities: physiology and discourse (conversation) – the former an individual phenomenon, the latter collective' (p. 345) – is reflected in Habermas's Vichian remark: 'what raises us out of nature is the only thing whose nature we can know: language.'[30]

The structure of Harré's argument for realism in EHU is three-fold:

1. What we can know [in science] is limited to the human Umwelt, our historically changing – generally enlarging – environment (p. 301), as technological advance enables us to access more of the totality of what there is [in the world].
2. What we can know must be seen [in philosophy] as the products of an interaction between a noumenal reality (unknowable to us) and the apparatus and techniques of observation devised by human beings (see p. 309).
3. We know [in philosophy] that such a [noumenal] reality exists independently of us because the world which we do experience and manipulate (our Umwelt) is only so far malleable to our wishes and interests (see p. 350).

From a Copernican standpoint this is a very limited ontological realism. From such a standpoint what we need to know is whether the kinds of entity and their ways of acting (expressed in laws) – ways of acting which we may call mechanisms – which the sciences have hitherto identified, exist and operate in the manner we have identified *outside and independently* of their identification, the conditions of their identification and human being(s). It is this stronger form of realism, sustaining the *transfactuality* of the objects of our knowledge, which I have argued for elsewhere.[31]

In addition to the pragmatic policy realism he advocated in VR, Harré is now willing to accept a qualified form of convergent realism on two grounds (see p. 318 below). The first is this: 'One would surely be irrational to spend huge sums of money and invest a great deal of time in looking for something one did not believe probably did exist. So to proceed with a policy realist project if one had in mind only the even-handed possibility of getting either determinate answer [yes or no] would be irrational. Looking for something as a project has the pragmatic presupposition that one is more likely to find it than not' (p. 318). It is this pragmatic presupposition that grounds research on coherent and plausible rather than incoherent and implausible research programmes. The second argument turns on the existence of a revisability hierarchy, defined by the sequence: attribute, kind, category (pp. 318–9; cf. also pp. 315–6). Only rarely will we be forced to revise metaphysical category, but the fact that this may always – and sometimes does – happen means that the argument for Harré's convergent realism remains only 'weak' (pp. 297, 319).

The primary human reality in the social world is the conversation (pp. 341, 350–1), accessible to us as our social Umwelten and only so far amenable to the influence of individual speakers (p. 351). It is not quite clear how this striking image, present from PB on, relates to the duality, in SB, between the practical and expressive orders. Is the practical order too constituted through conversation? Or does this depend on the workings of individual physiology? – surely an implausible position, but physiology is pronounced the only other human reality (p. 345). And how in any case does the conversation have material effects, if norms cannot be causes (p. 342)? Further, 'if what causes movements and noises to occur and what endows them with this or that significance' are treated as totally separate questions (p. 351), is Harré not going to end up with a social/material dichotomy as unacceptable as Kant's split between the moral and the phenomenal realms? Perhaps *Physical Being* will resolve these questions with a robust account of materially embodied agency. But for the moment they remain troubling ones.

EHU, like much of Harré's recent work, is infused with great moral feeling. This can be illustrated with a final quote from Rom's commentary with which I pass the conversation on to the contributors and Rom himself:

> [In *Social Being*] I argued that in a social world in which the primary social and psychological reality was conversation, there was necessarily one in-alienable right that must accrue to any creature that purports to be a human being, a member of some society or other. That right is the right to be heard as a contributor to the conversation that defines the social moiety to which the putative social actor belongs. The pathological condition of a psychologi-cally symbiotic dyad occurs when the senior member persistently talks for the junior member, performing all the necessary psychological acts to sustain an appearance of personhood vicariously. On our view this is a kind of ultimate evil. *(p. 359)*

Roy Bhaskar
Linacre College, Oxford

NOTES

1   Anarkali Press, Lahore, 1954.
2   Sheed & Ward, London, 1961.
3   Macmillan, London, 1970.
4   Blackwell, Oxford, 1975.
5   Blackwell, Oxford, 1986.
6   Blackwell, Oxford, 1972.
7   Blackwell, Oxford, 1979.
8   Blackwell, Oxford, 1983.
9   Blackwell, Oxford, forthcoming.
10 With J. Morgan and C. O'Neill, Routledge, London, 1977.
11 *The Rules of Disorder*, with P. Marsh and E. Rosser, Routledge, 1977.
12 *The Meaning of Primate Signals*, edited with V. Reynolds, Cambridge University Press, Cambridge, 1983.
13 Good background reading for these chapters are contained in VR, chapter 6, and G. Nerlich, *The Shape of Space*, Cambridge University Press, Cambridge, 1976; VR, Part 5, and M. Redhead, *Incompleteness, Non-Locality and Realism*, Cambridge University Press, Cambridge, 1987; and N. Rescher, *Dialectics*, State University of New York Press, Albany, 1977, and M. Kosok 'The formalisation of Hegel's dialectical logic', *Hegel*, ed. A. MacIntyre, University of Notre Dame Press, Notre Dame, 1976.
14 A position further developed in his *A History and Philosophy of the Social Sciences*, Basil Blackwell, Oxford, 1987, especially Part III.
15 *Auctions: The Social Construction of Value*, Free Press, New York, 1989.
16 For the theories, see my *A Realist Theory of Science*, 2nd edition, Harvester Press, Hassocks/Hemel Hempstead, 1978, Appendix to chapter 2; for the problems, see ibid., chapter 3, and CP, passim.
17 Cf. *A Realist Theory of Science*, pp. 164–5, n. 36.
18 See ibid., p. 145.
19 See ibid., chapter 3, section 2.
20 This is a feature shared with Kant, whose own work often reveals a similar knife-edge balance. Cf. J. Findlay, *Kant and the Transcendental Object*, Clarendon Press, Oxford, 1981, especially chapter VII.
21 For further remarks on the Copernican Revolution in the philosophy of science, see my *Reclaiming Reality*, Verso, London, 1989, chapter 9, especially p. 181.
22 See my *The Possibility of Naturalism*, 2nd edition, Harvester-Wheatsheaf, Hemel Hempstead, 1989, chapter 4, especially sections 3–5.
23 A Giddens, *New Rules of Sociological Method*, Hutchinson, London, 1976, chapter 4.
24 See my *Scientific Realism and Human Emancipation*, Verso, London, 1986, chapter 2, section 2.
25 G. Bachelard, *Le Nouvel esprit scientifique*, Presses Universitaires de France Paris, 1934, p. 11.
26 *La Formation de l'esprit scientifique*, Vrin, Paris, 1938, p. 61.

27   *Le Nouvel esprit scientifique*, p. 13.

28   Ibid., p. 9.

29   J. Habermas, *Theorie des Kommunikativen Handelns*, Suhrkamp Verlag, Frankfurt, 1981.

30   J. Habermas, *Knowledge and Human Interest*, Heinemann, London, 1972, p. 314.

31   See my *A Realist Theory of Science* and *Reclaiming Reality*, especially chapters 2–3 and 8–9.

Part I

Issues in Realist Philosophy of Science

1

Perception and Human Reality

Marjorie Grene

A priori, human reality might be best exemplified by the state of participation in the Platonic forms or the possession of Spinoza's third kind of knowledge, or what you will. In the present context, however, I presume we can take it that human reality, like the reality of other Animalia, is rooted somehow or other in the contact with our environments mediated by our perceptual systems. Taking that premise as given, therefore, I want to compare two theories of perception and their implications for our conception of human being-in-the-world. The first is traditional: what Hatfield and Epstein call 'the theory of the sensory core', deriving in its modern form from Berkeley through Helmholtz and well exemplified still, for example, in the writings of Richard Gregory (Hatfield and Epstein, 1979; Gregory, 1972, 1974). The second is the ecological theory developed by J. J. Gibson from 1950 to 1979. (I could have chosen other representatives of the tradition, particularly from the so-called 'functionalist' school, but both Gregory's facility at summarizing the standard view and the fact that there exists a clear and pithy exchange between Gregory and Gibson (in fact, between Gregory and J. J. and E. J. Gibson) from which I shall want to quote, makes my choice an obvious one.) Harré has often declared his adherence to the Gibsonian theory; and although it is possible, admittedly, to take a realist position, ontologically and epistemologically, in terms of the older view, realism certainly comes much more naturally from the Gibsonian perspective. Indeed, philosophically, that is one of the major points in its favour.

Perception, it is agreed by both camps, is our path to information about the world. How is it acquired: from what source and by what means? On the older view, the stimuli from which perception must be initiated are meaningless sensory signals which will have to be worked up, indirectly, into perceptions. The distinction between sensation and perception is fundamental and sensations are the necessary material from which perceptions are built. Sensations, moreover, are atomistic and momentary; for vision, they are identical with the famous upside-down, flat, retinal images that provide the impoverished 'pictures' out of which we have somehow to construct perceptions. Gregory writes: 'information given by eyes is only of indirect use to living creatures. To make use of it, a good deal of computing is required' (Gregory, 1974, p. 603). For Gibson, the situation is quite different. From his point of view, sensation is unimportant. Indeed, he argues, it was in asserting that point sensations are necessary to perception, 'are the basis of perception', that Berkeley went wrong and so led astray the major tradition of experimental psychology to this day (Gibson, 1969). On the contrary, as Gibson sees it, the information necessary to perception is conveyed in structures and deformations picked up by perceptual systems: in the case of vision, the eye, hand, brain, body system. As E. J. and J. J. Gibson have put it:

> In life, the sea of stimulus energy in which an observer is immersed is always an array and always a flow. The stimuli as such, the pin-pricks of light or sound or touch, do not carry information about their sources. But the invariant properties of the flowing array of stimulation do carry information. They specify the objects of the world and the layout of its surfaces. They are invariants under transformation, non-change underlying change. Note that they are not in any sense pictures or images of objects and of layouts as so many psychologists have been tempted to think. Nor are they signals from the objects and surfaces of the environment like dots and dashes in a code. They are mathematical relations in a flowing array; nothing less. *(Gibson and Gibson, 1972)*

What is presented, therefore, is relational: spatially, an array, temporally, a flow. Images are irrelevant in such presentations, nor is it a question of *re*presentation, but of a direct being-with of organism and external reality.

In the traditional model, further, the bits we start from have to be pulled together by association. Hume has given the classic account of this alleged process. On the ecological view, in contrast, the primary process involved in perceptual activity is differentiation. E. J. Gibson's work on perceptual development may be taken as definitive here (E. J. Gibson, 1969). The myth that association is the necessary forerunner of perception can at long last be forgotten: the idea that animals from butterflies to babies have built up associations from many instances before they perceive anything can be dismissed for the nonsense it patently is. Out of the infinite complexity of potentially available information, organisms can discriminate information that is species-specifically relevant to their survival in their environments. Some of this information pick-up may take place 'innately', but in many cases much is also learned, *perceptually* learned through the organism's own active exploration.

What emerges out of this contrast, unfortunately, is information in two different senses. Much of the misunderstanding of Gibson by his critics, and even by some of his alleged supporters, springs from this semantic difference. For Gregory and the majority of theoretical and experimental psychologists, information in perception is identified with the calculations of information theory and, even worse, with work in artificial intelligence. But perception is an activity of animals, which are natural entities, not artifacts, and however cunningly machines may simulate such processes, they miss, on principle, the bodily reality indispensable to it (Polanyi, 1958; Dreyfus, 1972). Gibson's 'information', in contrast, is much more biological: it is what is available to particular real organisms, squirrels, bluebirds, eels or people, in the particular real environments which permit them to be, and even define them as, the particular sorts of real organisms they are.

What, then, is perception on these two views? For Gregory – and although he puts the case more extremely than some, he is in fact echoing the standard view – perceptions are hypotheses, or even fictions. Thus he declares:

> perceptions are constructed, by complex brain processes, from fleeting fragmentary scraps of data signalled by the senses and drawn from the brain's memory banks – themselves constructions from snippets from the past. On this view, normal everyday perceptions are not selections of reality but are rather imaginative constructions – fictions – based (as indeed is science fiction also) more on the stored past than on the present. On this view all perceptions are essentially fictions: fictions based on past experience selected by present sensory data. *(Gregory, 1972)*

For Gibson, on the other hand, perceptions are explorations of an array, a process of the extraction of available information and the optimization of its pick-up. In the same exchange with Gregory already quoted, the Gibsons write:

> Perception therefore does not have to be conceived as the interpreting of messages or the learning of the so-called 'sensory code'. It is the exploring of an array, the extracting of available information, and the optimizing of its pickup. The eyes, for example, look around, focus their lenses on details of the world, and modulate the intensity of the light when the illumination is too high or too low. For listening, the head turns to equalize intensity of input to the two ears so as to point the head towards the source of sound. *(Gibson and Gibson, 1972)*

A number of crucial differences are contained in, or follow from, these contrasting definitions. On the traditional view, perception has to be mediated; for Gibson, it is direct. For the tradition, perception is sensation plus judgement, or some form of cognitive activity. There is a sharp break, therefore, between sensation and perception. Hamlyn, for instance, failing to understand the existence of any other possible view, lamented that poor Aristotle had only one word for the two processes (Hamlyn, 1961). Gibsonians, like Harré or the present writer, might rather think him fortunate. True, there are sensations, fleeting bits that can be captured perhaps by drug addicts, perhaps by experimental psychologists; but it is the full-blooded process of perception that matters in the life of organisms and its distinction from sensation, in drawing attention away from what ought to be the central subject matter of perceptual psychology, has done more harm than good. Witness the fact that perceptionists like Gregory spend infinite time in the study of illusions: the hollow face, impossible objects and such, and little in the examination of real, everyday perceptions. Gibson and his school, in contrast, are concerned with the analysis of real-life perceptual situations: driving a car, crossing a street, jumping a long jump, the early perceptions of infants, and so on.

Gregory and other traditionalists celebrate their theory as active, since passive sensations must be used as data for the active computation of the fictions that count as perceptions, and they condemn Gibson's theory as passive because it takes perception to be direct. This is a crass misunderstanding since, as we have seen, Gibson's theory stresses from the start the exploratory activity of the perceiver (Harré, 1983). It is every bit as 'active' a theory as the other, only it places the cut between direct and indirect perceptual awareness at a different place, and therefore reads differently the place of cognition in perception and the difference between different kinds of cognition. For Gregory and others, sensation is passive and non-cognitive, perception (based on unconscious inference) distinctively cognitive. For Gibson, the primary perceptual process is already cognitive, and I think one could argue, further, although this is not the place to do it, that all cognition is, in the last analysis, at least in part perceptual. For him, the break between the direct and indirect (though not between passive and active) comes at the juncture, in human perception, where words and pictures come to mediate perception.

Another contrast which I can touch on only fleetingly here, but which deserves more careful exposition, is the difference in the evolutionary premises of the two theories. Both theories are Darwinian, taking perception as the product of natural selection, through which organisms have 'learned', so to speak, phylogenetically, to adapt to the demands and opportunities of their environments. The evolutionary basis for the traditional theory, however, is externalistic and mechanistic, stressing the machine model of the organism that has always been one feature (though by no means the whole) of selection theory. And in line with its machine-minded stance, it explains the origin of sense organs and their activities in terms of classical linear causality. Gibson's theory, on the other hand, follows the richer and more adequate ecological aspect of the Darwinian tradition, seeing animals as *in* their environments, and interprets their phylogenetic as well as developmental histories in interrelational, thoroughly functional, terms.

How does human reality fare on these two theories? Basically, the traditional view suggests a phenomenalist position. We are not in a real world, but construct one out of disconnected bits and pieces. A Humean propensity to feign supports, not only human, but all animal experience. When it comes to our particular case, moreover, our artifacts, languages and other products of culture add a further dimension of artificiality to an already unreal scene. Not so much a Humean as a Hobbesian vision is suggested here. For Gibson – and for us; I may on such an occasion as this confess to preaching to the converted – to us human reality is one version of animal reality. We are, indeed, peculiarly dependent on the artifacts of culture, artifacts, in the last analysis, of our own making and whose authority we accept on our own recognizances. But culture, rather than being a mere addendum to nature, a fiction supervenient on the naturally induced fiction of perception – culture, on our reading, while expressing a need inherent in our nature, is itself a part of nature. There is no culture, and therefore no human reality, not made from natural materials and itself contained in nature, in the natural environment of mother earth on whose existence we all depend. Let Gibson speak in conclusion: the human environment, he adjures us,

is not a *new* environment – an artificial environment distinct from the natural environment – but the same old environment modified by man. It is a mistake to separate the natural from the artificial as if there were two environments; artifacts have to be manufactured from natural substances. It is also a mistake to separate the cultural environment from the natural environment, as if there were a world of mental products distinct from the world of material products. There is only one world, however diverse, and all animals live in it, although we human animals have altered it to suit ourselves. We have done so wastefully, thoughtlessly, and, if we do not mend our ways, fatally.

The fundamentals of the environment – the substances, the medium, and the surfaces – are the same for all animals. No matter how powerful men become they are not going to alter the fact of earth, air and water – the lithosphere, the atmosphere, and the hydrosphere, together with the interfaces that separate them. For terrestrial animals like us, the earth and the sky are a basic structure on which all lesser structures depend. We all fit into the substructures of the environment in various ways, for we were all, in fact, formed by them. We were created by the world we live in. *(Gibson, 1979, p. 130)*

REFERENCES

Dreyfus, H. (1972) *What Computers Can't Do: A Critique of Artificial Reason*, New York, Harper & Row.

Gibson, E. J. (1969) *Principles of Perceptual Learning and Development*, Englewood Cliffs, N.J.: Prentice Hall.

Gibson, E. J. and Gibson, J. J. (1972) *TLS*, 23 June, pp. 707–8.

Gibson, J. J. (1969) 'Transparency and occlusion, or how Bishop Berkeley went wrong in the first place', MS, Cornell Archives.

Gibson, J. J. (1979) *The Ecological Approach to Visual Perception*, New York, Houghton Mifflin.

Gregory, R. L. (1972) *TLS*, 23 June, pp. 707–8.

Gregory, R. L. (1974) 'The evolution of eyes and brains – a hen-and-egg problem'. In R. L. Gregory, *Concepts and Mechanisms of Perception*, London, Duckworth, pp. 602–13.

Hamlyn, D. W. (1961) *Sensation and Perception: A History of the Philosophy of Perception*, London: Routledge & Kegan Paul.

Harré, R. (1983) *Great Scientific Experiments*, Oxford, Oxford University Press.

Hatfield, G. C. and Epstein, W. (1979). 'The sensory core and the medieval foundations of early modern perceptual theory', *Isis* 70, pp. 363–84.

Polanyi, M. (1958) *Personal Knowledge*, London, Routledge.

2

Modest Realism, Experience and Evolution

Peter Manicas

When Rom Harré set out some twenty years ago to make a 'Copernican Revolution' in the philosophy of science, he probably did not realize that he would initiate as well an entirely fresh way to look at the history of philosophy. In 1964, when most philosophers were still firmly committed to variant forms of 'empiricism', he and Maurice Mandelbaum both published books which forced us to look again at the beginnings of early modern philosophy.[1] While everyone knows that Descartes, Leibniz, Locke and the so-called 'empiricists' were doing their thinking against the background of the revolution in modern science – were indeed part of this – Harré and Mandelbaum suggested, in different ways, that we misread them badly if we fail to grasp the *scientific* problems in terms of which their putative 'epistemologies' were composed.

In this paper, I follow in Harré's footsteps and turn my attention to Herbert Spencer and William James. I suggest that we take them seriously as psychologists, struggling against a tide to recover problems for psychology that had been appropriated by the post-modern inquiry we call 'epistemology'. I hope that this paper is not merely of historical interest, a dispute between two late nineteenth-century philosopher/psychologists. On the contrary, I want to use them as background for some current problems, but especially as counters for Harré's rich 'rationale for the natural sciences' as developed in his recent *Varieties of Realism*.

William James and the Tradition

In the remarkable final chapter of his remarkable two-volume *Principles of Psychology* (1890), James defines a project which demolishes one hundred years of debate between 'apriorists' and 'the empirical school'. He offers to 'make plain' three things:

1. That, taking the word experience as it is univerally understood, the experience of the race can no more account for our necessary or *a priori* judgments than the experience of the individual can;
2. That there is no good evidence for the belief that our instinctive reactions are fruits of our ancestors' education in the midst of the same environment, transmitted to us at birth.
3. That the features of our organic mental structure cannot be explained at all by our conscious intercourse with the outer environment, but must rather be understood as congenital variations, 'accidental' in the first instance, but then transmitted as fixed features of the race.[2]

The first claim is aimed at both 'associationist' psychology, the empiricism of Hume, Bain and Mill, and at the empiricism of Spencer, who seeing that the standard empiricist treatment would no longer suffice, amended it by adding a critical evolutionary component. Rejection of both of these alternatives, of course, put James on the side of the apriorists. As he says, 'on the whole . . . the account of which the apriorists give of the facts is that which I defend; although I should contend . . . for a naturalistic view of their cause' (ibid.). The second claim rejects, of course, Lamarckian biology, and the third, as a footnote makes clear, affirms Darwinian biology. 'Accidental', he writes, is used in the Darwinian sense, 'as belonging to a cycle of causation inaccessible to the present order of research' (ibid.).

We cannot allow the title of this chapter, 'Necessary Truths and the Effects of Experience', to throw us off. The problem James is addressing is more general than might appear. The issue is not merely 'analyticity' as contemporary writers have it, nor *a priori* judgments like '2 + 2 = 4', but the Kantian question of whether in any cognition there are necessarily *a priori* elements, features that cannot in any useful sense be learned.

James can barely take the associationist account seriously. He offers an extremely long text from Spencer in which he allows Spencer to refute this and to state his own view, a view that is both important and too often overlooked. Spencer argues that if all mental connections were the results of experience, then antecedent to experience, 'the mind is a blank'. But if so, 'whence comes the power of organizing experiences? whence arise the difference degrees of that power possessed by different races of organisms, and different individuals of the same race? . . . Why is not a horse as educable as a man?'[3]

But it is not necessary to jump to the transcendentalist (Kantian) hypothesis, which, argues Spencer, presents us with 'insurmountable difficulties'. Rather, all we need to say is that 'the ability to coordinate impressions and to perform the appropriate actions always implies the pre-existence of certain nerves arranged in a certain way'. But – and this is the critical point – these 'result from the registration of experiences continued for numberless generations'. 'The genius of instinct, the development of memory and reason out of it, and the consolidation of rational actions and inferences into instinctive ones, are alike explicable on the single principle that the cohesion between psychical states is proportionate to the frequency which the relation between the answering external phenomena has been repeated in experience.' 'In a sense, then, that there exist in the nervous system certain pre-established relations answering to relations in the environment, there is truth in the doctrine of "forms of intuition" – not the truth which its defenders suppose, but a parallel truth. Corresponding to absolute external relations, there are established in the structure of the nervous system absolute internal relations – relations that are potentially present before birth in the shape of definite nervous connections; that are antecedent to, and independent of, individual experiences.'

James calls this 'a brilliant and seductive statement', but finally, as least as he reads Spencer, it is fundamentally mistaken. Yet before I turn directly to James' criticism and alternative account, it will pay to sketch the basic assumptions of Spencer's conception of psychology.

Spencer's Transfigured Realism

Spencer was sensitive to what had become profoundly difficult epistemological problems standing in the way of a scientific psychology. First, there was the Kantian distinction between 'science' and metaphysics. For Kantian motivations, Spencer was content to accept, on Kantian grounds, 'thing-in-itself' realism, the idea that any reality lying beyond experience is unknowable. Second, there was the problem of causality. Here, as an 'empiricist', he sided with Hume. The idea that causes were 'productive' of their affects and necessary was a metaphysical idea. Third, there was the mind/body problem. On this, he anticipated later empiricisms – Mach's and Carnap's.[4]

Spencer distinguished between physiology, 'aestho-physiology' and psychology. Physiology had to exclude *all* reference to consciousness: 'Physiology is an objective science; and is limited to such data as can be reached by observations made on sensible objects.' 'It cannot . . . properly appropriate subjective data; or data wholly inaccessible to external observations.'[5] On the other hand, *versus* the mentalism of associationist psychology, inquiry could not be restricted to the laws of the successive states of the mind since one needed to show how these were connected with changes in the central nervous system and then in the environment.

Another kind of inquiry, called by him 'aestho-physiology', was required. It had as its aim the discovery of the connections between the data of consciousness and objective phenomena *within* the organism, data generated by physiology. Eventually, then, these had to be connected with what goes on in the environment *outside* the organism. This then would comprise psychology, a science which *depends* upon both physiology *and* aestho-physiology:

> that which distinguishes Psychology from the sciences on which it rests, is, that each of its propositions takes account both of the connected internal phenomena and of the connected external phenomena to which they refer. ... [A psychological proposition] is the connection between these two connections. . . . The distinction may be best explained in symbols. Suppose that A and B are two related manifestations in the environment – say, the colour and taste of a fruit; then so long as we contemplate their relation by itself, or as associated with other external phenomena, we are occupied with a portion of physical science. Now suppose that *a* and *b* are the sensations produced in the organism by this peculiar light which the fruit reflects and by the chemical reaction of its juice on the palate; then, so long as we study the action of the light on the retina and optic nerves, and consider how the juice sets up in other centres a nervous change known as sweetness, we are occupied with facts belong to the sciences of Physiology and Aestho-physiology. But we pass into the domain of Psychology the moment we inquire how there comes to exist within the organism a relation between *a* and *b* that in some way or other corresponds to the relation between A and B. Psychology is exclusively concerned with this connection between (A B) and (*a b*) – has to investigate its nature, its origin, its meaning. *(Spencer, I: 132–3)*

Having lost his epistemological innocence, Spencer was profoundly sensitive to what were by then obvious objections to his programme. He observed that 'each individual is absolutely incapable of knowing any feelings but his own', that accordingly it is only through one's 'reasonings' that one can infer that with the actions of other bodies 'there go internal states of consciousness like those accompanying [the] external actions of one's own body'; that even if this is true – as he does not seriously doubt – it is still not experientially demonstrable that 'what he knows under its subjective aspect as feeling, is, under its objective aspect nervous action'; and, finally, having 'learnt at second hand, though the remotely-inferential interpretation of verbal signs', that others 'like himself' have a nervous system, he further infers that he has a nervous system like those others and reasons finally that his own sensations are due to 'disturbances which the outer world sets up at the periphery'. This whole business only begins to suggest 'the remotely-inferential character of the belief that feeling and nervous action are correlated' (I: 98–100). But however indirect and 'remotely inferential', 'the evidence of this connection is so large in amount, presents such a congruity under so great a variety of circumstances, and is so continually confirmed by the correct anticipations to which it leads, that we can entertain nothing more than a theoretical doubt of its truth' (ibid.).

This means, however, that we must hold to a 'transfigured realism'. This 'simply asserts objective existence as separate from and independent of subjective existence' (Spencer, II: 494). This is not 'the Realism of common life – the realism of the child or the rustic', since critically, no relation in consciousness can 'resemble, or be in any way akin, to its source beyond consciousness' (ibid; see also *The Relativity of Relations between Feelings* I, ch. IV). While 'internal feeling' – the phenomenon of consciousness – 'habitually depends upon external agent, yet there is no likeness between them in either kind or degree' (I: 194). Even if 'ideas' correspond to 'things', they are not themselves things.

As noted, Spencer is still fully under the grip of Hume in his assumptions about causality. This was critical. It was not within the province of science to show *how* things in the external world 'produce' changes in the sensory and central nervous system and how, in turn, these 'produce' the subjective experiences. But if so, then one could but 'correlate' introspectively 'inner relations' and brain processes; and in turn correlate these with 'outer relations' in the independently existing world.

One final step could then be taken. An evolutionary story could be told which guaranteed that our experience gave us *knowledge* of the world outside of mind. If our 'ideas' were different than 'reality', evolution did guarantee veridical cognition via 'adjustment of inner to outer relations'.

James' Criticism of Spencer

James shared much with Spencer, much more than is usually appreciated. But he fundamentally disagreed with this last claim. Indeed, I believe that it was the point of departure for those views that he came to call 'pragmatism'. But to see what is at issue, we can return to the account of *Principles*. There are, however, some different questions which are easily conflated.

First, there is a point of significant *agreement*. Putting aside for a moment the strong parallels in their respective overall programmes, Spencer and James agreed that evolution gave humans what Kant had called 'the categories of the understanding', that these preceded *any individual* learning and were presupposed by it. James' formulation of this is both clear and careful:

> In its dumb awakening to the consciousness of something there, a mere this as yet (or something for which even the term this would perhaps be too discriminative, and the intellectual acknowledgement of which would be better expressed by the bare interjection 'lo!') the infant encounters an object in which (though it be given in pure sensation) all the 'categories of the understanding' are contained. It has objectivity, unity, substantiality, causality, in the full sense in which any later object or system of objects has these things. *(James, Principles, II: 8)*

The infant's sensations include Kantian schemata, even if prior to learning, experience is a 'blooming, buzzing confusion' in that the infant is yet unable to make any judgements about its objects.[6]

Second, there is the question of how this has come to be. Here James and Spencer *differ*. Spencer seems committed to a Lamarckian view. Third, there is the question of whether evolution could provide any sort of guarantee for the veridicality of perceptual *judgements*. This is, perhaps, the most critical point of difference, related to James' disagreement as regards the second problem, the genesis of the Kantian categories.

Evolution and Experience

We need to reproduce here a simple diagram provided by James:

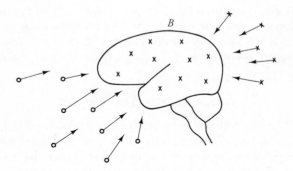

Figure 2.1

All the o's are 'natural objects', for example, sunsets, etc., which 'impress us through the senses'. In the strict sense, they gives us *experience*. James is willing to accept something like the associationist's story to explain how these 'mould' the brain to cognition. The x's inside the brain and outside it are other natural objects and processes, for example, in the ovum from whence develops the brained organism, in the blood, etc. In epigenesis, these make and modify the brain, but 'mould it to no cognition of *themselves*' (James, *Principles*, II: 626). In evolution, then, there are said to be 'two modes in which an animal race may grow to be a better match for its environment'.

In the first way, the environment modifies its inhabitant by 'exercising, hardening, and habituating him to certain sequences'. As regards the present problem, the first way is 'front-door', the way of the little o's in the diagram. The second way is Darwinian, the way of the little x's: 'Certain young are born with peculiarities that help them and their progeny to survive.'

Now James has no doubt that as regards *individuals*, the front-door way explains 'an immense number of our mental habitudes, many of our abstract beliefs, and all our ideas of concrete things, and their ways of behavior', beliefs that, for example, fire burns, water wets, etc. (II: 632). But for James, it cannot explain the preconditions for learning, including critically, the Kantian 'categories of understanding'. Spencer's view acknowledges that for *experience* to do its work, it takes 'numberless generations' and if so, then, it seems that *learned* habits can be inherited. This would fit neatly into Spencer's optimistic scheme. For if we can assume this, then evolution would guarantee that there would be a converging correspondence between 'inner' and 'outer'. Successful learning would give species advantages which would, through time, improve the fit between 'inner' and 'outer'. At some point, the fit would be nearly perfect! As Spencer had said: 'Scientific progress is progress in that equilibration of thought and things which we saw is going on, and must continue to go on, but which cannot arrive at perfection in any finite period.'[7]

In his 'Remarks on Spencer's definition of mind as correspondence' (1878),[8] James gave a devastating critique of Spencer's principle, the 'adjustment of inner to outer relations'. James argued that if 'the ascertainment of outward fact' is supposed to be the evolutionary task of organisms, then the principle cannot be true: '"Mind," as we actually find it, contains all sorts of laws – those of logic, of fancy, of wit, of taste, decorum, beauty, morals, and so forth, as well as perception of fact' (p. 8). But if 'correspondence' is loosened to avoid absurdity, the principle is quickly seen to be *vacuous*: 'Everything corresponds in some way with everything else that co-exists in the same world with it' (p. 10). Indeed, Spencer offers us 'the unassailable', but 'barren truism' that mind 'must think rightly'; 'thought must correspond with truth; but whether that truth be actual or ideal is left undecided' (p. 20). In this early text and as an explicit alternative to any sort of 'correspondence' view, James offered what is perhaps the best statement of his evolving (much misunderstood and abused) pragmatic conception of truth:

> the knower is not simply a mirror floating with no foot-hold anywhere, and passively reflecting an order that he comes upon and finds simply existing. The knower is an actor, and co-efficient of truth on one side, whilst on the other he registers the truth which he helps to create. Mental interests, hypotheses, postulates, so far as they are bases for human action – action which to great extent transforms the world – help to *make* the truth which they declare . . . The only objective criterion of reality is coerciveness, in the long run, over thought. Objective facts, Spencer's outward relations, are real only because they coerce sensation. *(p. 21)*

I hope that the context of this remark makes clear that this is by no means a sketch of the mildly interesting view that 'interests' enter into cognition and thus 'alter' or 'distort' veridical experience. James is suggesting that in the most elementary human judgements, *there need be no single, interest-free and culturally neutral 'adequation' of 'concept' and 'reality'*.

This view, a critical feature of his account in *Principles*, is rooted, he says, in Locke's distinction between real and nominal essence, even though 'none of his successors' has grasped the point. For James, it is not that there are *no* true judgements, but that 'all the ways of conceiving a concrete fact, if they are true ways at all, are equally true ways'. In a formulation which he had used several times previously, he concludes, 'the only meaning of essence is teleological, and . . . classification and conception are purely teleological weapons of the mind' (II: 332, 335). This is a rejection of traditional 'essentialism', but more than this it is a rejection of the classical realist view that knowledge of universals is the result of passive experience. Put in other terms, James is not denying 'real essences' but denying first, that they are absolute, and second that what they are is independent of our 'interests'.[9] To be sure, like the polyp, the fact of continuing human existence shows that human cognitions are *true enough*, that no 'cognition' is true which is inconsistent with the continued reproduction of the species, but that beyond this, there is an extraordinary openness as regards what counts as true enough.

We can get at the bottom of this by returning now to that second way that 'an animal race may grow to be a better match for its environment'. This way is the 'back-door' way, the way of the x's. This way may be 'adaptive' but in no useful sense are the changes in mental structure derived from experience. Indeed, 'the original elements of consciousness, sensation, space, time, resemblence, difference' may all come into being by 'the back door method, by such physical processes as lie more in the sphere of morphological accident than in that of the "sensible presence" of objects' (II: 631). The mechanisms here are *extremely indirect* and because they are, the entire picture changes.

In the first place, this way allows us to explain evolutionary continuities in rudimentary perceptual experiencing, since by virtue of evolutionary necessity, we can expect (now appropriating Harré's term), the 'coarse-grained' features of perception to be widely shared by living organisms. Ecologically considered, 'the physics' of the world would need to be grasped by any organism, no matter how simple or complex. But it would also give us a way to account for the range of cognitive capacities displayed by different species, including the distinctly human cognitive capacities. This is something that the front door way *cannot* do. Apart from the logical difficulties and the dubious Lamarckian assumptions, in the human case, it cannot since the distinctly human ways of thinking, including our 'scientific' ways of thinking, dramatically transcend what could possibly be derived or acquired from the front door way – from 'experience'. As I suggested earlier, the epistemological consequence of this would be enormous. Thus, our brain and perceptual system is adapted to the world for the same reasons as the foot of a horse, but it hardly follows from this that everything, indeed, anything of what is *learned* stands in some sort of 'correspondence' to the world.[10]

First, as to the account of the distinctly human capacities. In some complicated way, evolution made a human brain. But what happens in the brain

> is what happens in every material mass which has been fashioned by an outward force – in every pudding or mortar, which I make with my hands. The fashioning from without brings the elements into collocations which set new internal forces free to exert their effects in turn. And the random irradiations and resettlements of our ideas, which *supervene upon experience*, and constitute our free mental play, are due entirely to these secondary internal processes.... The higher thought processes owe their being to causes which correspond far more to the sourings and fermentations of the dough, the setting of mortar, or the subsidence of sediments in mixtures, than to the manipulations by which these physical aggregates can be compounded. *(II: 638)*

James does not, of course, try to flesh out the complicated story of how the human brain came to be or how it does what it does. Instead, he devotes the remainder of the last chapter of *Principles* to a programatic account of the psychogenesis of the natural sciences, the 'pure sciences', of metaphysics *and* of aesthetic and moral principles. The point of this, usually unnoticed or underplayed, is to show that, in the terms of repetitious experience, no account of these distinctly human systems of thought could possibly suffice. But if so, traditional epistemologies, rooted in assumptions that truth is a 'correspondence' of belief to *experienced* reality will not suffice either.

The Motivation and Character of Human Systems of Thought

It is James' view that 'the back door' gave us powers to discriminate and compare, that this is the basis of all classification and thence of judging, predicating and subsuming, that all so-called 'rational propositions' merely express the results of comparison, that *versus* classical realisms, 'the eternal verities which the very structure of our mind lays hold of do not necessarily themselves lay hold of extra-mental being, nor have they, as Kant pretended later, a legislating character even for all possible experience' (II: 664–5). Rather, it is his view that these 'higher powers' enable humans to articulate 'ideal prototypes of a rational order' *and* that there are genuine alternatives among these.

For James 'the sentiment of rationality', 'the 'theoretic interest' (which as a psychologist, he confesses he cannot explain) motivates all abstract systems of thought.[11] Each aim at 'ideal and inward relations' which can 'in no intelligible sense whatever be interpreted as reproductions of the order of outer experience' (II: 639). 'Nowhere', he writes, 'does the account of inner relations produced by outer ones in proportion to the frequency with which the later have been met, more egregiously break down than in the case of scientific conceptions.' 'The essence of things for science is not to be what they seem, but to be atoms and molecules moving to and from each other according to strange laws' (II: 633–4).

Indeed, not only do the concepts of modern science have their genesis in the same *need* as metaphysics or moral philosophy, but for James, they have the same essential epistemology as well:

> Now the peculiarity of those relations among the objects of our thought which are dubbed 'scientific' is this, that although they no more are inward reproductions of the outer order than the ethical and aesthetic relations are, yet they do not conflict with that order, but, once having sprung up by the play of inward forces, are found – some of them at least, namely the only ones which have survived long enough to be matters of record – to be *congruent* with the time- and space-relations which our impressions affect.
>
> In other words, though nature's materials lend themselves slowly and discouragingly to our translation of them into ethical forms, but more readily into aesthetic forms; to translation into scientific forms with relative ease and completeness. The translation, it is true, will probably never be ended. The perceptive order does not give way, nor the right conceptive substitute for it arise, at our bare word of command. It is often a deadly fight;

and many a man of science can say, like Johannes Müller, after an investigation, '*Es klebt Blut an der Arbeit*'. *(II: 640)*

While the 'things of Nature turn out to act as if they were the kind assumed' (II: 668), 'the original investigator always preserves a healthy sense of how plastic the materials are in his hands' (II: 667).[12]

Prospects for a Scientific Psychology

This was, I think, an exceptional and richly provocative beginning, and while I make no effort here to compare and develop it against present views, I believe that in outline at least, it stands up extremely well. Still, there were some genuine tensions in James' *Principles*, tensions that finally led him to despair.

At times, he accepted Spencer's 'thing-in-itself realism' and at other times he seemed to hold that the 'world' contains relatively enduring 'things', which exist independently of us, *and* that for purposes of a scientific psychology, these are the 'objects' at the object end of the 'subject/object' dichotomy. From the point of view of the scientific interest, these are the theorized *and hence knowable* objects of natural science.[13] The problem then was to show how these become the stable, common objects of ordinary experience. But he failed to carry through the implications of this for scientific psychology exactly because, like Spencer, he was caught in the notion that scientific causality was merely *empirical invariance*. In the language of the foregoing, if 'inner relations' did not correspond to 'outer relations' and if there was no way to show *how* they were *related*, then the problem of knowledge *was* insoluble.

James' 1894 Presidential address to the American Psychological Association, 'The Knowing of Things Together', was a clear acknowledgement of the tensions of the *Principles*. In that essay, he returned to the problem that was at the very bottom of the warfare between 'empiricists' and 'spiritualists', 'the nature of the synthetic unity of consciousness'. He concluded that for various reasons, *none* of the theories can be accepted. But what of his own view in the *Principles*? He there had proposed 'to simply eliminate from psychology "considered as a natural science" the whole business of ascertaining how we come to know things together or to know them at all'.[14] 'That we do know things, sometimes singly and sometimes together, is a fact. That states of consciousness are the vehicle of knowledge, and depend on brain states, are two other facts.' At that time he supposed that 'a natural science of psychology might legitimately confine itself to tracing the *functional variations* of these three sorts of fact'. But indeed, he now saw that this road was a dead-end. Remarkably, after some twelve years of struggle to write his great book, James had concluded that it was 'a loathsome, distended, tumefied, bloated dropsical mass, testifying to nothing but two facts; 1st, that there is no such thing as *science* of psychology, and 2nd, that W.J. is an incapable.' [15] Of the latter, W.J. was surely mistaken; but if indeed a psychological science had to solve the problems which James had posed for it, his appraisal, then and probably now, was not far off the mark!

In a Jamesian spirit, then, I want to conclude with some views of Harré's regarding the defence of science, but in particular with the pertinence of some suggestions which he appropriates from J. J. Gibson, a theorist who claims inspiration from James and who, certainly, is one of most interesting of recent theorists to attempt to solve those problems which James found so intractable.

Harré's Defence of Common Sense and Science

In his recent and deep *Varieties of Realism*, Harré mounts an attack on 'representationalism', neatly summarized by the formula:

> O (object) causes S (sensation) which is interpreted (non-inferentially) as P (percept).[16]

Harré would seem to be entirely correct in holding that this formula (which owes to Reid, 1787) also applies to almost every major figure in the tradition from Locke, including Müller, his student Helmholtz, to Spencer, but I think not to James. All these theories founder, finally, on the assumption that what O causes is the sensation which then must be transformed into a percept. It is just this which is challenged by Gibson.

It will not be possible here, plainly, to give much of a summary of the version of Gibsonian theory which Harré adopts, still less to notice the several alternative versions of this held by self-named Gibsonians. The critical points may be best brought out by appeal to an example:

> Sharks electrically detect things to eat. . . . An edible living thing such as a flatfish differs in ionic composition from the surrounding water, producing a bioelectric field partially modulated in the rhythm of the living thing's respiratory movements. A flatfish that has buried itself in the sand will be detectable by a shark swimming just above it. Reproducing the bioelectic field of the flatfish artificially, by passing a current between two electrodes buried in the sand, invites the same predatory behavior. . . . Now there is no intelligible sense in which it can be claimed that source ought to have appeared inedible . . . In the niche of the shark 'an edible thing' and 'electric

field of, say, type F' are nomically related. To predicate of the shark (a) 'detects electric field of type F' and (b) 'takes to be an edible thing' is not to refer to different states of affairs, one (viz. (b)) that is reached by the other (viz. (a)) by an inference. Rather it is to make reference in two ways to single state of affairs of the shark-niche system. The linking of (a) and (b) is not something that goes on in the 'mind' of the shark. The linking of (a) and (b) is in the physics of an ecological world, namely, that system given by the complementation of the shark and its niche.[17]

The perception of 'edible thing' is direct; it involves no interpretative, constructive, operations. It involves no concepts in the usual sense of the word. The nomic relation between organism and properties of the environment are 'affordances', specific bounded dispositions determined by the specific sensory mechanisms of living things standing in complementary relation to mechanisms in the physical world. Thus this is an ecological theory of perception. Patterns of energy exist independently of systems that may receive it. But patterns are information only in so far as they have significance for receivers, only as they stand in specific nomic relations to a certain kind of living thing. The problem for an ecology theory, then, is the specification of these nomic relations, 'the empirical delineation of affordances', a combination of evolutionary ecology and ecological physics.

Because these points are perfectly general, they apply to human perception. But it is critical to notice that as regards the human animal there are some troublesome complications. In particular because humans are social beings, concepts and beliefs which are cultural products *infect* human perception. Accordingly, as Harré writes, the world which we *directly* perceive is 'coarse-grained'. It answers closely to Kantian schemata, as James had it, 'things', events, spatial, temporal and causal relations. In terms of the foregoing, evolution equipped us with brains and sensory systems. It had to give us discriminative and comparative capacities, the *basis* of judging, predicating or subsuming. It could, contrary to the entire representative tradition, give us direct perception of orderly patterns in the external world. But it could not give us *concepts*, still less *veridical* concepts, concepts true of the world which exists independently of us.

I believe that Harré would agree with this formulation. As he argues, Gibsonian theory (as I think we both understand it), yields no 'recognizably corrigible statements'. But – and this is where my difficulties begin – he also asserts that 'without some basis in veridical perception scientific realism, whether it be based on 'truth' [which he rejects] or upon 'reference' [which he affirms] must founder in a mess of relativism' (p. 161).[18]

I am unclear about this 'mess of relativism'. First, as I have suggested, even if Gibsonian perception gives us direct access to the external world (and thus guarantees communication), this is no epistemological 'bridge-head' exactly because there are no incorrigibles. Human percepts are 'blind' with respect to linguistically articulated knowledge.

Second, Harré acknowledges that he seeks not 'foundations' but *grounds* and these are found, not in statements, but in material practices: 'We trust beliefs that have been produced by reliable people using reliable methods' (p. 166). His line of argument seems to go something like this: Gibsonian perception sanctions the practical reliability of scientific knowledge; practical reliability is required to sustain the 'moral order' of the scientific community. *Hence*, we escape relativism. If this is the gist of the argument (and I am by no means clear that it is), I doubt that the conclusion follows. Relativism of the sort defended by the 'strong pro-gramme' and assumed by Bhaskar,[19] more recently by Margolis[20] and, sketchily, by myself,[21] seems to be fully consistent with both Gibsonian perception and the requisite 'practical reliability'.

Indeed, as Harré's provocative account of the *moral* order which sus-tains science suggests, it seems to me that the problem is not so much relativism, but the desire to privilege epistemically just those material practices which Harré so brilliantly analyses in his wonderful book. One must be careful here. It is not anything called 'science' which Harré contends is to be preferred over other possible knowledge-producing practices, but the specific practices of what is perhaps best called the 'theoretical sciences'. Since he convinces me that Realm 1 discourse is but proto-science whose instabilities are remedied only by including refer-ence to unobservable things and processes, and since his brilliant defence of Realm 2 discourse, policy realism, takes the form a inductive argument which, finally, is a *recommendation*, I just cannot see what he believes is at stake in his appeal to Gibsonian theory. Relativists like William James, Barry Barnes and David Bloor, Roy Bhaskar, Joe Margolis and myself (each different in this way or that) reject absolutism as regards knowledge, but so does Harré. Nor can I see how this group is more subject to sceptical challenges than is he. That is, even if Gibsonian theory is correct, as Harré seems at least to assent, the 'epistemic access' it yields cannot discriminate between alternative epistemic practices. As he says, there are convincing arguments against the attempt (*à la* Spencer) to provide a selectionist-adaptationist account of the conventional practices of particular ways of 'finding out' even while there are sound grounds (as in James) for giv-ing a biological account of our capacity to employ the 'generic' cat-egorical scheme which Kant had mistakenly located in the transcendental ego.

NOTES

1   See R. Harré, *Matter and Method* (London: Macmillan, 1964); Maurice Mandelbaum, *Philosophy, Science and Sense Perception* (Baltimore, MD: Johns Hopkins, 1974).
2   William James, *Principles of Psychology* (New York: Dover, 1950), Vol. II. pp. 617–18, hereafter referenced in the text by volume and page.
3   James is quoting from para. 207 of Spencer's *Principles of Psychology*, 2 volumes (New York: Appleton). The first edition of this was published in 1855, the second, from which James is presumably quoting, was radically rewritten and published in 1870. A third edition came out in 1902.
4   'Ultimate scientific ideas', for example, force, matter, space and time, 'are all representations of realities that cannot be comprehended' (Herbert Spencer, *First Principles*, 4th edition (New York: Caldwell, 1880), p. 55).

   Thing-in-itself realism' is, as Kant says, an empirical realism (though the converse does not hold). See Moritz Schlick's response to Planck's realism in which he argues that 'nature, and everything of which the physicist can and must speak belongs, according to Kant, to empirical reality, and what this means is ... explained by him in just the way it must be for us. Atoms in Kant's system have not transcendent reality, they are not "things in themselves"' ('Positivism and Realism', in A. J. Ayer (ed.), *Logical Positivism* (New York: Free Press, 1959)).

   In my 'Pragmatic philosophy of science and the charge of scientism', (in *Transactions of the Charles S. Peirce Society* 24 (1988), pp. 179–222), I argue that James waffled on all three ideas, holding, in *Principles*, for a form of realism in which the theoretical objects of physical science (including atoms and non-observable brain processes) were real, had causal powers *and* were beyond experience. Convincing himself that within the framework he had set for himself, the psychological problems he set out to solve were insoluble, he opted for an entirely new approach, radical empiricism. A form of thing-in-itself realism, his 'postulate' of radical empiricism assserted that 'the only things that shall be debateable among philosophers shall be things definable in terms drawn from experience. [Things of an unexperienceable nature may exist ad libitum, but they form no part of the material for philosophic debate.]' See below.
5   Herbert Spencer, *Principles of Psychology* (New York: Appleton, 1902), Vol. 1, p. 48, hereafter cited in the text by volume and page number.
6   Throughout *Principles*, James argued that *everyone* impoverishes 'sensation', the point of departure of the 'warfare' between 'sensationalists' (empiricists) and 'spiritualists' (Kantians). (This was, of course, also a critical feature of radical empiricism, and a source of the belief that the continuities in the later James are more important than the discontinuities. On my view, this is emphatically not the case.) He is willing to countenance *some* distinction between perception and sensation. 'Sensation ..., so long as we take the analytic point of view, differs from Perception only in the extreme simplicity of its object or content' (II: 1–2). This is but a relative matter and both

sensation and perception, to emphasize, are organized. On the other hand, for James, concepts, 'thoughts', and 'judgements' are to be sharply distinguished from sensations, both psychologically and physiologically. See below, p. 35.

7   Spencer, *First Principles*, p. 467. Compare Peirce who, unlike Spencer, did not leave scientific progress up to *evolution*. Peirce held that only if we consciously adopt scientific method, which we will perhaps *not* do, was there hope of a convergence to the truth of things. But in any case, Peirce's views on evolution are most complicated.

8   In *Essays in Philosophy*, *Works of William James*, Frederick Burkhardt (general ed.), Cambridge, Mass.: Harvard University Press, 1978, pp. 7–22.

9   That is, as Peirce had insisted, the 'objects' of the external world have some 'character' *or other*, even though they need not be self-identifying to be cognized. If they are not self-identifying, however, the way they get identified can be largely a function of human purposes, *generically understood*. Thus, 'readers brought up on Popular Science may think that the molecular structure of things is their real essence in an absolute sense, and that water is H–O–H more deeply and truly than it is a solvent of sugar or slaker of thirst. Not a whit! It is all of these things with equal reality, and the reason why *for the chemist* it is H–O–H primarily, and only secondarily the other things, is that *for his purpose of deduction and compendious definition* the H–O–H aspect of it is the more useful one to bear in mind' (II: 334–5n). More generally, as I note below, because H–O–H satisfies the *theoretic* interest it is primary.

10 At least in part because it is hard to make intelligible the view that 'ideas' stand in 'correspondence' with the world, it is very often difficult to know what is being claimed. For example, Konrad Lorenz writes that 'nearly all natural scientists of today ... consciously or unconsciously assume in their daily work a real relationship between the thing-in-itself and the phenomena of our subjective experience, but a relationship which is by no means a 'purely' ideal one in the Kantian sense.... Adaptation has provided our thought with an innate structuralization which corresponds to a considerable degree to the reality of the external world.... Our categories and forms of perception, fixed prior to individual experiences, are adapted to the external world for exactly the same reasons as the hoof of the horse is already adapted to the ground of the steppe ... ('Kant's doctrine of the *a priori* in the light of contemporary biology', in H. C. Plotkin (ed.), *Learning, Development and Culture: Essays in Evolutionary Epistemology*, New York: Wiley, 1982, pp. 124–5). Is this Spencer or James?

11 There is deep irony in American pragmatism. Considered, typically, to be the supremely practical philosophy, Peirce argued that 'true science is distinctively the study of useless things' and James persistently insisted that what motivated science was not practical interests, technologies, but 'to think with perfect fluency'. This was the *central* thesis of his 1879 'The sentiment of rationality', summarized in *Principles* as follows: 'The craving to believe that the things of the world belong to kinds which are related by an inward rationality together, is the parent of Science as well as of sentimental philosophy' (II: 667). Similarly, in his 1881 'Reflex action and theism' (quoted in

Principles), he wrote: 'The conceiving or theorizing faculty works exclusively for the sake of ends that do not exist at all in the work of the impressions received by way of our senses, but are set by our emotional and practical subjectivity. It is a transformer of the world of our impressions into a totally different world . . . and the transformation is effected in the interests of our volitional nature, and for no other purpose whatever' (II: p. 634n). I try to explain pragmatisms ambiguous role in 'Pragmatic philosophy of science and the charge of scientism'.

12   James argued that although theoretical claims must 'harmonize' with the more practical 'truths', they are 'declarations that the experienced form is false and the ideal form true, declarations which are justified by the appearance of new sensible experiences at just those times and places at which we logically infer that their ideal correlates ought to be' (II: 669). The 'plasticity' enters, of course, in many places.

13   In his notes for the 1879 'The sentiment of rationality' there is a neat argument for the pragmatic pertinence of the idea of a *knowable* non-experienceable reality. James says:

> The principle of 'pragmatism', which allows for all assumptions to be of identical value so long as they equally save the appearances will of course be satisfied by this empiricist explanation . . . [viz., as according to Mill, that no mysterious 'outness' needs to be postulated]. But common sense is not assuaged. She says, yes, I get all the particulars, am cheated out of none of my expectations. And yet the principle of *intelligibility* is gone. Real outness makes everything simple as the day, but the troops of ideas marching and falling perpetually into order, which you now ask me to adopt, have no *reason* in them – their whole existence is *de facto* and not *de jure*. (*Essays in Philosophy, p. 364*)

Nevertheless, if British phenonmenalism did not suffice, neither could he accept a 'more' beyond the actual as it functioned in Spencer and Kant. Appealing to Peirce's arguments, he first notes that 'most scientific readers of Spencer wholly fail to catch the destructive import of his theory. . . . They are willing to believe with the Master that the deepest reality is the absolutely irrational, because that reality is unknowable, but few of them ultimately realize that the knowable of their philosophy forms a world of Chance pure and simple' (*Essays*, p. 369). Spencer's 'unknowable' cannot function to give order, since to do this it must be *known* to have properties which could *explain* the orderliness of experience. It was thus that the 'plus ultra in many philosophies – in Mr Spencer's and in Kant's e.g., the noumenon is a dog in the manger, it does nothing for us itself but merely stands and blasts with its breath the actual' (p. 371). James agreed here with Peirce that the real could not be reduced to he actual: 'There are still other forces at work in the mind which lead it to suppose something over and above the mere actuality of things'.

14   In *Essays in Philosophy* (p. 87). In *Principles*, James had asserted that '*the*

relation of knowing is the most mysterious thing in the world', that 'if we ask how one thing *can* know another we are led into the heart of *Erkenntniss-theorie and metaphysics*' (I: 212). By his 1904 'Does consciousness exist?', after abandoning those assumptions he had shared with Spencer, he was prepared to assert that 'if we start with the supposition that there was only one primal stuff or material of the world, a stuff of which everything is composed, and if we call that stuff "pure experience", then *knowing can easily be explained* as a particular sort of relation towards one another into which portions of pure experience may enter' (*Essays in Radical Empiricism, Works of William James,* Fr. Burkhardt general editor), Cambridge, Mass.: Harvard University Press, 1976, p. 4, my emphasis).

15   Letter to his publisher, Henry Holt, May 1890, quoted from Ralph Barton Perry, *The Thought and Character of Williams James,* 2 vols (Boston: Little, Brown, 1935).

16   Rom Harré, *Varieties of Realism* (Oxford: Basil Blackwell, 1986), p. 155.

17   M. T. Turvey, R. E. Shaw, E. S. Reed and W. M. Mace, 'Ecological laws of perceiving and acting: in reply to Fodor and Pylyshyn (1981)', *Cognition,* 9 (1981), p. 276–7. This is a brilliant, if difficult, overview of what I take to be an extremely plausible version of Gibsonian theory. While the authors may hold that I step into the same trap which they are at pains to display, I appeal to it in what follows.

18   I may miss here Harré's critical point. He notes, properly, that 'the nearer we get to the generic Gibsonian level we take ourselves to be, the more trustworthy we take perception to be' (gelignite sticks for a stove platform!). But as I understand foundationism, the issue is not merely the possibility of mis-identification which is a consequence of the fact that memory and recognition is fallible, but that as he earlier notes, foundational statements must be incorrigible in the sense that they are 'decideable independently of general theoretical beliefs'. James's remark gets it right. In the absence of concepts there is veridical perception, but we are restricted to the interjection 'lo'! I think that the point, finally, may be irrelevant to the point I want to make since, in any case, relativism of the sort I want to defend is perfectly consistent with what in humans would seem to be *universal learned beliefs,* fire burns, etc.

19   See, e.g., David Bloor, *Knowledge and Social Imagery* (London: Routledge & Kegan Paul, 1976; Barry Barnes, *T. S. Kuhn and Social Science* (New York: Columbia University Press, 1983; Roy Bhaskar, *A Realist Theory of Science,* 2nd edition (Sussex: Harvester Press, 1978).

20   Joseph Margolis, *Pragmatism without Foundations* (Oxford and New York: Basil Blackwell, 1986).

21   P. T. Manicas, *A History and Philosophy of the Social Sciences* (Oxford and New York: Basil Blackwell, 1987), chapter 12.

3

Reason and Reality: a Prolegomenon to their Varieties

J. R. Lucas

The concepts of reason and reality are difficult to elucidate, not least because they are related in pairs of opposed ways. Since the time of Plato we have been inclined to regard rationality as a mark of reality, and to accept as completely real only what is completely intelligible; and in the same tradition the Schoolmen identified the *Ens Realissimum* with the divine λόγος, and modern physicists think that the grand unified theory, when we have it, will be transparently rational as well as the fundamental reality. But at the same time we have been impelled to contrast reality with reason, and think of it as a brute opaque fact which we just have to accept willy-nilly; which we cannot hope to understand, but must just conform ourselves to, as part of the brute contingency of things, to be acknowledged but incapable of being fully known. In a second opposition we sometimes think of reality as transcending rationality, and as constituting the real truth that goes beyond our limited apprehension of it: there is a gap between our rational methodology and what is really the case, which imports a tincture of fallibility into everything we assert. Sceptics then seize on this gap, and argue it into a great gulf, so that reality not merely may transcend reason, but must be utterly inaccessible to it. In the one understanding, reason can approximate to reality, but can never sew it up completely, so that we should always be modest, and acknowledge that our statements, however well warranted, could conceivably be wrong, and are in principle corrigible: in the other, reason cannot even approximate to reality, which must remain forever unknowable, and about which the only rational attitude must be one of decent agnosticism.

These crude antitheses are misconceived, but are influential none the less. They bear on our intimations of reality, sometimes refining them, more often distorting them, and need to be disentangled if we are to follow out all the ramifications of that protean concept. I shall attempt, with only partial success, to reveal the roots of the variant understandings of reality. The different realisms that Rom Harré distinguishes are not chance misconceptions of different philosophers, but the outcome of conceptual pressures that can be properly evaluated only if we are fully conscious of them. Consciousness, therefore, needs to be raised.

John Austin recognized the protean quality of the word 'real'. A number of homely examples showed that the force of the word varied very much with context: real silk as opposed to artificial silk or rayon; real butter as opposed to margarine; real cream as opposed to synthetic cream or sodium glycerophosphate; real gentleman as opposed to *faux bon homme,* and the like. Austin concluded that the meaning of the word was to be elucidated entirely in terms of everyday examples, and that it should be understood simply in terms of what it excluded rather than any positive assertion. The conclusions do not follow, but the initial point is well taken: the word 'real' is like the word 'good'; just as a good x is an x which performs well the tasks that x's typically do, or rates high on the criteria by which we normally judge x's, so a real x is one which exemplifies in all respects the characteristics we expect x's to possess. Only when we know what x is – under what description it is being referred to – can we address the question whether it is a good x or a bad one.

Thus far Austin's exegesis is valuable, and we need always to keep in mind what sort of entities they are whose reality is being discussed and the respects in which they may or may not come up to scratch. Austin's further contention, that in doing this we should always be guided by ordinary usage, is, however, mistaken. The word 'real' did not originate in ordinary language, but was a philosophers' word. It was coined by the Schoolmen, *realis*, thing-like, from *res*, a thing. Along with 'quality', 'quantity', 'substance' and 'essence', it has proved its worth in a multitude of everyday applications, but has not lost the logic of its original *locale*. Everyday use is a valuable corrective to philosophical assertion, but cannot constitute an exhaustive elucidation of meaning. We need to know not only what men say but what they want to say, and therefore need to empathize with their metaphysical moods and logical inclinations. The Greeks and the Schoolmen may have been wrong in their ontological aspirations, and Quantum Field Theory may lead us to revise our realism in some new third realm that passes almost all understanding; but that revision will be achieved by a hard intellectual reassessment of our science and metaphysics, not a mere examination of current usage.

Austin's second conclusion, that the word 'real' should be understood simply in terms of what it excluded rather than any positive assertion, is helpful but not profound. Often we do ask whether an x is a real x when ther is some particular respect in which it may well not be real, in which case there is a particular contrast in mind, and usage crystallizes that opposition as canonical. But it does not have to be so, and in asking whether it is real butter I may be seeking to exclude not the possibility of its being genuine marg, but of its being a fake foodstuff placed on a Scandinavian sideboard in a furniture showroom, or its being a delusory delicacy gracing the table of a mad Macbeth, or its being a philosopher's fantasy which looks like butter, tastes like butter, feels like butter, and possesses all the primary and secondary qualities of butter, but lacks something, I know not what, that constitutes the real essence of butter. Unreality need not always wear the trousers. Although often there is some particular potential defect we are concerned with, we may be embarking on a general quest for reality where not just one particular, but any defect whatever, will be relevant.

In their quest for complete thing-likeness, philosophers have been concerned on different occasions to exclude different potential defects, but have had commonly had one fundamental opposition in mind, which in turn gives rise to two others. Things are *what* they are – and not what I, or others, might think them to be. From this it can follow that things are *more than* they seem, and perhaps altogether remote and incomprehensible: and that things are *as* they are – and not as they might have been. The first is a personal opposition between omnipersonal objectivity and first-personal subjectivity: the second an opposition between what is true and what is knowable, which may be simply a recognition of our fallibility but can easily become in the hands of the sceptic a blanket denial of the very possibility of knowledge: the third a modal opposition between actuality and mere potentiality.

Things are what they are. There is a certain objectivity about them that contrasts with every sort of subjectivity. But subjectivity is of many sorts, and the unrecognized shift from one subjectivity to another can make reality seem more *recherché* and remote than it really is. What is subjective may be my egocentricity, or yours, or ours, or his, or theirs; and while we are reasonably clear who I am, and have some idea of your identity, third persons are often indeterminate, and we are systematically ambiguous about the boundaries of 'we'. If 'we' includes all rational agents, what is acknowledged by us all is really so, but if 'we' refers only to those of us who happen to be talking together at one particular time in one particular place, intersubjective agreement falls far short of objective truth, and reflects only the limitations of our culture, age and situation. Objectivity is omni-personal, and so is contrasted with what is merely first-, or second- or third-personal singular, or second- or third-personal plural, but not necessarily, though often in fact, with the first-personal plural. If we define objective reality only by contrast, we invite confusion. Reality, we begin by saying, it is not what appears to me, or to you, or to any chance selection of them or us; and reality, we end by supposing, cannot even be what appears to everyone and all of us, but must be something separate, a thing-in-itself divorced from all appearances, utterly inaccessible to all sentient subjects, behind and beyond all phenomena. The confusion arises from a combination of the negative approach with the ambiguity of the first-person plural. It is reasonable to contrast what is really the case with what I think, or what some limited selection of us think, but not with what we, all rational beings whatsoever, think. If 'we' are confined to any limited range, then it is always possible that we are in error, and so pertinent to draw a distinction between what we think and what is really the case: but as the range of 'we' increases, so what is left by excluding us all is diminished, until at the limit there is no contrast at all. To avoid such vacuity, we should eschew the negative approach, and construe objective reality not as opposed to subjective appearances, but as embracing them all. The real shape of an object is not the shape that is not apparent to anyone, but what is invariant as between all apparent shapes. To me the penny may seem oval, and to you it may appear very elliptical: if each of us were to characterize the exact eccentricity of the apparent elliptical shape of the penny, we should be unable to agree on a common description, or ascribe to the penny the same shape; but there is a common shape, invariant under different perspectives of perception, and if we talk about that, since it is the same for us all, it can be characterized in the same way by us all. Invariance under interchange from one person to another yields invariance from one point of view to another, which leads at a very simple level to the Euclidean nature of ordinary space,[1] and at a more sophisticated one to 'certain necessary conditions for a concept to denote something real'.[2] Reality is thing-like not in being non-personal, but in not being confined to any one particular person, and therefore being the same for all persons, and in this sense omni-personal and universal.

The different applications of the word 'all' explain the gap between rational methodology and a complete apprehension of reality. Methods are what we, here and now, have adopted. Our methods may be rational, in as much as we have chosen them with care in the past, and are prepared to improve them in the future, but they are defined by, and so limited to, the approbation of our own culture, age and situation. Because of this limitation, they cannot be constitutive of reality, though we can reasonably hope that they will in general approximate to reality, and may sometimes attain it. The gap, though it cannot be closed by argument, does not have to be a gulf. Although we always may be wrong, and must acknowledge that all our assertions are in principle corrigible, it does not follow that we may be always wrong, or that our assertions cannot ever be correct. The sceptic resorts to many arguments to make out that this conclusion does indeed follow, and these arguments can be conclusively refuted only as they are adduced, but besides showing up the ambiguity in his application of the word 'all', we can argue generally that there is no sense in a concept of reality divorced from all appearances, and it is only if phenomena are some sort of guide to reality, albeit a fallible one, that we can construct a contrast at all. Cartesian certitude we can forgo: but a reasonably reliable knowledge of reality under favourable conditions must be at least possible if we are to make any sense of the concept at all.

Things are as they are. There is a certain actuality about them that obtrudes on the free-flowing fantasy of subjective opining and optating. Neither our conceiving nor our wishing makes them so, and reality stands in contrast both to appearance on the one hand and to aspiration on the other. The two contrasts have different modal implications. When what is actually the case is contrasted with what appears to be the case, appearances are perfectly possible, and there is no suggestion that reality is necessarily as it is. It just happens to be so, and we, perpetually fallible as we are, just happen to be wrong. When our aspirations are confined by reality, however, the constraint is in some way a necessary one. No matter what we do, our actions cannot achieve what we would wish. Reality is what it is impossible to avoid. We may discover it by trial and bitter experience, or we may reach a recognition of necessity by ratiocination. In the latter case our wishes may alter as we comprehend more fully what is involved and we cease seeking the unattainable because we no longer want what we should have to want were we seriously trying to bring it about: the feeling of freedom is preserved by tailoring our aspirations to fit the available options; as we change our reasoning, so we change the modal aspect of reality, and instead of being an opaque constraint on what what we can achieve, it becomes a rational restriction on what we can reasonably want.

We may, as a first approximation, correlate the two modal aspects of reality with boundary conditions and with natural laws. Boundary conditions are what they actually are but could perfectly well have been otherwise. Natural laws, by contrast, are not merely actual but in some sense necessary. If boundary conditions are not as we think them to be, that merely falsifies our opinions, but the necessity of natural laws cannot be obviated no matter how we alter the actual conditions. Such a correlation, however, helpful though it is, needs to be refined. In particular, we need to refine necessity further, and distinguish between the contingently necessary natural necessities of Realm 2 discourse from the necessarily necessary conceptual necessities that underlie Realm 1 discourse, and to distinguish further the different necessities arising in the various discourses of Realm 3.[3] The key is reason. There are different styles of rationality, giving rise to different applications of necessity. What is legally necessary is that for which there is overwhelming legal reason for doing: what is morally necessary is that for which there is overwhelming moral reason for doing. Logical necessity is interdefinable with deductive necessity, physical necessity with the reasoning of physical theories. As these theories become more abstruse, so the nature of its reasoning, and hence the associated necessity, and with it the appropriate ontology, become more abstruse also. Contrary to the tenets of Logical Positivism, no complete and exact criterion of rationality can be formulated: not even Elementary Number Theory can be finitely axiomatized, and *a fortiori* not the various theories of mathematical physics. But this need occasion no despair. Although we cannot axiomatize completely, we can for many purposes give an adequate account. What is important for an elucidation of reality is not to give an exhaustive account of different types of physical reasoning, but to recognize that there are different types, and hence that there are different modes of necessity.

It is because of their being different modes of necessity that Rom Harré's characterization of natural necessities as only contingently necessary is not a contradiction in terms, and some reconciliation between the opposing modal implications of reality may be looked for. Although natural necessities cannot in practice be avoided, they could conceivably be different. At the very least then, they are practically necessary but logically contingent. The concept of a reality which is one sense necessary but in another contingent may resolve a serious incompatibility that emerges if we adopt a possible-worlds interpretation of modality. What is necessary is what holds in all possible worlds in the relevant range, whereas the particular actual world is only one among the possible ones. Necessity is expressed by a universal A-type proposition, whereas actuality is expressed by a particular I-type proposition. A partial resolution can be reached if we recognize different types of modality, so that a natural law can be in one sense necessary, while in another contingent. And in the pursuit of scientific understanding we are led to just such a position. For though natural laws present themselves at first as ineluctable constraints on what conjunctions of natural phenomena we can bring about, we seek explanations of them, and in so far as we are successful, they cease to be brute opaque facts about the natural world, and become rationally transparent features we no longer find puzzling or obtrusive. They become necessary with respect to the explanatory theory. But the question always can be raised why it should be this theory rather than some other conceivable alternative, and to that extent it is only contingently the case that it is this that is true rather than that. Yet, though the question always can be raised, it cannot always be pressed. The irrationality of some alternatives is so great that they only have to be stated for it to become evident. Neither the Special Theory of Relativity nor Quantum Field Theory are tautologically true, but logically possible alternatives are not serious rivals, and the contingency of Relativistic, or Quantum Field Theory, necessities is a diminishing one. The contingent necessity of natural laws is thus not a vulnerable one. In acknowledging that it is not tautologically necessary, we are not seriously impugning its necessity, but only indicating what sort of necessity it is. It arises not from the law of non-contradiction, that to deny it would be to mouth a mere inconsistency, but from our knowledge of physics, as we seek to understand it better. It is ineluctable, but not altogether opaque. Although our understanding of physics is incomplete, it is not negligible, and the laws of physics present themselves neither as vacuous tautologies nor as mere brute facts, but as substantial principles we can begin to comprehend.

The concept of the thing-like, which is not so much impersonal as omni-personal, gives rise by a natural logical development to its being a standard of truth against which the methodologies of our own age and culture may be tested and corrected, and to its having some modal status more solid than that of mere possibility. The interplay of the different strands of rationality, universality and modality is much more complex than this brief account can accommodate. Rom Harré has followed out many of them, and disentangled them carefully for our benefit. The aim of this chapter is to go back to the roots of the concept in order to understand why it has developed in the way it has, in the hope of its serving for some as a useful prolegomenon to his work.

NOTES

1 J. R. Lucas, *Space, Time and Causality*, Oxford, Oxford University Press 1985, ch. 7, pp. 111–14.
2 Rom Harré, *Varieties of Realism*, Oxford: Basil Blackwell 1986, ch. 13, p. 245.
3 Rom Harré, *Varieties of Realism*, Oxford: Basil Blackwell 1986, ch. 17, pp. 338–41.

4

Experimental Realism

Jerry Aronson

In *Varieties of Realism*, Rom Harré presents an ingenious argument for scientific realism. What is especially interesting about this argument is that is based on empirical considerations, considerations that even the anti-realist cannot overlook. Even though Harré believes that he has presented an argument for a more modest form of realism, I shall argue that his defence can be extended to support a full-blown convergent realism.

It is true that various attacks have put convergent realism on the defensive. It has been argued, for example, that the history of science has shown numerous cases where the success of a theory does not indicate that it is getting closer to the truth while others claim that scientific progress can be accounted for without having to appeal to verisimilitude. Finally, the anti-realist maintains that defending realism by claiming it provides the only plausible explanation of scientific progress simply begs the question.

In response to this onslaught, some realists, including Harré, have sought to characterize their philosophy in such a way as to avoid these criticisms, by making their position more modest but retaining other essential features. While some have given up reference others have given up truth, limiting realism to the assertion that there simply exists a mind-independent world out there. According to this view, the epistemological aspects of the doctrine are to be dropped, for they cannot be defended against the above attacks anyway. Others feel that the notion of approximate truth has been open to the charge of being vague, beyond repair; it is simply a cross which the realist need not bear. For example, Harrés's defence is restricted to policy realism, with the intent to skirt those problems created by clinging to verisimilitude.

Of course, it is the classic version of realism, the one developed by Boyd and Putnam, that has taken the brunt of these recent attacks. As we all know by now, their defence is based on inference to the best explanation, viz., the best possible explanation for scientific progress is that our theories are approximating truth, whereas the anti-realists cannot come up with an equally adequate account, if they can come up with any at all.

Recent Attacks of Realism

Let us briefly review the various critiques of the above defence of realism. In the first place, Laudan (1981, pp. 29–32) and others have called into question the very notion of getting closer to the truth, and rightly so. Although much literature has been devoted to the semantics of verisimilitude, it seems that little or no consensus on the matter has been reached. On this issue, I agree with Devitt that 'a large and very technical literature shows that assigning degrees of truth and comparing truth (falsity) contents are much more difficult than it as first appeared' (Devitt, 1984, p. 115). There is yet the further problem of precisely relating verisimilitude to scientific progress, something any convergent realist must do.

Even if we can come up with a clear and precise formulation of verisimilitude, in what way would it constitute an explanation of scientific progress or, at least, as the best explanation of progress? Both Laudan (1981, pp. 25–31) and van Fraassen (1980) argue that success need not entail that our theories are getting closer to the truth, that one can come up with anti-realist models of scientific progress, the major gap in the realist's argument being the failure to provide this link between verisimilitude and inference to the best explanation.

This leads to what many have taken to be a crowning blow to the realism-explaining-success defence, viz., the circularity argument provided by Fine (1984, pp. 85–91) (and Laudan, 1981, pp. 45–6). The realist claims that theoretical entities must be posited in order to explain scientific progress; yet they must establish a much stronger claim, viz., the truth of their existence. But the realist never establishes a connection between the best explanation and the truth of the explanans; he simply assumes it. It appears that the only technique the realist can use to establish the connection on the meta level between the truth of realism and its being the best explanation of progress is to appeal to a connection between the truth of theoretical entities and the explanation they provide of observables. Making such an appeal would glaringly beg the question.

Finally, we must not forget the meta-induction argument against realism (Laudan, 1981, pp. 22–6). It goes simply like this. In the past, there have been several cases of successful theories where it subsequently turned out that the central terms of these theories were non-referring. So, by induction, we are probably wrong about unobservables that are posited today.

Since this line of argumentation has been adopted by the anti-realists, the defenders of realism have reacted quickly and firmly. For example, Hardin and Rosenberg re-analyse many of the cases cited by Laudan in such a way as to render them harmless. Realism is limited to 'mature' or 'take-off' theories, whereas many of these cases are not part of a sequence of theories that constitutes a mature science. Non-starters pose no threat to the realist's position (Hardin and Rosenberg, 1982, pp. 608–10). Devitt makes the same point (1984, p. 146). Even if it is found that theoretical terms like 'gene' do not, in fact, successfully refer, this kind of case is distinguishable from cases like the failure of phlogiston theory, and in such a way that the realist need not be concerned (Hardin and Rosenberg, 1982, pp. 611–14)

Harrés's answer to the meta-induction argument is along the same line. The natural kinds which are built into our various empirical theories form a 'referential grid' in such a way as retroactively to determine the reference in previous theories. On the basis of this grid, we can determine that yesterday's theoretical entities are identified with today's observed referents: 'To have demonstrated that capillaries exist is to settle the question of the referential force of the term "capillary." As a theoretical term in Harvey's theory of the circulation of the blood *it must have already referred*' (Harré, 1986, p. 74). Thus, no series of take-off theories can be used as inductive evidence against referential realism.

Devitt presents another answer to the meta-induction argument. He claims that if we examine the argument more carefully, we shall see that it is not even a good induction, for scientists can be wrong more often than right about unobservables in the past, in such a way that being mostly wrong then is perfectly compatible with our theories being mostly right today.

> we can see that scientists in the past were often *wrong* to have confidently accepted theories given the evidence available to them. We have the view that not only are scientists learning more and more about the world but also that they are learning more and more about how to find out about the world; there is an improvement in methodology. As a result the success rate of confident posits has tended to improve. (*Devitt, 1984, p. 146*)

So, even if scientists may often have been wrong in the past, with methodological progress, they can improve to the extent of being mostly right about today's unobservables.

Devitt maintains that the realism issue should be settled before the semantic and epistemic issues. While I agree with him on the former, I cannot assent to the latter. If anything, it would mean that convergent realism would have to be given up or not defended. But both he and Harré feel that the major reason why realism has fallen onto hard times recently is because verisimilitude and convergence have been combined as major premisses of any defence of realism, and that this can not work.

Instead of using inference to the best explanation of scientific progress to defend the truth of realism, he uses it instead to support the journey from appearances to the existence of theoretical entities underlying them. On the one hand, we are justified in believing that observables exist because 'by supposing they exist we can give good explanations of the behavior and characteristics of observed entities, behavior and characteristics which would otherwise remain completely inexplicable' (Devitt, 1984, p. 105). But why can this very same reasoning not be used to justify our belief in theoretical entities? After all, the world of observables appears to us in a particular way and what postulating unobservables (= realism) does is to provide us with the only means of explaining the way observable things look, appear or behave. Not only that, anti-realist theories are straitjacketed to explaining observables in terms of other observable entities, which places them at a decisive disadvantage.

> Suppose that a theory posits unobservable xs, but there are in fact no xs. Why is the observed world as if there are xs? The question is not disturbing to the Realist. He expects some theories to be wrong. He seeks an answer in terms of other unobservable entities. Such an answer is not available to the anti-Realist because he denies not only xs but unobservables in general. *(Devitt, 1984, p. 108)*

So, by switching from using 'Realism is true' to explain scientific progress to using 'There exist unobservable entities, having such and such properties' to explain the observable world, Devitt maintains that this use of inference to the best explanation will free the realist from the above-mentioned attacks.

While I believe that Devitt does an admirable job of destroying the meta-inductive argument against realism, I think that there are two insurmountable problems that plague his own argument in support of realism. The first is the well-known positivist retort that observables plus many correlations among them can explain the observable world just as well as theoretical entities. I have attempted to answer this criticism (Aronson, 1984, pp. 163–206), but space limitations do not permit such a long and detailed story.[1]

Even if it can be demonstrated that unobservables plus laws can do a better job of explaining the observable world than postulating observables alone and a variety of laws relating observables only, there is still the circularity problem. Again, why must there be a connection between the best explanation and truth? Perhaps, in the spirit of anti-realism, we may discover that our best explanations are not based on true postulates at all! It is true that the best explanation of why my tie looks red under white light may be that it *is* red. But we all know that if this account is to be any good, it must be based on theories (optics, biology, etc.) that are *true*, theories that are about the ways things appear, look and behave in relation to the way they *are*, theories whose truth of which the anti-realist will call into question because of their reference to unobservables.

The pont is that Devitt may have violated one of his own maxims, in particular, Maxim 3, which says: 'Settle the realism issue before any epistemic or semantic issue' (Devitt, 1984, p. 4). But if his defence of realism is based on inference to the best explanation and the belief that the best explanation is the one which is closest to the truth, how can he possibly avoid making a strong epistemological and semantic claim – viz., we are justified in believing that the hypothesis that best explains the data is the one closest to the truth – as the ultimate premiss underlying his justification? Thus, I do not think that we can settle the realism issue before any epistemic or semantic issues if we use inference to the best explanation.

I think that the outcome of all this is that one cannot come up with a viable defence of realism by means of inference to the best explanation. Otherwise, the realist will have to weather many of the above attacks. Instead of using a connection between truth and the best explanation to underpin a realist philosophy, I contend it should be the other way around: we use realism to establish the link between the best explanation and truth. This requires that we come up with a new approach to justifying realism, one that does not use inference to the best explanation. Harré has provided us with just such an approach.

Harrés's Defence of Policy Realism

Harré distinguishes three different referential realms: Realm 1, the world of common experience; Realm 2, that of possible experiences; and Realm 3, the world beyond all possible experience. Now, if we view these realms from an historical perspective, we notice immediately that their boundaries are constantly shifting: the subsets of Realm 2 shift to Realm 1; and, with the developments of new theories and the overthrow of others, some subsets of Realm 3 shift over to Realm 2 (Harré, 1986, pp. 59–61). Today's theoretical impossibility may be tomorrow's practicality. This point is in complete accordance with a major tenet of traditional realism, viz., the boundaries of possibility and experience are an empirical question, i.e. they cannot be drawn *a priori*.

The realism that Harré defends is of the more modest variety, which he refers to as 'policy realism'. Instead of using inference to the best explanation to establish the truth of theories about unobservables or that any theoretical term successfully refers (referential realism), the realism established here concerns the rationality of certain scientific procedures or practices, viz. taking the referring expressions of a theory seriously, to the extent that we find it reasonable to mount a material search for such entities. Whether we succeed in locating them is an empirical question but rationality dictates that the scientist proceed *as if* these entities do actually exist, are out there, waiting to be discovered (Harré, 1986, pp. 67–9, 223–5, 312).

The basis for policy realism is inductive: we have observed how past applications of policy realism has paid off by successfully shifting objects from Realms 2 and 3 to Realm 1. In other words, the history of science provides us with innumerable case-studies where a theory postulates the existence of a class of entities which are subsequently found to exist after many years of speculation about them. It could be the discovery of a new continent, the observation of micro-organisms under a microscope or seeing a new planet with the aid of a telescope. The scenario, then, is to have theory predict these new entities, giving us good reason to go out and search for them; and, with the advent of new technology, we often end up observing them to exist or, sometimes, failing to find them under circumstances where theory says we should. Notice that even if many things the prevailing theory says about these entities turn out to be false, theory can still be vindicated in that its postulated objects have neverthe-less been discovered. The point is that pursuing Realm 2 and 3 objects has been most successful in the history of science in most startling and important ways. So, we have good inductive reason to believe that continuing this pursuit with our latest theories should pay off as well. Thus, policy realism has a rational foundation (Harré, 1986, pp. 222–36).

So, Harré presents us with a defence of a pragmatic version of realism, one that neither claims truth nor guarantees reference but, instead, the wisdom of serious attempts to locate objects in Realms 2 and 3. Thus, he feels, many of the arguments against the other versions of realism become irrelevant in light of policy realism. What is especially nice about this defence is that it does not rely in the least on inference to the best explanation and, hence, it is not open to the above circularity charge. On the contrary, it is an argument based on induction, something even the constructive empiricist must accept, for the constructivist empiricist must allow for induction if science is to function at all. (See Boyd, 1984, p. 67.)

The major problem, I fear, with Harré's defence is that the constructive empiricist may actually embrace the conclusion of the inductive inference, claiming that policy realism has watered down scientific realism to the extent that the end-result is perfectly compatible with constructive empiricism. 'After all,' the empiricist might reply, 'we think that it is rational to pursue the eventual observation of theoretical entities as well. But this does not mean we think that past success spells evidence for the *truth* of theories about unobservables; it only means that such theories lead to better instrumental reliability. What better way, then, to extend the realm of observables than to behave *as if* there were such entities out there? But this does not mean we are forced to concede that it is true they are out there. Thus, we constructive empiricists are proud to be policy realists although we would like to call it policy empiricism.'

What this shows, I think, is that conclusion of Harré's argument is too modest, that his induction is more powerful than he realized when he proposed it in support of policy realism. In fact, I contend that it can be used to establish the stronger conclusion of convergent realism. After all, if the above kind of induction can be used to support policy realism, why can't the very same evidence support convergent realism? Below, I shall provide the reader with such an extrapolation.

Representing Epistemic Invariance and Convergent Realism

It is my contention that the key to Harré's defence is the idea that realism can be open to experimental considerations. The trick is to convert such data into an argument for evidence that does not beg the question. In order to do so, however, we must supplement the induction with another principle, one which I believe the anti-realist can not possible deny, viz. the principle of epistemic invariance: when it comes to gathering evidence for our beliefs, *the epistemological situation remains the same for observables and unobservables alike*, no matter what realm we happen to be dealing with at the time. More will be said about this principle immediately below.

Suppose we represent convergent realism in the following way. Let 'A' stand for the way nature actually is while 'T' stands for the way our theories depict nature. Letting 'B' denote the way nature actually behaves and 'P' stand for the behaviour T predicts about nature, we can simply construct the absolute values, $|T-A|$ and $|P-B|$, and use these quantities to graph or represent convergent realism (see figure 4.1).

This graph says that there is a functional relationship between verisimilitude and scientific progress, viz. scientific progress serves as a measure of the extent our theories are getting closer to the truth. In other words, the increase in accuracy of our predictions and measurements is a function of how well the theories upon which these predictions and measurements are based depict nature. While convergent realism is not

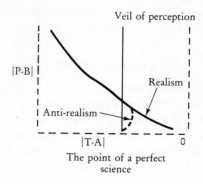

Figure 4.1 *Convergent realism*

necessarily committed to using verisimilitude to *explain* scientific progress, it is committed to the view that there is a functional *relationship* between the two, that as our theories are getting closer to the truth we are cutting down on the error of our predictions and measurements *and vice versa*. In contrast, the anti-realist holds that it is a real possibility for |T–A| to increase while |P–B| decreases (dotted line on the graph).[2]

Now, using the vertical line to represent the 'veil of perception', we can represent the principle of epistemic invariance in terms of a symmetry principle: the functional relationship between |P–B| and |T–A| will remain invariant as the veil of perception shifts to the right of the graph. In other words, the relationship between theory and prediction, on the one hand, between nature and the way it behaves, on the other, remains the same as we move from observables to unobservables, from unobservables to in principle unobservables.

I do not think there is anything controversial about this claim unless the anti-realist is prepared to maintain the view that an observable nature behaves differently than the world of unobservables (if there were such a world, that is). Putting problematic interpretations of quantum mechanics aside, what difference could there be between these two worlds, except the trivial one that one is observable while the other is not?

I admit that I have not presented the reader with a characterization of verisimilitude. Nevertheless, I do think verisimilitude can be characterized. The issue I think ought to be emphasized, here, is not what verisimilitude is but the relationship between getting closer to the truth and scientific progress; it is the relationship that really matters in the realism debate. In fact, I believe that the empiricist demand for a characterization of verisimilitude is a red herring. As I shall maintain below, the kind of verisimilitude I have in mind can, in many cases, be directly observed, and it is the same kind of verisimilitude the realist holds for unobservables.

Experimental Realism

Is the convergent realist correct to maintain that the degree in error in our predictions and measurements is a function of how closely our theories depict nature, and that this function is such that our theories are getting closer to the truth as our predictions and measurements are getting more and more accurate? Contrary to the traditional realist and the anti-realist, I contend that this question can be empirically settled using Harré's line of argumentation.

What would such an empirical justification look like? To begin with, those who maintain that success need not imply the truth of a theory must allow their own *theory* to be applied, at least, to observable situations. And this is something the anti-realist position completely overlooks: we construct and confirm innumerable theories about observable things, *theories that can be directly observed to be true or false*. It is just that we often construct theories about observables prior to being in position to directly observe their truth value. Most importantly, however, we often make predictions (and measurements) on the basis of these theories, again, before we can go to the trouble to observe directly whether or not they are true. This kind of situation in science is the source of the power underlying Harrés's induction.

Let us consider this case in point. Something goes wrong with your car; suppose you have trouble starting it. You call your mechanic and describe the symptoms to him. He hypothesizes that something is wrong with the starter and asks you to try to do other things to start the car. On the basis of his hypothesis, he predicts what will happen and, sure enough, he is right. He then goes even further by theorizing what is wrong with the starter and asks you to try even more things and he is right again about what subsequently happens. Let us say what he claims that a particular part in the starter is worn. Remember, your mechanic is doing this over the telephone.[3] Even so, you have the impression that he is zeroing in on the truth about your car. You take the car in, the starter is removed, that particular part is taken out and examined and, sure enough, it is worn beyond repair. The part is replaced, the starter put back in the engine and the car starts like new. What this example shows, besides my ignorance of auto mechanics, is that a hypothesis can *later* be observed to be true – and, hence, cease to be an hypothesis – *after it has been used to make many successful predictions*.

Surely, Laudan and van Fraassen cannot deny the possibility of many theories about observables which, in turn, can be settled directly by observation. As Boyd has emphasized, their kind of anti-realism does not call for a Humean type of scepticism. Otherwise, their position would be bogus.

So, we are left with this situation. The convergent realist wants to maintain that success and verisimilitude are interlinked. The anti-realist maintains that it is *possible* for our theories to make progress while even getting further away from the truth about nature. Can such a fundamental dispute be decided? What we have here are two rival *hypotheses* about the relationship between theories, progress measured in terms of pre-dictability and accuracy of measurement, and the truth or accuracy of description of these theories. So, why can we not decide between these rival theories by *testing* them? How can we test them? By taking theories which can eventually be observed to be true or false and testing to see if any false theories can systematically lead to better predictions and measurement in spite of their being false. It is my contention that the anti-realist position will be shown to be empirically false by such testing.

Is it a real possibility that a progressive series of theories about a given subject-matter could wander from the truth, even if predictions, measure-ments and inventions get better with each successive theory? Let us put it to the test, then. Instead of considering the contentious cases in the history of science that, for example, Laudan cites, cases such as phlogiston and the ether, we should set up some type of controlled experimentation. After all, Laudan accuses the realist of being dogmatic on the basis of his claim that, for each case of scientific progress, it is *possible* that we are getting further from the truth. But how can he establish such a possibility? It seems that he feels that such a possibility is established by showing these cases have actually occurred in the history of science. However, if these cases are contentious at best, why look for them in the history of science when we should be able to produce them right now under controlled circum-stances? All I am proposing, then, is a fair test of his hypothesis, a crucial experiment on the connection between progress and verisimilitude.

So, let us see if this issue can be empirically settled. Prepare a series of black boxes. The preparers will try to design the inside of each box in such a way that its observable behaviour will systematically mislead a researcher into formulating false hypotheses about what is going on inside the box. But the preparer is not just trying to get the researcher to come up with a false hypothesis in the beginning. That would be too easy. The preparer wants the examiner to come up with a series of (more refined) hypotheses about the box, hypotheses that end up going astray, *even though he has been making better and better predictions about the behaviour of the box all the while*. We can then play this little game, one very much like Turing's limitation game; only, this time, we trick the scientist into making false hypotheses about the box while believing that he is getting closer to the truth because these hypotheses are yielding better and better predictions. If we are clever enough to succeed, then we have evidence for the anti-realist hypothesis, for all the researcher actually achieved was to come up with a series of hypotheses which only saved appearances but failed to get at the truth about the inside of the box. After the boxes are constructed, we seal them and have scientists examine each one. While they can not open the box and observe what is inside, they can use any means at their disposal to test the behavior of each box.

Then we gather the fruits of their labour. We are only interested in those hypotheses that yield better and better predictions about the behaviour of the box being examined. The judges compare each such hypothesis with reality by opening the corresponding box. Now all we have to do is determine the ratio of cases of successful series of hypotheses that have actually strayed further from the truth over the total number of successful series of hypotheses.

I bet that the ratio will approach zero. My reason for this is that we are all familiar with cases of everyday hypotheses about observables which are highly successful and are subsequently confirmed by direct observation. I do not think any of us can come up with a case where a highly success-ful *series* of hypotheses, with each successive hypothesis yielding better predictions, actually ends up getting further from the truth in the long run. So, why should we expect things to be different for a series of hypotheses that makes better and better predictions upon refinement, only, this time, we cannot directly observe if it is getting closer to the truth?

This is also why I think that the anti-realist demand for a precise formulation of verisimilitude is a red herring. In the above cases, the judges can observe for themselves if a sequence of hypotheses is getting closer or further from the truth. If 'getting closer to the truth' makes sense in these empirical cases, and it is fairly clear that it does, realists can always maintain that it is the exact same sense of 'getting closer to the truth' they have in mind for theories about unobservables. There is simply no justification for maintaining two different senses of 'verisimilitude,' one for observables and one for unobservables. To do so would clearly confuse semantics with epistemology.

We come back to the above postulate that there is no difference in the relationship between truth and the progress of theories when it comes to a nature which is observed or unobserved. It should not make any differ-ence. In fact, this postulate is open to empirical considerations as well. Is it not true that in the above cases of confirming empirical theories we have a transition between a theory about an unobserved nature (relative to the examiner) to a nature which is observed (when each box is opened for all to see)? Has the relationship between truth and successful prediction been altered by this transition? I think not.

It is true that the anti-realist may still question the principle of epistemic invariance by insisting that we have no reason whatsoever to believe that it applies to theories about Realm 3, where the entities in question cannot, *in principle*, be observed. The anti-realist would maintain that even if the above argument works, it only allows for an extrapolation from observables to unobservables but not from observables to *in principle* unobservables. Yet, some of our most important theoretical entities are just unobservable in principle (for example, virtual particles). So, the anti-realist would insist that the above argument does not really come to grips with the problem of making such a great inductive leap.

In reply to this criticism, I think that the onus is really on the anti-realist to show that, while the inductive leap from Realm 1 to Realm 2 may be justified, it is not justified in the observable–in-principle-unobservable case. The realist maintains that the relationship between verisimilitude and predictive progress is independent of whether theoretical entities are unobservable in practice or in principle. So, the anti-realist must show that the *in principle* unobservable case does affect the relationship between verisimilitude and progress. But this amounts to showing, I think, that *whatever it is about nature that renders certain entities in principle unobservable also opens up the possibility that our theories may go haywire while yielding better predictions*.

But how can the anti-realist show, inductively or otherwise, that those features of nature that are responsible for it being impossible to observe certain entities also upset the relationship between verisimilitude and progress in such a way that is it possible for a sequence of theories that lead to better and better predictions are actually getting further from the truth? We all know that 'in principle unobservable' is a theoretical notion. All we can do, then, is to examine, on a case-by-case basis, *how* nature determines that certain entities are unobservable in principle. By this means, we shall be able to tell if these features also negatively effect the relationship between getting closer to the truth and increased accuracy.

As a case in point, virtual particles are, in principle, unobservable in that their observation would violate the laws of quantum mechanics (in particular, the uncertainty principle). But what is it about the uncertainty principle that should lead us to believe that it is *possible* for the relationship between verisimilitude and increased success to be different in the case of theories about virtual particles, that is, what is it about the uncertainty principle that makes it possible for these theories to get further from the truth as their predictions get better? I do not think the anti-realist could ever come up with a theoretical reason for linking up the uncertainty principle with the breakdown of verisimilitude; and I am sure other cases will show the same lack of success for the anti-realist. Besides, is the anti-realist not getting dangerously close to accepting the realist's position by attempting to establish a link between in principle unobservables and the possibility of our theories getting further from the truth?

So, ther are two reasons why the above objection fails. The only way the anti-realist can make his case is to appeal to theory. But the realist can use that theory to come up with a positive reason for believing that the relationship between truth and progress will remain unchanged as we go from observables to certain in principle unobservables. Secondly, the anti-realist ends up in the ironic position of having to play the realist's game, i.e. having to appeal to the workings of the very entities he refuses to recognize in order to exploit the distinction between unobservable in practice and in principle; on the other hand, it is the realist who is advocating that these cases should be empirically settled.

The anti-realist has another charge to level against my induction for convergent realism.[4] I have claimed to come up with evidence for a functional relationship, f, between increased accuracy and verisimilitude; yet the empiricist will argue that any experimental data I come up with are not evidence for anything of the sort. On the contrary, what I may take to be evidence for the truth of f, the anti-realist will insist that I only have evidence for instrumental reliability. If I construe the results of the above experiments as evidence for the truth of f *vis-à-vis* its reliability, then I have simply begged the question; for opting for the former assumes realism is true in the first place.

In response to this criticism, I should like to emphasize that nowhere do I claim to supply evidence for f, if by 'evidence' we mean some version of inference to the best explanation, for example, in the sense that tracks in a Wilson cloud chamber are evidence that a certain type of particle has passed through. In all cases, the item for which the evidence is of is not directly observed. Claiming evidence for realism in this sense would surely beg the question.

But f and not-f are tested in the above game by making *direct observations* in each test case and then counting up the results. I emphasize that, in each case, we directly observe if f holds or not. Whether f holds *in general* or not – the realist claims 'yes' while the anti-realist claims that we cannot tell – is now a function of inductive reasoning, how fair the tests were, how good the samples were, and so on. This is within the spirit of experimental realism. But inductive reasoning, fair tests and good sampling are considerations that even the constructive empiricist must accept if his position is to avoid collapsing into Humean scepticism.

So, I really do not have to claim that evidence always bears on truth in order to say that f is borne out by these tests, for such a claim is based on direct observation and induction. It is true that evidence-gathering takes place during the course of formulating and evaluating a particular hypothesis about what is inside each box. In no way are these data supposed to be construed as evidence for or against f. Direct observation decides that question.

This means that my defence is not to be taken as a proof of f. Rather, the principle of epistemic invariance is to be construed simply as a demand for consistency in reasoning, that the anti-realist must reason about unobservables in the same way he does about observables. Unless the anti-realist can show that there is something about the unobservable world that renders f false, he *should* think about the unobservable world in the way he does the observable one. Otherwise, the anti-realist is like the creationist who may behave quite rationally at the supermarket and in his automobile but changes the rules of the game when it comes to evolution.

I submit that the situation in many natural sciences is like this. We have a string of successful reductions where we have 'opened up the boxes' along the line, except at the end of the line. It is just that we have not (and may never) opened the last box. For example, in physics, tables and chairs are identified with atomic lattices, atoms have been found to be made up of protons, neutrons and electrons, protons and neutrons consist of quarks, and so on. Even if we happen to be wrong about depicting the most recently discovered constituent of matter, it really should not make any difference, for we were headed in the right direction all along, except for this last turn away from the truth. Even if quarks, for example, turn out to be other than the way physics describes them to be, we can still say that tables and chairs are atomic lattices, atoms consist of protons, neutrons and electrons, and so on. We were, in this case, just incorrect about quarks, i.e. we were getting closer to the truth all along, having just slipped up at this one level; but we can surely get our theories back on the right path again. I cannot see any difference between this situation and the car mechanic being wrong about what part in the starter is the cause of the problem.

In conclusion I have presented an adaptation of Harrés's inductive argument for policy realism in order to extend it to convergent realism. Simply put, the argument maintains that the relationship between verisimilitude and progress in observable cases is as realism depicts it to be. But there is no reason to believe that this relationship changes as we go from observable cases to unobservables. Hence, realism correctly depicts the relationship between scientific progress and theories getting closer to the truth.

This argument has several advantages over the traditional line of argumentation. In the first place, in contrast to more recent defences which end up watering down the realist position, the realism argued for here is a full-blown convergent realism. In addition to this, unlike past justifications which have been open to the charge of circularity, it is not based on inference to the best explanation. Not only is this defence free from circularity charges, the long-sought connection between verisimilitude and the best explanation trivially follows. Once the functional relationship between truth and progress is empirically established, then all that has to be done is to maintain that the best explanation is the one that assigns the highest probability to the explanandum phenomena, and hence it is the one that leads to the best predictions and measurements, i.e. the most progress.[5]

The argument also frees us from hermeneutics in the history of science. Why debate interpretations of the sciences of the past when the question of the relationship between truth and progress can be independently, empirically settled in the present? But the best virtue of the above argument is that it meets the anti-realists on their own empiricist terms. Laudan (1981) presents the realist with these challenges:

> What, then, of realism itself as a 'scientific' hypothesis? ... If realism has made some novel predictions or been subjected to carefully controlled tests, one does not learn about it from the literature of contemporary realism. *(p. 46)*

He then goes on to say:

> No proponent of realism has sought to show that realism satisfies those stringent empirical demands which the realist himself minimally insists on when appraising scientific theories. *(ibid., p. 46)*

Not only do I fully endorse what Laudan says in these passages, I think the above defence of realism goes a long way to meeting these challenges. On the contrary, my defence of realism shows that empiricists ought to be more empirical.

NOTES

*A shorter version of this paper was presented at the Pacific Division Meetings of the American Philosophical Association, 1987.

1   Even so, I cannot find any passages in Devitt's work that attempt to meet this challenge head-on. It seems that he simply assumes that correlations among

observables, no matter how rich and varied, can never replace theoretical entities.

2   Notice that, according to this representation, each successive theory can be false while getting closer to the truth. In addition to this, the functional relationship between verisimilitude and progress may be stochastic in nature. For example, it may exhibit a random walk but one which approaches 0 in the long run.

3   It turns out that there are mechanics on call-in radio shows where things like this actually happen. For example, there's the 'Click and Clack' show, which can be heard on National Public Radio's 'Weekend Edition' in the United States. What happens is that the caller gives the mechanics the year and make of his car and the symptoms. They, in turn, suggest that the caller tries certain things out. On the basis of the results, the radio mechanics 'bet' what's wrong with the car, give an estimate of repair costs, all of this being open to future confirmation by the caller's mechanic.

4   I am grateful to Arthur Fine for articulating this criticism.

5   This link-up between the best explanation and maximum likelihood is argued for in detail in Aronson (1984, pp. 141–61, 191–9).

REFERENCES

Aronson, Jerrold L., *A Realist Philosophy of Science*, New York, St Martin's Press, 1984.

Boyd, Richard, 'The current status of scientific realism', in Jarrett Leplin (ed.), *Scientific Realism*, Berkeley: University of California Press, 1984.

Devitt, Michael, *Realism and Truth*, Princeton: Princeton University Press, 1984.

Fine, Arthur, 'The natural ontological attitude', in Jarrett Leplin (ed.), *Scientific Realism*, Berkeley: University of California Press, 1984.

Harré, Rom, *Varieties of Realism*, Oxford, Basil Blackwell, 1986.

Hardin, Clyde, L. and Rosenberg, Alexander, 'In defense of convergent realism', *Philosophy of Science*, Vol. 49, No. 4, 1982.

Laudan, Larry, 'A confutation of convergent realism', *Philosophy of Science*, Vol. 48, No. 1, 1981.

van Fraassen, Bas C., *The Scientific Image*, New York, Oxford University Press, 1980.

5

The Scientist as *Homo Loquens*

Roy Harris

*The mistake of traditional metaphysics was not so much to say that
metaphysics is about what exists, but in supposing that it was a science.*

Rom Harré

Introduction

There is a causal chain which links this paper on the language of science to
my first making Rom Harré's acquaintance in the late 1950s, when we both
found ourselves newly appointed lecturers at the same university, and
lectured to the same audiences from the same rostrum on a number of
occasions. For me, as a total non-scientist, this sparked an interest in
philosophy of science and related linguistic questions which is reflected in
what follows below. Although Rom's later work subsequently moved in
other directions, his views of language, of logic and of science do not seem
to me to have shifted radically from those which I frequently heard him
expound some thirty years ago. I also heard him expound in those days,
and with some panache, a thesis to the effect that 'by definition, in the
academic world anyone over forty must be wrong'. I was never quite sure
whether this thesis bore upon the definition of the phrase *academic world*
or the definition of the word *forty*. In retrospect, I now see that Rom was
right; but that either he has opted out of the academic world, or else he is
much younger than I had imagined.

In setting out the following historical sketch of the twentieth-century
scientist as *homo loquens*, I present what is no doubt a crude and
controversial picture of an essentially Cratyline figure. The Cratylus in
question is the Cratylus of Plato's dialogue, whose view of language is
essentially surrogationalist. The central tenets of surrogationalism I take to
be (i) that words have meanings by 'standing for' entities, properties,
relations, etc., and (ii) that the entities, properties, relations, etc., are given
independently of the words standing for them. Various versions of

surrogationalism may be distinguished, depending on the status assigned to the items words are taken to stand for, and on the exact interpretation given to the surrogational connexion, the 'standing for' (Harris 1980: 33ff., Baker and Hacker 1980: 1ff.). But these subtleties get a look-in here only by courtesy of the traditional rhetorical device of *praeteritio*. The particular form of surrogationalism which Cratylus made famous was the thesis that utterances are meaningless unless formulated in words which are 'naturally correct'. The history of Western linguistic thought ever since is strewn with the debris of unsuccessful attempts to spell out a principle of 'natural correctness'.

The sceptical standpoint from which my sketch is drawn could perhaps best be indicated by modifying the epigraph at the head of the paper to read:

> The mistake of modern science was not so much to say that science is about reality, but in supposing that it was a metaphysics.

And by calling something a metaphysics I equate it with a metalinguistics. In other words, modern science made – and still makes – the mistake of thinking it speaks a language we have no option but to accept. And that is not only a form of hubris but a mistake about language: for there is no such language.

This hubristic error has a long previous history, which I allude to only briefly. But it has been exacerbated in the present century by the social contradiction between the power which the natural sciences wield within the confines of academia and the more or less menial role allotted to them by the governments of the Western world. Science is funded, to be sure: but only because it is deemed to be 'useful' either for civil or for military purposes. Caught in this situation, scientists have fallen victims to schizophrenia of the Kiplingesque variety: taking the cash, but trying to take the credit too. All this is understandable. It is understandable, for instance, that when in 1874 the Prussian government decided to establish permanent chairs of geography in all Prussian universities, the academic geographers of Prussia did not inquire too closely into the reasons for this sudden interest in geography on the part of their political masters. It is equally understandable that, in order to preserve their self-respect, scientists should reject a lowly utilitarian role and prefer a nobler picture of themselves as engaged in an eternal 'quest for truth'. In painting this picture, unfortunately, they have been led to espouse what many non-scientists would regard as a quite untenable theory of language and of the linguistic role of the scientist in modern civilization.

If it should be objected that what I have drawn instead is not a sketch but a mere caricature, I would be inclined to plead guilty, albeit with reservations about the word 'mere'. For caricature is as good an art form as any for 'capturing reality', and arguably better than most. Although Cratylus, almost certainly, would not have agreed.

Science and Philosophy of Science

There is a remarkable lacuna in Sir Peter Medawar's much acclaimed book *The Limits of Science* (Medawar, 1985): no account is given of any *linguistic* limits. The lacuna is all the more remarkable on three counts. First, Medawar evidently assumes scientists to be normal human beings in at least one respect; namely, they are language-users. Rash though this assumption may be, Medawar does not question it, and it will not be questioned here. The point is, though, that normal human beings do in their saner moments realize that there are linguistic limits to the questions they can sensibly ask and to their capacity for understanding answers. But Medawar makes no reference to this in the case of the scientist, even though he evidently wishes to present science as a quintessentially human inquiry. Second, Medawar also wishes to claim that scientific truth is not any special kind of truth. Science, according to him, adopts the ordinary, everyday notion of truth. This 'humbly commonsensical conception of truth' he believes to have been formulated with great insight by Tarski in the crystalline dictum: 'A true sentence is one which states that a state of affairs is so and so and the state of affairs is indeed so and so' (Medawar, 1985, p. 5). (This already lays the ground for Medawar's version of what will be referred to below as 'semantic continuity theory'.) Third, Medawar *does* claim that there are certain questions which science cannot answer, because they belong to a different 'world of discourse'; and not temporarily or adventitiously so, but intrinsically so.

If we wish to put Medawar's position in some kind of historical perspective, we would do well to start with the twentieth-century lay view of 'science'. This, roughly, is the view that science began when the cleverest of our forebears 'stopped discoursing of the origin and destiny of man and began to roll balls down slopes, to swing pendulums, and to weigh the water which dripped from a bottle' (Dingle, 1947, p. 2). A scientist, in other words, is archetypally a person who believes that there is at least one department of human experience in which reasonable certainty may be attained, and that is 'our experience of the movement of bodies' (ibid., p. 2). That, among other things, allegedly distinguishes the scientist from the philosopher. The philosopher is professionally unsure that there is *any* department of human experience in which reasonable certainty may be attained. So unsure are philosophers of this that they have erected their collective doubts into a special branch of their subject and called it 'epistemology'.

Although the philosopher thus described sounds even less like an ordinary human being than the scientist, the philosopher too is a language-user. Indeed, philosophers are commonly believed to be even more dependent than scientists on using language for their livelihood. This is seen as being because the philosopher, unlike the scientist, needs to be able to talk about *all* human experience – about, for instance, the beauty of sunsets, moral dilemmas, religious faith, the meaning of life, and many other things of which science knows nothing. At least, this is the lay view.

Dissenters from this view have included some notable scientists. Einstein, for example, gave his approval to the opinion that 'in this materialistic age of ours the serious scientific workers are the only profoundly religious people' (Einstein, 1940, p. 28). The scientist, according to Einstein, has a deep conviction of the rationality of the universe. He is 'possessed by the sense of universal causation', by 'a rapturous amazement at the harmony of natural law, which reveals an intelligence of such superiority that, compared with it, all the systematic thinking and acting of human beings is an utterly insignificant reflection' (ibid., p. 29). It presumably follows that the beauty of sunsets, the value of religious experience, etc., are as much chords of the cosmic harmony as the behaviour of balls rolling down slopes. Anyone motivated by such a lofty idealization will, understandably, refuse to accept that science deals only with one limited part or aspect of the world as mortals understand it; for science is constantly expanding its domain to take in more and more of the marvels of the universe. It is also predictable that such a person will refuse to admit that science is validated by its practical successes in facilitating human control over the environment, toothache, etc., but will insist that science is totally independent of its practical applications. This is indeed precisely what Einstein claims. Science, he asserts, 'must have no practical end in view' (ibid., p. 30). *No* practical end? That is what Einstein says: and if we take his philosophy of science seriously at all, then we must take that claim and its deepest implications seriously too. Einstein would doubtless have agreed with T. H. Huxley, who once said that he wished the term *applied science* had never been invented, since it gave rise to the misconception 'that there is a sort of sicentific knowledge of direct practical use'. For Huxley 'pure science' was not a kind of higher-order systematization from lower-order inquiries of immediate practical utility: on the contrary. 'What people call applied science is nothing but the application of pure science to particular classes of problems' (Huxley, 1893, p. 145). In short, for partisans of this view, science is 'pure' *by definition*, and potentially unlilmited in scope.

Medawar, by contrast, is an unashamed utilitarian, or, if this sounds too harsh a term, a 'Baconian'. He does not actually say that the purpose of science is to increase our standard of living, but he goes out of his way to quote Bacon's preface to *The Great Instauration*, in which we are reminded that it was the desire of power that brought about the fall of the angels, and the desire for knowledge the fall of man. Bacon, according to Medawar, 'believed that the purpose of science is to make the world a better place to live in' (Medawar, 1985, p. 39). That too is his own view. If the picture presented in the present paper is at all credible, the semantic crisis of modern science arose essentially because (for historical and cultural reasons) many scientists were not willing to be Baconians.

The Baconian attitude long preceded Bacon. Strabo in his *Geographica* had already given a very Baconian justification of geography not merely as 'useful' knowledge but as contributing to human happiness. There were also many varieties of anti-Baconian posture, including the justification of the pursuit of science purely as an intellectual challenge (irrespective of the 'discovery of truth'). For example, when Jacobi was reproached by Fourier for wasting time on the study of elliptic functions when there were still practical problems in heat conduction to be solved, Jacobi replied: 'It is true that M. Fourier had the opinion that the principal aim of mathematics was public utility and the explanation of natural phenomena; but a philosopher like him should have known that the sole end of science is the honour of the human mind' (Bell, 1937, p. 372). All this is part of the intellectual history of the distinction between 'pure' and 'applied' knowledge, which cannot be pursued further here.

The polarity of this traditional opposition has continued to structure much twentieth-century discussion of the history and function of science. On the one hand, scientific progress is seen as the cumulative acquisition of a limited but rock-solid body of more or less incontrovertible facts about how various parts of the physical world work, with practical 'mastery over natural' (Bernal, 1939) as its goal. On the other hand, science, as distinct from technology, is presented as a completely disinterested pursuit of answers to questions posed by the ultimate nature and structure of the universe. Nothing prevents the two from going hand in hand; but that is not the point. The polarity itself is a feature of our conceptualization of what is going on, or has been going on. Projected back into the past, for example, this polarity generates one account of the history of Greek thought in which the pre-Socratics of the Milesian school feature as scientists of the former kind (albeit given to making foolhardy generalizations), as opposed to Socrates and Plato, who feature as scientists of the latter kind; but another account according to which Socrates and Plato were, precisely, not scientists at all but philosophers. The thrust of their intellectual inquiry, powerful as it was, was anti-scientific (Farrington, 1944). No pupil at the Academy was ever recommended to start rolling balls down slopes in the pursuit of truth.

The same polarity has informed many twentieth-century debates about the social duties and responsibilities of the scientist. For example, in a paper on 'The Present Crisis in the Mathematical Sciences' presented to the Second International Congress of the History of Science and Technology in 1931 one of the delegates of the USSR began by asserting: 'The position of mathematics, as that of any science, is at bottom determined by the development and the position of the forces of production, of technology and economy' (Colman, 1931, p. 1). He went on to argue that these forces affect mathematics both directly and indirectly; directly by creating the supply and demand for mathematics (in the form of practical problems to be solved and the training of mathematicians able to tackle them), and indirectly through the prevailing 'philosophy of the ruling class'. Here we are presented with a view of science in which scientific endeavour is automatically guided by and subordinated to the practical needs of the state or the community. Whatever the particular political background to such a view may be, it manifestly stands in contrast to a position from which the scientist's first and last allegiance is seen as being to an a-social 'higher truth', as a result of which the scientist may sometimes become engaged in head-on conflict with the government or other temporal authorities. As one might expect, scientists who acknowledge the possibility of such a conflict take care to enrol science on the side of the angels. Thus, for example, J. Robert Oppenheimer, in his essay 'Physics in the Contemporary World', writes 'Tyranny, when it gets to be absolute, or when it tends so to become, finds it impossible to continue to live with science' (Oppenheimer, 1955, p. 202). But there is no mention in Oppenheimer's script of any possible conflict between democracy and science. That would indeed be surprising in a script written by a scientist who masterminded the atomic bomb.

It is not the political implications of the polarity but the linguistic implications which are of primary interest in this paper. For it is a polarity which generates two conflicting attitudes to the perceived disjunction (nowadays, some would say, an ever-widening gulf) between the language of science and the language of every day. According to one view the disjunction is both natural and necessary, because the world the modern scientist mainly describes is quite simply *not* the world of daily experience. But according to an alternative view there ought at some level to be a viable translation or transition between the two languages, because science deals with the whole universe, which must by definition include the phenomena of daily experience. Adherents to the latter view sometimes speak of the need to construct a 'conceptual system that embraces both common sense and science' (Harré and Madden, 1975, p. 2). For want of any established teminology, let us call those who accept this latter view 'semantic continuity theorists' and those who accept the opposite view 'semantic discontinuity theorists'.

In a famous simile Wittgenstein once compared the language of science and the language of every day to patterns of urban topography.

> Our language can be seen as an ancient city: a maze of little streets and squares, of old and new houses, and of houses with additions from various periods; and this surrounded by a multitude of new boroughs with straight regular streets and uniform houses. *(Wittgenstein, 1953, p. 18)*

According to Wittgenstein 'the symbolism of chemistry and the notation of the infinitesimal calculus' are 'suburbs of our language' (ibid., p. 18).

This simile will at least serve to clarify the distinction between theorists of semantic continuity and discontinuity. Wittgenstein's comparison is one which we would expect to get a sympathetic reception from the former group. Following Wittgenstein's map, the honest citizen proceeds from the central maze of little streets out to the suburbs on foot. There is no Berlin wall. The suburbs are further from the centre; but they are not on the other side of the ocean, and certainly not on a distant planet. For semantic discontinuity theorists, on the other hand, nothing could be more misleading than Wittgenstein's picture. A chemist or a mathematician, the separatist maintains, really does have to learn a different language, a different conceptual system, in order to do chemistry or mathematics. It is in no sense just an extension or suburb of the more central communication system of daily life. Wittgenstein's map juxtaposes, and thereby confuses, two fundamentally different cartographies.

Thus we find projected two profoundly different accounts of the scientist as *homo loquens*; hence of the scientist as a human being; and hence of human beings in general. According to one account, the scientist belongs to an elite, a priesthood speaking a sacred language in which great truths are enshrined, beyond the comprehension of the common populace. According to the other account, the scientist is simply a technical specialist, whose obscure jargon is of no more significance than the jargon of any trade or craft, and useful only in its limited domain. That dichotomy, however, runs in tandem with another. For the scientist sometimes also speaks to us in non-scientific language *about* the language of science. These two roles must be carefully distinguished, for roughly the same reason that what politicians say is by no means to be judged on the same footing as what politicians claim they say.

Physics and Stamp Collecting

Are scientists themselves the most reliable authorities on the status and functions of the language of science? This question takes us back again to the epigraph at the head of this paper. The paragraph quoted continues:

> This is completely to misunderstand its role in intellectual constructions. Descriptive metaphysics concerns itself with the existence presuppositions and priorities of our conceptual schemes as they are: *prescriptive* metaphysics with the existence presuppositions and priorities of conceptual schemes we might or should adopt. In neither branch are we doing any kind of science. You can take or leave a metaphysical view in a way which you can't exercise options in science. *(Harré, 1961, pp. 1–2)*

The implications of this, clearly, is that scientists should stick to their scientific last, and not try to set up in business as metaphysicians as well. Or if they do, there is no rank they can pull qua scientists, any more than Ian Botham can rely on his prowess as an England cricketer to guarantee his selection to play football for Scunthorpe United.

Anyone who wishes to object to the 'scientists must stick to their last' policy will probably complain that this is just the line we would expect from an official of the philosophers' trade union. For philosophers would not be in business at all unless they could claim to tell everybody else how to conduct themselves. So why does the scientist (or the artist, or the prophet, or the milkman ...) have to stand for the philosopher's academic arrogance? Some philosophers tried to forestall this objection by claiming that philosophy is actually the most general, and hence the most basic, of the sciences. In the present century, this view is particularly associated with Russell. Wittgenstein disagreed radically with Russell on precisely that issue. But in retrospect this clash of swords on the philosophical stage has a wooden ring to it. Both Russell and Wittgenstein can in hindsight be seen as philosophers desperately keen to defend the besieged citadel of philosophy, but disagreeing about the best strategy. The beleaguering forces are in both cases those of science.

Who, then, is qualified to pronounce on the language of science? Perhaps, one might venture to say, linguists. But here again there is a trade union problem. The currently accepted trade union doctrine in academia is that chemists, mathematicians, etc., are the experts on chemistry, mathematics, etc.; and by the same token linguists are the experts on language. But the expert witness of the linguist is admissible in court if, and only if, linguistics is itself a science. Otherwise the jury might just as well rush out into the street and canvas the opinion of the nearest passer-by.

The snag here is that the scientist in intransigent mood may simply decree *ex cathedra* that those who study languages, albeit in a systematic and scholarly way, simply do not produce anything that count as scientific theories about langauge. For in order to count as scientific, a theory (whether about language or anything else) has to be in certain crucial respects like theories in physics. That is the view epitomized in Rutherford's celebrated dictum: 'There is physics and there is stamp collecting.' What underlies this dichotomy between physics and stamp collecting is the claim that unless we are dealing with statements that can or could in principle be reduced to statements about elements, events and processes that physics can handle, then we are not in the domain of science at all.

For purposes of assessing the dichotomist's claim, one does not need to be too pernickety about defining 'physics', or about defining 'stamp collecting' either. For physics, the investigation of 'matter in motion' will do well enough, provided one is willing to grant that matter includes living matter, and that living matter includes us. Then the claim will run roughly as follows: that anything we can justly call a science of life, or of part thereof, must ultimately be translatable into statements of the kind the physicist uses to describe matter, its constitution and the laws which govern it. Nor can the direction of reduction be reversed. Nature is such that everything resolves into combinations of material elements of a certain sort, but these elements do not in turn resolve into elements of a previously encountered kind. That is why sociology or psychology might in the end boil down to a rather specialized kind of physics; but physics will never boil down to a rather specialized kind of sociology or psychology. Now what, on this view, are the prospects for achieving a genuinely scientific account of language?

The most promising path will presumably lead into the experimental study of the various kinds of neurophysiological programming underlying verbal behaviour. Taking that path might suggest that it will be impossible to avoid the range of controversies surrounding the relationship between mind and body, and the theses known to philosophers as 'physicalism' or 'central state materialism'. If so, then the case of language becomes simply one particular example of a more general type of problem already familiar. Because it is so familiar, and because nothing in this paper hinges on taking a stand on it, let us agree to shortcut it by the rather high-handed strategy of treating all those issues which divide the partisans in the mind–body debates as being 'merely terminological'. That is not a strategy that will appeal to everybody, but the point of adopting it here is to highlight the fact that *even if* those issues were merely terminological, there would still be left an important question about the status of language in relation to scientific theorizing.

The question concerns meaning. Physics needs language; whereas stamp collecting does not. The stamp collector is free to arrange a collection of stamps in any groupings he or she pleases, or in none. No justification need be given for such groupings, or for why certain stamps appear in the collection but not others. Any such justification is extraneous to stamp collecting itself, and reflects a personal preference on the part of this or that collector. But in the end, every stamp collection speaks for itself, in so far as it speaks at all. An experiment in physics, by contrast, does not speak for itself. Physics, however generously or narrowly defined, needs language because the physicist has need of words and word-related symbolisms in order to state conclusions. However meticulously I roll a ball down a slope, it does not count as a scientific activity until I say something about it; and what is said has to be something more than 'Well, well!' or 'Isn't it pretty?'. Only if it did not matter *what* I said would physics and stamp collecting be on a par.

This, however, places the dichotomist in an uncomfortable situation. At some point an explication will be required of the meaning of the words in which the statements of physics are formulated. Failing such an account, what the physicist has neglected is the most essential part of the whole scientific enterprise: for it remains unclear what the statements of physics mean. The physicist cannot at this juncture appeal to the neurolinguist. The point is not that neurolinguistics is in no position to offer anything remotely resembling an account of the meaning of even the simplest of the sentences in Newton's *Opticks*, but rather that even if such an account were available and were manifestly 'scientific', that sub-part of science would be the cornerstone of the whole scientific edifice. This remains so even if the entire body–mind problem is just a misguided terminological controversy. The reason why is simple. A physics which claimed to be able to dispense with any account of the meaning of what physicists say would just not be a rational explanatory activity of the kind that most physicists, presumably, would want us to believe it is. The distinction between physics and stamp collecting would collapse at a more fundamental level than any which Rutherford had in mind.

This was the realization which led to the 'semantic crisis' of twentieth-century science. The intellectual structure of that crisis will be examined in the following section. But first it is relevant to point out how it links up with the polarity discussed above (pp. 66–70). It is not much good for physics to hold the key to unlocking the mysteries of the universe if science itself cannot give a scientific account of what the statements of science mean. Science automatically loses any claim to priority in the hierarchy of human inquiry; for it emerges as dependent upon knowledge of a non-scientific kind for its interpretation. On the other hand, this does not matter much if the status of science is merely banausic. Why should it matter? Nothing important turns on the fact that the man from the Gas Board who tells us that the leak is not serious because his test shows only a drop in pressure of three millibars cannot, when asked, give a definition of *millibar*. He can just point to the dial on his instrument and say, '*That's* three millibars'. So the semantic incompetence of science is only cause for concern if coupled with the view that the scientist is *not* just a technical specialist. It does become a problem, however, if coupled with the more exalted pansophic view of science.

Precisely at this critical point the semantic continuity theorist comes to the rescue. If the language of science is semantically continuous with the language of every day, that lets the scientist at least temporarily off the hook of having to give any general account of meaning, other than producing definitions of special scientific terms. But not only that. In so far as the terminology of science is more carefully and exactly defined than non-scientific usage, it acquires the status of a superior part of language, the attractive, regular suburbs of Wittgenstein's simile. Such suburbs are clearly not only 'better' from a town-planner's point of view than the chaotic jumble of streets in the old city centre, but provide a paradigm for judging and analysing all urban development. Thus by espousing continuity theory science can even offer a model which will show the linguist how to do descriptive semantics 'scientifically'. Furthermore, it supplies a basis for arguing the case that what is wrong with ordinary language is that in certain respects it falls short of the standard which is set – and shown to be attainable – by the language of science. Why not just demolish that old city centre, and build a neatly laid-out shopping mall instead?

Science as Semantics

The semantic crisis of modern science was in one sense an inheritance from the seventeenth century, when Locke, in his role as epistemologist to the Royal Society (Aarsleff, 1982), rightly perceived the necessity of providing an account of language as part of the theoretical foundations of any systematic inquiry into Nature. Book III of the *Essay on Human Understanding* may be regarded as the Bible of semantic continuity theory. The twentieth century's problems with the semantics of science can all be seen as arising from the belated realisation that Locke's solution does not work.

Locke saw ordinary language as being quite inadequate for the purposes of science – a view which has never since been seriously challenged. But he believed that these inadequacies could be overcome in a scientific language if scientists took the simple precaution of agreeing on the definitions of all the key terms. There are various reasons why this was always a somewhat utopian solution, but only one need concern us here. Locke's solution was based on his belief that all scientists share (along with all non-scientists), by reason of the physiological constitution of *homo sapiens*, a common fund of 'simple ideas'. This simultaneously provides the basis for postulating continuity between ordinary language and scientific language. In fact, if Locke's assumption about 'simple ideas' is correct there *must* be semantic continuity, because this universal fund of simple ideas is the only ultimate source of linguistic communication. Furthermore, it underwrites Locke's celebrated distinction between 'nominal essences' and 'real essences': the former are derived from 'simple ideas' whereas the latter are independent of them.

Once Locke's foundational assumption is rejected, a double disaster ensues for his surrogational language of science. Not only is there no assurance of communication between, say, physicists and biologists, or between either group and the general public, but there is no way this can be remedied by agreement on definitions. For the definitions themselves will be subject to all the uncertainties and inadequacies which beset their definienda (in common with the terms of ordinary language). A definitional regress opens up, which science is powerless to halt.

Again, for practical purposes, this does not much matter provided scientists are prepared to accept the humble role of technical experts and regard their technical terminology as having no more important a function in our understanding of the world than the technical terminology of dress designers or cabinet-makers. But it matters a great deal for any more ambitious thesis about the role of science and its discovery of the ultimate secrets of the universe.

What was eventually to provide the conceptual touch-paper for the semantic crisis in twentieth-century science emerges from a line of thinking that goes back to Ernst Mach, whose name is usually associated with the doctrine called 'neutral monism'. This is commonly distinguished from the more hard-line reductionist position in philosophy of science called 'physical monism'. Physical monism takes the extreme view that only matter exists and all so-called mental and psychological phenomena are ultimately governed by the laws of matter. There is thus no separate realm of the mind, with laws of its own. Neutral monism is perhaps best thought of as an attempt to repair a rather large philosophical hole in physical monism. Physical monism is all very well, provided we are not at all worried about how the laws of matter can be known consciously by a human agent, or whether they can be known at all. If they cannot be known, then whatever physicists may think they are doing or claim they are doing, it can hardly be discovering how Nature really works. And this is a conclusion which physics in its role as scientific flagship of the human race clearly cannot countenance.

Neutral monism bails physics out, by providing not only an account of what physics is, but also of how it is possible to be a physicist. Neutral monism takes the view that Nature can be known only by human observation, and through the construction and testing of hypotheses by reference to what is observed. It is often regarded as a complete reversal of the position of the physical monist, because it is associated with the philosophy that all is mind, and matter is merely a construction of the mind. But that is not essential. One can formulate the central thesis of neutral monism in a way that does not rely on taking an anti-materialist stance. One can say simply: whatever exists, its nature is such that it is scientifically knowable only by constructing and testing hypotheses by reference to observables.

The linguistic implications of this were developed in a very striking and controversial manner by the Vienna Circle from the late 1920s onwards. The central tenet of Vienna Circular semantics was that in order to have any meaning a statement had to be objectively verifiable. Strictly interpreted, this had the consequence that statements like 'God exists', or 'Truth is beauty', or 'Fascism is evil', for which no plausible means of empirical verification could even be suggested, had to be counted as meaningless. Not only was this comforting for the physicist but it was also good news for the linguist; at least, for those linguists who were aware that the weak link in the claim of linguistics to be recognized as a science was its manifest inability to deal convincingly with semantics. For if the verificationists were right, then there simply was no account to be given of the meaning of very many sentences used in everyday speech, because they had no meaning. And in so far as everyday words and sentences *were* meaningful, then the natural sciences would – sooner or later – be able to give the appropriate definitions.

Among linguistic theorists this brand of reductionism was associated particularly with Bloomfield. According to Bloomfield (1935) only people's observable linguistic behaviour was available as scientific evidence to the linguist. Consequently, the only case in which the meaning of a word could be analysed with any certainty was when the word referred to some objectively investigable thing. Thus, for example, according to Bloomfield, the word *salt* has a meaning, and it is possible to say quite precisely what that meaning is, because what salt is has been discovered by science: it is the substance sodium chloride. But words like *love* and *hate* do not have meanings that can be precisely stated, if they have meanings at all: because science has not yet reached the stage where the objective correlates of these terms, if they have any, are available to analysis. So whereas linguistics can give an accurate account of the meaning of a sentence like *This is salt*, it cannot do the same for a sentence like *I love you*. What *I love you* means, if anything, the linguist does not know. But then, nor does anyone else. Thus in effect a position is reached where it is proposed that the linguist should hand over descriptive semantics lock, stock and barrel to the physicist, the chemist, the biologist and their colleagues in the natural sciences.

The irony of this situation in which science was set to take over semantics lay in the deep divisions which were beginning to emerge within science on fundamental semantic issues. Bloomfieldian behaviourism and Vienna Circle verificationism both stem from taking a certain view about the nature of scientific inquiry and then worrying about he status of the resultant statements. But the worries could be pursued in different ways and to different extremes. The concept of 'observation' was crucial here. According to one interpretation, all the scientist in the end can do is measure things. This led directly to Bridgman's 'operationalism' (Bridgman, 1927), in which the meaning of a scientific statement is ultimately cashed in terms of the measuring operations from which it was derived. A closely related view was that of Eddington (1928), who saw the scientist as ultimately reporting on the readings of instruments. Thus the man from the Gas Board who responds to our query by pointing to the dial and saying '*That's* three millibars' is giving an impeccably Eddingtonian semantic analysis. On either of these views, Bloomfieldian semantics, although on the right lines, did not go far enough: for what remained to be explained was the meaning of the statement 'Salt is sodium choloride'.

Bridgman's operationalism led in linguistics to Zellig Harris's 'distributionalism', which was modelled upon it (Harris, 1951). Bridgman also laid the basis for one of the more sophisticated forms of continuity theory. Consider, for example, phrases such as *the length of a cricket pitch* and *the length of a radio wave*. The operationalist, defining concepts by reference to techniques of measurement, will maintain that different concepts of 'length' are involved in the two cases. (The head groundsman at Lord's is not in a position to pronounce on whether or not the BBC's cricket commentary is broadcast on the right wavelength; but he *is* in a position to settle disputes about whether the wickets are the right distance apart.) However, although these are operationally different concepts of 'length' there is semantic continuity between them, inasmuch as 1500 metres is 'longer' than 22 metres in both cases.

A different line was taken by those who, while agreeing that 'observation' is the *sine qua non* of science, held that because the scientist is after all a mere mortal, a finite observer, no scientist can hope to take account simultaneously of everything that is going on in what is observable.

Consequently science must constantly have recourse to a kind of make-believe: this is the role of 'theory'. The scientist, in other words, can do no more than formulate accounts of what *would* be the case if there were nothing interfering with the operation of just those elements and forces which have been selected for investigation. Since this 'no interference' assurance can never be given, the scientist is led to construct idealized abstractions of what ought to be available for observation if Nature were not actually quite so complicated as it unfortunately seems to be.

This view of the relationship between observation and theory in science also had a marked influence on the development of modern linguistics. The aim of the descriptive linguist came to be seen not as the direct investigation of speech behaviour but as the construction of an ideal language which would represent the essential features of whatever actual language the linguist happened to be studying. Thus according to Carnap (1937) the structure of

> a particular word language, such as English, or of particular classes of word languages, or of a particular sublanguage of a word language, is best represented and investigated by comparison with a constructed language which serves as a system of reference.

What Carnap means by that is explained as follows:

> The direct analysis of [languages], which has been prevalent hitherto must inevitably fail . . . just as a physicist would be frustrated were he from the outset to attempt to relate his laws to natural things – trees, stones and so on. In the first place, the physicist relates his laws to the simplest of constructed forms; to a thin straight lever, to a simple pendulum, to punctiform masses, etc. Thus, with the help of the laws relating to these constructed forms, he is later in a position to analyze into suitable elements the complicated behaviour of real bodies . . . *(Carnap, 1937, p. 8)*

Subsequently generative grammarians took over exactly the same view of the relationship between scientific observation and theory construction. Indeed, the criticism which generativists levelled at Carnap's generation was precisely that of failing to carry through the proclaimed programme. Katz commented on Carnap's proposals:

> On this conception an artificial language is construed as an idealization of a natural language in just the sense in which ideal gases, perfectly rigid rods, complete vacuums, etc., are idealizations of physical phenomena. Its function is this to reduce the complexity of such phenomena to manageable proportions, so that regularities can be described in terms of simple laws.

But although this analogy correctly represents the ideal character of a scientific theory of language, it is misleading as an interpretation of the results actually produced by the logical empiricists ... *(Katz, 1966, p. 63)*

What is important here is to note the claim that 'this analogy correctly represents the ideal character of a scientific theory of language'.

Why, then, did the logical empiricists fail? According to Katz, there were two reasons.

the artificial languages developed by Carnap and his followers are, unlike successful idealizations in physics, under no strict empirical controls that determine their adequacy. A scientist who proposes an idealization must demonstrate that it predicts accurately within a reasonable margin of error and that the closer actual conditions approximate the ideal, the smaller this margin of error becomes. *(Katz, 1966, p. 64)*

So the first reason was the failure to provide an adequate account of what observable linguistic behaviour the hypotheses were intended to predict, with the result that they were not strictly testable.

The second reason, according to Katz, was that the logical empiricists never properly defined their terms. Although they described linguistic properties of various expressions, as being, for example, 'synonymous' or 'analytic', they failed to define what was meant by calling expressions 'synonymous' or 'analytic'. So these descriptions in fact were vacuous. It was as if

the Newtonian theory of mechanics were to specify examples of bodies, states of motion and rest, forces, actions and reactions, etc., but were to offer no laws of motion to explain the physical principles relating mechanical causes to mechanical effects. Hence, we know no more about a language after we find out that a Carnapian idealization 'predicts' that certain of its constructions have certain linguistic properties ... than we did before the idealization was formulated. The analogy with idealization in physics only conceals this fact behind a facade of scientism. *(Katz 1966, p. 65)*

The upshot of this criticism is clear. What Katz is complaining about is not that the logical empiricists made theories in linguistics too much like theories in physics; but, on the contrary, that they did not make theories in linguistics *enough* like theories in physics. And this criticism came, it should be noted, from a school of linguistics which prided itself in having shaken off the linguistic misconceptions of the Bloomfieldian era.

Here the semantic crisis of modern science spiralled ever deeper into a maelstrom. Science now knew (supposedly) what a scientific theory of language ought to look like. But science seemed powerless to define the theoretical linguistic terminology which was *ex hypothesi* required.

The Survival of Surrogationalism

What lay behind the semantic crisis of modern science was a deep reluctance on the part of scientists and philosophers of science to abandon a surrogationalist view of language. The reason for this was that abandoning surrogationalism seemed tantamount to letting go of any claim that the statements of science were *true* statements. For many scientists it was deeply disturbing to be able to say no more than that their conclusions were 'useful', or 'systematic', or 'consistent', or even 'productive'. They hankered after something more. And in the wake of positivism it was fairly clear that they would not get anything more except by adopting a surrogational semantics. This was the principal attraction of the semantics which Bloomfield had proposed. It could claim to be a 'realist' semantics, but its realism was of the Cratyline variety. In addition, like all forms of surrogationalism from Plato's *Cratylus* onwards, it was covertly prescriptivist. Thus, for example, the Bloomfieldian characterization of the meaning of *salt* as 'sodium chloride' implied that uses of the word other than in that meaning are *pro tanto* incorrect. This is all of a piece with the surrogationalist doctrine that the ultimate 'incorrectness' in language is to have words for things that do not exist at all (like *phlogiston*).

It is a sure sign of Cratyline prescriptivism to dismiss the ways in which others may use words as 'abuses'; and in particular the way they use words like *meaning*. This complaint has now become routine in philosophy of science. The Vienna Circle started the ball rolling by claiming that many words which others thought meaningful were meaningless. But that is a game any two prescriptivists can play. A more recent instance is Putnam's objection to Feyerabend's views on the language of science. Putnam writes:

> It is evident that Feyerabend is misusing the term 'meaning'. He is not alone in such misuse: in the last thirty years, misusing the term 'meaning' has been one of the most common, if least successful, ways of 'establishing' philosophical propositions. *(Putnam, 1975, p. 122)*

How did this regrettable logomachy over what we mean by *meaning* come about? Putnam, with no apparent tongue in cheek, says: 'The blame must be placed squarely upon the Logical Positivists.' Pot calling the kettle black was always one of the commonest forms of prescriptivist accusation.

The prescriptivism of latter-day Bloomfieldians in philosophy of science is sometimes disguised under a veneer of permissiveness. Putnam again provides an eloquent example: 'I cannot ... think of anything that *every* user of the term "electricity" *has* to know except that electricity is (associated with the notion of being) a physical magnitude of some sort, and, possibly, that "electricity" (or electrical charge or charges) is capable of flow or motion' (Putnam, 1975, p. 199). Now the relevant point about this eccentric piece of semantics is not that the conditions as stated fail to distinguish what is going on in a telephone cable from what is going on in a glass of lemonade, or either of these from what is going on in the chorus line at the Folies Bergères, but that when we inspect Putnam's claim (and even set aside its question-begging conflation of knowing with believing) it still emerges as a claim about what '*every* user of the term "electricity" *has* to know'; and this does not make much sense unless we insert 'in order to use that term correctly'. In other words, Putnam is still apparently pronouncing on necessary conditions governing the usage of the word *electricity* in the English-speaking community in general, and doing so not on the basis of any empirical investigation of that usage but on the basis, as he puts it, of what he can 'think of'. This admits two interpretations. On one interpretation, what Putnam can think of about the term *electricitiy qua* native speaker of English is merely introspective evidence; in which case there is no warrant for advancing it as a claim about '*every* user of the term'. The alternative, and more plausible, interpretation is that the conditions Putnam states are prescriptive conditions. The ultimate authority for this prescriptivism is presumably Nature, to whose dictates on the subject of electricity the 'scientific' lexicographer is deemed to have privileged access, just as Bloomfield supposed.

Bloomfield *qua* linguist had told the scientists exactly what they wanted to hear. (In return, he expected his brand of linguistics to be officially recognized as 'scientific'.) The 'Bloomfieldian era' in linguistics lasted for a quarter of a century. Bloomfieldian authority waned only when the behaviourism on which it was based came under attack. What is interesting is that even then something very close to the Bloomfieldian programme (in which scientists would eventually write the linguist's descriptive lexicon) survived in philosophy of science. And still survives. More curiously still, Bloomfieldian semantics was used to attack positivism itself: a strategy rather like trying to defeat a dragon by tying the beast's own tail round its neck. Or perhaps inducing the beast to choke by swallowing its own tongue would be a more meticulous simile.

An interesting example was the argument from so-called 'ontological experiments' (Harré, 1961). This involved a typically surrogationalist fallacy. Purportedly, ontological experiments are of the kind which, at least in favourable cases, allow the scientist to convert a metaphor into a literal statement of fact. We begin with a proposition of the form 'It is as if p' (or 'It is p-like') and proceed via ontological experiment to a proposition of the form 'It is the case that p'. (Roughly speaking, the scientific scenario one is invited to envisage is analogous to the progress of a visitor who begins by looking out of your kitchen window and saying, 'What's that thing like a spaceship doing at the bottom of your garden?', and ends up running down your garden path shouting 'Good heavens! Look! It *is* a spaceship!')

The way the scenario is supposed to develop is as follows. The scientist constructs a model (= 'hypothetical mechanism') which includes a component tentatively designated by a term t. This model is then tested experimentally in order to determine whether the component in question 'really is a t' (= the 'ontological experiment'). There are three possible outcomes: (i) The component proves not to be a t. In that case, the term t may be discarded. Or it may be kept 'in inverted commas', because it happens to be useful for scientific purposes to think of the component 'as if it were a t'. (ii) The component proves in fact to be a t. In that case, the term t is retained as its designation, but now has a meaning in certain sentences which it did not have before the conclusive experiment, when it was used only metaphorically. (iii) The experiment is inconclusive, in which case the term t retains its metaphorical status.

The following examples (from Harré, 1961) illustrate the difference between two uses of a term having a different status conferred upon it by ontological experiment. (A) In the theory often used to account for the behaviour of drops of liquid, the drop is said to be covered by a 'skin'. On this supposition, the drop can be treated from the physicist's point of view as if it were a balloon. But in fact, the physicist knows that this is only a metaphor. Tests show that a drop of liquid has no skin. (B) In the theory which sought to explain how aluminium resisted corrosion, it was hypothesized that when the metal was attacked by acid or alkali a protective 'skin' was formed. That is to say, what happened or failed to happen was as if there were a skin protecting the metal. But then, by experiment, it was shown that this explanation was literally correct, and the skin formed could be physically separated from the underlying metal.

This is not pure Bloomfield; but it is not a million miles away either. The point is that the argument from ontological experiment carries no punch against positivism at all *unless* we accept its linguistic presuppositions: and these are strictly surrogationalist. (We have to accept that the experiment proves that whatever protects the aluminium is 'correctly' called *skin*. This is exactly like Cratylus inquiring into Hermogenes' financial affairs in order to determine whether he is 'correctly' called *Hermogenes*.) In short, the scientist turns up once again in the familiar role of lexicographer, and a surrogationalist view of words is employed to validate a form of continuity theory. (For it would actually *defeat* the thrust of the argument if what was claimed was merely that for experimental purposes the scientist should be allowed to redefine the word *skin*.)

Thus surrogationalism is employed to outpositivize the positivist. It is the finding of a physical object which is deemed to provide the ultimate validation of the use of the term. The scientist has found not just *a* thing which the word *can* stand for, but *the* thing it *did* stand for. If the ontological experiment fails to reveal the thing, this is not taken to settle the issue definitvely: all that may happen is that the word continues to be tolerated as a metaphor. It is regarded as inferior in some way, as not having its 'full' or 'proper' meaning in these cases. Metaphor thus becomes a kind of linguistic limbo, from which words can escape by passing the test of science.

To savour the full historical irony of this move, one must bear in mind both (i) that the argument from ontological experiment was here being used *against* the forms of positivism espoused by Bridgman, Eddington & Co., and (ii) that all this was in the context of beating a Popperian retreat from diehard allegiance to the verification principle. Here we see surrogationalism caught in the Popperian bind which rejects verifiability in favour of falsifiability. The way out is breathtakingly barefaced. In effect, we are told that Bridgman, Eddington & Co. rushed to panic stations prematurely when confronted with a semantic crisis. They should have stayed at their posts and remained calm. For all that was needed to avert the semantic bankruptcy of modern science was a long-term loan from the metaphysical bank. The bank simply slips into existence-claims a proviso about language. From now on, existential cheques will be cashed only on the understanding that they read:

> According to theory T, experiment X demonstrates the existence of . . . in universe of discourse U. (*Harré 1961, p. 50*)

Surrogationalism is dead: long live surrogationalism.

By this stage one might well ask: why not go the whole hog and resuscitate Locke's distinction between real and nominal essences? Why be shy about being a semantic essentialist? After all, the Greeks thought it was permissible (between consenting adults). The step was indeed boldly taken (Harré and Madden, 1975) and admirably backed up by citing the history of successive definitions of the word *copper*. These, apparently, have been continuously improving as the definition moved away from the 'nominal' towards the 'real'.

The current state of semantic play with the word *copper*, we are told, is the following.

For the scientist this term refers to something having the properties of malleability, fusibility, ductility, electric conductivity, density 8.92, atomic weight 63.54, and atomic number 29. All but the last of these properties are dispositional, ascribing powers and liabilities to the substance and hence already have a force over and above the attribution of manifest properties. But since the properties set out above serve to specify what a substance has to be, and to be capable of doing to be copper, if an entity lacked any of these properties it would not properly be called 'copper'. *(Harré and Madden, 1975, pp. 12–13)*

This is much closer to unadulterated Bloomfieldian semantics, and overtly prescriptivist. Doubtless in the local ironmongers they do not know what the atomic number of copper is. But that is because they are ignorant and consequently the everyday semantics of the word *copper* is pretty sloppy. The surrogationalist lexicographer-scientist knows better: *copper* really means 'substance having the properties so-and-so . . . and atomic number 29', because that is what copper *is*. The everyday meaning is connected to the real meaning, but rather loosely.

Thus the most recent version of surrogationalism to become fashionable involves the claim that terms for basic natural substances (like *water* and *gold*) together with certain basic theoretical terms in science (like *electrical charge*) are not arbitrary. That is to say, what these terms mean is not a matter of definitional convention in the sense that, say, what counts as a goal in football is laid down arbitrarily in the rules of the game. Rather, the meanings of those basic terms are derived causally or ostensively from the realities they designate, without it necessarily being possible to formulate their true definition. The terminology may nevertheless be introduced by exemplification, prior to any discovery of the properties which a correct definition would need to mention. Thus it is perfectly possible in a linguistic community for words to be used, and used sensibly and appropriately, without anybody in the community knowing what they mean. Putnam has even glorified this into a linuigistic principle: the 'Principle of Reasonable Ignorance' (Putnam, 1975, p. 278). One can dimly glimpse the shade of Bloomfield in the underworld nodding approval.

When it takes this form, surrogationalism promotes the scientist from the role of descriptive lexicographer to that of general linguistic theorist. The implication, clearly, is that any linguistics which takes the arbitrariness of the linguistic sign as its foundational principle is not 'correctly' representing the nature of language. For it fails to capture the fact that slowly but surely the human race is working towards that ideal state which pioneers like Bishop Wilkins rashly tried to rush us into. The linguistic utopia ultimately promised is one in which language is not arbitrary at all; for its structure will indeed reflect the structure of reality. In that linguistic paradise, not only shall the lion lie down with the lamb, but the linguists will all agree, and a scientist shall lead them.

The survival of surrogationalism in twentieth-century science and philosophy of science is thus not the mystery it at first appears to be. One can safely predict not only its survival but its deeper entrenchment in the foreseeable future. For it is the only view of language Western culture has ever made available which bolsters that flattering self-portrait which modern science likes to present to the world. It is the portrait of a ceaseless quest for truth, in which tireless researchers dig ever deeper into the ultimate nature of physical reality. The bedrock may not yet have been reached. But however deep the digging goes, the scientist can send back up to the surface reliable descriptions of what has most recently been discovered down at that level. This is possible because the language of science, in spite of appearances, is semantically continuous with the language of every day, and because the latter like the former also rests on surrogational foundations. That is the only semantic theory on offer which fits the notion that the linguistic task of the scientist as *homo loquens* is the 'accommodation of language to the causal structure of the world' (Boyd, 1979). Or, as Cratylus would have put it to Einstein, making sure that our names are correct.

REFERENCES

Aarsleff, H., *From Locke to Saussure*, London, 1982.

Baker, G. F. and Hacker, P. M. S., *Wittgenstein: Meaning and Understanding*, Oxford, 1980.

Bell, E. T., *Men of Mathematics*, London, 1937.

Bernal, J. D., *The Social Function of Science*, London, 1939.

Bloomfield, L., *Language*, London, 1935.

Boyd, R., 'Metaphor and theory change: What is "metaphor" a metaphor for?', *Metaphor and Thought*, ed. A. Ortony, Cambridge, 1979.

Bridgman, P. W., *The Logic of Modern Physics*, New York, 1927.

Carnap, R., *The Logical Syntax of Language*, London, 1937.

Colman, E., *The Present Crisis in the Mathematical Sciences and General Outline for their Reconstruction*, London, 1931.

Dingle, H., *The Missing Factor in Science*, London, 1947.

Eddington, A. S., *The Nature of the Physical World*, Cambridge, 1928.

Einstein, A., *Mein Weltbild* (trans. A. Harris, *The World As I See It*), London, 1940.

Farrington, B., *Greek Science*, Harmondsworth, 1944.

Harré, H. R., *Theories and Things*, London, 1961.

Harré, H. R. and Madden, E. H., *Causal Powers*, Oxford, 1975

Harris, R., *The Language-Makers*, London, 1980.

Harris, Z. S., *Methods in Structural Linguistics*, Chicago, 1951.

Huxley, T. H., 'Science and culture', 1893. Reprinted in Gardner, M., *The Sacred Beetle*, Oxford, 1985.

Katz, J. J., *The Philosophy of Language*, New York, 1966.

Locke, J., An Essay Concerning Human Understanding, 5th edn, London, 1706.

Mach, E. W. J. W., *Populärwissenschaftliche Vorlesungen*, Leipzig, 1896.

Medawar, P., *The Limits of Science*, Oxford, 1985.

Oppenheimer, J. R., 'Physics in the contemporary world', 1955. Reprinted in Gardner, M., *The Sacred Beetle*, Oxford, 1985.

Putnam, H., *Mind, Language and Reality. Philosophical Papers*, Vol. 2, Cambridge, 1975.

Wittgenstein, L., *Philosophische Untersuchungen*, ed. G. E. M. Anscombe and R. Rhees, trans, G. E. M. Anscombe, Oxford, 1953.

Part II

Controveries in the
Philosophy of Physics

6

New Tasks for the Philosophy of Physics

John Roche

Neglected Areas of Research

In the course of research over the past ten years on the history and concepts of electromagnetism, it gradually became clear to me that at least two areas of philosophical research in physics are virtually untouched today. One such area is the scheme of descriptive, analytical and explanatory strategies used by the working physicist. Familiar examples include the concept of 'line of action' of a force, the notional division in two of a bubble in order to calculate its internal pressure, and the concept of 'dynamic equilibrium'.

The second area requiring clarificatory analysis by the philosopher encompasses many of the technical concepts of physics, including, for example, scalar potential, centripetal acceleration, rotary momentum and the phase velocity of a wave. Since a satisfactory analysis of the conceptual products of physics is not possible without a prior examination of its conceptual tools the present article will concentrate on the latter.

This kind of research is much more neglected in classical physics than in quantum physics. Since it involves a detailed clarificatory analysis of interpretative schema and the resulting technical concepts, I shall call it the 'analytical philosophy of classical physics'. In those aspects dealt with here it attempts to understand and clarify the techniques and terms used within physics to distinguish, describe, enhance, classify, manipulate and explain the structures, systems, phenomena, processes, laws, properties, mathematics and notation of classical physics.

It can hardly be doubted that the understanding of classicial physics at this level of detail is a necessary prolegomenon to any clear understanding of quantum physics in the future.

The analytical philosophy of physics might study, for example, concrete examples of the use by the physicist of the distinction between 'intensive' and 'extensive' properties. By linking present usage to its historical origins, it could elaborate a general account of that distinction which would clarify the received usage and allow it to be used with greater confidence, precision and generality, primarily by the practitioner of physics, but also, of course, by the general philosopher of physics.

Another example might be a systematic study of the use of classical symmetry in physics. A natural history table could be drawn up of examples from mechanics, gravitation, geometry, electrostatics and so forth. The distinction between symmetry as a physical property and symmetry as a principle of explanation, proof, problem-solving, theory construction, instrument design and theoretical and experimental exploration could be studied. The difference between physical symmetry and analytical symmetry requires explanation, as does the nature of polar symmetry, and of taxonomic symmetry. The justification of arguments from symmetry needs to be studied. These and many other questions concerning classical symmetry require clarification within physics.

Such concepts, many of which are listed below, are, of course, created in the first instance by the working physicist as a response to the need to organize and interpret a given complex of theory and phenomena. However, the application of these concepts in physics is not always accompanied by a critical investigatin of their suitability and conditions of validity. Perhaps such an examination is not even properly the task of the practitioner. In carrying through such an analysis the philosopher can function as a critical physicist. His research would also be invaluable to the intelligent popularizer of science.

Rom Harré has actively encouraged this research from the very beginning. It seems appropriate, therefore, to use the opportunity of this *Festchrift* to discuss the objectives, methods, professional training, audience and publication outlets of this new or renewed departure in the philosophy of physics.

Reviving the Art of Verbal Explanation in Physics

Several movements of thought have conspired over the past three centuries to weaken the role of verbal explanation in modern physics. These include the rejection of the qualitative physics of Aristotle in the seventeenth century; the pursuit of novelty in Nature which also developed at that time and which deflected attention away from the task of consolidating and clarifying that which is already known; the emphasis on experiment and mathematics as sources of knowledge; the replacement of geometry and proportion by algebra and mathematical analysis as the dominant language of mathmatical physics, and the growing perception of science as concerned with what is useful rather than with what is true in nature. As a result of all of this the resources of terms and verbal techniques available to the physicist for the interpretation and explanation of physics are now severely impoverished.

Today physics needs to develop a much richer and more flexible verbal language which can cope with the wealth of subtle phenomena and concepts which have flooded into the subject over the past three centuries. The analytical philosophy of physics can make a highly significant contribution to this task by clarifying and extending, in the first instance, the interpretative instruments of the physicist. The philosopher could then, of course, go ahead and apply this improved explanatory apparatus to clarifying and restructuring particular theoretical concepts in physics. It must be emphasized, however, that it would be premature and ineffective to attempt to do this without a deep understanding of the subject in question, without preparing the necessary conceptual tools and without a framework of supporting concepts. These considerations will now be developed further.

The Education of the Analytical Philosopher of Physics

Together with the excellent training now provided in the general philosophy of physics, other skills are required for the philosophic art described here. These include what I shall term an 'historical understanding' of the concepts in question, together with a thorough familiarity with those areas of physics which exemplify the interpretative schema or technical concepts of interest. I shall consider the latter requirement first.

If the investigator proposes to study, for example, the general role of sign conventions in physics, he (or she) will need to be familiar with their application to geometrical optics, statics, translatory and rotary dynamics, electrostatics, electromagnetism, angular measurement, the calculus and so forth. It will also be necessary to decide when they are a hindrance and when a help.

Clearly, the minimum requirement here is an academic qualification in physics. But that alone is not enough. A mature understanding of the relevant areas of physics is needed and this requires a steady diet of reading, teaching and pondering, solving problems and even carrying out physics research on that topic, if possible. This takes time, because the digestion and clarification of concepts cannot be hastened. I should be very surprised if less than ten years of professional immersion in physics were adequate to prepare the analytical philosopher of physics to make a contribution which would be taken seriously by the physicist. This is not, therefore, a task for precocious youth. It is sometimes enough for the ill-prepared philosopher to make a small slip to reveal a depth of misunderstanding of basic physics concepts sufficient to exasperate and alienate the professional physicist or any philosopher who possesses a mature understanding of physics.

The second, non-philosophical skill required by our philosopher is a detailed historical knowledge of his chosen areas of research in physics. Some philosophers of science seem to suppose that the critique of received concepts in physics can be carried out independently of their historical origins. This might be true in an ideal world in which physics purifies all of its received concepts before handing them on to the next generation. But this is hardly ever the case. Physics sees itself as a pioneering subject always pressing forward to new frontiers, with little time to correct and consolidate the gains already made. As a result, almost every theory and every category in physics today is either flawed by foundational errors which have never been cleared up or represents a loose convergence of competing traditions whose differences have never been resolved.

Virtually every concept in physics, therefore, is a working but indis-criminating fusion of imperfect or incompatible elements. This is almost an inevitable consequence of the haphazard historical evolution of these concepts. In brief, therefore, the received concepts of physics are 'noisy' concepts. This is no fit beginning for immediate philosophical analysis.

Historical study helps to resolve such concepts into their constituent elements and it lays bare the roots of remaining difficulties. The detailed study of the historical evolution of a schema or concept in physics is also, perhaps, the best way to understand it quickly and deeply. All of this leads to what I have called the 'historical understanding' of concepts in physics. It is, sadly, a missing dimension in physics education, at present, but it is possible to be a good physicist without it. It is not possible, however, to practise the analytical philosophy of physics in a fully professional manner without it.

It might be objected that one is already asking far too much of the analytical philosopher of physics by expecting him or her to be thoroughly familiar with certain aspects of physics and of the history of physics, in addition to the required philosophical skills. But keeping in mind the inner logic of the task, the intended audience of physicists and the need to do it professionally, I can see no other way. Furthermore, all three sets of skills are complementary and mutually illuminating, and form a kind of natural intellectual harmony. Dedication is, of course, required to acquire them, but philosophers of physics, in general, appear to be enthusiastically dedicated to their subject. Recent contributions by scientists to natural theology set a marvellous example here by their impressive mastery of all branches of modern physics, of modern astronomy and cosmology, of molecular biology, of evolution and of the history of the debate.

The Rational Style of the Analytical Philosophy of Physics

Since external discipline is also helpful the most appropriate outlet for the analytical philosopher of physics is physics journals and physics conferences. This will mean that articles are refereed by professional physicists and this will sharpen the focus of the language employed by the philosopher. To be effective it is necessary to discover an idiom which is generally acceptable to the physics profession on its own terms. Furthermore, there should not be a journal, I believe, of the analytical philosophy of physics. A general audience of physicists should be aimed at, not some new group of specialists created and cultivated by the philosopher. Such a group could only too easily become alienated from mainstream physics.

If the clarifying philosopher is to have the maximum impact on physics, the physicist must see in his writings a refinement and an extension of the language of physics itself. This means that the more technical language of philosphy must be avoided. Terms like 'counterfactual', 'nomological', 'explanadum', 'ontological', 'epistemological' and 'Humean' should be excluded. Sometimes they will not be understood by the physicist, but even if they are, they immediately place the text in an alien philosophical (rather than in a physics) register and the sympathy of commonality will be lost. Furthermore, since the aim of the philosopher here is to clarify and generalize further the explanatory categories already rough-hewn and used by the practitioner of physics, there will rarely be any need to introduce such specialized philosophical terms. The excellence of the art will lie in its invisibility.

The style of papers and books in the general philosophy of physics at present is not always attractive to the professional physicist. While it is only to be expected that a large part of the literature of the philosophy of physics should be addressed to other philosphers of science there is surely a place for a literature addressed directly to the physicist in a language which he can immediately comprehend. Many philosophical movements throughout history have, of course, profoundly influenced the very content of physics in this manner.

The task of the analytical philosophy of physics as it is understood here is not, therefore, to refine further the various in-house debates which are of interest only to the professional philosopher of physics. Its primary goal is to create user-friendly concepts for the working physicist, that is, physics concepts crafted in a philosophical workshop.

Elaborating further on the rational style which I believe is required of the analytical philosophy of physics, it is most important that philosophical hypotheses should not be mixed in with the clarificatory analysis of physics schema and theoretical concepts. If they are introduced inadvertently the pen of the physics referee or the reaction of a physics audience may draw attention to them. Even if certain philosophical hypotheses are consciously adhered to, however (some form of philosophical scepticism, for example), it may be possible to avoid obtruding these into the kind of analysis we have been discussing. If such hypotheses have been so irremediably internalized that they inevitably structure and pervade all investigations by the philosopher, then it is doubtful whether the uncontroversial exposition of physics concepts before the general physicist will be possible for that philosopher.

The main features of the register of thought or explanatory style which is most acceptable to the physicist seem to be as follows. For most physicists, as well as for other professionals such as the chemist, the engineer, the biologist the medical scientist and the environmental scientist, scientific knowledge is an amalgam of much factual knowledge about artefacts, natural objects and laws, together with much approximate, hypothetical and conventional knowledge, many skills both rational and manual, and a recognition of many areas of perplexity, doubt, ignorance and possible error.

The ontology and epistemology implicit in all of this might be described as that of 'critical common sense'. Provided the philosopher keeps to the same register of thought a physics audience should find the presuppositions of his approach generally acceptable.

Some philosophers of science feel it their duty to undermine the epistemological confidence of the physicist and there is, of course, a place for such an approach. But it is no less necessary and relevant to cultivate a philosophical approach to physics which goes along with the common-sense ontology of most physicists and attempts to clarify its concepts from within that setting. Such a programme offers vast opportunities for useful research and it can be carried through with remarkable consistency and intellectual satisfaction.

Philosophical Hypotheses Embedded in Contemporary Physics

At the margins of the mainstream interpretation of physics today there are fragments of various philosophical systems which have worked their way into physics at different times in the past and which remain attached to various concepts and theories today. These include Pythagoreanism, Platonism and Neoplatonism, positivism and operationalism, conventionalism and instrumentalism, Kantian ideas, Darwinism and a new Romanticism. Most of these movements are now strongly associated with philosophical scepticism and relativism.

Physicists are sometimes unaware of the presence and influence of these philosophical undercurrents. Physicists may sometimes argue at cross-purposes with each other concerning a particular topic in physics without any hope of resolving the dispute because at bottom it is based on unconsciously absorbed and conflicting philosophical hypotheses. Any philosopher of physics, well versed in the history of philosophical movements in science, can be very helpful to the physicist here.

For example, he can point out the operationlism which sometimes attaches today to the concept of scales of temperature, or Kirchhoff's reduction of force, kinetic energy and momentum to mathematical formulae, or the influence of Poincaré's mathematically derived conventionalism on some interpretations of Newton's laws of motion, or the strange mixture of positivism and Kantian ideas in quantum theory, or the Pythagoreanism which latterly influenced Heisenberg. A knowledge of those influences will also help the analytical philosopher of physics to distinguish more clearly between the traditional or mainstream interpretations of physics and those interpretations which are heavily influenced by philosophical hypotheses.

I shall now provide a list of interpretative schema which, I believe, merit careful philosophical attention. I have attempted to make it as broad as possible but, inevitably, it represents my own perspectives and limitations. I have also appended a list of theoretical concepts in physics which seem to require clarification.

Interpretative Concepts of Physics

The distinction between the 'qualitative' and the 'quantitative' in physics

Fewer distinctions are more frequently made in physics. When are they used? What do they mean? To what extent has macroscopic physics really reduced quality to quantity? How much qualitative meaning still attaches to the so-called 'quantities' of physics? Is temperature not qualitatively different from density or the electric field from the stress field in a supporting beam? How are two physical 'quantities', which have the same numerical values, distinguished?

The concept of a 'regime' in physics

Examples include the Hooke regime in a stretched wire, the Boyle regime in a compressed gas; the harmonic regime in a pendulum, the Coulomb regime in the law of force between electric charges, the radiation regime in the field due to an accelerating electric charge, and, in general, the regimes of validity of the macroscopic or 'classical' laws of physics.

Differing behaviour in different regimes.

Levels of order in physical nature.

The distinction between explanatory and measuring definitions

Measuring definitions of physical quantities, such as the defining expression for entropy, $dS = dQ/T$, do not of themselves represent an explanatory definition of that quantity. A full physical definition of a given quantity provides both an explanatory and a measuring definition. This distinction is reflected in physics textbooks, in examination papers and also, of course, in physics dictionaries.

The structure of qualitative explanations in physics requires careful analysis. Examples include the definition of a saturated vapour, the explanation of moment of inertia, the definition of electric charge, the justification of Lenz's law in terms of the conservation of energy, and the verbal explanation of why the effective resistance of a capacitor to alternating current reduces with frequency. The regimes of validity of law-based indirect measuring definitions also require general analysis. For example, Newton's second law of motion expressed in the form $F = ma$ can be used as a valid indirect measuring definition of force only at non-relativistic speeds and, only then, when the mass is constant.

Can a distinction ever be drawn between conventional and proper measuring definitions? The conventional scales of temperature such as the Celsius scale which begin from a conventional zero seem to differ in this manner for the physicist from the absolute scale beginning from the natural zero of temperature. Perhaps the task of the applied philosopher of science here is not to insist to the physicist that no such distinction exists, but to examine whether it is actually made and what are the reasons in physics for making it.

The different kinds of measuring definition require careful classification. In analogue definitions, for example, the measuring number is zero when the physical quantity is zero, and doubles when the latter doubles, that is, when like is added to like. Length, volume, weight, angle, and many other quantities seem to fit this description. But there are other measuring definitions, such as that for refractive index or decibel sound level, which do not fit this description. Yet other definitions seem to be counterintuitive or improper. The measuring number for the resolving power of a telescope decreases, for example, when the resolution improves. Is mathematical convenience here being preferred to natural expectations, or is a deeper principle at work?

The distinction between informal, non-numerical and numerical measurement

I find that the philosophy of physics this century has rarely analysed measurement in terms of the purpose of measurement as it is understood in physics and technology. Measurements are usually made so that a particular physical state can be reproduced or recognized subsequently. This was the historical motivation for the introduction of absolute measurement by Gauss. The philosophical analysis of measurement from this perspective organises the subject in a new way.

Informal measurement, by means of visual judgement or touch, or by a combination of sense and experience unaided by instruments, requires analysis. Informal quantitative knowledge is a result of the immediate cognitive encounter between object and subject. The study of non-numerical measurement, by means of a template or pieces of string, for example, needs to be compared with informal measurement and also with numerical measurement. Why is numerical measurement usually superior to other kinds of measurement?

Dimensional analysis

Dimensional analysis is a striking example of the need for philosophical analysis to go hand in hand with historical understanding. A careful study of the historical evolution of dimensional theory will reveal that what passes under the name of dimensional analysis today confuses four separate branches of the calculus of measurement. These are as follows. The dimensional theory of Fourier is a calculus of conversion factors between different systems of base units.

The quantity calculus of Gauss introduces a non-algebraic symbolism for units in which the symbols, like the symbolism of nuclear physics or chemical reactions, stand for the physical thing immediately. In mathematical physics the algebraic symbol also stands for a physical quantity, but not immediately, only through the medium of its measuring number.

The mensurational calculus of Weber relates every quantity which is mensurationally derivative to the ultimate measuring base, through a system of algebraic measuring definitions.

Finally, there is a scaling calculus which shows how physical properties in a system alter relatively when the scale or magnitude of any quantity in the system alters. Each of these branches of the calculus of measurement needs to be carefully distinguished, developed and rationalized. This leads on to further issues and questions. For example, was Fourier's choice of the term 'dimension' fortunate? Which quantities are 'dimensionless' in all systems of measurement (such as a count of discrete objects or a ratio of like quantities), and which are dimensionless only in some systems of measurement (such as the fine structure constant)? Why is the discovery of certain functional laws possible by means of dimensional analysis?

The analytical philosophy of physics can do much to dispel number mysticism here.

Systems of measurement in physics

The technical language of this subject requires much clarification. For example, surely it is better to contrast 'derived' and 'base' quantities rather than 'derived' and 'fundamental' quantities? Electric current is a base quantity of measurement and electric charge is not, but electric charge is physically fundamental while electric current is not. Are not the base quantities chosen for convenience and accuracy of measurement rather than for their 'fundamental' nature?

Is it not better to speak of a 'system of measurement' rather than simply of a 'system of units'? The *Système Internationale*, for example, chooses a general set of base quantities, involves a comprehensive scheme of general measuring definitions of 'derived' quantities, together, of course, with its specification of the sizes of the base units and derived units. There is much more to a system of measurement, therefore, than the specification of units.

The concept of an internally coherent system of measurement needs careful definition, as also does the concept of compatible and incompatible schemes. Supplementary and auxiliary units need to be distinguished more clearly. Are derived units not also 'absolute' units?

Perhaps the concept of a 'standard measuring definition' of each derived quantity needs to be introduced to mensurational science, together with a table of these definitions for every branch of physics.

Is the modern symbolism for derived units (e.g. m kg s^{-2}) not a confusion of Gauss's quantity calculus and Fourier's calculus of conversion factors? Can it, or should it, be replaced by a more rational and intelligible system?

The classification of properties in physics

Physics has developed a very rich but unsystematic language of classification of its properties. I shall simply describe some of these terms since a comprehensive table is needed before systematic analysis can begin.

The term physical 'property' or 'quantity' is sometimes used very broadly to include every quantifiable feature of a body or system of interest to physics. In other contexts physical 'properties' such as density are carefully distinguished from 'processes' such as mechanical work, 'states' such as the excited state of an atom, 'events' such as nuclear disintegration, 'structures' such as crystalline structure, 'phenomena' such as a virtual image, and 'relations' such as the relational length of an object moving at a relativistic speed.

Physical properties in this narrower sense are classified in physics from various perspectives.

With respect to direction they are classified into scalars, vectors and tensors. Some quantities fall between categories, however. E.m.f., Magnetic flux and electric current, for example, are directed scalars. Axial vectors, such as angular momentum, are tensors masquerading as vectors.

With respect to the distribution of a property in an extended body there are 'bulk' and 'distributed' properties, or 'extensive' and 'intensive' properties. Volume is extensive, for example, and temperature intensive. Some properties, however, seem to be a mixture of both categories. Density, for example, is clearly a distributed or intensive property but it is defined not as a point, strictly speaking, but over a volume in the neighbourhood of each point. Similarly, pressure and velocity gradient are in a certain sense both intensive and extensive properties.

Physics has borrowed a variety of metaphors and terms from everyday use and from other subjects to describe and classify its processes and systems.

'Dynamic equilibrium', for example, is used to describe the state of a saturated vapour in equilibrium contact with its own liquid.

The motion of an 'effectively' rigid body is classified into 'pure translation', 'pure rotation' and 'mixed motion'.

The 'excited' state of an atom or nucleus is distinguished from its 'ground' state.

'Anomalous' behaviour is distinguished from 'normal' behaviour. Vibrational 'modes' and 'regimes' are distinguished from each other. Forces are distinguished into 'active' and 'reactive' types. The 'primary' coil of a transformer is distinguished from the 'secondary', and 'self' induction from 'mutual' induction.

Semi-conductors are classified into 'natural' or 'intrinsic' and 'artificial' or 'extrinsic' semi-conductors.

A careful reading of the text-book and research literature of physics will add greatly to this brief lexicon of descriptive and classificatory terms.

The classification of the laws of physics

In contrast to the existing but undeveloped language of the classification of properties, a terminology of classification of quantitative and qualitative laws hardly exists in physics. Coulomb's law of force between two electric charges is, of course, an example of a quantitative law and Lenz's law of electromagnetic induction is a purely qualitative law. A tentative classification of quantitative laws follows in terms of the causal status of each law. There are many other perspectives, of course, such as degree of generality, accuracy, verification, range and semantic content, to mention but a few. However, it is difficult to think of a more fundamental viewpoint than that of causal status.

Classification, if badly done or if it is inflexible, can, of course, be misleading and sterile. The history of classification in the life sciences shows that it is a slow and arduous process. When it succeeds however, it brings about a great improvement in the descriptive and explanatory power of a subject.

If an algebraically expressed law of physics is to be interpreted correctly most of its symbols cannot be understood as having fixed values. They must be allowed to run in thought through a range of possible values. The interpretation of the law then emerges as a steady feature of the running system.

(a)   *Cause–effect laws.* Newton's second law of motion, in the form which relates a force to the rate of change of mementum which it generates, is commonly interpreted as a cause-effect relation. The first law of thermodynamics is similarly understood.

(b)   *Cause–effect–control.* When Newton's second law of motion is expressed in the form 'force equals mass times aceleration', force is the cause, acceleration the effect and the mass acts as the control on their relationship. Similarly, in the classical understanding of Newton's law of gavity, $F_2 = GM_1 M_2/r^2$, M_1 is the cause of the force F_2 on M_2, M_2 and r are ordinary controls, and the gravitational interaction constant G is a universal control on the magnitude of F_2.

(c)   *Pure correlations.* In such laws the quantities related are caused simultaneously by a process which does not appear explicitly in the equation. In Hooke's law, for example, both tension and extension are produced simultaneously by the stretching force. Maxwell's electric vorticity law $\underline{\nabla} \times \underline{E} = -\partial \underline{B}/\partial t$ is another example of a pure correlation since the induced electric field on the left of the equation and the changing magnetic field on the right of the equation are joint effects of a current system which does not appear explicitly in the equation. The changing magnetic field here does not 'cause' the induced electric field.

(d) The four causal categories established so far, cause, effect, correlation and control or condition will be found mixed together explicitly in every imaginable way in the quantitative laws of physics. Some examples of this mixing of categories follows. In the work law $W = F \times d$, the force F causes the correlated effects W(ork) and d(isplacement). Maxwell's magnetic vorticity law $\underline{\nabla} \times \underline{B} = \mu_0 \underline{J} + (1/c^2) (\partial \underline{E}/\partial t)$ mixes cause, effect and correlation in an even more subtle manner. In Ohm's law $V = RI$ both V (the energy supplied per unit current) and the current I are correlated processes and joint effects of the local surface charges and ultimately of the source e.m.f. The resistance R controls the relationship between these correlates. Note that the voltage does not 'cause' the current. Ohm's law, therefore, mixes correlation and control. Similarly, in the pendulum law $T = 2\pi \sqrt{l/g}$ both T and g are effects of the Earth's gravity acting upon the pendulum, and g controls the relationship between the 'independent' variable l and the 'dependent' variable T.

The causal interpretation of many laws varies with circumstance. For example, the equation $W = Mg$ holds good when a body is in free fall or at rest or moving arbitrarily. In free fall g represents the acceleration of gravity and the law relates cause to effect. If the body is at rest then g may be interpreted as the intensity of gravity that is, the applied force per unit mass. The law $W = Mg$ then relates the total force to the sum of partial forces. Finally, when the body is at rest g may again be interpreted as representing the magnitude of the acceleration of gravity, which is the usual interpretation. In this case the best reading seems to be that W and g are correlated (though not simultaneous) quantities with m as the control.

(e) *Laws which mix auxiliary mathematical quantities with physical quantities.* The equation for the displacement of a particle undergoing simple harmonic motion, $x = A \sin \omega t$, includes the amplitude A and the time t which are genuine physical properties of the motion, but it also includes ω the 'angular velocity' of the associated imaginary auxiliary circle, which is not a true physical property of the motion. In the alternative expression, $x = A \sin 2\pi ft$, (where f is the frequency) all of the variables are physical properties of the motion.

(f) *Laws which mix pure mathematics and physics.* Gauss's electric flux law seems to graft pure mathematics onto physics because the area over which the flux is calculated is commonly an imaginary area only. The circulation law for the magnetic intensity of an electric current is another example and action principles may be yet another. Quite frequently the strictly descriptive quantitative laws of physics seem to generate a penumbra of such useful semi-mathematical laws.

(g)   *Laws which are purely mathematical.* Many integral transformations, such as Green's transformations, appear to have this character.

The distinction between latent and active (or actual) properties in physics

The concept of a predisposition or dispositional property, usually called a latent, virtual or potential property in physics is, perhaps, one of the most important distinctions made in physics. Examples include the latent heat of fusion, virtual work, electrostatic potential energy, nuclear binding energy, and the vector potential understood as a latent momentum in the electromagnetic field. Other examples include the resistance of an electric conductor considered as an authentic physical property even in the absence of a current, the heat capacity of a body in the absence of an inflow of heat; the refractive index of glass in the absence of light; the time constants of a circuit in the absence of any charge or current; the natural modes of a body in the absence of any vibrations and the virtual presence of sinusoidal components in a travelling wave.

Another neglected area is the study of the external properties of bodies such as the focus of a lens or the centre of gravity of an arc. Bodies are thought of in physics as having extrinsic properties *with respect to* such external points.

Descriptive mathematics in physics

Since the seventeenth century physicists have distinguished between descriptive mathematics and auxiliary mathematics. A well-known example of the latter is the imaginary auxiliary circular motion introduced to deduce the equations of a linear simple harmonic motion more easily. Auxiliary mathematics in physics seems to be derived historically from the construction lines of geometry and the intermediate functions of algebra.

What is the relationship of descriptive mathematics to nature, to pure mathematics and to auxiliary mathematics? How does the semantic reference of these three kinds of mathematics differ from each other? How is the 'transduction' from natural laws into their more artificial algebraic surrogates carried out? Many case histories and much careful analysis is required here.

What is the semantically optimum manner of presenting the mathematical laws of physics, the first law of thermodynamics, for example, or Ohm's law?

The expression $dU = dQ - dW$ would appear to be semantically superior to the more usual expression $dQ = dU + dW$. In the former version the effect dU is carefully distinguished from its two causes, dQ and dW. In the latter version, however, cause and effect are not clearly distinguished. Students find the first version easier to understand.

Similarly $V = RI$ seems to be better than $R = V/I$ as the most semantically perspicuous version of Ohm's law. In most applications R is a fixed quantity controlling the correlated variables V and I. Although it is, of course, quantitatively correct to write $R = V/I$ it seems to be categorically and semantically opaque. Of course, $R = V/I$ is the correst way to write the measuring definition of resistance, but the use of a law to provide indirect measuring definitions of physical quantities must be carefully distinguished from the proper statement of the law itself.

Why are proportionality factors introduced into the mathematics of physics? When have they physical meaning and when are they purely scaling factors only?

How much information is implicit and how much is explicit in the mathematical laws of physics? For example, the mathematical expression $F = (1/4\pi\varepsilon_0) \cdot (Q_1 Q_2 / r^2)$ for Coulomb's law of force between electric charges, does not make it explicit that two forces are involved, that they are equal and opposite, that the transmission of force is retarded, and that the equation holds good only when the charges are at rest, in a vacuum and small compared with their separation. How is such implicit information read into the equations of physics?

How does physical understanding control the construction, choice and manipulation of equations? What dictates the selection of a physically meaningful solution from the array of solutions offered by mathematics?

What is the significance of the fundamental ambiguity of the bare mathematical laws of physics?

What information is given by 'rationalization', that is, by the introduction of 4π in the denominator of Coulomb's law above? How is the semantic content of the equations of physics maximized?

How are notational devices used to signal physical distinctions, for example, vector and scalar notation, Latin and Greek letters, capitals and lower case letters, positive and negative signs, unit notation, ordering of characters, operator notation, complex algebra, the symbols dy/dt, $\partial y/\partial t$, $\Delta y/\Delta t$?

In the course of mathematical manipulation do the equations of physics temporarily lose semantic reference?

How and when do they recover it?

How do the various mathematical idioms used by the physicist differ from each other, namely, proportion, geometry, algebra, graphics, numerical analysis, computer modelling and so forth? What decides which idiom is to be used?

Auxiliary mathematics and representations in physics

What are the reasons for the use of auxiliary mathematics in physics? The study of specific examples is needed here, including phasor diagrams, the complex analysis of alternating currents, the inertia ellipsoid in mechanics, the phase 'space' of Lagrange and Hamilton, momentum 'space', Fermi 'space', Hilbert 'space', the general concept of an auxiliary 'space' in physics, the Lagrangian function, Gibbs function, Poisson brackets and gauge transformations in electromagnetism. Other examples include the velocity potential function of hydrodymanics, the magnetic scalar potential function, electric flux and Hertz vectors.

The infinite line of action of a force, the orbits of planets conceived as existing ellipses, the auxiliary area of a coil or of an orbit, the network of lines of longitude and latitude, the magnetic meridean conceived as an imaginary plane, the parallelogram of forces, the passage of time as represented by a line, and Fletcher's indicatrix in crystal optics all seem to mix together descriptive with auxiliary mathematics and are usually called 'representations'.

It is difficult to exaggerate the importance of this topic for a better understanding of quantum physics and general relativity.

Approximations in physics

This includes the study of intrinsically inexact quantities in classical physics such as room temperature, room humidity, coefficient of friction, heat capacity of auxiliary calorimetric apparatus, the polychromatic refractive index of glass, the focus of a lens, the capacitance of a gold-leaf electroscope, and the position of magnetic poles. It also includes the approximate laws and theories of physics, such as Newton's law of cooling, the thin lens formula, Van der Waal's equation, many of the instrument equations (for example, the comparator) the laws of friction, the intermolecular force equation, and the Hartree–Fock approximation.

Approximate measurement requires analysis also. When is measurement exact, approximate or inaccurate in physics?

It is necessary to examine the distinction between physical laws with both theoretical and experimental foundation and 'purely empirical laws' such as Bode's law.

'Phenomenological' theories are established laws with contrived modifications so that they are enabled to account for unexplained phenomena, and which have no theoretical justification. They, therefore, blend exact laws with *ad hoc* and trial modifications.

It is, of course, important to build up understanding gradually from simple examples and not to begin with very advanced examples.

The distinction made by the physicist between conventional entities and physical entities

Examples include Ampère's conventional current in a wire as opposed to the true electron flow in that wire; the conventional north magnetic pole of the Earth, which is really a south pole; and Huygen's 'construction'. Why are such concepts, which are known to be false, or partly false, seemingly necessary in physics?

Other examples would include the root-mean-square current in a.c. theory; the conventionally infinite starting-point of the measuring definition of electrostatic potential; the conventional movement of positive charge during electrostatic induction in a metallic conductor; and virtual objects and virtual images.

Sometimes physics makes use of entities which it would describe as 'fictions' rather than conventions, for example, the analysis of the forces between bar magnets in terms of magnetic poles; the interpretation of the Earth's magnetic field as due to a small bar magnet at its centre; Huygen's centrifugal force; the polarization charges which 'appear' on the end faces of a polarized delectric; and the 'phase' velocity of electromagnetic waves in a wave-guide.

The notional processing of phenomena in physics

The physicist rarely takes natural phenomena as he finds them but frequently simplifies or modifies them in thought to make them more amenable to explanation or mathematical handling. I shall attempt a rough and necessarily incomplete classification of the various forms which this takes.

(a) *Partitioning.* The notional division of a soap bubble in two in order to calculate its internal pressure; the partitioning of a liquid into uniformly moving layers; the partition of the gravitational force at a point inside the earth into two parts, one due to the outer spherical shell, the other due to the inner sphere; the partition of a force into notional components; the resolution of a wave profile into harmonic components; the partition of moving gas molecules into three mutually perpendicular and non-colliding groups. What are the conditions of validity of each of these procedures? Why are they used? Why do they 'work'?

(b) *Notional surrogates.* The pull of gravity on a body is, in reality, a force distributed all over the material of the body. This is commonly replaced in thought by a single force acting through the centre of gravity, a point which may not even lie within the volume of the body.

The notional resultant of any two forces.

Equivalent circuits; the equivalent brick thickness of a layer of air in heat flow; the 'effective' resistance of an alternating current circuit; the 'reduced' momentum of a rotating flywheel; the 'effective' mass of a body moving in a liquid; the 'standardized' length of a barometer mercury column; the 'optical path' of a light ray through a liquid;

(c) *The notional enhancement of the natural.* Examples include the lines of magnetic force drawn about a magnet; lines of longitude and latitude on the Earth.

Exaggeration in diagrams as a means of simplifying explanations. The grip rule.

Fleming's left- and right-hand rules;

Sign conventions in mechanics, optics, thermodynamics, and electromagnetism.

Phenomena themselves, can, of course, be enhanced or highlighted in the laboratory, for example, the 'decoration' of magnetic domains by Bitter patterns.

By using the letters of the Greek or Roman alphabet to represent such widely different things as points and displacement vectors, objects and their magnitudes, intensive and extensive quantities, space and time, static and dynamic conditions, descriptive, auxiliary and pure mathematics, is there not a danger than an immersion in mathematical physics might reduce awareness of the qualitative diversity of nature?

Cognitive judgements in physics

How are terms such as 'law', 'theory', 'hypothesis', 'postulate', 'speculation', 'belief', 'true' 'false', 'real', 'correct', 'verified' and 'cause' used by the working physicist? It is most important that the philosopher should not use those terms with philosophically-laden meanings if he wishes to address the physicist on the latter's territory.

How does the physics profession achieve a broad consensus that a particular phenomenon or quantitative law has been verified within a certain regime?

When is an hypothesis regarded as a candidate for physical reality or simply as a 'heuristic' or working hypothesis?

It is important also to study case histories of past hypotheses which have now been verified such as the roundness of the Earth, the spin of the Earth, Archimedes' principle, the existence of Neptune and Helium, the laws of mechanics and electrostatics within classical regimes, Lenz's law, Avogadro's 'hypothesis' and the existence of atoms and molecules.

Hypotheses which seem about to be verified, such as the existence of black holes and of other planetary systems are particularly interesting.

What is the distinction between a postulate and an hypothesis as it is employed by the physicist?

The uses of idealization, analogues and models in classical physics

This involves the study of examples of idealization such as point masses, continuous media, line charges, two-dimensional surface charges, ideal gases, frictionless surfaces and the perfect radiator. What is their present function within physics? Are they necessary? What is the difference between an ideal gas, an 'effectively' ideal gas and a 'standard' gas?

There is a considerable literature in physics on formal resemblances and analogies between different processes and systems. The traditional philosophy of science has, of course, always taken an interest in this subject. The analytical philosopher of physics, by studying many case histories of analogies may be able to define more clearly the conditions in which analogy is used as an instrument of discovery, of explanation, of description, or of illustration. Equally important would be a study of the circumstances in which analogy has been misleading in physics.

Models are analogous *systems*, that is they are independent systems which seem to bear some structural resemblance to the system being studied but are, or appear to be, physically distinct from it. The literature of physics today, and sometimes even of the philosophy of science, shows that the term 'model' is frequently used inaccurately and misleadingly.

The explanatory interaction between the model and the system being modelled requires careful investigation. The different uses of models. Maxwell, for example, used models in at least three ways, to stimulate analogical cross-fertilization, to discuss hypothetical explanations and to provide teaching illustrations.

What is the nature of computer modelling (of Jupiter's atmosphere, for example)?

Again this needs to be studied in the context of many case histories. Clarification of the rational process involved is more important here than a dry classification of types of model.

Clarifying the technical concepts of physics

It is impossible to separate clearly the elucidation of the general descriptive and interpretative schema of physics from the analysis of the technical concepts of physics themselves. As I have suggested earlier the programme of clarification of the latter concepts should begin with classical physics. No concept should be ignored as unworthy of examination since it is not possible to know in advance which property, if better understood, might illuminate some poorly understood area of physics. Each of the concepts listed below was found to be difficult to teach, in certain respects at least, to physics students. The list, of course, represents a limited and personal selection.

The distinction between the physical meaning and measuring definition of velocity.

The concept of acceleration, especially centripetal acceleration.

The nature of the activity of forces which are in equilibrium.

The equilibrium of forces acting on a uniformly moving body.

Self-propulsive forces, such as those in an air-rifle or motor car.

The distinction between the physical meaning and measuring definition of linear momentum, work and kinetic energy.

The concept of mass as the seat of mechanical inertia and the reception of gravitational attraction and also as the source of gravitational attraction.

The concepts of torque, moment of a force, rotary inertia and rotary momentum.

The concept of the 'radius of gyration' of a body.

What is the relationship between the components of a force and the force itself?

When is a resultant a notional surrogate and when is it a true union of parts?

What is the physical meaning of the concept of 'tensor' in physics, as applied, for example, to the tension in a wire, the pressure of a liquid, and the stress-system in a solid?

The concept of the 'reduced momentum' of a flywheel.

The concept of virtual work.

The mathematical description and explanation of simple harmonic motion needs clarification.

The semi-autonomous relationship of a wave to the medium in which it travels is one of the most subtle and least developed concepts of classical physics.

The distinction between phase velocity, group velocity and particle velocity in a wave.

The nature of standing waves, the relationship between the incident wave and the reflected wave at the point of reflection, the transport of energy in a wave and the extra-ordinary ability of sound and water waves to pass through each other without scattering one another.

The relationship of the Fourier analysis of a wave to the actual wave.

The nature of the concept of 'ray' in a light ray.

The reason for the effectiveness of construction lines in geometrical optics.

The distinction between object and image space in a mirror, lens, telescope and microscope.

Why are different sign conventions possible in geometrical optics?

The nature of virtual objects and images and the concept of an object or image at 'infinity'.

The nature of the 'virtual' process occurring on the *far* side of a transparent interface when the angle of incidence on the near side is greater than the critical angle.

The light reflected from a glass block appears to be reflected at each surface. In fact it is scattered by each atom in the body of the block but the phases of the scattered light conspire to give an *appearance* of superficial reflection. What is the significance of this seeming 'deception' built in to the laws of optics? The study of other cases of 'natural deceptions' in physics such as the apparent poles at the ends of a bar magnet and the manner in which the components of the retarded field of a uniformly moving charge unite to give the impression that the field of the charge derives from the present position of charge only.

The concept of the 'intensity' of a current or field is difficult to grasp.

Ampère's sign convention for electric currents.

The concept of an equivalent circuit.

The concept of phase difference between the various properties of an alternating current.

The concepts of reactance and impedance.

The concept of root-mean-square alternating current.

The concepts of electric potential, mutual potential energy and individual potential energy.

The concept of electromagnetic vector potential.

The concept of a 'line of force' in electrostatics, magnetism, induced and radiation fields.

The distinction between non-radiation and radiation fields in electro-magnetism.

Force explanations seem to describe an efficient cause whereas energy and entropy explanations appear to be teleonomic. The analysis of cases where both types of explanation can be applied to a single process, for example, electrostatic induction in an insulated conductor.

Distinguishing the real from the conventional force distribution between bar-magnets.

The relationship between a multipole expansion and the actual structure of a charge or current system.

Surface tension. The causes of surface tension phenomena.

How are the various deductions of surface tension effects inter related?

The concepts of change of phase and phase equilibrium of a substance.

The concept of a mole of substance.

The concepts of latent heat of fusion and evaporation.

The concept of specific heat capacity.

The 'water equivalent' of a calorimeter.

The concept of an ideal gas.

The natural zero of temperature; a limiting, or an ideal concept?

How are conventional and absolute scales of temperature inter related?

The macroscopic concepts of heat, temperature and work in thermo-dynamics.

The concept of degrees of freedom of a solid, liquid, gas.

The concept of internal energy.

The concepts of adiabatic and isothermal change.

The concept of reversibility in thermodynamics.

Entropy: a macroscopic or a microscopic concept, or both, or neither?

Defining macroscopic thermodynamics.

The relationship between the macroscopic and miscroscopic in thermodynamics.

The logical relationship between the kinetic theory and the macroscopic gas laws.

The ergodic principle.

The concepts of enthalphy, free energy and Gibb's function. Are these physical states or mathematical artefacts?

The concepts of binding energy and self-energy.

When is the latter concept empirically justified and when is it purely speculative?

The concept of parity in physics.

The concepts of 'information' and 'noise'.

The study of apparently teleonomic laws such as Le Chatelier's principle, Lenz's law, the principle of last action, certain energy principles and certain applications of the second law of thermodynamics.

Why does the parallelogram of forces 'work'?

The physical meaning of 'divergence', 'gradient', 'curl', the laplacian algorithm, and the d'Alembertian algorithm.

The physical meaning of vector algebra.

The meaning of scalar, vector and tensor products.

Do vector identities or integral transformations ever have any direct physical significance?

How is perturbation analysis related to the actual structure of a system? Is it an artificial or a natural analysis into components?

The physical significance of complex numbers in physics. Are they always auxiliary or can they have a descriptive function?

The concept of a frame of reference in mathematical physics requires clarification. What is the physical significance of choosing different systems of coordinates, different frames of reference, the transformation from one frame to another, and scale transformations?

It is important to emphasize that each problem should be treated as part of a coherent strategy of general clarification and not simply as a casual item in a jumble of puzzles in physics.

7

Realism and the Global Topology of Space–Time

Robert Weingard

In this paper I want to discuss an interpretive problem concerning the global structure of space–time. This problem is discussed by Rom Harré in his *Varieties of Realism*, and there he proposes a solution. But for a book that presents three varieties of realism, his solution is surprisingly non-realistic. In contrast, I shall argue that this anti-realism is unnecessary. The facts about space–time structure he discusses offer no good reason for rejecting the straightforward realist solution to this problem.

We shall begin with our problem as it is presented by Rom in *Varieties of Realism*. Consider, then, flat space–time rolled up into a cylinder with a space-like axis (with two spatial dimensions suppressed). In this space–time, time is closed in the following sense. There is a frame in which time has the topology of a circle, namely one in which the spatial slices are parallel to the cylinder axis as pictured.[1] Therefore, there are closed time-like world-lines along which one can travel into the past just by going far enough into the future! Minkowski (i.e. unrolled up or topologically Euclidean flat) space–time, on the other hand, does not contain such closed time-like curves. None the less, it is clear that for each such cylinder space–time, there exists a Minkowski space–time that is empirically indistinguishable from it. This Minkowski space–time will consist of an infinite number of identical strips which fit together in a continuous way, and each of which is a copy of the developed or unrolled cylinder.

Cylinder space–time and its repeated strip Minkowski partner are empirically indistinguishable in the sense that any observations or measurements that are compatible with one, are compatible with the other. That is, any observations or measurements that can be interpreted in terms of one of them can be interpreted in terms of the other. It is true that, as we have seen, cylinder space–time allows a kind of time travel into the past, and it might be argued that because of the paradoxes of time travel, cylinder space–time is not a coherent hypothesis. But I think this is wrong, and I am going to rely here on arguments that I and others have given

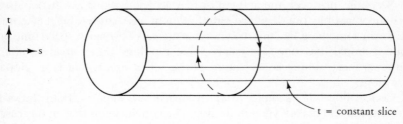

t = constant slice

Figure 7.1

elsewhere, to the effect that closed time and backward time travel are not paradoxical or incoherent.[2]

Furthermore, I do not want to claim that in general, if H_1 and H_2 are two hypotheses that are both compatible with observations O, then O provides equal support (or confirmation) to H_1 and H_2.[3] For example, in our case one might argue that even with its closed time and associated time travel, cylinder space−time is a more plausible hypothesis than its repeated strip partner, in which all physical processes, down to all the details concerning elementary particles and fields, are repeated infinitely often. Indeed, later I shall develop this point by arguing that there is a different in the explanatory power of our two topologies.

The question Rom raises concerning our example is the familiar one. Are the two hypotheses of cylinder space-time and its repeated strip partner incompatible and genuinely distinct hypothesis about the global structure of space-time, just one of which is true? Or are they merely different ways of presenting the same physical facts, the difference in the global topology being the difference between two different frameworks for describing the world. We can call the first alternative the realist answer, the second the anti-realist answer.

As it stands, the idea of the global topology being an aspect of our 'descriptive framework' could be explained in a number of ways. Let me mention just two of these. One is a conventionalist position modelled on Reichenbach's view concerning the metrical geometry of space. Whether space is curved or flat makes sense only relative to a coordinative definition which determines how the lengths of spatially separated objects are to be compared. Relative to one such definition, space is curved, relative to another it is flat, and it is just a matter of convention which definition we adopt. On this view, then, the two hypotheses of cylinder space-time and its repeated strip partner would not be genuinely incompatible. Rather, there would be an equivocation on some of the key geometrical terms involved, as there is[4] in the notion of 'x is equal in length to y' in the metrical geometry case.

Secondly, however, the anti-realist may accept that our two hypotheses are incompatible, but deny that either of them has a truth value. I take this to mean something like this. It is not that the set of events in space-time, in our example, has one particular global topology rather than another. Instead, there simply is no feature of the set of events that is its global topology.

Concerning our example, Rom, in *Varieties of Realism*, both draws a conclusion and makes a generalization. The conclusion is that, in this case, the anti-realist is correct concerning the global topology of space-time. The generalization is that for arbitrary space–times, the anti-realist account of the global topology is the correct one. Let us consider the generalization first. Seeing how it goes wrong will help us then to see why the conclusion concerning our particular example is mistaken as well.

Begin by noting that the relationship between cylinder space–time and Minkowski space–time is not a reciprocal one. For each cylinder space–time there is a repeated strip Minkowski partner that is empirically indistinguishable from the cylinder. But there are many Minkowski space–times which have no empirically indistinguishable cylinder partners. A simple example would be a Minkowski sapce–time M containing just a single container from which gas has been escaping in all directions. Assuming n molecules of the gas, no flat spatial slice in M is intersected more than n times by molecule world lines. But in any cylinder space–time containing such a container, each flat spatial slice would be inter-sected an infinite number of times. Assuming that the flat metric of M is given, it is clear that it cannot be interpreted in terms of a cylindrical topology.

For a slight variation on our case of cylinder and repeated strip space–time, we have the following empirically indistinguishable pair I and II, where we have repeated cycles of spherical space, S^3, expanding and contracting in I, but just a single stage of I in II:

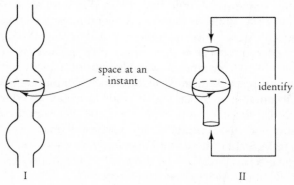

Figure 7.2

As in the flat space–time case, for each space–time II, there is an empirically indistinguishable type I space–time, but not vice versa.

However, consider tear-drop space–time, in which spherical space expands from an initial singularity to a maximum radius, and then collapses to a final singularity, rather than being truncated as in II,

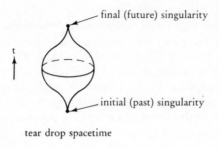

final (future) singularity

t

initial (past) singularity

tear drop spacetime

Figure 7.3

If we regard the two singular points as unphysical, so that the cosmic time t is defined only on an open interval, then there is no compact version analogous to II, nor a 'sausage' space–time analogous to I.[5] If we regard the two singularities as physical points,[6] then it might be thought that whatever is evidence for tear-drop space–time is also compatible with a sausage space–time of the form:

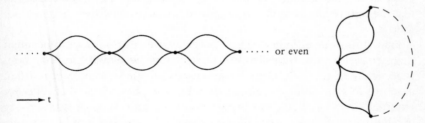

or even

t

Figure 7.4

with any number of links. Maybe so, but this sausage is not empirically indistinguishable from the tear-drop in the sense of our earliar examples. Since no observer can exist in more than one region, the question here is simply, are there any other links than the one the observer lives in.[7]

All this is not to say, of course, that current evidence for the global structure of space–time cannot be interpreted in more than one way. For example, among the most important evidence for the standard cosmological model of constant curvature space expanding from an initial singularity, are the cosmological red shift and the three degree background radiation.[8] The three degree radiation is taken to be radiation left over from the initial fireball, that has cooled due to the expansion of space. While the red shift is due to the recession of the galaxies, again due to the expansion.

But Ellis[9] has argued that an inhomogeneous, closed model, in which space has just two centres of spherical symmetry, one of which is a singularity and the other is our location, can explain both the observed background radiation and the cosmological red shift. The background radiation is due to hot gases surrounding the singularity and the galactic red shift is due to gravitation (and maybe expansion).[10] But this does not support a non-realist interpretation of global space–time structure. It merely reminds us that, from a cosmological perspective, we have information from just one point (or small region) of space, and that our grounds for assuming that all of space is like this point are not that secure.

The simple examples we have discussed show that the empirical indistinguishability of cylinder and repeated strip space–time is not general. There are space–times without empirially indistinguisable partners (with a different global topology), and therefore, considerations of empirical indistinguishability do not support the general conclusion of anti-realism concerning the global topology of space–time. This conclusion, however, is still compatible with empirical indistinguishability establishing the anti-realist account for the case of cylinder space–time and its repeated strip partner. Let us turn, then, to this special case of empirically indistinguishable global topologies. Here I also want to argue that the anti-realist account of the global topology of spacetime does not follow.

First, it must be admitted that Rom really gives us no reason other than their empirical indistinuishability, for treating the global topology non-realistically in the case of the space–times of our special case. But that alone cannot be sufficient. Once we admit, as physicalists, that different external states of affairs can bring about the same state of our sensory apparatus (or sensory areas of the brain), I do not see how empirically indistinguishable, but objectively different states of affairs can be ruled out, just on the basis of their indistinguishability.

Second, consider a somewhat analogous dispute to the one we are considering, the dispute between substantival and relational space. This is the dispute between space conceived as an entity or structure that exists in addition to, and distinct from, material bodies, and space conceived as a system of relations between material entities. Without going into all the details, one argument that used to be[11] brought against substantivalists is based on Leibniz's law of the identity of indiscernibles.

Namely, if substantival space existed, there would be no discernible different between the state of the universe now, and its state if all material bodies were rigidly displaced, say, ten feet in a given direction. By Leibniz's law, there cannot be such distinct states, and thus, substantival space is impossible. But this argument assumes space must be constantly curved. In a substantival space of variable curvature, a rigid displacement of all material bodies ten feet in some direction would be discernible from the state of the universe before the displacement.

But once we realize the objection does not work against variably curved substantival space, even one that deviates just a little from constant curvature, it is not convincing against substantival space of constant curvature as well. The point is, just as in the case of variably curved space, where we can explain, in terms of the variable curvature, why a rigid displacement will lead to a discernible state, in a constantly curved space, the constant curvature explains why the two states, while distinct, are not discernible.

This is analogous to our case of cylinder and Minkowski space—time. We know that the global topology of a non-repeated strip Minkowski space—time is discernibly distinct from that of any cylinder space—time. This is true even for a Minkowski space—time that is of the repeated strip form except for one point (or small region of space—time). For example, suppose space—time contains just a single periodic process, like a blinking light that skips a single period. The anti-realist claims that if just this single period had not been skipped, the global Euclidean topology would no longer be objectively distinct from the cylindrical topology. Is this any more plausible than the claim that an almost constantly curved substantival space could not have existed if it had instead been constantly curved? In my opinion, both of these claims are incredible and involve the same mistake. Namely, they both involve an illegitimate use of Leibniz's law of the identity of indiscernibles.

Third, we have seen that each cylinder space—time has an empirically indistinguishable repeated strip partner. The same is true if we considered a space—time in which the cylindrical dimension is spatial instead of temporal. A particular case would be Minkowski space—time rolled up along a space-like rather than a time-like direction. But more generally, the space—time does not have to be flat. As long a space—time has the global toplogy $H \times S^1$, S^1 being a space-like circle, it can be developed into an indistinguishable repeated strip partner.[12]

In this case the empirically indistinguishable partner is repetitive in a space-like rather than a time-like direction. And if anti-realism about the global topology is correct for the case in which the cylindrical dimension is time-like, clearly, it must also be correct for the case where the cylindrical dimension is space-like. But in this latter case, I think we can see that the assumption of a space-like cylindrical dimension has a different explanatory power, or status, than the assumption that the same dimension is topologically Euclidean with a repetitive structure.

For example, consider the Kaluza–Klein account of an electromagnetic field in four-dimensional space–time. A fourth, extra flat spatial dimension is assumed, and the electromagnetic potentials are identified with the γ_{4u}, u = 0 to 3, components of the five dimensional metric γ. Assuming the extra spatial dimension is compact, with a very small radius, explains why we haven't noticed the extra dimension.[13]

We shall now add quantum mechanics to Kaluza–Klein theory. Then because the extra compact dimension imposes a boundary condition on the modes of the metric field in the extra dimension, we get a gravitational Casimir effect. This drives the radius of the extra dimension down to the order of the planck length.[14] However, suppose we unroll the fourth space-like dimension before quantizing. Then space–time structure does not impose periodic boundary conditions, when we quantize fluctuations of the metric about this classical background. Of course, we could just assume suitable boundary conditions, but they would not be explained as they are when the extra dimension is compact.

These are my reasons, then, for thinking that even in the special case of cylinder and repeated strip space–time, the anti-realist account is not justified. Let me finish this paper by briefly contrasting the empirical indistinguishability of cylinder space–time and its repeated strip partner, with space–times which are observationally indistinguishable, in the technical sense of Glymour and Malament.[15] In order to do this, I need to say a few words about event horizons.

Even horizons exist because of the light cone structure of relativistic space–times. Consider, for example, a future directed inextendible time-like curve α, which we can think of as the world line of an idealized observer O, with an unlimited lifetime. At any point p on α, O can receive information only from points on, or within, the past light cone of p (which we can call the past of p). During O's whole life, the total region of space–time that O can gather information from is just the union, P(α), of all the pasts of all the points of α (which we call the past of α). The boundary of this set of points is the world lines future event horizon, and it can easily be seen to be the limiting past cone of α in the future direction.

In Minkowski space–time, since all the light cones are parallel, the limiting past cone in the future direction of a geodesic observer contains all of space-time, as we see from the diagram:

Thus, all of Minkowski space–time is observable to this observer. But this is not generally true for relativistic space–times. For example, in the current popular cosmological models for the universe, space[16] is expand-

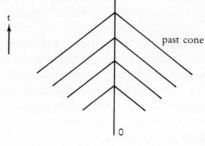

Figure 7.5

ing at a rate faster than light, so that the worldlines of points of space eventually leave the future event horizon of a geodesic observer,

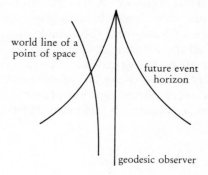

Figure 7.6

The observer cannot receive information from a point of space after it leaves his future event horizon, and thus the observers future horizon contains only a portion of the whole space—time. This is the importance of future event horizons. If an observers world line has a future event horizon, then that observer can observe, even in the ideal case of an unlimited lifetime and unlimited information, only a portion of the entire space—time.

In general, however, the part of space—time contained within the future horizon of a worldline α, can be embedded isometrically within quite different space—time geometries. And this is why there are observationally indistinguishable spacetimes. That is, two space—times M and M̂ are observationally indistinguishable if for each ideal observer O in M with worldline α, there exists an ideal observer Ô with worldline α̂ in M̂, such that P(α) and P(α̂) are isometric, and the same for M̂ with respect to M.[17]

If M and M̂ are observationally indistinguishable, then no observer in either M or M̂, even if he observes as large a region of space–time as is physically possible, can tell if that region is part of M or M̂. Interesting examples of distinct space–times that are observationally indistinguishable can be found in Malament's paper.[18] I only want to point out that empirical indistinguishability, in the sense we have been using it in this paper, does not imply observational indistinguishability.

In particular, cylinder space–time and its repeated strip Minkowski partner are not observationally indistinguishable. This is because the future event horizon of any geodesic in either space–time contains all of space–time, and the two space–times are not (globally) isometric. The empirical indistinguishability of cylinder space–time and its repeated strip partner is a question of the interpretation of observable regions. The same region of observable space–time (here all of it) can be interpreted to have one or the other global topology. But in the case of observationally indistinguishable space–times, there is no dispute over the geometry of any observable region of space–time (observable by a single observer). Rather, the pasts of all the different observers can be fitted together, or embedded, in more than one space–time structure. Because observationally indistinguishable space–times do not involve different interpretations of what can be observed, they are less plausible candidates for the anti-realists case than are empirically indistinguishable space–times.

NOTES

1 Note that there is also a slicing of cylinder space–time with respect to which time is open. This has been emphasized by Earman (1977).
2 See Lewis (1976), Weingard (1979; and forthcoming).
3 See Glymour (1977a).
4 That is, it is alleged by conventionalists that there is such an equivocation on the phrase, 'x is equal in length to y'.
5 By identifying antipodal points on each t = constant slice, we get a space–time 'observationally' indistinguishable from the tear-drop. This is explained later in the paper.
6 That this is plausible is suggested by the work of Smith and Bergmann (1986). In their quantum version of the Robertson–Walker space–times, there is a kind of tunnelling through the singularities.
7 I am ignoring horizons which I discuss later.
8 Even within the standard model, current evidence does not decide between open and closed space.
9 See Ellis (1978).
10 Originally Ellis proposed a static inhomogeneous closed space model, but could not fit it to the observed data.

11   And maybe still is. See Forbes (1987).
12   There are no restrictions on H.
13   Interestingly, one can also give a geometrical account of the electromagnetic field by assuming an extra time-like dimension, rather than a fourth space-like one. But the extra dimension is not compact and the metric is velocity-dependent. Rather than a Reimannian metric, we have a Finsler space. See Beil (1987).
14   For more about the gravitational Casimir effect, see Appelquist and Chodos (1983).
15   Glymour (1977b) and Malament (1977).
16   Space relative to the galactic frame, in which the world lines of the points of space are the galaxy world lines.
17   The exact definition is: Two space—times M and $\hat{M}$ are observationally indistinguishable if for every future directed, future inextendible, time-like curve α in M there is a curve $\hat{\alpha}$ of the same type in $\hat{M}$ such that $P(\alpha)$ and $P(\alpha)$ are isometric, and correspondingly, with the roles of M and $\hat{M}$ interchanged.
18   In the example given in note 15, one of the observationally indistinguishable pair is the covering space for the other. Malament gives examples that do not involve a space and its covering space.

REFERENCES

Appelquist, T. and Chodos, A. 'Quantum dynamics of Kaluza—Klein Theories', *Physical Review D* 28 (1983), pp. 772–84.
Beil, R. G. 'Electrodynamics from a metric', *International Journal of Theoretical Physics*, 26 (1987), pp. 189–97.
Earman, J. 'How to talk about the topology of time', *Nous* XI (1977), pp. 211–26.
Ellis, G. F. R. 'Is the universe expanding?', *General Relativity and Gravitation* 9 (1978), pp. 87–94.
Forbes, G. 'Places as possibilities of location', *Nous* XXI (1987), pp. 295–318.
Glymour, C. 'The epistemology of geometry', *Nous* XI (1977a), pp. 227–51.
Glymour, C. 'Indistinguishable space—times and the fundamental group'. In Earman, J., Glymour, C. and Stachel, J. (eds) *Foundations of Space—Times Theories* (1977b), University of Minnesota Press, Minneapolis, pp. 50–60.
Harré, R. *Varieties of Realism* (1986), Basil Blackwell, Oxford.
Lewis, D. 'The paradoxes of time travel', *American Philosophical Quarterly* 13 (1976), pp. 145–52.
Malament, D. 'Observationally indistinguishable space—times'. In Earman, J., Glymour, C. and Stachel, J. (eds) (1977) *Foundations of Space—Time Theories*, University of Minnesota Press, Minneapolis, pp. 61–80.
Smith, G. J. and Bergmann, P. G. 'Quantum blurring of cosmological singularities', *Physical Review D* (1986), pp. 3570–2.
Weingard, R. 'General relativity and the conceivability of time travel', *Philosophy of Science* 30 (1979), pp. 170–2.
Weingard, R. 'Spacetime, time travel, and the nature of time', *Dialectics and Humanism*, forthcoming.

8

Undressing Baby Bell

Michael Redhead

Abstract

The proofs of the Bell Inequality have been getting simpler and simpler. Junior Bell has been replaced by Baby Bell. But the discussion about the assumptions behind these proofs and the connection with non-locality goes on.

I visited the Magic Circle the other night. There was a new trick on by John Quell. As I arrived I noticed some of my friends in the audience. There was Arthur Shine, Bernard d'Espair and that old codger Bedhead, who always seems interested in these puzzles. Quell produced a large cabinet with two slots in it marked A and B. He explained there were a lot of counters in the box, all coloured red on one side and green on the other and on each side of each counter was written either $+1$ or -1. Quell would not say how the figures got written on the counters – we imagined it must all happen somehow inside the box.

'Now this is what is going to happen,' said Quell. 'I want two volunteers to stand one each side of the box. Let's have John Laurel and Elie Dada up on the stage. Now Laurel you stand beside slot A and Dada you stand beside slot B. In a minute the counters will come out in pairs through the slots. Both of you can choose which side of your counter to look at and then note down whether you see a $+1$ or a -1. We will do it a 1000 times, and we want to build up some correlations, so make sure you do not always choose the red side or the green side to look at. You can decide in advance if you like which colour each of you is going to look at, or change your mind at the last minute, it does not matter to me.'

Let us define for the nth pair of counters

a_n is the number on the red side of the counter from slot A
a'_n is the number on the green side of the counter from slot A

b_n is the number on the red side of the counter from slot B
b_n' is the number on the green side of the counter from slot B

Now define the correlations

$$c(a,b) = \lim_{N\to\infty} \sum_{n=1}^{N} a_n b_n$$

$$c(a,b') = \lim_{N\to\infty} \sum_{n=1}^{N} a_n b_n'$$

$$c(a',b) = \lim_{N\to\infty} \sum_{n=1}^{N} a_n' b_n$$

$$c(a',b') = \lim_{N\to\infty} \sum_{n=1}^{N} a_n' b_n'$$

Then what can you say about these four correlations?'
'That's easy,' said Bedhead. 'If you add together $c(a,b)$ $c(a,b')$ and $c(a',b)$ and subtract $c(a',b')$ and take the modulus, the number you get will always be less than or equal to 2. If you prefer it in symbols $|c(a,b) + c(a,b') + c(a',b) - c(a',b')| \leq 2$.'
'That's right,' said Quell, 'Would you like to explain it to the audience? There's a blackboard over there if you want to use it.'
'It's like this,' said Bedhead, 'write

$$\gamma_n = a_n b_n + a_n b_n' + a_n' b_n - a_n' b_n'$$
$$= a_n (b_n + b_n') + a_n' (b_n + b_n')$$

Since b_n and b_n' either have the same sign or opposite sign, only one term does not vanish and the value of the non-vanishing term is obviously ± 2. So

$\gamma_n = \pm 2$. But then for any N

$$\left| \frac{1}{N} \sum_{r=1}^{N} \gamma_n \right| \leq \frac{1}{N} \sum_{n=1}^{n} |\gamma_n| = 2$$

So taking the limit as $N\to\infty$ we get the inequality I said.'
'Right, now we can begin,' said Quell. 'First observe that the sequences a_n, a_n' and b_n and b_n' are all random (Colin Growson will explain that if you don't understand – he spends his life shuffling packs of cards and knows all about random sequences) and we assume the four correlations all exist,

that is to say the limits exist. With 1000 gos we should be able to estimate the limiting values pretty accurately.'

An hour passed and 1000 pairs of counters came out of the box. Quell did the sums as Laurel and Dada noted the numbers and he triumphantly added and subtracted the various correlations and lo and behold he got the result 2 1/2 ≤ 2!

'That's *real* magic for you,' said Quell.

The conjurors were all amazed. Either Laurel or Dada must have cheated. They must have altered the numbers on the counters after they saw how things were turning out. But Quell said that this was not how it was done.

'Let's look at it more carefully,' said Bedhead. 'There must be a catch somewhere. I wish John Shotkins was here. He always works these things out. First of all let us look at the table of results again.

n	I		II		III		IV	
	a_n	b_n	d_n	b_n'	a_n'	b_n	a_n'	b_n'
1	.	.	.	.	.	.	.	.
2	.	.	.	.	.	.	.	.
.								
.								
.								
	$c(a,b)$		$c(a,b')$		$c(a',b)$		$c(a',b')$	

We have really been doing four different experiments. But when I derived that inequality for the correlations the crucial assumption was that the number on the red side say of Laurel's counter did not change its value according as Dada chose to look at the red or green side of his counter. But Quell assures us there was no collusion here. Dada had a perfectly free choice and Laurel never tampered with the counters anyway. Can you confirm that Laurel?'

'Yes.'

'But there are some other points to consider,' Bedhead continued.

'First only part of the table is filled up. To get it complete we must put in the numbers for sides of the counters that were not looked at.' 'I was thinking about that myself,' interposed Shine. 'Are you sure the sample of numbers from each column we need to compute the correlation is not biased in some way?'

'I agree with you that we have to be very careful,' replied Bedhead. 'But I don't see how any bias could be introduced. After all Laurel and Dada chose which side of the counter to look at it *before* they looked. But, to continue, the beauty of the proof I gave is that nothing depends on what those numbers actually are – just that each counter has a definite fixed value written on both sides. But there *is* a counterfactual statement involved, for example, 'If Dada had looked at the green rather than the red side of his counter, when, in fact, he looked at the red side, Laurel would have recorded the same number as he actually did for the side he actually looked at'. Philosophers often worry about counterfactuals but that looks all right to me. Wait a minute, though. I have got an idea. Suppose there is something funny about the counters themselves. Suppose the numbers on each face are changing randomly until Laurel and Dada looked. Then the counterfactual might not be true. After all, think of a truly indeterministic roulette wheel which turns up No. 17. If the roulette wheel was spun again, in another world, with everything else as near as possible the same, would 17 still turn up? I am not at all sure that it would. But that stops me proving the inequality. I wonder if Quell would let us have a peek at the counters before Laurel and Dada and see if that is what is going on.'

'I have got a difficulty,' said one of the conjurors. 'If the numbers are changing randomly as you say how come we get those non-vanishing correlations?'

'Look at it like this,' replied Bedhead. 'Suppose there is some parameter, call it λ, inside the cabinet which is controlling the numbers on the counters, but only in a stochastic fashion. So if Prob (a,b) stands for the probability for getting the result $a = \pm 1$ on the red side of the counter from slot A together with the result $b = \pm 1$ on the red side of the counter from slot B, then let me write

$$\text{Prob}(a,b) = \int_\Lambda \text{Prob}(a/\lambda) \cdot \text{Prob}(b/\lambda) \cdot \varrho(\lambda)\,d\lambda$$

where Prob (a/λ) is the probability of getting the result a given λ and Prob (b/λ) is the probability of getting b given λ and ϱ is the probability density for the value λ itself. The integration extends over the whole collection Λ of values for λ. Then

$$c(a,b) = \sum_{\substack{a=\pm 1 \\ b=\pm 1}} ab\,\text{Prob}(a,b)$$

and this can easily be non-vanishing if Prob (a/λ) and Prob (b/λ) always peak at the same numerical value for a and b. In fact, reflected Bedhead, 'I can use these formulae to get a proof of the inequality. Do you want to see the details?'

'No! we believe you,' chorused the audience.

'Wait a minute,' said Shine. 'If you can prove the inequality with your randomized numbers on the counters, are we not back to square one?' 'No,' replied Bedhead. 'Because the new proof makes more assumptions than the old one. It assumes joint distributions for a_n and a'_n, for example. So we could block the new proof by denying that these joints exist (remember we were never asked to look at *both* sides of the counter) and the old proof would be blocked by the counterfactuals. Howzat!'

'It appeals to me,' said Shine, 'but there is another point against your new proof, as you call it. Does that curious factorization in the integrand correspond to the assumption of no-collusion between Dada and Laurel. It looks a rather stronger assumption to me.'

'I think it is all right,' said Bedhead. 'After all, we could always write

$$\text{Prob}(a, b) = \int_\Lambda \text{Prob}(a/b \,\&\, \lambda) \cdot \text{Prob}(b/\lambda) \cdot \varrho(\lambda) \, d\lambda$$

and then I am assuming $\text{Prob}(a/b \,\&\, \lambda)$ does not depend on b for a fixed λ.

'Yes, but when you integrate over λ

$$\text{Prob}(a/b) = \text{Prob}(a, b)/\text{Prob}(b)$$

does depend on b. So your factorization or independence assumption is not generally true, only at the λ – level of description, so it can't be simply identified with the no-collusion condition.'

'Things are more complicated than I thought,' said Bedhead. 'I don't think Abner Bemony agrees with you – he is shaking his head. But I admit you have got me worried now. But the point is I was not relying on the *new* proof anyway. So you are helping me, with what I said at the beginning – there is *no* convincing proof of the inequality if the numbers on the counters are changing in this stochastic manner.'

At that moment Quell intervened. 'Bedhead's idea can't be right. I did not tell you before, but there is another slot B' alongside B. Dada can choose to take a counter from B or B' – they can come out of either slot you see. And he can choose which slot to use, B or B', after the counter has come out of slot A. But with the B' counters the numbers on each side always agree exactly with the numbers on the corresponding side of the counters from the A – slot. So Dada, open the B' – slot and look at the red side. See, it is +1. Then *whenever* Laurel looks at the red side of his counter it will always be +1, so the numbers on his counter *cannot* be changing in the way Bedhead suggested. They must be fixed as you thought originally.'

'But then,' said Bedhead ruefully, 'we are back to the original proof, and we can't block it.

'Aha' – there was a sudden cry from Shine. 'I have just been doing some calculations on the back of the programme for tonight's meeting, and I have discovered a wonderful result. The inequality is a necessary and sufficient condition for the existence of a 4-joint distribution Prob (a, a', b, b') which returns all the observed joint distributions as marginals. But this means that joint distributions like Prob (a, a') must exist. So Bedhead *must* have made a mistake in saying his original proof did not assume these joints. And now,' said Shine triumphantly, 'we can block the original proof by denying that these joints exist, just what Bedhead said about the *new* proof, before I raised the extra difficulties about that funny factorization.'

'Not so fast,' said Bedhead. 'Let me look at your calculations. Yes I thought so. You have proved that if the inequality holds then there must exist a Kolmogorov probability space for which all the joint distributions exist and there is another theorem of Wald that if the spaces are not too big, and that is certainly true in this case with just a small finite number of possible events, then there is always a relative frequency model of such a space, again with all the joints defined.

Schematically Shine has shown

Inequality $\rightarrow \exists$ K (J (K))
$\rightarrow \exists$ r (J (r))
$\rightarrow$ J(y)

for some y from the set $\{r\}$.

K is a variable ranging over Kolmogorov spaces, r is a variable ranging over relative frequency models and J is the property of having all the joint distributions defined.

But what I proved was that in the relative frequency structure, call it x, of the actual experiment, I could derive the inequality under the assumption that J(x) was false. So putting everything together

$\sim$ J (x) $\rightarrow$ Inequality $\rightarrow$ J (y)

But since x $\neq$ y we cannot go on to claim $\sim (\sim J(x)) \equiv$ J (x) which is what Shine wanted us to believe.' 'I give up,' said Shine.

There was a stunned silence. Then Bernard d'Espair remarked, 'I have just finished a book on conjuring with a chapter in it entitled "Veiled Reality". Quell's cabinet illustrates the idea exactly.'

Most of the conjurors had drifted off by now. I waited until they had all gone. Then I approached Quell. 'Look,' I said, 'tell me how the trick is done! I am really fascinated to know. There must have been some collusion between Dada and Laurel.'

'No,' said Quell, 'and I can prove it. The same results happen if Dada and Laurel had looked at their counters absolutely simultaneously – then there is no time to signal to each other. Don't you remember that old member Albert Einstock who did the trick with the two pocket watches. One was sent round the back of the stage and then it was ten minutes behind the other!'

'I never understood that trick either,' I confessed. 'But what has it got to do with instantaneous collusion between Laurel and Dada?'

'Well Einstock said his trick proved that was not possible – otherwise you could have checked out the two watches against one another even at opposite ends of the stage – I forget the details but I know I was convinced at the time. But', continued Quell, 'I will let you into a secret. I don't know how the trick works mystlf! I bought the cabinet originally from a physicist called Professor Bell at CERN. He said it worked with photons. I am not a physicist, just a conjuror. If you really want to know how the trick is done you had better ask him.'

I shrugged my shoulders, buttoned my coat and walked out into the gathering dark.

NOTE

An early version of this paper was read in the Department of Philosophy, Logic and Scientific Method, the London School of Economics, in February 1984. No attempt should be made to identify positively any of the characters referred to. In particular the arguments should be interpreted only as a rational reconstruction of current debates.

Part III

Controversies in the Philosophy of the Human Sciences

9

An Empirical Interpretation of Ethogenics

Michael Argyle

Social psychology has seen a remarkable growth in cognitive approaches to the subject, partly under the influence of Rom Harré. However, this has become somewhat divorced from the study and explanation of social behaviour, and especially of social interaction. I shall examine the analysis of interaction in terms of cognitive processes, and show that some of the ideas of ethogenics, and of similar approaches like symbolic interactionism, are needed to deal with it. However, I shall also show that detailed experimental studies of social behaviour enable us to give a verifiable empirical interpretation of these phenomena.

Some of the key ideas of ethogenics are that social behaviour consists of intentional social actions with subjective meaning, that communication is symbolic, needed for cooperation and survival, there is joint construction of social behaviour, and that rigorous and especially experimental research is neither necessary nor desirable.

However it should be pointed out that ethogenics and symbolic interactionism are not the most widely recognized approaches to cognitive social psychology. Two other approaches are more familiar, though as we shall see both have their shortcomings.

'Hard-line Cognitive Social Psychology'

This sees social behaviour as a kind of rational problem-solving, performed by computer-like processes in the head. This position is largely a man of straw attacked by many, believed by few, but the textbook by Fiske and Taylor (1984) comes close to it. However, even they admit that 'The social perceiver has been viewed as somewhat of a hermit, isolated from the social environment. Missing from much research in social cognition have been other people in a status other than that of a stimulus' (Fiske and Taylor, 1984, p. 416).

'Reformed Cognitive Social Psychology'

This is now the dominant approach, and arises out of a stream of criticisms of hard-line CSP. In addition to purely cognitive processes, it is admitted that emotion and motivation play a part, that shared cognitions and awareness of such intersubjectivity are important, that some behaviour is *not* primarily governed by intentions or other cognitions, and there is concern about trends towards 'cognitive imperialism' (Forgas, 1981; Markus and Zajonc, 1985; Eiser, 1986).

Both of these more orthodox approaches are represented by large bodies of experimental research. Much of this is directed towards studying the causes and explanations of cognitive, i.e.

S → cognitions

This has taken attitudes, beliefs, concepts or other cognitions as the dependent variables. The question which I want to discuss is how far they can account for social *behaviour*.

Meanwhile it must be recognized that some of the criticisms made by Rom Harré of earlier research in social psychology have been to some extent taken into account and averted by the use of different (rigorous) research methods, such as quasi-experimental field studies, attribution-type experiments where the subjects act as judges but do not engage in social behaviour themselves, and the use of new forms of cognitive assessment like the repertory grid and multi-dimensional scaling. However the idea of joint construction of behaviour has not been taken up seriously, and I shall return to it later.

Cognition and Social Behaviour

Can cognitive social psychology explain the phenomena of social interaction? The problem arises because there has been something of a split between those social psychologists who are primarily interested in cognition, and those more interested in social interaction. I want to bring the two sides together by considering the contribution of the former to the latter. There are several ways in which cognition could be related to social behaviour.

Model 1: S → R

This is the model which CSP rejected, and which supposed that stimuli, or antecedent conditions generally, including personality factors, determine behaviour, without being mediated by intentions or other cognitive factors. Reformed CSP has come to recognize that such influences occur, and this model has made something of a comeback recently (Nisbett and Wilson, 1977). The main instances are: (a) addictions, (b) classical conditioning, (c) language, where grammar is buried so deep as to be inaccessible to cognition, (d) skills, where focusing attention often disrupts skilled performance, and (e) small non-verbal signals, which will be described later. As McClure (1983) observed, people can report their intentions and plans, but not the causes or motives for their behaviour. Langer (1978) produced evidence to show that a great deal of social behaviour is 'mindless', i.e. conducted without conscious attention, for example, by following familiar scripts. There may be cognition here, but there is no thinking. In one experiment, for example, 68 per cent of office workers complied with the request to return a sheet of paper to a room number, even thought the request to do so was the only information on it.

Model 2: S → cog. → R

This is the model assumed by CSP. An example is the effect of attributions for another's behaviour on helping behaviour and other reactions (Kelley and Michela, 1980). Another is the successful prediction of behaviour from intentions, as by Fishbein and Ajzen (1975).

Combinations of Models 1 and 2

Research using causal modelling has found that a combination of these models is needed, though the weighting varies with the behaviour being predicted. Bentler and Speckart (1979) found that behaviour is partly predictable from intentions, but also partly from past behaviour and from attitudes, independently of intentions. Health-related behaviour, like taking exercise, was more predictable via this second route.

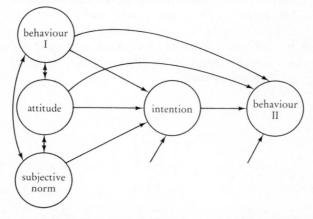

Figure 9.1   *A model of the attitude–behaviour relation incorporating previous behaviour* (from Bentler and Speckart, 1979)

Models 1 and 2 also combine in another way. Schachter and Singer (1962) proposed, for example, that emotion is the product of a physiological state, and cognitive processes which result in this state being labelled in a way related to appraisal of the situation.

Model 3: S $\nearrow$ R $\searrow$ cog.

It has been argued that sometimes quite different processes are involved in the production of behaviour and cognition, and that one does not cause the other. Zajonc (1980) has shown that affective reactions are sometimes not predictable from cognitions, and are faster. The beliefs of paranoid patients provide no guide to the true causes of their behaviour, and appear to be the result of independent processes.

Model 4. S → R → cog

Here cognition is a reaction to behaviour, produced initially without cognitive mediation. Examples are (a) rationalization, as after post-hypnotic suggestion, (b) self-attributions, after false feed back, (c) expression of attitudes after observing own behaviour (Bem, 1967), and (d) cognitive dissonance experiments, using forced compliance. Subjects who had been coerced to eat fried grasshoppers had no insight into the cognitive processes behind their new liking for this food – 'Well, it was no big deal whether I ate a grasshopper or not' (Zimbardo, 1969).

Model 5

Later in this chapter I shall show that social interaction requires a further model, similar to that of ethogenics, to deal with the close coordination, the joint production of behaviour, by two people engaged in social interaction. It is not simply that A responds to B, since most of the action is simultaneous; each is continuously monitoring and responding to the jointly created ongoing situation.

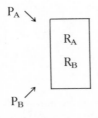

The Cognitive Analysis of Social Interaction

Non-verbal communication (NVC)

There are some clear cases of model 1 operating. Many small NV signals are sent without conscious intention and are received and reacted to without awareness – small head-nods, shifts of gaze, small non-verbal vocalizations, for example. A striking example is pupil dilation in sexual arousal, which communicates without intention on the part of the sender or awareness by the receiver (Hess, 1972). Infants provide examples of model 1: early smiling is a physiological reflex to physical stimuli – dot patterns will do (Malatesta, 1985). Non-human primates reared in isolation are able to send and receive facial expressions for emotion. There is extensive evidence for the innateness of human facial expressions for emotion (Ekman, 1982). It is generally assumed that the capacities to send and receive NV signals have evolved together – one would be useless without the other.

Decoding the NVC of others probably involves Model 1, when the NV signals of others produce a direct effect on observers. Model 2 also operates, for example, if subjects are shown photographs of faces, and

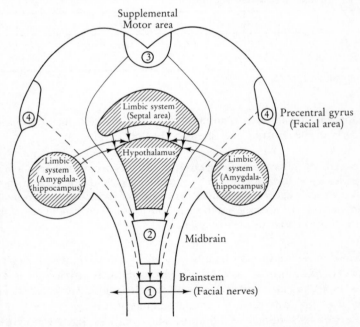

Figure 9.2 *Neural bases of emotional expression* (from Buck 1984)

given conflicting information about the situation in which the expression occurred, they do their best to make sense of this information, using their common-sense knowledge, e.g. that people do not usually pretend to be sad (Spignesi and Shor, 1981).

The combination of models 1 and 2 is typical in the generation of NVC. Facial expression is the result of spontaneous emotions, and of attempts to control expression, under the influence of 'display rules' (Ekman and Friesen, 1975), and other sources of intentional expression. The two processes use two different neural routes: spontaneous emotions reach the facial nerves from the hypothalamus, intentional control from the motor cortex (Rinn, 1984).

However the full explanation of NVC takes us beyond these simple cognitive models, to something more similar to ethogenics and symbolic interactionism. To begin with, NVC is primarily a matter of *communication* rather than *expression*. By communication I mean signals which are intended to be received by and to influence others. Kraut and Johnstone (1979) found that at a bowling alley players rarely smiled at the skittles when they hit or missed, but often smiled at their companions.

Table 9.1   *Smiling at the bowling alley (%)*

	hit	*missed*
at people	42	28
at skittles	4	3

(from Kraut and Johnston, 1979)

Infants engage in such communication (rather than just 'expression') very early in life. Bruner and Sherwood (1981) said

> A pattern of inborn initial response ... is soon converted into a very complex joint anticipatory system .... Mother and child develop a variety of procedures for operating jointly and in support of each other.... From the start children are predisposed to share with others their experience of the world – before they can use language. *(pp. 32, 47)*

It looks as if, for human infants as well as animals, there is an innate capacity to communicate with others, just as there is physiological equipment – especially face and voice – with which to do it. However socialization is also very important, for human infants at least.

Observational studies of children and mothers have found that if behaviour is categorized in one-second units, the two individuals often shift to similar behaviour simultaneously by three months. Murray and Trevarthen (1985) found that 6–12-week-old infants would happily interact with their mothers over CCTV from another room, but were distressed if they were simply shown a replay from an earlier period: it was the *interaction* that they enjoyed. Stern (1985) analysed interactions of 8–9-month-old infants with their mothers and concluded that intersubjectivity for them involved 'affect attunement', the precise sharing of affect. By twelve months there is turn-taking, and by two years there is integration of vocalization and gazer in 'conversation' (Tronick et al. 1980). Children learn turn-taking before they can speak: mothers treat any vocalization as a turn, and respond verbally, so that between 3 and 18 months children learn to take turns at the same time as they learn to speak (Snow, 1977).

Adults cooperate very closely while interacting, and the more they adopt congruent postures and make similar bodily movements, the stronger the feeling of rapport they have (La France, 1979). Dabbs (1969) found that subjects liked an experimental confederate more if he deliberately copied their bodily posture and movements – showing that coordination causes liking. There is a basic property of social behaviour, which this non-verbal coordination demonstrates – that it takes two to do it. However we must not exaggerate the extent of this non-verbal fine-tuning: early claims of a 'gestural dance' at fractions of a second have not survived careful statistical analysis (McDowall, 1978). But there is quite close coordination at the time-scale of clauses and utterances, as well shall see next. This is a time-scale of seconds and half-seconds – well above the usual reaction time of 0.15 secs or so.

Coordination of bodily posture and movements is probably one of the main ways of signalling and sustaining social engagement and mutual attraction. There are several other ways, and in an earlier paper we suggested that these include: gaze, smiling, proximity, orientation, touch and tone of voice (Argyle and Dean, 1965). Later research has confirmed that under many conditions these signals can substitute for each other.

Verbal communication

Examples of Model 1 here are the use of grammar, and the Markov analysis of sequences of types of utterance, e.g. showing reciprocity of length of utterances, or use of words like 'a' and 'the'. An example of Model 2, and its rivalry with Model 1, is the phenomenon of 'operant verbal reinforcement' – increasing a subject's frequency of using a certain kind of utterance by means of head-nods, or other reinforcements. This only works well when the subject has become aware of what is going on (Spielberger, 1965).

Verbal communication depends on the availability of words with similar meanings, and awareness of such 'intersubjectivity' – an extension of cognitive social psychology which is generally accepted. As conversation proceeds there is also a build-up of shared information, and each utterance contains a combination of old and new, the new building on the old (Rommetveit, 1974; Clark, 1985).

However, close cooperation is needed for conversation; this takes us beyond the framework of cognitive psychology. As G. H. Mead and others had said, others do not stand still during a social act, but they fit their lines of action together (Deutscher, 1984). As Goffman (1956) said, impression management depends on cooperation from the other.

However, it is the analysis of speech acts which shows most clearly how this is accomplished. A speech act is a piece of behaviour which is intended to communicate with, to be understood by, a listener, and it is designed to influence him in some way (Grice, 1968). Speech acts must be 'felicitious', a request for example only makes sense if the speaker really wants the other to do, and the other can do it (Austin, 1962). Grice (1975) proposed his 'cooperative principle' a set of rules for acceptable conversation – make your contribution as informative as required and no more, it should be true and relevant, and not ambiguous or obscure.

While the speaker A is speaking, the other person, or persons, B helps them. A looks up at grammatical pauses, and B responds with head-nods, smiles and frowns, and short vocalizations. In these ways B (a) indicates that he is attending, willing for A to carry on, (b) provides back-channel comments on his reactions to A's utterance, (c) may simply reflect A's feelings, and (d) may help to complete the utterance. The speaker A monitors B's reactions closely while he is speaking, and often changes an utterance from that originally planned while he is delivering it, if he sees that B does not understand it, or agree with it, for example. For some reason the Japanese are particularly rigorous in back-channel behaviour, producing twice the number of head-nods and vocalizations than we do (Clarke and Kanatami, 1980).

Interactors are able to take turns in speaking with great efficiency; often the interval between utterances is less than the usual reaction time, and there is little interruption. How is this achieved? Terminal gaze is one of the signals used to indicate the ending of an utterance; others are falling pitch, ending of gestures, and the grammatical structure of the utterance (Argyle, 1987b).

One speech act leads to another, and the 'adjacency pair' is one of the building blocks of conversation. One speech act 'projects' the next, by creating an obligation to complete the pair, question–answer, request–promise, etc. (Clark, 1985).

However conversations have more complex sequences than can be

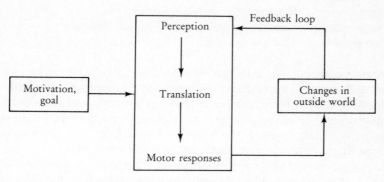

Figure 9.3 *Motor skill model*

accounted for by adjacency pairs. Just as sentences have intricate phrase structures and generative grammars, so do conversations. Examples of these structures are (1) higher-order Markov chains, (2) repeated cycles, (3) four-step social skill sequences, with corrected action to elicit a response from the other (see below, figure 9.4). It has been found that people have tacit shared knowledge of such principles, as shown by their ability to reconstruct the original sequence of utterances after these have been scrambled (Clarke, 1983).

The social skill model provides some explanation of how coordination is achieved. The model compares the social behaviour of an individual to the performance of a motor skill. However in a conversation both parties are pursuing their goals simultaneously, while adhering to the rules of sequencing, Here is an example:

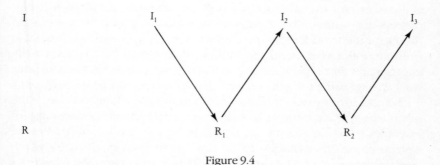

Figure 9.4

Interviewer$_1$: How well did you do at physics at school?
Respondent$_1$: Not very well, I was better at chemistry.

Interviewer$_2$:   What were your A-level results?
Respondent$_2$:   I got a C in physics, and an A in chemsitry.
Interviewer$_3$:   That's very good.

Social behaviour has a hierarchical structure, where the larger, high-level units consist of integrated sequences and groupings of lower-level units. An interview has a number of phases, each with a certain sequence of questions, each question consisting of a number of words, and accompanying non-verbal signals. The sequences making up small units tend to become habitual and 'automatized', i.e. independent of external feedback; more attention is given to the performance of the larger units on the other hand – they are carefully planned, and are controlled by rules and conventions (Argyle, 1983).

Conversation is central to most human social interaction. I have tried to show some of the ways in which conversation is a joint, cooperative product of two people.

Social relationships

One of the best examples of Model 1 is the effect of reinforcement on interpersonal attraction. For example, if children are rewarded by an experimenter in the presence of other children, they are found to like the other children more (Lott and Lott, 1974). However some process other than reinforcement is responsible for attachment in monkeys at least, as Harlow and Harlow (1965) found – infant monkeys clinged when frightened to the artificial mother with the right fur, not the one with the milk. A good example of Model 2 is the finding by La Gaipa and Wood (1981) that disturbed adolescents, who have no friends, have an inadequate concept of friendship – lacking the ideas of loyalty, commitment and concern for the other's welfare. (I am assuming that these cognitive concepts are causal.) The combination of Models 1 and 2 is seen in the two-factor theory of love, as the combination of physiological arousal and (mis)attribution (Berscheid and Walster, 1974). Model 3 can be seen in the efforts made after separation or divorce to develop an explanation of what went wrong, partly to justify oneself, part to understand it (Harvey, 1982).

The cognitive model can be extended to include taking the role of the other, either in cognition or feeling. This is important in relationships: for example, when people are in love they have a great concern for the welfare of the other (Rubin, 1970). One of the main mechanisms which generate helping behaviour is empathy (Batson and Coke, 1981); there is a good correlation between helping and ability to see another person's point of view (Underwood and Moore, 1982). This is one explanation for the high level of help in close relationships (Argyle and Henderson, 1985).

The coordinated interaction model takes us into further important issues in the analysis of relationships. What is the explanation of bonding, long-term attachment, between parents and children, siblings, spouses and others? Genetic predispositions to favour those who share genes may be part of the explanation as has been shown for animals. More important probably is the effect of a long period of close intimacy, during which close coordination becomes established. Favourite cousins are those who were childhood playmates (Adams, 1968). Lovers are people who have attained and sustained a high level of intimacy, and this requires close coordination. In love and marriage sex is a powerful source of attraction and reinforcement, but can also be seen as a case of close coordination and intimacy, which may be its true importance. Sequences of interaction are important too. Unhappily married couples make more negative verbal and non-verbal acts, and these are reciprocated more often compared with happily married couples (Gottman, 1979).

What is the role of reinforcement in establishing relationships? Part of the answer is that relationships are very rewarding – but only if some coordination is achieved. Otherwise they are a source of conflict and frustration.

Friends have a degree of bonding. They share a lot of enjoyable activities – eating, drinking, joint leisure (Argyle and Furnham, 1982). These activities are more enjoyable than doing the same things alone, but only if a coordinated relationship has been established.

Rules develop for all relationships to maintain coordination, by avoiding sources of friction. The rules for friendship for example include a number of 'third party' rules, for maintaining the network – friends should keep confidences, not criticize one another in public, etc. If they do so, the friendship is liable to lapse (Argyle and Henderson, 1984).

In all relationships between human adults conversation is important, and this produces self-disclosure, and the building up of a shared outlook on matters of common concern. It is particularly important for pairs of female friends, and for husbands and wives. (Male friends talk less, but engage in more joint activities.) Where there is found to be disagreement, young lovers have to work this through, and may go through periods of conflict (Argyle and Henderson, 1985).

In a particular encounter individuals adopt and present a working self concept, or 'situated identity', a social construction of the self which is acceptable to the others present – another case of coordination and shared cognitions (Alexander and Wiley, 1981).

Coordination has been used in therapy, both for individuals and couples. Autistic children can be helped by re-establishing feeding and play routines with their mothers (Clancy and McBride, 1969). Marital therapy

Table 9.2   *Rules of friendship*

Exchange

13   Seek to repay debts, favours or compliments, no matter how small.
17   Share news of success with the other.
20   Show emotional support.
25   Volunteer help in time of need.
27   Strive to make him/her happy while in each other's company.

Intimacy

24   Trust and confide in each other.

Coordination

18   Respect privacy.
21   Don't nag.

Third party

10   Don't criticize other in public.
11   Stand up for the other person in their absence.
12   Keep confidences.
23   Be tolerant of each other's friends.
26   Don't be jealous or critical of other relationships.

---

includes joint role-playing to improve interactive patterns, individual training in negotiating disagreements more constructively, and learning the rules for this relationship (Argyle and Henderson, 1985).

Practical Applications of the Coordinated Interaction Model (CIM)

I believe that an important test of a theory or approach in social psychology is whether it leads to new practical applications which can be shown to work. This shows that a theory is more than just a new way of talking about the phenomena. It has an implication which is inconsistent with ethogenics however, since application usually depends on the establishment of cause–effect relationships, and this needs either experiments, or quasi-experimental designs across time, such as cross-lagged panel designs. It is also inconsistent with ethogenic's emphasis on the meaning of actions to the actor: for most practical purposes it is his *behaviour* which is important – as in social hostility and crime. In other cases emotional or physiological reactions are important, as in health and mental health. Understanding the reasons for behaviour is not enough; we need to be able to control it.

Inter-group conflict

Most accounts of this phenomenon have assumed a model 2 pattern of causation. The best-known theory is Tajfel's Social Identity Theory (1978), that group members exaggerate inter-group differences, on characteristics which favour the in-group, in order to enhance self-esteem. However, this has so far led to no practical application, though some suggestions have been made, for example of encouraging mutual recognition of positive features, or bringing about 'decategorization' of group members (Hewstone and Brown, 1987). The rival theory ,which SIT was claimed to supplant, was Sherif's Realistic Conflict Theory (1966), and this *does* have a practical application – discover or create superordinate goals, as was done in the Robbers' Cave study.

The coordinated interaction theory suggests that an important source of inter-group conflict is difficulty of interaction between members of the two groups. This may be because there are different languages, different gestures or other NV signals, or simply different rules of behaviour – how to conduct particular social encounters, the forms of politeness, etc. It is not denied that real conflict may also be important. This simple hypothesis is rich in suggestions for improving relationships between groups.

Language learning. The greatest obstacle to harmonious relations between two groups can be the lack of a common language. If one side has a partial mastery of the other's language, this helps a lot but coordination is still greatly impaired. There can be serious difficulties within a culture due to different dialects, different social class styles, and differences in pragmatics. Examples are class differences in Britain (Bernstein, 1959), and black–white differences in the USA.

NVC learning. A major source of friction is differences in proximity, orientation, touch, gaze, gestures, etc. For example some Italian gestures may be meaningless (Figure 5). Other gestures can cause great offence, unintentionally. Touching, standing too close or too far away, is disconcerting. Black Americans give few back-channel signals, Japanese give a great many (Argyle, 1988).

An inability to decode the expressions or gestures of another group can make taking the role of the other impossible, and as a result there is no empathy, and the others are seen as incomprehensible or even sub-human. It is quite easy to learn to recognize, or even to use, the NVC of another culture, and this greatly enhances acceptance (Collett, 1971).

Frequency of interaction has long been known to be an important means of improving attitudes to another group, though the conditions must be right – especially equal status (Hewstone and Brown, 1987). From the point of view of CIM, the reason is that each side is able to become accustomed to, adapt to and learn to coordinate with the other. It would

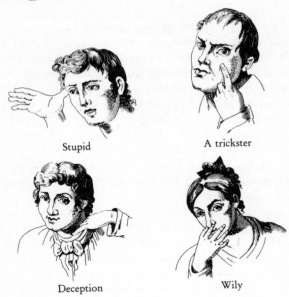

Stupid   A trickster

Deception   Wily

Figure 9.5   *Some gestures in Naples* (from De Jorio, 1832)

be expected that meeting under conditions requiring intimacy and cooperation would be most effective.

Inter-cultural skills training is now widely used, with success, for many people who are going to work abroad. A method which has been used with some success is the Culture Assimilator, which can teach the rules of the second culture, and teach people how to avoid the most common difficulties experienced there, by means of a tutor-text (Fiedler et al., 1971). Other methods commonly used are further educational methods, meeting returned expatriates and members of the other culture.

Negotiating perception of the situation. Sometimes it is possible for a positive or negative interpretation of events to be developed. For example, in industry a minor annoyance may or may not lead to a strike. Management promotes the wrong person, or disciplines someone; shop stewards may or may not build this up into a coherent protest, there may or may nor be some degree of go slow or stoppage, management may or may not label this as a strike (Batstone et al., 1978).

The pursuit of happiness

Happiness, positive moods, subjective well-being, are partly the result of Model 1 processes, like the sun shining (Schwarz and Clore, 1985). They are partly due to Model 2 processes, as in the 'Michigan model': satisfaction is predicted by the goal-achievement gap, which in turn is caused by comparisons with own past life, and the state of 'average folks' (Michaelos, 1980), We have found that happy people have a special style of attribution – internal, global and stable for happy events, and the opposite for unhappy events, just as depressed people are found to make internal, global and stable attributions for unhappy events. It is not known how far cognition is causal in the case of happiness; it is more a dependent variable in the case of depression, though it helps to sustain the condition (Williams, 1984).

The CIM predicts that happiness will be generated by close relationships with other people. Many studies have shown that the main cause of positive moods is encounters with friends and others in close relationships (Scherer et al., 1986). What is the explanation of this finding? (1) One possibility is that, as we have seen, people smile at friends; this has two consequences – they smile back, which is rewarding, via facial feedback, positive mood is enhanced. (2) It is found that extraverts are happier than others ($r = .40$), but only when in the company of others (Emmons and Diener, 1983). This may be because they smile, look and talk more, or because they generate joy on social occasions in other ways, such as making jokes, or because they make greater efforts to establish close relationships (Thorne, 1987; Argyle, 1988). This suggests an extension of the CIM: extraverts engage in closely coordinated interaction, and also increase the level of arousal, because they are normally at a lower level of arousal than introverts. Several studies have shown how people at work, especially those engaged in boring work, engage in a great deal of jokes, games and fooling about, presumably for similar reasons (Roy, 1959).

A second component of happiness is satisfaction – a cognitive state which we have seen is partly the product of cognitive processes. It is also the product of certain kinds of social relationship, especially instrumental help, emotional support, and shared interests and activities (Argyle and Furnham, 1983).

Our approach generates a number of new ideas for enhancing happiness, which could be used in 'happiness therapy'.

(a) Train people in the social skills of extraverts, including closely synchronized interaction and the generation of arousal.
(b) Strengthen social relationships generally, by social skills training.
(c) Spend more time in enjoyable activities in the presence of others, both at work and leisure.
(d) However, there are other sources of positive emotions and happiness, other forms of happiness therapy. The latter include regular

arousal of positive moods by self-suggestion, modifying styles of attribution and habits of thinking, and discovering the activities which have the most positive effects and doing them more often. These often include physical exercise, which induces positive moods by releasing endorphines (Argyle, 1987).

Social Factors in Health

Health and health-related behaviour are partly due to Model 1 processes. Whether or not a person goes to the clinic when directed, or takes exercise, or stops taking drugs, is strongly affected by processes outside intention or conscious control. They are also affected by cognitive factors like health beliefs, and by intentions (Bentler and Speckart, 1981; Eiser, 1986).

CIM predicts that close relationships will be good for health. Many studies have already shown the benefits for physical health of supportive social relationships – on death rate, especially from heart disease, but also from many other illnesses, including several forms of cancer. The forms of social support which are most effective are an intimate relationship, with a confidant, social integration into a larger group, the provision of help, affection and self-esteem. Social support works primarily through 'buffering' the effects of stress, i.e. it becomes effective in the presence of stress, though there may be main effects as well (Cohen and McKay, 1984). There is a lot of evidence that stress damages the immune system, while social support restores it. This demonstrates a direct biological effect of CIM (Jemmott and Locke, 1984).

Social support has even stronger effects on mental health. As Brown and Harris showed (1978), stressful life-events make depression more likely, but a close attachment or confidant can almost eliminate this effect. The explanation here may be rather different from that for physical health. Stressful life-events produce depression, anxiety, loss of self-esteem and eventually mental illness, but social support can remove these negative emotions and cognitions. Thus CIM has a direct effect on mental health as well as physical health.

It is found that married people are in better physical and mental health than those who are single or widowed, and much better than the divorced, and that this difference is at least partly causal. However the benefits for husbands are about twice as great as for wives. The most likely explanation is that wives are better sympathetic listeners and confidants than are husbands (Argyle, 1987a).

We can generate some practical implications of CIM for health and mental health.

(a) Establish and maintain one close, supportive relationship, and a social network. It is already known that social skills training is good for mental health (Hollin and Trower, 1986).
(b) Similar considerations apply to physical health. More use could be made of social relationships inside medical institutions.

Extensions of social skills training (SST)

This is now widely used both for mental patients of a variety of kinds, and for the professional training of teachers, doctors and others (Argyle, 1985). The effects of SST are partly due to Model 1 processes, and behaviour therapists often carry out SST in terms of 'reinforcement schedules' for smiling, talking, etc., especially for severely impaired patients. Other trainers operate under Model 2 and emphasize understanding, and bringing hitherto automatic processes under cognitive control. Classical role-playing methods can be seen in this light. Some of the research discussed above shows that educational methods can be quite successful here – for example, in teaching the rules of situations, the true nature of relationships, the ways of other cultures. Training to take the role of the other in an extension of orthodox cognitive thinking.

The coordinated interaction model suggests some new directions for SST.

(a) Marital therapy and other relationship training is sometimes done by joint role-playing, to improve coordination between a pair of individuals.
(b) Several lines of research have shown that coordination is necessary at a relatively fine time-scale, so that the use of slowed-down video-recording in feedback is desirable.

The Levels of Explanation of Social Behaviour

I have argued that social behaviour can be only partly explained at the cognitive level, and have hinted at the other levels needed. To illustrate this theme I shall discuss the explanation of one simple phenomenon, and ask: 'Why do people smile?' (Argyle, 1988).

Physiology. The first, and most essential, part of the answer is that people smile because they have faces and these are equipped with muscles like the *zygomatic*, which pulls up the corners of the mouth, and these are controlled by the facial nerve, which is controlled partly from the hypothalamus, partly from the motor cortex.

Evolution. Why do we have faces? Because during the course of evolution the area for looking, breathing and eating has gradually changed to become a specialized area for communication, with finer muscular control, that eventually became essential for cooperation and communication in groups of non-human primates.

Socialization. We have seen how the smile develops in children from a physiological reflex to a controlled social signal. This is partly the result of imitation, partly of parental influence. For example, women are more expressive than men – they smile 50 per cent more. But it is boy babies who are the more expressive; mothers do not respond favourably to this, whereas they do respond to the emotional displays of little girls (Malatesta, 1985).

Cognition. Socialization consists partly of learning the display rules of the culture, and occupational training may take this further, for example, air hostesses have to learn how to be able to smile at passengers regardless of their feelings (Hochschild, 1983).

Social interaction. This is a distinct level of analysis, describing the close coordination needed for social behaviour. Smiling plays a central role here; it is one of the first social signals to develop, it is the most powerful reinforcer, and it becomes intricately linked with gaze, speech and other social signals.

Personality. There are systematic individual differences in social behaviour; smiling, gaze and other-directed gestures form an approach dimension, positively correlated with extraversion, negatively with neuroticism and other mental disorders.

Culture. There are minor differences in how smiling is performed, so-called 'facial dialects' (Seaford, 1975). Far more important however are cultural display rules, mediated by socialization, and derived from past cultural history. In Japan people often smile when experiencing negative emotions, probably because of the influence of the Samurais.

Conclusions

I have tried to examine the contributions of cognitive social psychology to the analysis of social interaction. The traditional Model 2 has some application, but a lot of social behaviour takes place without cognitive mediation, and sometimes cognition is a result of behaviour. I have suggested that the analysis of social interaction needs a different kind of model, which is very much in line with ethogenics and symbolic interactionism, except that it is supported by detailed empirical research and makes a number of specific predictions concerning practical problems.

Finally I would like to recall the story of the blind Indians and the elephant – one thought it was a rope, another a snake, a tree, a spear, etc. It is equally difficult to see social behaviour as a whole.

(a) For CSP it is like two people thinking, solving problems.
(b) In some ways it is like a motor skill (Argyle, 1969).
(c) It is also like two people playing a game, taking turns, following the rules, using the approved moves (Argyle, Furnham and Graham, 1983).
(d) It has been compared to a language, with complex rules of sequence (Clarke, 1983).
(e) Now I am arguing that it is like two people cooperating to produce a joint product: building a house, sawing a tree, dancing, and sexual intercourse are models for social behaviour in general.

REFERENCES

Adams, B. N. (1968) *Kinship in an Urban Setting*, Chicago: Markham.
Alexander, C. N. and Wiley, M. G. (1981) Situated identity and identity formation. In M. Rosenberg and R. H. Turner (eds) *Sociological Perspectives*, New York: Basic Books.
Argyle, M. (1969) *Social Interaction*, London: Methuen.
Argyle, M. (1983) *The Psychology of Interpersonal Behaviour*, 4th edition, Harmondsworth: Penguin.
Argyle, M. (1984) Some new developments in social skills training. *Bulletin of the British Psychological Society* 37, 405–10.
Argyle, M. (1987) *The Psychology of Happiness*, London: Methuen.
Argyle, M. (1988) *Bodily Communication*, 2nd edition, London: Methuen.
Argyle, M. and Dean, J. (1965) Eye-contact, distance and affiliation, *Sociometry* 28, 289–304.
Argyle, M. and Furnham, A. (1982) The ecology of relationships: choice of situation as a function of relationship, *British Journal of Social Psychology* 21, 259–62.
Argyle, M. and Furnham, A. (1983) Sources of satisfaction and conflict in long-term relationships, *Journal of Marriage and the Family* 45, 481–93.
Argyle, M. and Henderson, M. (1984) The rules of friendship, *Journal of Social and Personal Relationships* 1, 211–37.
Argyle, M. and Henderson, M. (1985) *The Anatomy of Relationships*, London: Heinemann.
Austin, J. (1962) *How to do Things with Words*, Oxford: Clarendon Press.
Batson, C. D. and Coke, J. S. (1981) Empathy: a source of altruistic motivation for helping? In J. P. Rushton and R. M. Sorrentino (eds) *Altruism and Helping Behavior*, Hillsdale, N. J.: Lawrence Erlbaum.
Batstone, E., Boraston, I. and Frenkel, S. (1978) *The Social Organization of Strikes*, Oxford: Basil Blackwell.
Bem, D. J. (1967) Self-perception: an alternative interpretation of cognitive dissonance phenomena, *Psychological Review* 74, 183–200.
Bentler, P. M. and Speckart, G. (1979) Models of attitude–behavior relations, *Psychological Review* 86, 452–64.

Bentler, P. M. and Speckart, G. (1981) Attitudes 'cause' behaviors: a structural equation analysis, *Journal of Personality and Social Psychology* 40, 226–38.

Bernstein, B. (1959) A public language: Some sociological implications of a linguistic form, *British Journal of Sociology* 10, 311–26.

Berscheid, E. And Walster, E. (1974) A little bit about love. In T. L. Huston (ed.) *Foundations of Interpersonal Attraction*, New York: Academic Press.

Brown, G. W. and Harris, T. (1978) *Social Origins of Depression: A Study of Psychiatric Disorders in Women*, New York: Free Press.

Bruner, J. S. and Sherwood, V. (1981) Thought, language and interaction in infancy. In J. P. Forgas (ed.) *Social Cognition*, London: Academic Press.

Buck, R. (1984) *The Communication of Emotion*, New York: Guilford.

Clancy, H. and McBride, G. (1969) The autistic process and its treatment, *Journal of Child Psychology and Psychiatry* 10, 233–44.

Clark, H. H. (1985) Language use and language users. In G. Lindzey and E. Aronson (eds) *Handbook of social Psychology*, 3rd edition, New York: Random House.

Clark, C. H. and Kanatami, K. (1980) Turn-taking in small group discussions: A cross cultural study, *Language Laboratory* 17, 12–24.

Clarke, D. D. (1983) *Language and Action*, Oxford: Pergamon.

Collett, P. (1971) On training Englishmen in the non-verbal behaviour of Arabs: an experiment in intercultural communication, *International Journal of Psychology* 6, 209–15.

Dabbs, J. M. (1969) Similarity of gestures and the structure of the nonverbal communication of emotion, *Journal of Personality* 45, 564–84.

De Jorio, A. (1832) *La Mimica degli Antichi Investigata nel Gestire Napoletano*, Naples: Associazione Napoletana.

Deutscher, I. (1984) Choosing ancestors: some consequences of the selection from intellectual traditions. In R. M. Farr and S. Moscovici (eds) *Social Representations*, Cambridge: Cambridge University Press.

Eiser, J. R. (1986) *Social Psychology*, Cambridge: Cambridge University Press.

Ekman, P. (1982) *Emotion in the Human Face*, 2nd edition, Cambridge: Cambridge University Press.

Emmons, R., Diener, E. and Larsen, R. (1986) Choice and avoidance of everyday situations and affect congruence: two models of reciprocal interactionism, *Journal of Personality and Social Psychology* 51, 815–26.

Fiedler, F. E., Mitchell, R. and Triandis, H. C. (1971) The culture assimilator: an approach to cross-cultural training, *Journal of Applied Psychology* 55, 95–102.

Fishbein, M. and Ajzen, I. (1980) *Belief, Attitude, Intention and Behavior: An Introduction to Theory and Research*, Reading, Mass.: Addison-Wesley.

Fiske, S. T. and Taylor, S. E. (1984) *Social Cognition*, Reading, Mass.: Addison-Wesley.

Forgas, J. P. (ed.) (1981) *Social Cognition*, London: Academic Press.

Goffman, E. (1956) *The Presentation of Self in Everyday Life*, New York: Doubleday Anchor Books.

Gottman, J. (1979) *Marital Interaction*, New York: Academic Press.

Grice, H. P. (1968) Utterer's meaning, sentence-meaning, and word-meaning, *Foundations of Language* 4, 225–42.

Grice, H. P. (1975) Logic and conversation. In P. Cole and J. L. Morgan (eds) *Syntax and Semantics*. Vol. 3: *Speech Acts*, New York and London: Academic Press.

Harlow, H. F. and Harlow, M. K. (1965) The affectional systems. In A. M. Schrier, H. F. Harlow and F. Stollnitz (eds) *Behavior of Nonhuman Primates*, New York and London: Academic Press.

Harvey, J. H. et al. (1972) An attributional approach to relationship breakdown. In S. Duck (ed.) *Personal Relationships*. Vol. 4: *Dissolving Personal Relationships*, London: Academic Press.

Hess, E. H. (1972) Pupilometrics. In N. Greenfield and R. Sternbach (eds) *Handbook of Psychophysiology*, New York: Holt, Rinehart & Winston.

Hewstone, M. and Brown, R. (1987) *Contact and Conflict in Intergroup Encounters*, Oxford: Basil Blackwell.

Hochschild, A. R. (1983) *The Managed Heart*, Berkeley, Calif.: University of California Press.

Hollin, C. R. and Trower, P. (eds) (1986) *Handbook of Social Skills Training*, Oxford: Pergamon.

Jemmott, J. B. and Locke, S. E. (1984) Psychosocial factors, immunology mediation, and human susceptibility to infectious diseases: how much do we know?, *Psychological Bulletin* 95, 78–108.

Kelley, H. H. and Michela, J. L. (1980) Attribution theory and research, Annual Review of Psychology 31, 457–501.

Kraut, R. E. and Johnston, R. E. (1979) Social and emotional messages of smiling: an ethological approach, *Journal of Personality and Social Psychology*, 37, 909–17.

LaFrance, M. (1985) Postural mirroring and intergroup relationships, *Personality and Social Psychology Bulletin* 11, 207–17.

La Gaipa, J. J. and Wood, H. D. (1981) Friendship in disturbed adolescents. In S. Duck and R. Gilmour (eds) *Personal Relationships. Vol. 3. Personal Relationships in Disorder*, London: Academic Press.

Langer, E. J. (1978) Rethinking the role of thought in social interaction. In J. Harvey, W. Ickes and R. Kidd (eds) *New Directions in Attribution Research*. Hillsdale, N. J.: Lawnrke Erlbaum.

Lott, A. J. and Lott, B. E. (1974) The role of reward in the formation of positive interpersonal attitudes. In T. L. Huston (ed.) *Foundations of Interpersonal Attraction*, New York: Academic Press.

McClure, J. (1983) Telling more than they can know: the positivist account of verbal reports and mental processes, *Journal for the Theory of Social Behaviour* 13, 111–27.

McDowall, J. J. (1978) Interactional synchrony: a reappraisal. *Journal of Personality and Social Psychology* 36, 963–75.

Malatesta, C. Z. (1981) Infant emotion and the vocal affect lexicon. *Motivation and Emotion* 5, 1–23.

Markus, H. and Zajonc, R. B. (1985) The cognitive perceptive in social psychology. In G. Lindzey and E. Aronson (eds) *Handbook of Social Psychology*, 3rd edition, New York: Random House.

Michalos, A. C. (1980) Satisfaction and happiness, *Social Indicators Research* 8, 385–422.

152 Michael Argyle

Murray, L. and Trevarthen, C. (1985) Emotional regulation of interactions between two-month-olds and their mothers. In T. M. Field and N. A. Fox (eds) *Social Perception in Infants*, Norwood, N. J.: Ablex.

Nisbett, R. E. and Wilson, T. D. (1977) Telling more than we can know: verbal reports on mental processes, *Psychological Review* 84, 231–59.

Rinn, W. E. (1984) The neuropsychology of facial expression: a review of the neurological and psychological mechanisms for producing facial expressions, *Psychological Bulletin* 95, 52–77.

Rommetveit, R. (1974) *On Message Structure: a Framework for the Study of Language*, London: John Wiley.

Roy, D. F. (1959) Banana time: job satisfaction and informal interaction, *Human Organization* 18, 158–68.

Rubin, A. (1970) Measurement of romantic love, *Journal of Personality and Social Psychology* 16, 265–83.

Schachter, S. and Singer, J. E. (1962) Cognitive, social and physiological determinants of emotional state, *Psychological Review* 69, 379–99.

Scherer, K. R., Walbott, H. G. and Summerfield, A. (1986) *Experiencing Emotion*, Cambridge: Cambridge University Press.

Schwarz, N. and Clore, G. L. (1983) Mood, misattribution and judgments of well-being: information and directive functions of affective states, *Journal of Personality and Social Psychology* 45, 513–23.

Seaford, H. W. (1978) Maximizing replicability in describing facial behavior, *Semiotica* 24, 1–32.

Sherif, M. (1966) *Group Conflict and Cooperation: their Social Psychology*, London: Routledge & Kegan Paul.

Snow, C. E. (1977) The development of conversation between mothers and babies, *Journal of Child Languague* 4, 1–22.

Spielberger, C. D. (1965) Theoretical and epistemological issues in verbal conditioning. In S. Rosenberg (ed.) *Directions in Psycholinguistics*, New York: Macmillan.

Spignesi, A. and Shor, R. E. (1981) The judgment of emotion from facial expressions, contexts, and their combination, *Journal of General Psychology* 104, 41–58.

Stern, D. N. (1985) *The Interpersonal World of the Infant*, New York: Basic Books.

Tajfel, H. (ed.) (1978) *Differentiation between Social Groups: Studies in the Social Psychology of Intergroup Relations*, London: Academic Press.

Thorne, A. (1987) The press of personality: a study of conversation between introverts and extraverts, *Journal of Personality and Social Psychology* 53, 718–26.

Tronick, E. Z., Als, H. and Brazelton, T. B. (1980) Monadic phases: a structure descriptive analysis of infant-mother face-to-face interaction, *Merrill-Palmer Quarterly* 26, 3–24.

Underwood, B. and Moore, B. (1982) Perspective-taking and altruism, *Psychological Bulletin* 91, 143–73.

Williams, J. M. G. (1984) *The Psychological Treatment of Depression*, London: Croom Helm.

Zajonc, R. B. (1980) Feeling and thinking: preference need no inferences, *American Psychologist* 35, 151–75.

Zimbardo, P. G. (1969) *The Cognitive Control of Motivation* Glenview, III.: Scott, Foresman.

10

I Don't Know Why I Did It

Tony Crowle

In 1972 Harré and Secord reminded us that we should try to seek the views of our informants/respondents/subjects. Instead of being indifferent to their views, as positivist social researchers were said to be, we were to ask for them and to treat them seriously. In this paper I want to talk about a type of informants' report that is routinely dismissed as evasive or misleading. I wish to argue that this type of report may well be true and therefore that it should be taken seriously.

When asked why they did something deviant, deviants often say, 'I don't know why I did it' (IDKWIDI). These two examples should make plain the problem:

1 Patients studied by John Bancroft (n.d.) were asked to account for their attempted suicides. The accounts were classified by the researchers into three main groups:
    a.   Getting away from it all.
    b.   Tried to get attention.
    c.   IDKWIDI.
   Bancroft viewed IDKWIDI as an evasion. The patients were thought to be reluctant to give the real reason for the suicide attempt.[1]
2 Sex offenders (e.g. rapists, indecent assaulters, indecent exposers) appearing before magistrates often plead guilty and claim that they are unable to offer an explanation for their conduct (Taylor, 1972). Laurie Taylor sees IDKWIDI as a device, a method for getting the benefit of the magistrates' doubt.

In both these cases the social researcher claims that the deviants really did know why they did what they did, and supplies a motive which explains why they deny their knowledge. I believe the deviants were telling the truth, and wish to argue two points:

1   Some deviants don't know why they do things – what the deviants said was true: they really did not know why they did it.
2   Researchers don't know why some deviants do things – the social analyst is no better able to figure out why deviants did things than the deviants are.

The basis of my argument is that the deviant cannot answer the question why he did what he did because he does not know the formula that links his act with his circumstances: he has many unknowns and only one equation.

The expository device I use here is to talk as though I were a rigorous empirical sociologist who has been asked the question that deviants are asked. I employ a very simple model of the processes which lead to a person being primed for deviance, as follows: every person is potentially at risk from exposure to some of the very many features of our culture that promote deviance. At the same time, the person is protected by some of the many features of our culture that inhibit deviance. If at any time the deviance-promoting features outweigh the deviance-inhibiting features then the person is primed for deviance. (Note that this is similar to saying, 'If you eat too much you get fat'.) What specific form this deviance may take is not my concern; in this discussion I am only interested in the enabling mechanism. (In terms of the analogy used earlier, in claiming that if you eat too much you get fat, I do not have to be able to specify exactly where on a body the fat will be deposited.)

The Total Attack Variable

Let us postulate a dependent variable TA (for 'Total Attack') which is the resultant of all the 'attack' variables that tend to promote deviance. For a middle-class, middle-aged male in this (British) culture, these attack variables might be such things as: loss of job; loss of spouse; receipt of rejection slips; bankruptcy; and so on. Suppose you ask me what the contributions of the various attack variables to TA are. I would have to say that I do not know, but that I know how to find out. The first thing the research would require would be a valid interval-level measure of the dependent variable TA. (I might have to spend a large amount of time and money on developing such a measure.) As this would be a pioneering effort, I would make my task easier by drastically pruning the list of independent attack variables until I had made it as short as possible. I would also simplify the handling of the attack variables by treating them as dichotomous variables (High versus Low or Presence versus Absence). I could carry out an experiment employing an Analysis of Variance (ANOVA) design which would enable me to get the most information out of the fewest resources. Suppose I were able to reduce the list of attack variables to three, called X, Y and Z. I would then have all the elements of a well-understood ANOVA design, namely a '2 to the power of 3' layout. In this design there are eight cells and eight effects. Each one of the eight cells is one of the eight possible combinations of two levels of the three independent variables. If we call the levels H and L for High and Low, then we can display the cells like this:

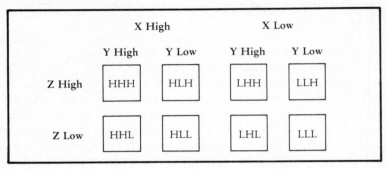

Figure 10.1

The eight effects are:
(i)   The average level of TA over all the cells of the design.
(ii) The X, Y, and Z main effects on TA (the main effect for X is the difference between the average of all the cells with X at a high level and the average of all the cells with X at a low level, ignoring the levels of variables Y and Z).
(iii) The XY, XZ, and YZ interaction effects on TA (the XY interaction effect may be thought of as showing whether or not the effect of a variable (X or Y)) depends on the level of the other variable (Y or X).
(iv) The XYZ interaction effect on TA (the XYZ interaction effect may be thought of as the difference between the averages in the cells and what we might have expected from adding together the three main effects and the three first-order interaction effects).

In order to obtain an estimate of the error term, we need to have at least two observations in each cell, that is we need to have sixteen experimental subjects. The actual conduct of the research is, in principle, quite routine. We randomly assign our sixteen subjects to the eight cells in such a way that we finish with exactly two in each cell. Then we expose them to the levels of the independent attack variables that are correct for their cells, e.g. one cell might have [mortgage called in + eldest daughter on drugs + safe job] while another might have [mortgage OK + eldest daughter OK + redundancy notice].

Some Problems with the Design

At this point we must take note of a few problems with our design. The first problem is merely practical, namely that we cannot in fact conduct experiments of this sort, e.g. we cannot cause people to lose or not lose their jobs depending on the outcome of the toss of a fair coin. The second problem is that the various independent attack variables are likely to impact on different people in different ways. Other things being equal, a person with a history of being in and out of work is presumably less upset by the loss of a job than someone without that history. A person who has known of a spouse's illness for some time is less shocked by the spouse's death than someone to whom it comes as a surprise. It seems evident that the effect of the independent attack variables is different from person to person, depending on the person's history. I call this the principle of *Different slopes for different folks.* Hence we could have two persons who are in the same cell of our ANOVA design (e.g. the cell with spouse's death and job loss) whose 'TA' levels though similar are the results of quite dissimilar patterns. As we are dealing with a set of responses that will vary from individual to individual, and what we wish to understand is how the various effects combine in individuals, what we need to do is 'use the subject as his own control'. That is, in order to to be able to estimate the effects of the three independent variables on the dependent variable, we must use the same subject twice in each of the cells of the design. This entails us in taking measurements of Mr S bankrupt and not bankrupt, spouse dead and not dead, job lost and not lost . . . and so for all eight combinations of levels of the three independent variables. If we decide that we can forgo estimating the highest order interaction term (XYZ), we can use it as an estimate of the error term, and then we can get away with using Mr S just once per cell.

At this point the difficulty arises that our experimental design requires us to be able to cause Mr S's job to be lost, then found, then lost again, and his spouse to die, and then be alive, then be dead again. Because of the nature of the 'fully crossed' factorial design that we are committed to, there is no way of ordering the cells in an incremental fashion – the independent variables have to be present, then absent, then present again, and so on. What is more, we do not want Mr S to be wise to the experiment – we want him somehow to be an uninformed subject while we perform our various experimental miracles, otherwise the study would be compromised because he would be exposed to his spouse's death knowing that she had died before (in some other cell) and had returned before (in yet another cell). All this is counter to what might be called *Charles' Principle*: When Ray Charles was asked if he thought his hard upbringing (due to his blindness and poverty) had helped him to stay on top in the world of popular music,[2] he replied, 'I'm glad you said "do I *think*" 'cause I certainly couldn't possibly *know* because I don't have anything to compare it with. In other words, it isn't like I was born both ways where I could compare one way against the other.' (Armed as we are with B. J. Winer's *Statistical Principles in Experimental Design* (1962), we note that a complete answer to the question would require there to have been four lives of Ray Charles: not blind and not poor; blind and not poor; not blind and poor; blind and poor.) Clearly, our experimental subject can only live the one life too.

It is evident that these experimental research projects are doomed. For practical and theoretical reasons, the effects of the three independent variables on the TA variable cannot be estimated, whether for a sample or for Mr S as an individual, because the various 'treatments' cannot be delivered in the required manner. It is important to note that, at any one time, we are only in one cell of the ANOVA design. That is, instead of having data from the eight cells that are necessary to analyse three variables each at two levels, we have data from just the one cell that Mr S is in at the time we happen to investigate him. As a statistician might say, in real life all the effects are 'totally confounded'. We can infer nothing from a single cell. To jump ahead a little, I suggest that when we ask deviants to account for their behaviour, we are indeed asking them to make inferences from single-cell designs. No wonder then that they so often reply IDKWIDI.

Observational TA

Though an ANOVA experimental study has many virtues, it is a method which presupposes very tight controls over resources and people. We ought to consider what non-experimental techniques could offer us, e.g. the sample survey as a means of obtaining the data and regression analysis as a way of estimating the relative effects of the various attack variables. We can dispose of sample surveys quickly by noting, as we did above, that the phenomenon we are interested in is an individual one, and that averaging over the several individuals in the sample is apt to lose information in the process of conglomerating responses. The use of regression techniques looks more hopeful, because it will enable us to handle interval-level attack variables in a familiar way, e.g.:

$$TA = A + B1X1 + B2X2 + \ldots BnXn + E$$

where TA is 'Total Attack' as before, 'A' is the regression intercept, the 'Bi' are weighting coefficients (slopes), the 'Xi' are the attack variables that are inluded in the equation, and 'E' is an error term. The coefficients A and Bi are to be estimated from the data. Here we find that we need at least as many sets of observations as there are unknowns. What we have is a multidimensional space, and Mr S's data taken at any particular time provide us with just one point in it. Hence, as before, we find that we require Mr S to have lived several lives.

Though we cannot in fact employ this model to analyse any data that we might get from Mr S, we can use it to order our thoughts. We can view Mr S as being exposed to a set of attack variables of varying magnitudes. What the variables are, and what their magnitudes are, will differ from person to person. These attack variables are attenuated by the various resistances which are also unique to Mr S. The attacks as attenuated by the resistances are summed to produce the 'Total Attack' variable. This TA variable can be thought of constantly on the move, as Mr S traverses through life, sitting in traffic jams, hearing about MCC defeats, seeing younger men with flashier cars and so on. Every so often the TA may move massively after particularly attackful events.

Total Defence

Let us now postulate a variable TD (for 'Total Defence') which is a function of all the variables that tend to promote adherence to straight and narrow paths. In this culture, these variables might be such things as: religious teachings; ethical teachings; respect for the law; fear of punishment; and so on. These various protective elements I call 'defences'.

As before I note that all the various contributers to TD would be mediated by different individuals' different experiences. The notion 're-spect for the law' takes on new meaning after you have been physically abused by policemen. The injunction 'Thou shalt not kill' is revalued after the regiment's padre has blessed the guns. The various experiences that attenuate the effect on TD of the defences I call 'underminings'. The relationship between all these quantities is represented by an equation that is similar to that used for TA:

$$TD = 1 + C1Z1 + C2Z2 + \ldots CmZm + E$$

where TD is 'Total Defence', 'I' is the regression intercept, the 'Ci' are weighting coefficients (slopes), the 'Zi' are the defence variables that are included in the equation, and 'E' is an error term. As before, we cannot actually estimate the various unknown quantities, but we can use the equation to order our thoughts. We can view Mr S as being exposed to a set of defence variables of varying magnitudes. As before, what the variables are, and what their magnitudes are, will differ from person to person. These defence variables are attenuated by the various underminings which are also unique to Mr S. The defences as attenuated by the underminings are summed to produce the 'Total Defence' variable.

The TD variable can also be thought of constantly on the move as Mr S moves through life, reading uplifting literature, hearing about severe punishments, viewing items about bent MPs and so on. What we have then is an environing population of defence variables. Any given individual will have been exposed to some subsample of this population, and this subsample will have been modified by the individual's collection of underminings.

Combining Total Attack and Total Defence

The last stage of this simple model says that when an individuals TA is greater than his TD then he is primed for deviance. This is best thought of graphically: we have a trace line for TA and a trace line for TD. When the line for TA crosses over the line for TD, i.e. when TA exceeds TD, then the individual is primed. (Being primed for deviance is analogous to a body's becoming 'run down', so that it is susceptible to whatever physiological threat comes along, whether it is viral, bacterial, chemical or what have you.)

Some Possible Patterns

Though there are many possible different trace line patterns, I would like to draw attention to a few that are of special interest.

a. TD constant, TA slowly rises and crosses.

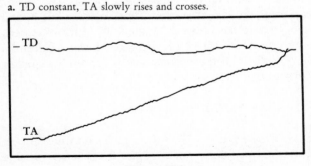

Figure 10.2

This is the 'war of attrition' pattern, in which the deviant reports that 'things kept building up until something snapped', and witnesses claim that they noticed the deviant gradually getting worse. The graphic representation makes it clear that a causal analysis in terms of the most recent known attack ('last straw' analysis) is misdirected. That is, it does not make much sense to look for explanations of the behaviour among the events in the immediate past. Nor is it sensible to single out any particular prior event, any more than it would be sensible for a fat person to blame a particular bun.

b. TD constant, TA sharply rises and crosses.

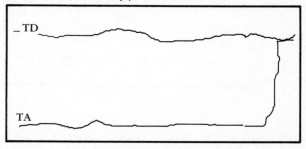

Figure 10.3

In this pattern, the Total Attack suddenly increases, as perhaps several things go wrong simultaneously. The deviant and every else is taken by surprise by this attack. 'I don't know what came over me' is the deviant's standard phrase, while the others say, 'She was a perfect wife and mother.' Here the social researcher's problem is that the near simultaneity of the several attacks, and their possible over-determination of the outcome, make it impossible to assign individual weights to them.

c. TD constant, TA at first sharply rises then slowly rises and crosses.

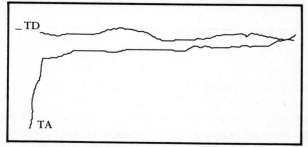

Figure 10.4

This pattern represents, e.g. the traumatic effects of early childhood experiences, followed by a relatively slight and slow effect of a multiplicity of little causes. Again, there will be nothing in the deviant's recent past to explain his actions, whether to himself or to others, while the events in the remote past may not be readily available or interpretable.

d. TA constant, TD slowly falls and crosses.

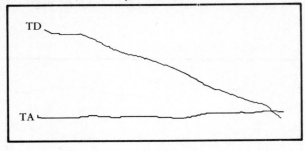

Figure 10.5

In this pattern there is no change in the Total Attack variable, and so onlookers are surprised when Mr S does something deviant as falling moral standards are reflected in his declining TD.

e. TA slowly rises, TD slowly falls until they cross.

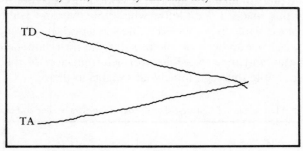

Figure 10.6

Presumably the most common pattern, as stresses cumulate while early moral teachings are eroded.

If TA and TD are somewhat homeostatic, we would expect exogenously induced fluctuations to be absorbed over time. However two simultaneous fluctuations could produce a crossover with non-absorbable conse-

f. Non-synchronized periodic fluctuations in TA and TD
eventually produce a crossover.

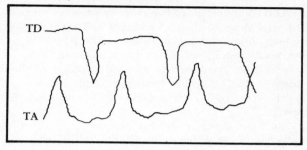

Figure 10.7

quences. Mr S, whose life, like a roller-coaster, is full of ups and downs,
goes off the rails.

We began with the fact that many deviants say 'I don't know why I did it'.
If saying why he did what he did implies assigning weights to a large
number of variables then, as we have seen, there are many possible
different patterns that lead to the conclusion that the doer cannot in truth
say why he did what he did. It would be too neat if all the persons who say
IDKWIDI reflected these patterns, while all the persons who do not say
IDKWIDI did not. It seems more plausible to suppose that at least some of
the persons who offer reasons why they did what they did (particularly
those who offer different reasons at different times) ought to be saying
IDKWIDI, but instead are offering a story that seems appropriate to them
in their circumstances.

In this paper I have not supported or criticized any particular theory of
deviance. The remarks I have made apply not only to true negative
confessions (IDKWIDI) and to false positive confessions, but also to many
other kinds of accounts. It is common in social research to attribute great
powers of recall and remarkable powers of self-analysis to our respon-
dents, not all of which are justified. Though we may tolerate these
practices, we surely should not be so forgiving as to honour the assumption that deviants can routinely do what we know is impossible to do.

NOTES

1   Bancroft and others' later research (1976, 1979) used a different technique
    (forced-choice questions) which precluded IDKWIDI.
2   Ray Charles interviewed by Jools Holland on ITV Channel 4.

REFERENCES

Bancroft, John (n.d.) *Accounts of Self-Poisoning Behaviour*, mimeo.

Bancroft, J. H. J., A. M. Skrimshire and S. Simkin (1976) 'The reasons people give for taking overdoses', *British Journal of Psychiatry* 128, pp. 538–48.

Bancroft, John, Keith Hawton, Sue Simkin, Breda Kingston, Clyde Cumming and David Whitwell (1979) 'The reasons people give for taking overdoses: a further inquiry', *British Journal Of Medical Psychology* 52, pp. 353–6.

Harré, R and P. F. Secord (1972) *The Explanation of Human Behaviour*, Oxford, Basil Blackwell.

Taylor, L. (1972) 'The significance and interpretation of replies to motivational questions: the case of sex offenders', *Sociology* 6, pp. 23–39.

Winer, B. J. (1962) *Statistical Principles in Experimental Design*, New York, McGraw-Hill.

11

'Subjects' *versus* 'Persons' in Social Psychological Research

Paul F. Secord

The manner in which investigators characterize participants in experiments and other types of research has a profound effect on the description of behaviour, the choice of methodology and the nature of theory. This characterization is not usually explicit, but may be sketched by teasing out the assumptions that underlie the way in which the research is carried out. The present discussion calls attention to a shift in social psychology over the past few decades from characterizing participants as 'subjects' to characterizing them as 'persons'. Clearly this shift is not explicit, but can be strongly inferred from changes in the way experiments are done and in particular from the kinds of manipulation that are carried out. Thinking of participants in psychological experiments as 'subjects' began relatively early in the history of psychology, and undoubtedly was the result of the way in which science was conceived. Not the least important was the success of physics – especially mechanics – as a model science. But what was copied from physics failed to display the real complexities of the physics model, and became a caricature that took the following form.

Inert or passive materials were the object of study by an observer who stood apart from the materials, not affected by them or affecting them. Most material objects do not act on their own, and in most circumstances do not change because they are observed. Only in the experiment did observers affect materials in carefully calculated ways. Logical empiricism and behaviourism are a legacy from this scientific history. Following the lead of physical science, psychologists chose the experimental method as their principal tool, and humans who participated in experiments were treated as passive subjects. Their behaviour was considered determined; every act had its cause: subjects were passive objects open to the pushes and pulls of their environment and even of their own body and the effects of past experiences.

This orientation towards participants in experiments was reflected in the early S–R (stimulus–response) formula of behaviourism, later modified to S–O–R (stimulus–organism–response). The introduction of O into the formula recognized that certain processes in the organism intervened between stimulus and response. These processes were thought of as mechanisms operating on variables, and initially were conceived in relatively simple terms (e.g. the organism had to attend to a stimulus before it could be reacted to). Later, as the reinforcement theory of Hull/Spence developed, processes associated with O became relatively complex. Then with the emergence of computer models and cognitive psychology, O mechanisms evolved into procedures for operating on information.

What is worth noting here is that O for organism is in no way an approximation of P for person. In reinforcement theory, the evolving behaviour of individuals is a mechanical process shaped entirely by what responses happen to be reinforced. Even in modern cognitive psychology, it is *information* that is processed and which results in certain behaviours, with almost no attention given to emotional and motivational aspects of the person.

Because it is extraordinarily difficult to treat humans as organisms or non-persons, this conception of participants has frequently been an uneasy one, especially in social psychology. Many social psychologists trained in sociology rather than psychology favoured a radically different view of participants, and typically thought of them as persons, although their favourite descriptive term for them was 'actor'. This orientation emphasized the ability of participants to interpret and define the situation, initiate action, or to pretend or deceive. But most social psychologists trained in psychology and even some sociologists preferred to think of participants as 'subjects' because that seemed more in keeping with 'doing sicence'.

What does it mean to treat a participant as a subject? Roughly, the *subject* perspective embraces the following assumptions:

1. Persons are organisms or subjects acted upon by forces in their environment.
2. The behaviour of subjects is partly an outcome of states and processes occurring in organisms.
3. The behaviour of subjects is partly an outcome of antecedent behaviours occurring under particular circumstances and which somehow change the organism.
4. Since the behaviours of subjects are determined by external and internal forces, subjects are incapable of analysing their situation or of initiating action – they are, in Garfinkel's (1967) words, 'judgemental dopes'.

Treating the research participant as a subject places the scientist in a privileged position: if the subject's behaviour is determined by various external and internal forces, then the scientist can identify these and explain the subject's behaviour in those terms. The scientist's version of what is going on is dominant. There is no place for the subject's version of the action; it is considered irrelevant to a scientific explanation. Moreover, this subject orientation leads the scientist/observer to design studies accordingly. Experiments are favoured over field studies because they allow more control over the causal factors impinging on the subject. In such experiments, moreover, it seems preferable to minimize verbalization by subjects; pushing a button or checking an alternative is preferred because the observer can unambiguously identify these simple behaviours. Options are shaped to fit the scientist/observer's interest in certain behaviours as relevant; non-relevant behaviours are constrained or discouraged as far as is possible. These activities are, of course, in the interests of experimental control and the exclusion of intruding conditions that might complicate the results and their interpretation. Their unintended effect, however, is that participants are more likely to behave in accord with the hypotheses of the experimenter, but their laboratory behaviour is less likely to have the same identity as their behaviour outside of the laboratory.

Within the subject orientation, emphasis is placed not only on external stimuli, but to the extent that processes occurring within the organism are considered, they are conceptualized relatively independently of the fact that they are something that a *person does*. For example, cognitive inconsistency is a state where cognitive elements, considered in isolation from the fact that they are thoughts or beliefs that a person holds, logically contradict one another. These processes are likened to computer subroutines that can function independently of the main program. Moreover, psychological states are postulated from externally observable situations involving the behaviour of the participant or the circumstances surrounding the behaviour. Ideally, information about psychological states is not obtained by asking the participant about thoughts or feelings.

Perhaps the 'subject' concept will be clearer when contrasted with that of 'person'. The following are characteristics that are typically attributed to persons:

1. Persons are capable of initiating performances or actions.
2. Persons perform actions with an intention or purpose.
3. Persons are typically but not invariably aware that their actions are rule-guided and goal-directed, and they monitor their progress in conforming to rules and towards achieving their goals.

4. Persons are capable of imagining how they would act in various situations, or of imagining how persons in general or how particular persons might act in those situations.
5. Persons often generate social action with a view as to how it will be received or reacted to by other persons.
6. None of the above is intended to deny that persons sometimes perform one act when they think they are doing another, or that persons often perform a series of acts in a routine or inattentive way.

Treating research participants as 'subjects' or as 'persons' represents two extremes, and only rarely if ever do investigations in social psychology adopt one extreme to the exclusion of the other. More often, the subject perspective is nominally adopted, but the person concept is covert and remains unexplicated. Under those circumstances, it is not surprising that many empirical studies mix elements of both perspectives without generating any awareness of the problems thereby created for interpreting the behaviour of the individuals under study. One example of this confusion is right up front: the very idea of an experiment in which *volunteer* subjects are used is a contradiction between the subject and person orientations.

Asking participants to serve in the *role of an experimental subject* is an action that itself recognizes individuals as actors. When asked to volunteer, participants can *accept* or *refuse*; if they accept, they must *cooperate* throughout the experiment. What this amounts to is a social contract between the experimenter and the participant. These contractual arrangements involve the intentional actions of persons; yet, paradoxically, during the very time that participants are cooperating they are treated by the experimenter as subject to a causal nexus, and it is only the latter that enters into the experimenter's theoretical framework. The experimenter often acts as if data had been obtained from the actions of unthinking robots, and whatever contribution was made to these actions by the participants acting as persons is ignored by the experimenter.

Before discussing further examples of this confusion in experimental work, several non-experimental approaches will be briefly discussed with respect to how they relate to the subject/person perspective.

Field experiments
It might be thought that field experiments are instances of pure person orientations, but such instances are relatively rare in social psychology. Typically, those who conduct field experiments do not treat participants as persons (e.g. most helping or bystander studies). Although they treat participants as having a choice, experimenters do not explore participants' views of what they are doing, but instead rely upon their own extrapola-

tions of what is occurring. Behaviour is treated in terms of the experimenter's theory, not the participant's theories. Moreover, the causal framework is one created by experimenters and is viewed in their terms.

Participants as judges

Using participants as judges might at first glance appear to be an explicit person orientation, yet such uses are typically markedly attenuated. The focus usually is not upon the *actions* of the participants; several different foci are possible. Participants might be asked how they would react in a prescribed situation. Given conditions a, b or c, what do they think they would do? Or what would other persons (unspecified) do under those conditions? Participants may simply be offering a cognitive judgement, not a performance. If the participants are not spontaneous and involved, such judgement experiments come close to adopting a subject perspective. This is one reason why non-participants hearing a mere description of the Milgram experiments on obedience to authority were radically wrong in guessing how Milgram's subjects actually behaved.

Participants as role players

The 'actor' label popular with sociologically-oriented social psychologists suggests another familiar activity, related to participants as judges: *playing a role*. Part of being human are such capabilities as detaching oneself from one's actions and trying to see them as an observer would, pretending or simulating, and the like. These capabilities sometimes enter into participating in experiments. This 'role-taking' is, of course, to be distinguished from describing a person's behaviour in terms of social role (e.g. a mother acting 'like a mother'). In some kinds of role playing (e.g. stage actors) another person or character is being acted out. But one important type of role playing in social psychological investigation involves *active* participants: a make-believe situation is created that enables them to act out a role in a spontaneous and involved manner (Mixon, 1971, 1972). Experimental realism can be achieved in role playing studies if the laboratory situation is properly structured. The antagonism toward role playing as a methodology expressed by some experimenters is based upon an assumed subject orientation and pertains largely to situations like those where participants are treated not as role players, but as judges.

'Subject' and 'Person' in Experimental Social Psychology

The great majority of studies in psychological social psychology are experimental in nature, and so the idea of participants as 'subjects' or as 'persons' needs close examination in that context. Some illustrative experimental programmes are discussed below, and in a later section, the manner in which subject/person orientations bear on the conceptualization and description of behaviour will be spelled out in more detail.

The Milgram studies of obedience to authority

Consider the classic experiments by Milgram (1969) from the dual perspective of subject/person. In these studies, participants are persons in that they respond to an advertisement, and participate in the experiment for pay. They are deceived in what they are doing: they are told that they are using the shock apparatus to 'teach' a 'learner' in the next room. From the experimenter's point of view, what they are doing is behaving aggressively in shocking the 'learner' in the next room (who is actually a confederate simulating being shocked by crying out or responding in other ways). Although many variants of this experiment were conducted, Milgram's chief interest was in how far subjects would turn up the shock in the face of considerable pain and possible danger presumably being experienced by the unseen but audible confederate in the next room. He suspected that his participants would be far more willing to shock the 'learner' than most people were willing to believe. Moreover, he regarded his experiments as an analogue of the situation in Nazi Germany whereby military personnel acting under orders tortured and put Jews to death.

Although participants are told that they are 'teaching a learner', clearly they are confronted with realistic and disturbing feedback from another person who is responding to actions that they are performing. They can see that their actions are upsetting or hurting the 'learner'. How to interpret their actions has been the subject of innumerable articles and it is not my intention to resolve the controversy here, but rather to use the situation to illustrate the interpretive problems that arise from adopting subject/person characterizations.

What is worth stressing here is that, in this research programme, as in so many social psychological experiments, from their point of view participants may be doing one thing, but from the experimenter's point of view they are doing another. What they are actually doing thus remains unclear and is heavily dependent on how the participants are conceived; this conception affects how human action is to be described. From the subject perspective which the experimenter adopts, participants are doing what they have been told to do: shock the learner (implying harm). They have been told to increase the shock with each 'error' made by the learner, and despite the feedback they are receiving concerning the learner's painful reactions, the majority of them continue to increase the shock. But if one remains within the subject perspective, it is difficult to go beyond this simple description of the actions of the participants and answer in any precise way the question of what the participants thought they were doing.

The subject perspective actually does not permit Milgram to draw the kinds of conclusion that he set out to investigate; to do so he must slip into thinking of the participants as persons, but that requires different experimental procedures.

Notice also that the experimental context sets up a situation with certain characteristics. The participants are anonymous with respect to the learner; there is no face-to-face confrontation. They know that their participation is short-lived; moreover, they will never see the experimenter again. Only to the extent that they carry with them in their memories what they have done do their actions have a possibility of affecting their future feelings or actions. The point is that, when one is anonymous and soon to leave a unique situation, one may feel freer about performing actions that might be self-censored under more enduring and more public circumstances. Later the importance of social context will be elaborated further, in a discussion of 'the social constitution of action'.

If the person perspective is adopted, and the criterion question is asked: 'What are the participants meaning to do?', a variety of answers that are not entirely consistent come to mind as possibilities. The participants are going along with the experimenter, they are trying to teach the learner, they are harming the learner, they are experiencing distress at the learner's responses but do not want to confront the experimenter (in some variations, a few do challenge him). Although it is true that participants are aware that the learner is apparently experiencing painful shocks (and in one condition, possibly even being permanently harmed), they also know that they are participating in an experiment, and in some variations, that the experimenter has taken responsibility for the safety of the learner.

In the main variations, about 60 per cent of the participants turned up the shock to the point labelled as 'WARNING! SEVERE SHOCK', while the other 40 per cent refused to amplify the shock to that point. The general implication that Milgram drew was that the majority of people are willing to harm others when placed in an authoritative situation of this sort. Unfortunately, this is a *normative* generalization, and it is not possible to draw normative generalizations from laboratory experiments: the *proportion* producing a particular response is bound to change under a variety of non-laboratory conditions. What experiments can do, though, is to reveal the capacities or powers of individuals – what they are capable of doing; and the Milgram programme does reveal that people are more capable of harming others than we might have thought. But note also that the condition in which participants received moral support from a confederate demonstrated the capacity to reject an authoritative command: most of these subjects refused to continue the shocks.

The aseptic design called for by a subject orientation and the misrepresentation of what an experiment is about prevents obtaining the extensive accounts from the participants that are necessary to ascertain what 'they were meaning to do'. But it should also be emphasized that such accounts by themselves would not necessarily settle the issue. Accounts can be distorted in the service of justifying one's actions. Moreover, if a research programme is to have implications that can be extended to conditions like the holocaust, what is needed in addition if a careful comparison of the features of the experiment with the features of the Nazi regime and the death camps. The differences between the laboratory and the holocaust are so great, though, that that comparison is virtually impossible.

Thirty years of dissonance research

Without resolving the interpretive problems of the Milgram research, enough has been said to illustrate the problems created by the subject/ person dialectic. Consideration of another line of research in social psychology, dissonance theory, may give us more definitive information on persons as experimental subjects. This research topic is especially fruitful for our discussion because it spans three decades and reveals the evolution of a social psychological theory that, in its most recent formulation, has little resemblance to the original. Even more importantly, the research is characterized by a gradual shift from viewing participants as subjects to viewing participants as persons.

Dissonance is said to occur when the obverse of one cognition follows from another. Familiar cognitions are beliefs or attitudes. But also invoked is a cognition that is *implied* by one's actions: for example, an act may be contrary to one's belief and thus create dissonance. The third statement below is an example. The three statements taken together illustrate cognitions that should create dissonance:

I don't want to get lung cancer.
I believe that smoking causes lung cancer.
I know that I smoke one pack of cigarettes per day.

When dissonance occurs, there is pressure to reduce it, and one way of doing this is to change a cognition. One of the most common experimental procedures (the *induced compliance* paradigm) leads participants to behave in a manner contrary to their attitude, creating pressure to reduce the dissonance by changing the attitude.

What is interesting about the paradigm is that experiments on dissonance, especially the initial ones, started out viewing participants more as subjects than as actors. This was true despite the fact that the theory is about cognitions that *persons* have! This claim may be illustrated in a number of ways. For example, the issue of whether or not dissonance needed to be a *felt experience* was not closely examined. Festinger thought of dissonance as a kind of drive state, like hunger, a vague but pressing state that was not necessarily associated with any articulate thoughts or feelings. But most experiments did not include a routine check for the presence of arousal, much less any exploration of the participants' felt experiences. Of course, this is not unreasonable; quite conceivably, participants could react to a dissonant situation even if they did not consciously experience it as such. But the failure to address the issue in the initial research suggests a subject orientation or a drastically reduced person orientation.

That the subject orientation was characteristic of early studies is suggested by the fact that intensive analysis of *why* any particular experimental treatment should create dissonance was seldom carried out. Typically, after naming an attitude and a behaviour that *appeared* to have a dissonant relation, the experimenter would apparently use common sense to create an experimental treatment that would cause dissonance, without examining conceptually exactly what cognitions and other conditions might be involved. This avoidance follows from a subject orientation; a person orientation would call for considerable analysis. Still another indication that the person orientation was to be avoided is illustrated by the famous Festinger and Carlsmith (1959) experiment, which led to ongoing studies of attitude change resulting from being induced to behave in a way contrary to one's attitude. The participant in a boring, seemingly meaningless task was offered a large or a small reward for telling the next participant that the task was interesting and scientifically important. Especially if the reward were small ($1.00), this behaviour was deemed to be dissonant with the participants' experience and thus to set them up to change their view of the task in order to resolve the dissonance. The large reward ($20.00) was considered sufficient in itself to justify the behaviour, thus arousing less dissonance and less attitude change. Yet, consistently with a subject orientation, no intensive analysis was conducted of what participants were meaning to do and how they felt about the reward and their action when they spoke to the next participant. Thus the issue of what processes actually brought about change in the participants' attitudes was ignored in favour of the simple view that 'dissonance', operationally defined, was the cause.

It was not long before rival theoretical interpretations appeared. Additional experiments were conducted to test these alternative interpretations, and ultimately, more than 1000 experiments on dissonance were eventually conducted. Some of these rival interpretations were more in keeping with a person orientation. In the classic Festinger and Carlsmith

(1959) induced compliance paradigm, for example, the possibility that those receiving they large reward might think they were being evaluated for honesty or independence or that they might become suspicious of the experimenter's motives was soon considered, and additional experiments were conducted to test these notions. Here is a clear reference to intentional elements characterizing the participants' states of mind that were believed to bear on the actions performed.

Over the last three decades, many different interpretations of the induced compliance paradigm were offered, along with experimental programmes to test their validity. What is especially interesting about these successive interpretations is that they move progressively away from a subject orientation towards an increasingly fleshed-out person orientation. This is apparent even from the language forms used in talking about the experiment. In 1957, for Festinger, two cognitive elements were in a dissonant relation if, considering these two alone, the obverse of one element would follow from the other. In 1984, Cooper and Fazio restated the initial theory this way: 'cognitive dissonance occurs when one cognition *that a person holds* follows from the obverse of another' (p. 230; emphasis added). Festinger speaks of 'cognitive elements' apart from the person; Cooper and Fazio talk of *persons* who *have* cognitions. Of course, in parts of his book, Festinger is perfectly clear that the cognitive elements belong to persons, but his language in defining dissonance reflects a desire to state the operations in a highly abstract way in which the person is left out. A small point, but a significant one.

This enormous volume of experimental research has finally reached a point where some fairly stable conclusions can be drawn about dissonance theory. Most of the results are consistent with a reformulation of dissonance theory offered by Cooper and Fazio (1984). Supported by hundreds of experiments, the successive discoveries briefly summarized below clearly reveal the progressive introduction of more and more attributes that imply that the experimental participants are persons rather than subjects. These attributes essentially amounted to necessary conditions for dissonance to occur; conditions that often involved thoughts, feelings or other processes occurring within the actor.

1.   Dissonance was found *not* to occur merely as a result of a logical contradiction between two cognitions. The consequences of acting contrary to one's attitude had to be aversive; e.g. one's action might be an unworthy one, such as persuading people of something one did not believe in. But if one's action had no effect on anyone, or if it affected only persons one disliked, no dissonance and no attitude change occurred.

2. Aversive consequences were crucial in bringing about attitude change only when they could be foreseen by participants, thus making them feel responsible (e.g. for misrepresenting how they felt).
3. Mere agreement to perform a counter-attitudinal act that could be seen to have potential aversive consequences aroused dissonance, even if the act later was not performed.
4. The aversive consequence had to be irrevocable; if it was possible for participants to rescind their action, dissonance was not aroused.
5. Participants had to feel personally responsible for creating the aversive consequences. If they were coerced by strong pressures into the counter-attitudinal act, they felt little dissonance even if their act created aversive consequences.
6. If the arousal of dissonance could plausibly be attributed to an external source rather than one's own counter-attitudinal act, participants did not change their attitude to reduce the dissonance.
7. Schlenker's (1982) research takes the paradigm still further into a person orientation. In his view, the participants' identities are involved in the dynamics of the induced compliance studies. First, like others, he found that participants had to believe that their actions would be known to an audience if dissonance were to occur. This makes clear that self-presentation is involved. The social meanings of the large and small payments derive from the implications that accepting them has for the participants' views of self. If the accepted payments are seen as illegitimate, participants need to take action to repair their identity, and changing one's attitude so that one's behavior was consistent with it is one way of accomplishing that (e.g. it may guard against the interpretation that one was bribed to say something one didn't believe). Experiments that varied the illegitimacy of the payments, along with other conditions, supported this interpretation.

It seems incontestable from this brief discussion of dissonance research that interpretations of experimental findings are firmly dependent on how the subject/person characterizations are treated. Treating participants as subjects inhibited thinking about how persons might think and feel about the induced compliance situation, and how those thoughts and feelings might affect attitude change. In the end, it became abundantly clear that participants engaging in counter-attitudinal behaviour are at least to some degree behaving like persons in that they feel responsible for actions that might adversely affect others or that might put themselves in a bad light, and that they act to mitigate these unpleasant effects.

This is a long way from the initial idea that logical inconsistencies between cognitions bring about attitude change all by themselves. The latter idea is rather mechanistic in form, while the former emphasizes that the cognitions are not isolable in any easy way, but depend upon the actor's psychology and the social context, as well as the social relations between the actor and the experimenter or other persons. The moral seems to be that, in designing experiments, it is best to assume that participants will behave like persons unless they are explicitly prevented from doing so. Moreover, placing severe constraints on them in the attempt to reduce them to passive subjects automatically limits what can be said about the phenomena under study. Adopting an explicit person orientation would always seem to be desirable and to result in a better controlled experiment in which the acts that are taking place can be more clearly identified for what they are.

The Description of Behaviour from a Person Perspective

The discussion so far has not dealt with observation *per se*, although the subject/person orientations have highly significant implications for observation and description. First, it should be noted that *naive* observers cannot read off and describe behaviour by merely observing it. All human observers have a vast store of knowledge that they use to describe what they see (Schutz, 1967). What they see depends upon what they know. That is one reason that thinking of participants as organisms producing responses became so popular with psychologists. This form of logical atomism fragmented behaviour into highly circumscribed units (often movements) that could nominally be readily identified by observers. Human actions, however, typically are much larger wholes and cannot be fragmented in this manner, especially if social behaviour is the topic of investigation. In fact, as Hampshire (1974) noted, over the past half-century *philosophers* have written volumes on the logic of behaviour description (usually referred to as human action), and, while progress has been made, the problems of such description are far from resolved. Reviewing this enormous literature is impossible here, but from it a number of important guidelines for psychologists can be extracted.

Behaviour cannot simply by read off by a naive observer, unless mere movements are the point of focus. Observers use their common-sense stock of knowledge – their knowledge of the world – to describe the action under observation. This means that experimenters too use their common sense to represent what is meant by the behaviours of their participants. The only exception would be where detailed theoretical conceptions of the behaviour had been spelled out in psychological terms, but such exceptions are virtually non-existent in social psychology.

Intentional behaviour

Much philosophical analysis of purposive or intentional behaviour has been published during the last few decades, and it is now fairly clear how such action may be characterized. A logical feature of the description of action is that the observer/scientist must describe or characterize actions in terms of the purpose or intention of the actor or agent. The question, 'What was the actor meaning to do?' must be answered. Postulation of a separate mental element called an intention is not necessary (but see pp. 179–81 below on reductionism). Often the purpose or intention is inherent in the description and is apparent to an observer. Clearly, even animals engage in intentional behaviour: a dog digging a hole under the fence may be seen as intending to get to the other side. No presumption that actors always have knowledge of their intention is required. Indeed, people may sometimes be not at all aware of their intention; e.g. the action may have become habitual, the motive may be repressed, etc.

For some actions, however, the actor's own account of what he or she were meaning to do may be crucial to correct identification of the action being performed. This complex issue has been extensively discussed in many sources, including Greenwood (1989), Harré and Secord (1972) and Shwayder (1965). Sometimes an observer can immediately attribute purpose to an action and identify it without difficulty. In other instances an account may be constructed by the observer only after intensive observation and interaction with the actor. In some cases the actor's own account is crucial, although it is rarely, if ever, sufficient by itself: the social context and other external circumstances are essential to establishing the identity of the action (Greenwood, 1989). Accounts not only help to identify the actor's intention, but also serve to relate the action to the context and background and thus give meaning to the action. Non-experimental methods such as participant observation, where the scientist-observer is only semi-independent of the observed and often interacts extensively with the observed, are frequently used where the agent's account is critical to the topic being investigated.

Meaning and socially constituted action

The subject/person confusion is one facet of hermeneutics – the principles of interpretation – and the meaning of human action has often been a basis for criticizing academic psychology. The fact that the subject orientation makes it impossible to grasp or describe most human action has been a powerful impetus for several familiar critiques of psychological social psychology: symbolic interactionism (Blumer, 1969), ethnomethodology (Garfinkel, 1967), ethogeny (Harré and Secord, 1972), social constructionism (Gergen and Davis, 1985), and contextualism (Rosnow and

Georgoudi, 1986). A central idea that underlies all of these critiques is that action is *socially constituted*. What this means is that actions have been codified by society, and that each of us has learned to identify and to perform these actions in the process of becoming socialized. What is essential is to recognize that these actions are identified by societal criteria: they are outcomes of particular types of interactive relations and thus can be readily identified by socially competent observers.

Hermeneutic critiques are not always clear themselves. Sometimes they argue that the participant's perspective is a necessary condition for identifying behaviour, and thus place great emphasis on the person's phenomenology. But this claim is clearly false. Many socially constituted actions (e.g. committing a crime, getting married, writing a cheque, taking an examination) are readily identifiable through external observation. Failure to recognize the importance of societal criteria and the typing of social actions has caused all sorts of misunderstandings. What has been clearly pointed out is that these socially constituted actions are difficult to study experimentally because the societal conditions that identify the act are hard to create in the laboratory. Instead, they are typically approached from an 'as if' perspective, essentially a role-playing scenario. Thus, jury behaviour may be studied by asking participants to imagine that they are members of a jury dealing with a specific court case which is presented to them. Clearly, this is an instance where the investigator must set up conditions compatible with the participants performing as persons, and must also establish as closely as possible the criteria that would constitute a real jury trial.

Moreover, it should not be assumed that the person's account is irrelevant to identifying action that is socially constituted. Sometimes certain attributes of the person are critical to a precise social definition of the action. For example, degrees of murder are recognized under the law primarily depending upon the murderer's intent. More simply, whether an act is assaultive depends on whether the actor intends to hurt. Although it is not necessary that actors represent to themselves every socially consti-tuted act as an instance of that kind, such representations are necessary for a subset of socially constituted acts. For example, if a man stood in for an absent friend who was the would-be groom in what he thought was a wedding rehearsal, he probably would not be considered legally married if it turned out that, unknown to him, what he participated in was a real wedding. Many socially constituted acts require certain intentions or commitments from the actors.

Finally, it should be understood that the criteria for particular human actions are not always clear, nor is everyone expertly competent. Thus, the identification of selected, more complex human actions would benefit if social psychologists and others did conceptual analyses of how such actions are socially constituted. An example of such work is found in Silver and Sabini's (1978) analysis of what it is to act out of envy.

Some Misunderstandings of the Person Perspective

Several possible ways of misunderstanding the person perspective are briefly discussed here. These include: (1) explaining away the person perspective through reductionist solutions, (2) the relevance of the person perspective to experimental realism, (3) the use of deception in experiments, (4) accounts versus experimental methodology as a means of identifying human actions, and (5) the supposed incompatibility of actions for a reason and causal analysis of the action.

Reductionist solutions to the person and subject dialectic

One potential way to resolve the conflict between person/subject perspectives would be to reduce or translate the person perspective to the subject perspective. Indeed, that objective – to reduce everything to physicalist terms – was central to the goal of the unity of science programme. But grave difficulties were encountered early in that philosophical programme, and it no longer seems viable to most philosophers or even to psychologists (Margolis, 1984). A salient difficulty is associated with those mental states such as beliefs, which are associated with intention, and which are indispensable when persons are conceived as actors. Intention is a complex philosophical concept, about which volumes have been written, and the issues cannot be sorted out here. But briefly and roughly, the difficulty confronting the would-be materialist can be identified.

The problem is that much of our behaviour is in linguistic form and, while many statements may be restated in the same sort of language that we use for describing overt behaviour, others contain 'psychological' terms that prevent such translation. These psychological terms (e.g. beliefs, attitudes, feelings, thoughts) are typically referred to as *intentional*. In 1874, Brentano (Sellars and Chisholm, 1958) pointed out that the mental was distinguished from the physical through a kind of reference or 'aboutness'. Verbs that express intention are about the propositional objects associated with them, but are not the objects themselves. For example, 'I am thinking about my son', 'I am thinking about tomorrow', or 'I am thinking about a unicorn'. These thoughts (or feelings or beliefs) exist independently of the object, as is especially clear in the case of non-existent objects. The point is that aboutness itself is a mental quality. Thinking, believing, desiring, intending, loving, hating, approving cannot be understood without invoking a concept of 'aboutness', because each state is about something and yet not the same thing as that something.

The upshot of this idea of intentionality is that, if we are to understand the behaviour of persons, we must be able to deal with all those actions that contain a psychological (or intentional) element. There is no way that we can ignore it and deal merely with overt behaviour. If, for example, an investigator chooses only to do research using a strictly behaviouristic language (almost an impossible task; e.g. Skinner, 1953; Quine, 1953; Margolis, 1984), the problem remains of how to translate the descriptions in terms of overt behaviour into a language that admits psychological terms *so that the action can be identified* in familiar language. In other words, descriptions solely in terms of overt behaviour are typically non-familiar and ambiguous.

Within the person perspective, there is always a *person* doing something, and that doing involves intention; from the subject perspective, there is only an organism responding to some stimulus under certain conditions. The former involves the point of view of the actor; in the latter, only the point of view of the observer counts. What is important for our purposes is that, from the person perspective, knowledge of the actors' subjective interpretations of their actions are usually necessary if the actions are to be correctly *identified*. The only exceptions are those actions that are wholly socially constituted. Many socially constituted actions, however, require for identification that the actor have certain intentions or that certain psychological states be present in the actor.

Often the actor has a goal or purpose in mind as well as a belief that certain ways or means will accomplish that goal, and has made a decision to perform the action. In those instances, ignoring the purpose with which behaviour is enacted produces confusion as to what the person is actually doing. A person who hurts another individual is acting aggressively only if that action is intended and not if it is accidental. Thus, reducing a person to a subject seems to fail, because actions are no longer identifiable. Although observers may sometimes know what an actor is thinking (believing, feeling, desiring) without asking the actor or without a verbal report, and actors themselves may not be clear on what they are thinking, the person perspective assumes that accounts provided by actors are often essential to describing the actions adequately.

The person orientation being discussed here should not be confused with phenomenological psychology. Many actions may be identified without using as criteria any elements of awareness or consciousness. Phenomenologists emphasize the phenomenal experience of actors as crucial for understanding behavior. Yet at least some phenomenologists treat experience as *received*, a consequence of forces acting on the person. In fact, behaviour is secondary to experience, which is primary. This suggests a modified kind of subject orientation rather than a person perspective. Phenomenal experience is something that *happens* to persons as a result of environmental stimulation, previous experiences, and the like.

Experimental realism

The concept of experimental realism, in contrast with mundane realism, is worth viewing in terms of the person/subject perspectives (Aronson, Carlsmith and Brewer, 1985). In social psychology, experimental realism is defined as the state attained when the participants become strongly involved in the experimental activity. Depending on the nature of the activity, they may become excited, upset, challenged. The activity need not be one commonly found outside of the laboratory; if it is, then mundane realism is also achieved. Mundane realism by itself is insufficient, experimental realism is thought to be necessary if the results from the experiment are to be taken seriously. Viewing this concept from our perspective tells us why: experimental realism makes the participant more of an agent and less of a subject.

Suppose we ask: (1) What are participants meaning to do? (2) How is the action to be identified? These two questions reveal why experimental realism is important. In a task not having experimental realism, the participants may well be only 'going through the motions'. The experiment has little meaning and is uninteresting; participants are only doing what they are told. In a sense, they are not being themselves. What then is the identity of their action? What are they meaning to do? Perhaps all that can be said is that they are meaning to cooperate with the experimenter. They are going through the motions, but their heart is not in what they are doing. In essence, they are doing something other than the intended experimental activity. How this changes the identity of the action depends upon its content, but in many instances it is obvious that the action would have a different identity. Experimental realism seems to require a person orientation. Participants are involved; they care what they are doing; more likely they are being themselves.

The consequences of deception

Experiments using deception frequently involve confusion between subject and person orientations. As Mixon (1972) has shown, deception is used so that participants will behave less like agents and more like passive subjects, but this very usage implies that they are active agents – unless they are deceived, they would do something other than what the experimenter wanted. The use of deception is apt to attenuate the person orientation, depending in part upon whether experimenters insist on accepting their version of what participants are doing or whether they consider how participants view their own actions. The actions of participants in experiments are often, in fact, constituted by the way they represent them – by what *they* think they are doing. Deception typically involves a cover story telling the subjects what they are doing; if they believe the story, they may not be performing the actions that the experimenter thinks they are really performing. Consequently, the experimenter who does not have an account from the participants cannot be sure what they are indeed doing.

No assumption is made here that actors can always provide adequate accounts for their actions; under some conditions their accounts are far from the mark (Nisbett and Wilson, 1977). But here we need to distinguish between different sorts of reports. Under most circumstances, persons should be able to report accurately what they are currently thinking and feeling without much difficulty and without appreciable distortion, and such accounts could well be helpful in identifying the acts that they are performing or the states they are experiencing. It is quite another thing to be able to report *why* one does what one does – to give a causal analysis of one's actions. No claim is made here to the effect that persons' accounts are reliable in that sense and, indeed, it is that kind of report that constitutes the substance of the work by Nisbett and Wilson and others who have worked on the problem. Moreover, Adair and Spinner (1981) have shown that, when the Nisbett and Wilson studies are reinterpreted in terms of demand characteristics, participants are in fact able to report accurately some of the causes of their behavior.

But, in keeping with the person orientation, the important claim made here is that participants *do* have access to their cognitive processes, and can include them in giving accounts. In fact, although they use stimulus-response language, Nisbett and Ross (1980, p. 223) apparently agree with the person orientation when they note that 'subjective accounts of stimuli and responses may often be crucial to understanding and explaining the actors' behavior' and that 'the scientist who manipulates the objective features of the actors' environment may simply lack the necessary insights about how the relevant stimuli or responses are perceived or interpreted by the actor.'

Indentification of behaviour through experimental methodology

Worth noting is that the methods typically used by experimenters to identify behaviour typically do not rely on extensive reporting from participants telling what they thought they were doing. Rather this information is obtained by placing participants in situations that are calculated to bring about certain states of mind. The discussion of dissonance theory research is a good illustration. Even though the eventual formulation of dissonance theory required that participants be thought of as persons, this result was not arrived at by obtaining accounts from experimental subjects.

The difference in procedure is important and should be spelled out. There are two alternative approaches, which may be illustrated by a concrete example: (1) The extent to which participants feel responsible for their counter-attitudinal action could be ascertained by asking them questions designed to reveal their feelings, or (2) Participants could be put in situations calculated either to make them feel responsible for their counter-attitudinal action, or to not make them feel responsible. Both procedures involve a person orientation, not a subject orientation. Thus, participants can be treated *conceptually* as actors rather than subjects within the experimental traditions of social psychology, without necessarily asking them about their thoughts, feelings and beliefs.

Each of these methods has their limitations. Often participants may not be able to provide adequate accounts of the actions. Sometimes the experimental design does not lend itself to such questioning. Moreover, accounts may be distorted to make one's behaviour appear more socially desirable. On the other hand, where the experimenter uses the alternative of constructing situations designed to create certain psychological states or to induce certain actions, typically common-sense knowledge of human action is the only tool available for such constructions. Thus, the experimenter has little scientific guidance for designing the experiment. A desirable alternative, the development of theory for conceptualizing the actions involved, is rarely practised.

What would seem best would be to use both methods. Obtaining accounts from participants would provide new hints of thoughts or feelings that might be affecting the behaviour; while putting participants in different experimental situations would test for the presence of thoughts or feelings that participants might not be reporting, as well as sometimes confirming the accounts that have been given. It might well be that, had intensive efforts been made in initial dissonance research to obtain accounts from participants, it would not have taken experimenters thirty years to bring dissonance theory to its present state. Such accounts would have provided rich information for designing experiments to test some of the person attributes that were only indirectly implied by experimental results. But, of course, subject orientations towards research were strongly supported by positivist views of psychological science implicitly or explicitly accepted by investigators.

Human action versus the causal analysis of behaviour

Within the philosophy of mind, human action has been explained largely in terms of persons doing things for a reason, and it has been argued that, if one describes and explains behaviour in such terms, behaviour cannot be explained by means of causal analysis. Very roughly, these two forms of explanation are closely identified with the person and the subject orientations discussed here. Causal analysis is usually identified with academic psychology, and human action orientations more with a certain logic of human behavior which especially involves the concept of intention (Peters, 1958; Louch, 1966). Similarly, discussions of free will have occasionally invoked concepts similar to the person and subject orientations, with proponents of free will pointing out the limitations of the subject orientation and the necessity of adopting a person concept (Melden, 1961; Ayers, 1968). Still another argument within philosophy has been between mechanism and responsibility, leaning towards the conclusion that if an act can be explained mechanistically, the individual is not responsible (thus, a person orientation is not appropriate for that act).

Progress has been made in resolving these philosophical arguments. Unless one is a dualist, one should assent to the idea that persons are organisms and that, if we knew enough, in principle their behaviour could be described in a neurophysiological language. Such a description would involve many causal processes. Yet the possibility or even the realization of such a description would not disqualify descriptions of purposive behaviour in a different language nor would it be advisable to dispense with them. Imagine, if you can, a neurophysiological description to substitute for a chessplayer's action described as: 'I pinned her knight against her queen, because I intend next to attack it with the king's pawn.' Such a description would be so enormously complex that we would still need the ordinary way of talking about chess moves. Even more telling, the neurophysiological description could be different for different persons even though the action in all instances were the same. Just as identical computer performances can be obtained by different computer programs, identical actions can be represented differently in the neurophysiology of different persons. Thus, the description in the language of the game could not be reduced to a neurophysiological one.

In the philosophy of mind, the argument that reasons cannot be causes of behaviour is generally conceded to have failed, as has the argument that, because human action is intentional, it cannot be caused. Dennett (1978) has suggested that the intentional stance comes into play when systems are too complex to comprehend in more physical terms. Thus it is sensible to speak of a computer as playing chess, or even as 'trying to win'. That it could in principle be explained mechanically does not render false the view of it in intentional terms. Moreover, human action is so complex that mechanistic explanations that might be conceivable in principle are at present remotely beyond our reach. Dennett observes that whenever an intentional explanation can be replaced by a mechanical one, it is the absence of rationality from the mechanistic orientation that makes the intentional explanation seem superfluous. But he argues that the absence of rationality is *not* the same thing as non-rational and, therefore, the intentional explanation is not refuted and still stands.

Just as one may treat a chess-playing computer either intentionally or mechanically, one can describe the intentional actions of a person, in terms of that person's motives, beliefs and knowledge about means and, at the same time without contradiction, consider what objective conditions make a particular motive salient, or what conditions contributed to the acquisition of a particular belief. Uncovering the causes of beliefs or of motives does not make description of the person's actions in intentional terms any less appropriate. In fact, intentional behaviour is *emergent*. That is to say that rational behaviour appears when the system is viewed on a particular level, and that in explanations at a lower, mechanical level, rationality is lost. Emergent properties cannot be reduced to lower levels without loss, therefore the higher level must be retained if explanation is to involve these properties. At present we do not have the slightest clue as to how social behaviour might be described in mechanical terms; in fact, our understanding of the human condition requires the intentional stance (along with other information) if it is to be intelligible. To adopt a mechanical stance would not explain social behaviour as we know it.

Persons are neither entirely free nor is their behaviour determined in any straightforward way by their circumstances. Instead, explaining some acts as done for a reason and explaining some behaviour in terms of causes does not entail any logical contradictions. There is no doubt that persons can initiate many actions whenever they choose. Moreover, the identity of their actions depends upon what they are intending to do as well as upon how their actions are socially constituted. At the same time, persons do not have total control over their behaviour. They may fail not only through lack of competence, but also through lack of will. Often we cannot cease some line of behaviour that we consider questionable nor can we talk ourselves into carrying out some activity that we know is desirable but are neglecting. Sometimes neurophysiology is directly involved, as in addictions.

Both reason and cause are necessary for adequate explanations of social behavior, but these need to be made explicit in ongoing research and typically are at different levels. That *social* behaviour is described in intentional terms does not preclude the identification of various conditions or antecedents that might have helped to bring about the action, nor does it eliminate neurophysiological states as possible contributors to the action. There is no logical contradiction involved in considering a person as an agent but at the same time assuming that some of that person's acts can be caused.

That we must treat persons as reasonable beings means that social psychologists must be constantly slert to the exercise of reason by the individuals they study. Experiments frequently are designed to place severe constraints on such exericse in the interest of determining the causal effect of certain conditions. But two unfortunate consequences sometimes occur: (1) despite constraints, participants use their reason to behave otherwise than expected; and (2) when participants behave as expected, the results obtained pertain to non-reasoning beings.

Social Action and the Social World

From the foregoing it seems clear that adopting a view of individuals as persons need not lead to an outright rejection of the experimental method, but that, indeed, viewing them as persons instead of subjects is desirable. Moreover, experiments do have their place in psychological science. But it is important to realize that that place is a limited one. Elsewhere I have noted that psychologically-trained social psychologists focus on a very narrow facet of human life (Secord, 1986). Two polarities can be identified: a focus on the individual versus a focus on society, and a focus on the 'inner' versus a focus on the 'outer'. Psychologists choose the individual and the inner ends of these polarities. Social psychologists are no exception, and thus are severely limited in what they can explain.

This claim can be illustrated with examples from dissonance theory, but the principle applies to many topics researched in the laboratory. Contemporary views of counter-attitudinal behaviour focus on the workings of internal processes with very limited attention to external relations. For example, we might expect that participants' reactions to behaving in a counter-attitudinal way would vary markedly depending upon the power relations between themselves and other involved persons, but these are seldom brought into the laboratory. In fact, one line of dissonance research suggests that possibly attitude change does not really take place, but is simply feigned because of the power of the experimenter (Tedeschi, Schlenker and Bonoma, 1971). Consider a more enduring relationship where one person has greater power over the other: a master–slave relationship, a woman with a powerful lover, or even a subordinate–superior relationship in the workplace. Does not the weaker party frequently engage in counter-attitudinal behaviour without experiencing dissonance and without changing attitudes? Of course the experimentalist might argue for an easy out here by asserting that compliance is so forced that there is no contradiction with dissonance theory. But that objection misses the point. The argument is that established relationships that we have with other people moderate and complicate our actions in ways that are difficult to explain if we only have a knowledge of internal processes:

we need to be able to characterize the relationships as well as the internal processes in order to fully understand social action.

Finally, it is possible to imagine societies other than ours where the situations created in experiments on dissonance would lead to different outcomes. Personal responsibility is high in some societies and low in others; similarly, threats to one's identity are more or less severe depending upon the society. But most of all, there may be many societies in which logical inconsistencies in thoughts or actions are of no moment, and where behaving counter-attitudinally has no adverse effects. The point is not that dissonance theory holds only for our society; rather, the point is that we do not know the ways in which what goes on in dissonance situations are tied to features of our society.

These comments are intended to illustrate the dilemmas of explanation that face social psychologists no matter what the focus of their experiments; dissonance experiments have only been used as an illustration. Most topics in experimental social psychology involve an uneasy, often implicit compromise between subject and person orientations, thus introducing uncertainty over the identity of the participants behaviors. Moreover, by not considering the social context and relational setting of the topic under investigation, the usefulness of the findings for explaining behaviour in natural settings is severely limited. These problems can be greatly mitigated by adopting an explicit person orientation towards participants in experiments.

REFERENCES

Adair, J. G. and Spinner, B. (1981) 'Subjects' access to cognitive processes: Demand characteristics and verbal report', *Journal for the Theory of Social Behavior* 11, 31–52.
Aronson, E., Brewer, M. and Carlsmith, J. M. (1985) 'Experimentation in social psychology'. In Lindzey, G. and Aronson, E. (eds), *Handbook of Social Psychology*. Vol. I: *Theory and Method* (3rd edn), New York: Random House.
Ayers, M. R. (1968) *The Refutation of Determinism*, London: Methuen.
Blumer, H. (1969) *Symbolic Interactionism: Perspective and method*, Englewood Cliffs, N. J.: Prentice Hall.
Cooper, J. and Fazio (1984) R. H. 'A new look at dissonance theory'. In L. Berkowitz (ed.), *Advances in Experimental Social Psychology* 17, 229–67.
Dennett, D. C. (1978) *Brainstorms*, Cambridge, Mass.: Bradford Books.
Festinger, L. (1957) *A Theory of Cognitive Dissonance*, New York: Harper.
Festinger, L. and Carlsmith, J. M. (1959) 'Cognitive consequences of forced compliance. *Journal of Abnormal and Social Psychology* 58, 203–11.
Garfinkel, H. (1967). *Studies in Ethnomethodology*. Englewood Cliffs, N. J.: Prentice Hall.

Gergen, K. J. and Davis, K. E. (eds) (1985) *The Social Construction of the Person*, New York: Springer-Verlag.

Greenwood, J. D. (1989) *Explanation and Experiment in Social Psychological Science: Realism and the social constitution of action*. New York: Springer-Verlag.

Hampshire, S. (1974) Description of behavior: A philosophical problem. In P. Collett (ed.), *Social Rules and Social Behavior*. Oxford University: Department of Experimental Psychology.

Harré, R. and Secord, P. F. (1972) *The Explanation of Social Behavior*, Oxford: Basil Blackwell.

Louch, A. (1966). *Explanation and Human Action*, Oxford: Basil Blackwell.

Margolis, J. (1984) *Philosophy of Psychology*, Englewood Cliffs, N. J.: Prentice Hall.

Melden, A. I. (1961) *Free Action*, London: Routledge & Kegan Paul.

Mixon, D. (1971) Behavior analysis treating subjects as actors rather than organisms, *Journal for the Theory of Social Behavior* 1, 19–32.

Mixon, D. (1972) Instead of deception, *Journal for the Theory of Social Behavior* 2, 145–78.

Milgram, S. (1969) *Obedience to Authority*, New York: Harper & Row.

Nisbett, R. E. and Wilson, R. D. (1977). Telling more than we can know: Verbal reports on mental processes, *Psychological Review* 84, 231–59.

Nisbett, R. E. and Ross, L. (1980) *Human Inference: Strategies and shortcomings in social judgment*, Englewood Cliffs, N. J.: Prentice Hall.

Quine, W. V. O. (1953) Two dogmas of empiricism. In *From a Logical Point of View*, Cambridge, Mass.: Harvard University Press.

Peters, R. S. (1958) *The Concept of Motivation*, London: Routledge & Kegan Paul.

Rosnow, R. L. and Georgoudi, M. (1986) (eds) *Contextualism and Understanding in Behavioral Science: Implications for research and theory*, New York: Praeger.

Schlenker, B. R. (1982) Translating actions into attitudes: An identity-analytic approach to the explanation of social conduct. In L. Berkowitz (ed.), *Advances in Experimental Social Psychology* 15, 194–248.

Schutz, A. (1967) *Collected Papers. I. The Problem of Social Reality*, The Hague: Martinus Nijhoff.

Secord, P. F. (1986) Social psychology as a science. In J. Margolis, P. T. Manicas, R. Harré and P. F. Secord, *Psychology: designing the discipline*, Oxford: Basil Blackwell.

Sellars, W. and Chisholm, R. M. (1958) Appendix: Intentionality and the mental. In Feigl, H., Scriven, M. and Maxwell, G. *Minnesota Studies in the Philosophy of Science*, Vol. II, Minneapolis, MN: University of Minnesota Press.

Shwayder, D. S. (1965) *The Stratification of Behavior*, New York: Humanities Press.

Silver, M. and Sabini, J. (1978) The social construction of envy, *Journal for the Theory of Social Behavior* 8, 313–32.

Skinner, B. F. (1953) *Science and Human Behavior*, New York: Macmillan.

Tedeschi, J. T., Schlenker, B. R. and Bonoma, T. V. (1971) Cognitive dissonance: Private ratiocination or public spectacle?, *American Psychologist* 26, 685–95.

12

A Concise Theory of Dialectics

Jean-Pierre de Waele

What does dialectics mean? Our starting-point is the definition given by Engels in his *Anti-Dühring*: 'Dialectics is the science of the most general laws of all kinds of movement; movement of nature, movement in the history of mankind or movement in thought.' In a more modern phrasing one would rather use 'evolutionary processes' instead of 'movement' and in order to avoid the positivist connotations attached to the term 'law', it is better to describe dialectics as the general theory of evolutionary processes. The field can be divided into (i) the objective, natural, biological, historical, social and psychological processes; (ii) knowledge and thought processes; (iii) the individual and collective actions which mediate between (i) and (ii). We are dealing here with material dialectics, first formulated by Hegel in his idealistic philosophy, whereas Marx and Engels outlined its principles on materialistic grounds.

For didactic reasons one usually follows the example of Engels who defined dialectics as consisting of three fundamental laws: (1) the law of the turning of quantitative changes into qualitative ones, (2) the law of the unity of opposites, (3) the law of the negation of negation. According to the first law each thing or system with its own specific nature exists only within the boundaries of certain quantitatively variable parameters. If the parameters quantitatively increase or decrease and thus overstep these boundaries, a discontinuity or 'jump' emerges in the thing or system subject to these quantitative changes which leads to a new qualitative condition.

The law of the unity of opposites means that every object or system consists of opposites responsible for its stable continuance and for its transformations. Stability occurs whenever the opposites balance each other, even though they are in constant interaction. Destabilization and evolution towards a new stable equilibrium occur when the qualitative increase of one of the opposites becomes so great that the other one has to change in order to maintain the original opposition in a new form.

The law of the negation of negation makes the existing connection between the moments of a dialectic evolutionary process explicit. By using a terminology borrowed from dialogic exchanges, the relation between the original opposites is being portrayed as one between affirmation and negation. That term of the opposition is called negative of which the quantitative intensification threatens the existence of the other term and therefore *ipso facto* the unity of the opposites on which the thing or original structure rests. The first opposite (or group of opposites) is thus being forced to mutate which can only result in a new affirmation, on condition that it negates the first negation and therefore acts as negation of the negation.

This summarized and for the most part intuitive presentation of dialectics differs from the usual expositions because the three laws are not treated separately but as terms of a conjunction which determines what is implied by 'dialectic evolution'. The term 'law' is once more a source of misunderstandings. In fact, we are dealing with three conditions which separately form a necessary condition but together in conjunction form a sufficient condition in a dialectic process.

We want to show that the problems that have to be solved in order to get to a theory of criminogenesis[1] demand that the criminogenetic processes are viewed as dialectic processes. Only in this way can we find a way out of the dilemma of continuity versus discontinuity and can criminogenesis be expressed in our taxonomy.

A preliminary analysis is required in order to realize this theoretical synthesis. But an analysis demands a suitable instrument so that this theoretical synthesis can be realized. The simplified presentation given above of dialectics cannot be used to fulfill the kind of analytical task we have in mind.

We shall therefore rely on a more differentiated formulation of dialectic processes, namely on a formalisation of dialectics worked out by J. Gorren and J. P. de Waele.[2]

Since we cannot refer at this moment to a published paper on this matter, we think it might be useful to give the reader a short introduction. We are aware that this enhances the danger of not being fully understood as a consequence of the incompleteness of our presentation.

First of all we want to draw the reader's attention to the fact that the 'objects' between which the interactions we are interested in occur, are persons. This peculiarity will offer no difficulty, however, because the concepts that have to be defined are very broad. We are dealing on the one hand with internal relations but on the other hand also with relations external to the objects we are studying. The internal relations are placed between square brackets, the external ones between round brackets. For example, '$>$' in

(P > Q)

represents an external relation between p and q whereas '>' in

[A > B]

represents an internal relation between A and B.

In other words, the square brackets are used to defined an object or an entity. The round brackets, on the other hand, define external relations between entities.

The formula

(P] v [Q) w (R] v [S)
  el   e2   e3

signifies that between the entities el and e2 and between e2 and e3 occurs the external relation 'v'. The relation 'w' however which exists between Q and R is an internal relation, inherent to entity e2. The terms P, Q, R and S represent facts or occurrences in which and through which capacities and qualities of the entities el, e2 and e3 are being manifested.

Facts and events do not occur outside time. Because of this one has to take into account that one external relation can take place between different facts during a certain period of time. In the meantime, however, the entities concerned remain the same. Therefore, such a succession must be represented unambiguously. Let us assume for example that fact P represents the manifestation of a certain quality of entity el which has an external relation '//' with fact Q through which a quality of e2 is expressed. It may be that, as a consequence of the existing internal relations in e2 (w), an analogue relation '//' will develop between fact R which belongs to e2 and fact S which is part of el. This sequence can be represented as follows:

(P] // [Q) w (R] // [S)
  el   e2   el

The open square brackets represent here two consecutive aspects of one and the same entity namely el.

These preliminary and very abstract remarks about the symbols we are going to use and their notation are none the less absolutely necessary in order to comprehend the following.

The entities, things or persons, distinguish themselves by their qualities manifested in their interactions. A quality is a capacity an entity has to generate certain effects. Which of the capacities an entity possesses will exercise a certain influence at a particular moment, depends on the special set of conditions which are present at that moment. One usually speaks of the capacities of an entity when they are not being exercised. There is not much point in using the truism that an entity can do precisely what we are observing it is doing.

Qualities or capacities can be categorized into different categories:[3] (1) capacity for activity of some kind; (2) capacity to be in a state of some kind; (3) capacity of an entity to affect another entity; (4) capacity of an entity to remain the same generically, notwithstanding the gain or loss of some capacities; (5) capacity of an entity to be affected by another entity; (6) the capacity to change into something generically different.

This conception of qualities and capacities is based on a causal interpretation of qualities and capacities which can be summarized in the following way. If under conditions I an entity e1 possesses quality P, this means that e1 is such that the occurrence of an event of the kind G which stands in relation r1 to e1, causes the occurrence of even F which stands in relation r2 to an entity e2 or to entity e1.

This makes it clear that if the content of interactions between entities is dependent on their qualities, these qualities are only expressed in causal processes and interplay. It is clear that we must examine these in order to define the kind of causations dialectical processes are made up of.

In the positive sciences the causal relation between cause and effect corresponds to a productive and generative process which sees to it that given C (cause), E (effect) is produced. In different scientific areas there exist numerous generative processes. The largest part of scientific research consists of drawing up models of generative processes and to correct them after testing. It is therefore impossible to give a general representation. If we want to represent concatenations of causal sequences, we can replace them by empirical verification relations that have to be met when a causal production process is supposed to exist. In other words, one replaces the description of a causal generative process by its testing-conditions, i.e. by the things one can empirically check as a logical consequence of their existence.

In order to construct such a representation one can start from events, i.e. ascertainable changes. Events that show analogies in their frequent occurrence are called facts. The frequencies facts display when they occur in series and their ratios will enable us to define some interesting relations.

A sequence in a series of terms is part of the series, beginning with a first term and ending in a last term. The frequence of a fact in a sequence is the ratio of the number of terms in which the fact occurs, to the number of terms in the sequence. In the sequence A, B, A, C, D, A, which has six terms, A occurs three times and therefore its frequence is 3/6. Two facts in a series are equivalent if they occur with the same frequency in all sequences of the series. This is noted as follows: A = B. A fact in a series of facts is nil if it does not occur in any sequence of the series, this is noted as A = 0. A fact is permanent if it occurs in every sequence of a series. This is represented as A = 1. From what precedes it follows that the frequence of a fact is a rational number between 0 and 1.

Several facts are in conjunction if they occur in the same term of a series. This means that if two facts are in conjunction, you cannot predict which one precedes the other. A conjunction is therefore dependent on the accuracy with which it is observed and also on the scale it is described upon.

Two similar facts which are conjunctional equal one single fact: AA = A. This is the principle of tautology. We must also mention that nil is the absorbing element in the conjunction while unity is the neutral one. Indeed, for each I you have:

$$XO = O \text{ and } X1 = X$$

A global fact is a set of facts which takes place whenever one of the elements of the set of facts occurs. A global fact is represented by A, B or C ... written with the sign used for a disjunction (v) AvBvCv. You can prove furthermore that, using z to denote absence,

$$Avb = 1 - zAzB$$
and that $$AvBvCv = 1 - zAzBzC$$
and $$AvB = A + B - AB$$

Conjunctional facts are the factors in a conjunction. Taking this terminological convention into account, you can define the principle of determinism as follows: a fact is determined by the conjunction of its factors. A determination is an equality with one member defining the other one. In the equality AB = C, it is the conjunction of A and B which determines C. This means that if AB = D occurred in the same series of facts, you would also get C = D.

The transition from a factor to the fact defined by the conjunction is a causation in which the factor is the cause and the determined fact the effect. In the determination ABCD = E, each factor can be looked upon as cause in this special causation. If you choose C as cause, the factors A, B and D form the circumstances in which the cause produces the effect. If X represents the conjunction of the circumstances, the determination is written thus: CX = E[4]

The principle of determinism we have just formulated has as corollary:

the same cause under the same circumstances produces the same effect. But the reciprocal proposition does not hold: the same cause can produce the same effect under different circumstances. This is what happens when

$$CX = CY \text{ if } X = Y$$

Let us go back to $CX = E$. By adding C to the two members, you get $CCX = CE$, which after applying the principle of tautology leads to $CX = CE$. You may replace CX by CE in $CX = E$. This gives you $CE = E$. This equality is nothing more than the immediate cause–effect relation.

Before going into matters further, we must first define the implication between facts. If $A = AB$, A implicates B. It is sufficient that A occurs for B to happen. A is a sufficient condition for B. But B can never happen without the occurrence of A. A therefore never occurs more frequently than B – 'never' meaning in none of the sequences of the series of facts. Because of this we write $A < B$ to indicate A implicates B.

The implication between facts is transitive. This means that if you have

$$A < B \text{ and } B < C, \text{ you also have } A < C.$$

This is written as

$$A < B \cdot B < C \rightarrow A < C.$$

The arrow we have introduced here indicates a deductive inference. It is an inference because you go from one relation of facts to another. The inference is called deductive because the first relation is sufficient in order to express the second one implicitly. Besides, proving an inference is only making what is implicit explicit.

The cause–effect relation $CE = E$ indicates that the effect implicated the cause. We have thus $E < C$. The cause precedes the effect however, so we write $C > E$ which means 'A causes E'.

The immediate cause is a necessary condition of the effect, without the cause the effect would not take place. Some examples: (1) there is no smoke without fire; the smoke implies the fire ($E < C$); the fire produces the smoke. (2) If electrical energy circulates, this implicates that the circuit is closed; in a closed circuit energy is produced and circulates. (3) If you exert power on a mobile, movement is accelerated; the acceleration implicates power and the power produces the acceleration.

This conception of the immediate cause as a necessary condition implies of course that the cause can occur without producing the effect. Should this 'always' be the case, you would have to add some conditions to the necessary one. These are the circumstances, their conjunction was indicated by the term X. The immediate cause C, in conjunction with the circumstances X, constitutes the necessary and sufficient condition for E to occur. If the circumstances can be considered permanent, you get $X = 1$ and $CX = E$ leads to $C = E$, i.e the cause forms the necessary and sufficient condition for the effect.

In scientific analysis you try to formulate model representations of generative processes which mediate between C and E and give a clear image of what we have called 'circumstances'. Otherwise an unlimited regression might develop and there would be no end to the circumstances you would have to take into account. The situation changes, however, when you want to test models of generative mechanisms for their capacity to produce a causal explanation. The testing implication is the following: if M as a generative process explains the production of E by C, you can deduce that $C'X = E'$ has to be empirically verifiable, on condition that C' and E' are good indices of C and E. But starting from $C'X = E$ you cannot come to a generative process. It might be useful, although it may seem as if we are drifting from our main issue, to point to this problem, because it has been widely discussed during the last years by philosophers of science (with the realists severely criticizing the underlying Humean presuppositions of neo-positivism).

A first form of 'negativity' is formed by 'absence' i.e. the absence of a fact. In a series of facts, the number of terms which contain A equal the sum of terms which contain A and B and those which contain A without B. The frequence of A is therefore always the same as the frequencies of AB and 'A without B'. 'A without B' is written as AzB, this leads to $A = AB + AzB$ and also to $AzB = A - AB$. The reader is reminded that the plus and minus signs refer to the frequencies of the mentioned facts. AzB is a conjunction of fact A with the fictitious fact zB (without B) which exists only as an idea but represents nothing objectively real.

For every X you have

$$XzA = X - XA \text{ and}$$

if $X = 1$

$$1zA = 1 - 1A$$

But $1zA = zA$ and $1A = A$, therefore $zA = 1 - A$. In this way we can introduce the fictitious fact zA as an element in our calculus. It could be interesting for example to examine what might be the meaning of zzA (without-without-A). By applying the preceding we get

$$zzA = 1 - (1 - A) = 1 - 1 + A = A$$

The answer to our question is as follows: the absence of the absence of a fact is equivalent to its presence.

There are three kinds of contraries: contraria, subcontraria and complements.

A is the contrary of B if A implies the absence of B. This is written as $A < zB$.
A is the subcontrary of B if A produces B's absence. This is written as $A > zB$.
A is B's complement if A is equivalent to the absence of B. This is noted as $A = zB$.

We must also add here that the terms for absence and occurrence are contradictory. Their conjunction (AzA) is a contradiction.

The three kinds of opposites show a special relation to the contradiction. Indeed, if A is B's contrary, this implies that their conjunction is a contradiction. Because,

$$A < zB \rightarrow AB < BzB$$

If A is B's subcontrary, the conjunction AB leads to a contradiction because

$$A > zB \rightarrow AB > BzB$$

Finally, if A is B's complement, the conjunction is equivalent to a contradiction, because

$$A = zB \rightarrow AB = BzB$$

The relationship between contraries and subcontraries is a reciprocal one. For contraries you get

$$A < zB \rightarrow zzB < zA \rightarrow B < zB$$

And for the subcontraries you get

$$A > zB \rightarrow zzB > zA \rightarrow B \rightarrow zA$$

You could also prove (what we shall not do here) that two contraries are exclusive and that whenever who facts are exclusive, they are also contraries. The term exclusive means that $AB = 0$.

Furthermore, we can show that two subcontraries are alternatives and also that two facts which are alternative, are subcontraries. Two facts are alternative if their disjunction is permanent i.e. $A \vee B = 1$.

Re complementarity is the sufficient and necessary condition for two facts A and B to be complementary.

$$A + B = 1$$

because

$(A = B = 1) \rightleftarrows (A = 1 - B) \rightleftarrows (B = 1 - A)^5$ and therefore $A = zB$ and $B = zA$

In addition to this, two complementary facts are exclusive and alternative, and two alternative and exclusive facts are complementary.

Two complementary facts that are complementary to a third fact are each other's equivalent because, if $A + B = 1$ and $A + C = 1$, it follows that $B = 1 - A$ and $C = 1 - A$ which means that $B = C$. Briefly put, a fact can have only one complement. But it is not evident that a fact has a complement, i.e. a real fact which is equivalent to the fictitious fact of its absence. A fact which has no complement in a series is unilateral in that particular series. If a fact does have a complement, it is called bilateral. For example the tossing of a coin leads to results that form a series of two-sided facts. Indeed, 'heads' is equivalent to the absence of 'tails' and 'tails' is equivalent to the absence of 'heads'. In order that the tossing of a coin would lead to a series of one-sided facts, you would only have to stretch the coin to twist it at one of its ends and put the two together. This way you would get a Moebius band which would always fall to one side because it has only got one.

The reader has already met a first form of negativity of facts in the form of the absence of a fact (without-A). Two other modalities of negativity are the negation of a fact and a fact's negative.

The negation of a fact is the disjunction of its contraries. It is a global fact that occurs evey time a contrary takes place. From this you can deduce that the contrary implies the negation and that the negation produces the contrary. The negation of A is noted as 'NA' and the negation of the negation as 'NNA'.

There are some fundamental theorems concerning the negation which we will briefly sum up here. But we shall not try to prove them here in order not to make the text too heavy.

Theorem 1: the negation implies the absence nl $NA < zA$
Theorem 2: a fact and its negation are exclusive i.e. $ANA = 0$.

198   *Jean-Pierre de Waele*

Theorem 3: contraposition of the negation i.e.
    A < B → NB < NA
Theorem 4: each fact implies the negation of its negation
    ANA = 0 → A < NNA
Theorem 5: regarding the negation, a fact can have only three positions A, NA and NNA.

This means that each uneven number of negations is equivalent to NA and that each even pair of negations is equivalent to NNA.

Theorem 6: a one-sided fact has three possible positions: A, NA and NNA. A two-sided fact has only two: A and NA. To put it in another way: a two-sided fact is equivalent to the negation of its negation.

Concerning the subcontraries, we already know that two facts A and B are each other's subcontraries if

A > zB → zB < A → zA < B

This means that the absence of one fact implies the occurrence of the other one. If a fact does not occur in a term of a series, all its subcontraries occur in a conjunction which is the negative of the fact. From this definition it follows that the negation implies the negative. Indeed, if the negative of A is represented by A', you get

NA < zA < A' → NA < A'.

We could also prove several important propositions concerning the negative of a fact. But we will only mention two of them very briefly.

Theorem 7: the negative of the negative of a fact implies the fact nl
    A'' < A
Theorem 8: a fact has only three positions with regard to the negative nl A, A' and A''.

At this point we finally have the formal apparatus we need in order to be able to give an analytical representation of a dialectical process. First of all, we shall pay attention to what is called the generalized law of action and reaction. Afterwards we shall come to the definition of a dialectical evolution.

In a causal chain, a cause produces an effect, this effect in turn becomes the cause of another effect, etc. Such a causal chain is formed out of immediate causes and effects which are connected in a transitive way. But it may be – and this will happen sooner or later – that a last effect 'bumps' into one of its contraries. This fact constitutes the starting-point of a 'reaction' whereby the original cause is negated.

Because of a contraposition of the negation you have

$$A > B \rightarrow NB > NA$$

This is the generalized law of action and reaction which can be phrased as follows: if a cause produces an effect, the negation of the effect causes the negation of the cause.

This law is a universal one because it can be applied to every possible field: nature, history, society, thought. You only have to define the nature of the generative process.

Action is represented by $(A > B)$ and reaction by $(NB > NA)$. It is very important to note that these two complex terms are bound by the sign used for a deductive inference $(\rightarrow)$ which means that you can logically deduce $(NB > NA)$ from $(A > B)$. But this is not an existential statement. It does not imply that if you have $(A > B)$ NB is also produced. If NB does occur, however, it follows that NB is the immediate cause of NA by applying the generalized law of action and reaction.

NB can occur in the following way. First you have $A > B$. At a certain moment it is bound to happen that B ceases to exist and then you have zB. But zB implies the conjunction B' of its subcontraries, $zB < B'$. We know that B' is the necessary cause of NB. Consequently, you finally get $zB < B'$ and $B' > NB$ and the term NB can introduce the reaction. The succession of action and reaction will be noted as:

$$A > B \text{————} NB > NA$$

(without the arrow pointed to the right, used for an inference). This leads us to a new type of causal relation. Until now we have only talked about immediate causality. But causality can also be 'mediate' which implies mediation. For example, a reaction $NB > NA$ can have as immediate effect C in such a way that you get $NB > NA > C$. Action and reaction can be represented thus:

$$A > B \text{————} NB > NA > C.$$

$A > B$ and the existing causal relation between NB, NB and C are immediate causations. Between A and C on the other hand, there exists a mediate, non-transitive causal relation. A mediate causal relation can be defined as a causal relation in which cause and effect are seperated from each other by a reaction. This type of causal relation should not be confused with an indirect cause. Indirect causes form part of a causal series composed of immediate causes. For example, if you have A > B > C, A is the indirect cause of C and C is the indirect effect of A.

The term 'interaction' is sometimes used too quickly, that is, without realizing that one is dealing with an intransitive and mediate relation. One says that X reacts to Y and that Y reacts to X without really understanding that, in case of transitivity, this would lead to the logical conclusion that X acts on its own.

If you wish to represent the process of action and reaction between two entities, you have to use the notation system we explained at the beginning of this exposition, that is for the sake of clarity. Let us suppose that two entities L1 and L2 are connected in such a way that L1 exercises a certain action on L2 to which L2 reacts.

L1 and L2 are separated from each other by the square brackets, while round brackets are used to define action and reaction. This is represented as follows:

$$(A] > [B) --- (NB] > [NA)$$
$$\quad L1 \qquad L2 \qquad\quad L1$$

This also makes it clear that the four terms used to express action and reaction are not 'separate facts'. They were only represented that way in the dialectics of facts in order to make the symbolism easier to handle. In reality, L1 and L2 are qualities or capacities of L2 which, under certain conditions, are manifested through causal processes. As an example we can take the original paradigm of the generalized law of action and reaction nl Newton's law on the equality of action and reaction. This law states that every time a body exercises some power on another body L2, this action produces an opposite but equal reaction from L2 to L1. Thus suppose L1 exercises a force A on L2 and, as a consequence of a collision, causes a transformation B of L2. Let us suppose now that this still happens within the boundaries of B's elasticity, then B's transformation is being followed by an expansion NB as a cause of which L2 takes back its original form and also by a force NA, the opposite of A, which exercises a force from L2 to L1.

Newton's law gives us the possibility defining the measure (m) of a force through the distortions of a dynamometer. If the forces act in the same direction, the measure of the conjunction XYZ . . . of the forces X, Y, Z . . . consists of the algebraic sum of the measures of these forces. This leads to

$$m(XYZ \ldots) = m(X) + m(Y) + m(Z) + \ldots$$

In particular: $m(XNX) = m(X) + m(NX)$.

The mechanical equilibrium is defined by $XNX = 0$. In consequence of this you get $m(XNX) = m(X) + m(NX)$.

In this example the two examined entities are two material bodies in motion. One of their qualities consists in exercising forces and undergoing elastic deformations. Under the mentioned conditions, these qualities are shown in the form of forces which act and react. We have to make a few remarks here. First of all, interactions are evidently not restricted to exercising force. In view of the correlation between qualities and causations, there are many other causations than those based on exercising a force. That's the reason why we talked about the *generalized* law of action and reaction.

Secondly, this generalized law of action and reaction and the resulting terms of mediate cause and effect are only the first step towards dialectic processes *stricto sensu*. Many authors mistakenly believe that the notion of dialectics can be reduced to the notion of interaction. But in fact, dialectics covers much more: it includes the defining and explaining of evolutionary processes and of the transcendence of the contradictions implied in the interactions. It is exactly this transcendence or '*Aufhebung*' (cf. Hegel) that has to be examined.

We have to confine ourselves to a minimum here, otherwise we would be able to show that the evolution by leaps which is inherent in the 'dissipative structures', studied by I. Prigogine and his school, can be seen as a dialectic process.

We have already mentioned that contraria are exclusive ($AB = 0$) and that exclusive facts form contraries. To this we can add that the disjunction of two contraries A and B equals the sum of their frequences. Indeed,

$$(A \vee B = A + B - AB) \to (AB = 0) \quad A \vee B = A + B$$

The exclusives A and B occur under the form of the global fact $A + B$. If the global fact is permanent, A and B are complementaries and one of the two always occurs. But if the global fact is not permanent, it may happen that A and B do not occur. What happens then is the conjunction of the negatives of each term i.e. $A'B'$. The contradictions of the contraries are transcended, exceeded or 'aufgehoben' by this conjunction $A'B'$. $A'B'$ is called the synthesis of the contradiction implied by the conjunction AB.

Because we have

$$A < zB < B' \to A < B' \text{ and}$$
$$B < zA < A' \to B < A'$$

we can conclude that two exclusive facts imply the factors of the synthesis of their conjunction.

To fall back on a terminology which originates not with Hegel but with Fichte, you can call the first of the exclusive terms thesis and the second one antithesis. The synthesis of both comes about according to the following schema:

$$\left. \begin{array}{l} \text{Thesis} < \text{negative of the antithesis} \\ \text{Antithesis} < \text{negative of the thesis} \end{array} \right\} \text{ synthesis}$$

We must still show how such a synthesis comes about in a process which consists of actions and reactions.

The sequence of actions and reactions for two-sided facts is limited to the form of

$$A > B \text{ ——— } NB > NA \text{ ——— } A > B \text{ ——— } NB > NA, \text{ etc.}$$

because the facts A and B can each have only two positions. Dialectic processes which build on one-sided facts occur under a more general form. Indeed, the reaction may be followed by a reaction to the reaction, different from the original reaction. One would be inclined to speak of a 're-reaction' if Spencer had not already used this expression to indicate a renewed action wich remains identical to the first one. But we are talking about a new action which, in a manner of speaking, jumps over the reaction and transcends the first two terms. You then have the result of two consecutive contrapositions.

$$A > B \to NB > NA \to NNA > NNB.$$

Using the notation which takes into account the fact that action and reaction are the 'emanation' of the entities, interacting with each other, you get

$$\begin{array}{llll} (A] > [B) & \text{——— } (NB] > [NA) & \text{——— } (NNA] > [NNB) \\ e1 & e2 & e1 & e2 \quad \text{for e1 and e2} \end{array}$$

It would be wrong to believe that a dialectic process could be equated with a rigid linear course. Indeed, the negations which occur in the reaction were defined as disjunctions of contraries. If there are n contraries for NA and NB, this means that there are n possible reactions to the same action. If you take the dialectic process as a whole, you have to take the disjunct contraries of the double negation into account. If they number nn, there are, starting from one action, $\times$ n possible reactions and nn possible double negations. In fact you get an increasing range of possibilities which in two consecutive steps can expand strongly.

The formula we just mentioned is only the analytical form of a dialectic process that can only develop further through a supply of new facts. The factual actualization of a dialectic process passes through a number of phases during which the mentioned relations are present but are grouped differently. We can distinguish the following steps.

1. Action followed by reaction: $A > B$ ———— $NB > NA$

2. Action and reaction occur at the same time as a result of repetition or duration:

$$A > B \text{ ———— } NB > NA \text{ ———— } (A > B) \cdot (NB > NA).$$

The adjunction of each term between brackets gives:

$$(A > B) \cdot (NB > NA) \rightarrow ANB > BNA.$$

It is worthwhile to note that the last conjunction (BNA) (because have $NA < NB$), can be equated with BNB; therefore $BNB = 0$ and $ANB > BNA$ leads to $ANB > 0$. The conjunction of the effect of the action with the effect of the reaction is nil. The conjunction of the cause of the action with the cause of the reaction produces nothing. In this case there exists an equilibrium between action and reaction.

3. Starting from the equilibrium formula $ANB > 0$, you can assume that either (i) the measured intensity of NB changes monotonously (either decreasing or increasing) while the quantitative inconstancy of A is limited in such a way that whenever this limit is reached, A ceases to exist; or (ii) while the frequency of NB increases, the frequency of A may decrease until A disappears from the conjunction, as a result of which you have zA and NB, i.e. the conjunction $(zA \cdot NB)$. This conjunction does not produce 0 anymore because you have $zA < A'$ and $A' > NA$. On the other hand, you also have $NB > NA$ and therefore also $(A' \cdot NB) > NA$.

4. The reaction $NB > NA$ develops further, under certain quantitative conditions, but it stands alone and since the generalized law of action and reaction can be universally applied, it functions as an action upon which a new reaction can follow and you get

$$(NB > NA) \text{ ———— } (NNA > NNB).$$

If the two causations coincide because of their duration or because they repeatedly occur, you have

$$(NB \cdot NNA) > (NA \cdot NNB)$$

and since $NA < NB$ and $NB \cdot NNB = 0$, you finally come to

$$NB \cdot NNA > 0$$

which means that a new equilibrium has been reached.

5. We can distinguish three phases in the factual progress of a dialectic process. First of all there emerges an equilibrium defined by $ANB > 0$. This is followed by a period of destabilization A'. NB NA during which the causation which was the reaction becomes the action. Then again a new equilibrium is reached nl $NB \cdot NNA$.

To sum it all up

$$(ANB > 0) \text{———} (A'NB > NA) \text{———} (NBNNA > 0).$$

The contrast between the two most important terms of this dialectic process is remarkable. NB occurs in every phase and in this way is constantly present but for A you first have A, then NA and finally NNA. Can we however consider the second equilibrium as a synthesis in the sense we earlier ascribed to the term?

The conjunction of action and reaction (cf. 2) is cause of a conjunction of exclusives: $BNA = 0$. According to the given definitions their synthesis must be the conjunction of their negatives i.e. $B' \cdot (NA)'$. As a result of the implications which exist between the three different kinds of negativity, you have $(NX < zX < X')$ $NB < B'$. If you replace X by NA in this series of implications, you get the implications $NNA < (NA)'$. If you form the conjunction of these two implications, you have

$$NB \cdot NNA < B' \cdot (NA)'$$

which means that the new equilibrium which emerges as a result of a dialectic development of an action and reaction process is a sufficient condition of the synthesis of the exclusives or contraries caused by the original equilibrium.

The factual progress of the dialectic process we examined offers us the possibility shedding new light on the previous representations of dialectics as a collection of fundamental 'laws'. It is clear, however, that the first and last phase can be seen as a 'unity' of opposites because the cause of the action and the negation of its effect constitute the cause of a conjunction of contraries. The permanent term NB can, because of this, vary continuously and monotonously. The double negation NNA shows no continuity with A. It is the new form of this term in which the qualitative change is shown.

NOTES

1 J. P. de Waele, *Homicidal Persons*, Kluwer, 1990 (in press).
2 J. P. de Waele, *Projet pour une théorie moderne de la dialectique*, Bruxelles, 1983. [*A Modern Theory of Dialectics* (in preparation).]
3 Cf. J. C. Ducasse *Truth, knowledge and causation*, (Routledge & Kegan Paul, London, 1968).
4 For a fuller discussion of 'causes' and 'conditions' cf. 'Causation and conditionals', in E. Sosa (ed.), *Oxford University Press, Oxford*, 1975.
5 ⇄ should be read as 'logically identical with'.

13

Rom Harré: Realism and the Turn to Social Constructionism

John Shotter

A simile that has been absorbed into the forms of our language produces a false appearance, and this disquiets us. 'But this isn't how it is! – *we say. 'Yet this is how it has to be!'*

Wittgenstein, 1953, no.112

What I want to do in this paper is to explore a tension in Rom's work between the tendencies to naturalism occasioned by his realist stance, and the anti-naturalistic tendencies occasioned by his very real (sic) concern in his recent socio-psychological writings, with the intricate workings of *moral* orders in the structuring of people's social activities. I mean the tension between, on the one hand, the claim that there is (or there can be) no essential difference between conducting investigations and warranting their results in the natural and in the social sciences (his Realism); and, on the other hand, the fact that quite different ways of formulating and warranting claims to knowledge seem to be required in the social sciences, if one takes his concern (in, for example, Harré, 1983, 1986a) with one's location in a moral order seriously (his turn to Social Constructionism). In other words, I want in the most friendly of deconstructionist spirits possible, to uncover some of the unresolved oppositions present in Rom's socio-psychological writing – to do with the polarities of individualism and collectivism, the dilemmas we all face in characterizing and coping with our relations to those around us – which open it up to yet further development and provide it with its dynamic. And I would like to begin to outline these polarities in greater detail by first mentioning a bit of personal history and the part played by Rom in it.

Powers

In 1969, after becoming depressed by the intellectual barrenness (though not, I hasten to add, the enormous challenges to one's ingenuity) in attempts to computer simulate supposed processes of language acquisition (Shotter, 1968), I turned from an interest in machines and mechanisms to a study of agency. What depressed me about a mechanistic psychology was the way in which it suppressed genuine individuality and led to us all being treated as indistinguishable atoms; but what also depressed me (to perhaps an even greater extent), was the way in which appeals to mechanism were used as a device to disclaim responsibility, and to avoid accountability for what were (to my mind), obviously political (and often morally obnoxious) proposals. While there was a good deal of dissatisfaction with this kind of academic psychology in those heady days around 1968–9, and many acquaintances who shared my feelings abandoned it because of this, few within academic psychology itself were admitting the fact, let alone attempting in any serious way to formulate a more adequate alternative – indeed, a vigorous and quite aggressive defence of the status quo was mounted, both academically (Broadbent, 1970, 1973) and institutionally.

A Nottingham friend, attending one of Rom's philosophy of science courses in Oxford at the time, told me of Rom's similar worries about psychology, and took him an early paper of mine which Rom read, commented upon, and sent back with an invitation for us to meet. Straightaway I was enlivened by Rom's tenacity, energy and verve, and by his determination to get some debate, somewhere, about psychology's fundamentals put on the agenda; and although Rom's own (official) situation in Oxford also had its rough sides (and has never, it seems to me, reflected the credit due to him), he was none the less generous in his attention to my predicament as well. And that mattered, and has continued to matter a lot to me.

At the time, Rom was still closely involved with his 'first love' – his realist philosophy of the natural sciences (Harré, 1970a, 1972) – and he gave me a paper of his on 'Powers' (Harré, 1970b), a 'generative' concept in both senses of the word, both in itself and for me in my thinking. And I set to work, trying to apply it in the new context in which I was now studying language acquisition: the (videotape records of) interactions between mothers and children. It was within this context that Rom's formulation of the concept of powers came to play a most important part. Influenced to an extent by Saussure's (1960) claim that linguistics could only become 'autonomous' and prosper academically if it could take as its subject-matter a circumscribed, humanly constructed product, it seemed to me that 'personal powers' could serve that same purpose in psychology. For the new 'twist' in Rom's way of formulating agency in terms of powers worked to separate the unlimited task of describing the whole of an agent's nature from the limited task of describing its powers. As he put it:

To ascribe a power to a thing or material is to say something specific about what it *will* or *can* do, but to say something unspecific about what it *is*. That is, to ascribe a power to a thing asserts only that it can do what it does in virtue of its nature, whatever that is. It leaves open the question of the exact specification of the nature or constitution in virtue of which it has the power. Perhaps that can be discovered by empirical investigation later. (Harré, 1970b, p. 85)

Furthermore, in relating 'power' to the notion of 'capability', he said

'Capability' as a positive concept expresses something of this idea: a capability is a power which can be acquired (or lost) without there being a change in the fundamental nature of the thing or material in question'. (1970b, p. 93)

For those with developmental concerns, this formulation seemed to provide a way in which they could be articulated: the nature of the development involved could be seen as a transformation of 'natural powers' into 'personal powers'. The possession of natural powers is, one can say, in the 'nature' of the child, and what requires explaining, is how children are helped by those around them, to 'appropriate' their own natural powers and to bring them under their own control as personal powers. And that is how I formulated the matter at that time (Shotter, 1974).

From the Natural to the Societal

However, although sharing an interest in agency and meaning, Rom and I soon found ourselves with a difference. Rom centred his initial attention upon what might be called the *already* socially aware person. And, influenced by the whole movement in the philosophy of human action in support of the 'rule-following model' and Chomsky's brilliant work on syntax, he took it that self-directed and self-monitored behaviour, performed by reference to rules, 'is the prototype of behaviour in ordinary daily living' (Harré and Secord, 1972, p. 9). For me, however, one of the reasons for my depression with the computer metaphor was the feeling that the rule-following model of meaning was inadequate: people do not just follow rules, they also create them (as well as challenge, change and correct them; and, in applying them, check with others whether they have applied them correctly.) Hence, in this respect, I was thinking along very different lines from Rom at this time.

Furthermore, given my concerns with how one became able to take *responsibility* for the outcome of at least some of the actions in which one is involved, and influenced among others by the Kantian, John Macmurray

(1957, 1961), I was worrying about *moral* issues, and how they affected
what Macmurray called the (logical) form of the personal. I was concerned
to formulate a *developmentally sensitive* account of it, to provide an
opening for rule-creation, i.e. at that time, not so much the creation of
rules *de novo*, as the re-creation in the child of already existing rules in the
possession of adults. And Macmurray's Kantian influence is apparent in the
formulation I produced. But so also are Rom's thoughts about *negotiations*, and it is these which, in the end, emerge as of central importance. In
taking a genuinely personal, as opposed to a mechanical or organic
approach, it seemed to me that:

> psychology is removed from the realm of the natural sciences and placed
> among the moral sciences. This alters its character entirely. It becomes
> concerned with *negotiations*. . . . Values, opinions, beliefs, feelings, inten-
> tions, etc., once again assume a crucial role in human affairs. . . . While
> classical science demands that everything by studied as if it were matter in
> motion according to an absent God's pre-established laws, *persons* seem
> able on occasions to act from a belief, a mere *conception* of a law . . . and in
> attempting to live thus, according to the conception of a law, people may fail;
> they may act inappropriately, rightly or wrongly, legitimately or illegitimately,
> etc., for conceptions decree only what *should* or *might be* the case, not what
> is. Attempting to live according to laws inevitably involves the judgement of
> other people. (Shotter, 1974, pp. 217–18).

In other words, how the source of an action is ascertained, and how the
attribution of a moral responsibility for it influences future action, struck
me as a fundamental, ineradicable and irreducible part of any proper
characterization of the nature of any genuinely *social* activity.

To move now to the next step: which was that, developmentally, the
view that the growth of social awareness and the self-determination of
action could be seen as the appropriation of powers from a 'natural' into
a 'personal' realm gave rise to a number of problems. One was that
in assuming essentially a rationalist formulation of the developmental
process – that the task of those around children is seen as being merely
that of helping to reveal what in some sense is already (innately?) in them
– almost everything of historical, moral and political importance is omit-
ted. It is not a genuinely *social* account of development, but an inter-
individualistic one, taking place within a featureless context, devoid of
psychological resources and valencies, i.e. in such a non-specific context
that it could be situated anywhere.

However, the basic approach contained a number of conceptual Trojan
horses which happily, when they began to discharge their contents,
changed its nature entirely. They were the claims which I have already
mentioned:

1. that psychology must be seen as essentially a *moral* science, because all our actions (even when acting all alone) must be performed with an awareness of how they will be *judged by others*; and
2. Rom's claim that such judgements involve *negotiation*. To these must be added:
3. Rom's Wittgensteinian claim that mental activity is not private, but available publicly in the activities in which people are involved with each other; hence, the problem of identifying it is not a matter of *access*, but of *authority*, and is to do with who has what rights in negotiating an account of its nature, and how that nature should then be attributed (Harre' and Secord, 1972, pp. 121–3).
4. Finally, there was both my own and Rom's adoption of Vygotsky's (1962, 1966, 1978) notion of 'appropriation', and a concern with what is involved in the process of one person, who lacks a skill, acquiring a mastery of it from those around them.

Vygotsky: From the Individual to the Collective

As Vygotsky's views have come to play a central part in Rom's more recent expositions of his social constructionist stance (Harré, 1983, 1986a, 1986c), it will be useful at this point to give their flavour by stating what might be called Vygotsky's two major laws of development: One is that 'consciousness and control appear only at a late stage in the development of a function, after it has been used and practiced unconsciously and spontaneously. In order to subject a function to intellectual control, we must first possess it' (Vygotsky, 1962, p. 90). Thus instructions do not face the task of attempting to teach us how to do something *de novo*, their task is only to 'stage manage' a context which 'calls out' what in some sense we can already do: and thus to help us recognize how to call it out for ourselves. Furthermore, the source of what we can already do spontaneously (what previously I had called our 'natural powers') lies in the general social activity in which we are all embedded. This is expressed in what Vygotsky calls 'the general genetic law of development' which can be, he says, formulated as follows:

> *any function if the child's cultural development appears on the stage twice, on two planes, first on the social plane and then on the psychological*, first among people as an *intermental category* and then within the child as an *intramental category*. (Vygotsky, 1966, p. 44; emphasis in original)

What Rom has drawn from these laws is, as he puts it, 'the insight (which history must surely ascribe to L. S. Vygotsky)' (Harré, 1986a, p. 120), that the personal psychology of each individual is created by them 'appropriating' the conversational forms and strategies available to them in the general clamour of everyday conversational activity around them. And 'insofar as individual people construct a personal discourse on the model of public discourse, they become complex 'mental' beings with unique "inner worlds"'' (Harré, 1986a, p. 120).

In developing his formulations in this sphere, Rom has set them out in terms of two polarities: one dimension he terms a mental activity's *manifestation*, and distinguishes between whether its performance is *publicly* available, or whether is occurs *privately*, i.e. in a way we make inaccessible to others; and the other he terms the activity's *location*, and distinguishes between whether it is located in the *collective* or in the *individual*. The two dimensions form what he calls a two-dimensional 'Vygotskian space' of four quadrants:

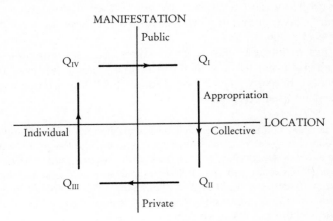

Figure 13.1   *Vygotsky 'space'*

To quote Harré:

according to the constructionist viewpoint, 'development' must occur through the transfer of rules and conventions that govern public conversation and other social practices from Quadrant I, via Quadrant II, to Quadrant III . . . The first step is the privatization of the language of the local social group.' But in fact, 'the Vygotskian space allows us to think of the mind of another person as spread out over all four quadrants. (1986a, pp. 121–2)

But what I think Rom has done here, in adopting this thoroughgoing social constructionist stance, albeit somewhat implicitly, is to have abandoned what might be called the 'things-ontology' he introduced in his original formulations of the concept of powers – and along with it what is seen as the strength of the realist position: the possibility of appealing, in warranting our claims to knowledge, to structured entities which exist independently of our knowledge or of our experience of them. It is no longer the case that mental powers are or can be ascribed to locatable things or entities in virtue of *their* natures (whatever they are). Their developmental trajectory must be thought of as originating in (and perhaps as terminating in) the diffusely spread-out activities within a collective. Even when they become privatized and localized within an individual, they can never be thought of as consisting in *complete* and hence describable structures, i.e. structures to which to refer in enabling and constraining the performance of actions. For all our actions must, if they are to have any proper social currency, be *open* in their performance to interpretation and evaluation by others (see in this connection the comments later about the necessary incorporation in one's talk of a 'rhetoric of reality').

But just to illustrate the depth of Rom's present commitment to this view, let me point to how in more recent writings he gives it further articulation. In Harré (1986c), he declares his Wittgensteinian stance on mental phenomena as follows:

> Wittgenstein's philosophy of language has prompted, directly or indirectly, the daring suggestion . . . that much, perhaps all of the *fine grain* of human psychological functioning is a product of the language that a person has acquired. For that reason psychology must from now on be thought of as much a collective as an individual phenomenon. The revival of interest in the theories and empirical researches of Vygotsky has added a further impetus to this movement. (p. 288)

Thus, as he now sees it (see, for instance, Harré, 1983, p. 58), 'the primary human reality is persons in conversation'. But this raises a number of questions for the realist philosophy of science he had previously helped to found.

From a Things-ontology to a Moral Activities-ontology?

Let me try to be more specific about what I think some of those questions are. Given his turn to a social constructionist stance, and given his current claims that many of 'the powerful particulars' of social life – like people's beliefs, their identities and even their minds – are socially constructed, and only have a continuously negotiated and reproduced existence in certain of our social activities, can his conception of the world as 'an interacting system of powerful particulars' (Harré and Madden, 1975, p. 7) be sustained? To what extent does it still make sense for him to maintain that causal powers should be seen (for the purposes of scientific investigation), not only as *located*, but also as actually located in *things*, which provides *in their natures* a basis for such powers? While the rhetoric of realism suggests the possibility of constructing and testing theories about the 'generative mechanisms' which are said to be the *causes* of the behaviour observed – the programme set out in Harré and Secord (1972), and still not wholly abandonned (Harré, Clarke and de Carlo, 1985) – by comparison, his social constructionist rhetoric is less clear-cut. Rather than a world of locatable, powerful particulars, it implies – I shall argue – a world of much more diffusely distributed, non-locatable, morally structured activities, which can only be investigated from a position of involvement within them. And this immediately raises the question of how the character of the involvements in which one is placed should best be characterized – (1) in terms just of a structure of locatable powers and competencies, or (2) in terms of diffuse, non-locatable powers, which are open to morally and politically significant *attributions*, which are contestable as to their nature and location?

Now what seems to be the strength of the realist's position in psychology – to quote Manicas and Secord (1983, p. 401), who have attempted to set out its implications for psychological research – is that realists accept that 'knowledge is a social and historical product; . . . [and] that there is no preinterpreted "given" and that the test of truth cannot be "correspondence".' But they still none the less insist that

> it is precisely the task of the sciences to invent theories that aim to represent the world. Thus in the spirit of Kuhn . . . the practices of the sciences generate their own *rational* criteria in terms of which theory is accepted or rejected. The crucial point is that it is possible for these criteria to be rational precisely because on realist terms, there is a world that exists independently of cognizing experience. Since our theories are constitutive of the known world but *not* of the *world*, we may always be wrong, but *not* anything goes.

By comparison, a thoughgoing social constructionist stance seems to lack such anchor points. It seems to suggest, that not only our knowledge of the world but the world itself is a social construction, and this seems to leave social constructionists whirling in a maelstrom of total relativity, bankrupt of any standards against which to judge the worth of their claims to knowledge.

Later in this paper, I shall argue (what might seem to be a bizarre claim) that the world in question for social constructionists *is* social constructed: for it is a world of mental powers and capacities, of mental liabilities and tendencies; of 'places', 'positions' and 'spaces'; of rights, duties, obligations and privileges; of identities, roles, personalities and selves; of different forms of human association: dyads, groups, institutions, bureaucracies, governments, industries, and so on. Such a social reality is articulated in terms both of the ways people can devise for relating themselves to one another, and of the kinds of people those modes of relationship allow or invite. But this does not mean to say that just 'anything goes'. And we *can* in fact find (prefigured in Rom's recent work in a social constructionist vein) *standards* in such constructions, in what can be called *responsibilities of communication* – where these are the responsibilities between people involved in maintaining our social constructions as the constructions they are. Here, however, let me continue with what I see as the main problem with a realist stance.

Rhetoric and the Cunning of Language

As I see it, the trouble is that a realist rhetoric or idiom authorizes a way of talking about certain 'things' and 'entities' – such as 'basic human powers and competencies and the structures that underlie them' (Manicas and Secord, 1983, p. 411) – when no such things, entities or structures may actually exist! Indeed, as Manicas and Secord themselves state it, the advantage of the approach is that 'It allows scientists to *believe* that they are grappling with entities that, although often not directly observable, are real enough' (Manicas and Secord, 1983, p. 412; emphasis added). Precisely! It allows scientists to warrant a way of talking about human mental phenomena *as if* they consisted in things like powers and competencies with describable underlying structures, without first questioning whether the source of their beliefs (about the existence of such locatable *entities*) is to be found solely in the nature of their talk, in the character of their own (non-locatable) communicative *activities*. They do not know whether the things they take to be *real enough* are in fact *false*, and/or *imaginary*. Furthermore, in treating language as primarily referential, they ignore its rhetorical power to 'move' one's feelings, to creat a sense of *commitment*, and make one feel that one *must* proceed in a certain way – that *this* is how something has to *be*.

Various comments of Wittgenstein's are relevant here: In one comment Wittgenstein warns against the unwarranted completion (in our descriptions) of essentially incomplete human activities still in progress:

> Mere description is so difficult because one believes that one needs to fill out the facts in order to understand them. It is as if one saw a screen with

scattered colour-patches, and said: the way they are here, they are unintelligible; they only make sense when one completes them into a shape. – Whereas I want to say: "Here *is* the whole. (If you complete it, you falsify it.) (1980, I, no. 257)

In other words, the unwarranted treatment of what is essentially ongoing activity as a completed object of knowledge, *falsifies* its (intentional) relations to other activites, past, present and future; and makes it impossible to understand how, besides having a meaning, one's speech may 'move' those to whom it is addressed. In another comment (Wittgenstein, 1981, no. 446), he asks why it is that we still feel driven to say that there *must be* some real, inner 'mental processes' going on when we understand something, when we have no experience of such processes:

> But don't think of understanding as a 'mental process' at all. – For *that* is the way of speaking that is confusing you. Rather ask yourself: in what kind of case, under what circumstances do we say 'Now I can go on ... [A] way of speaking is what prevents us from seeing the facts without prejudice.... *That* is how it comes about that the means of representation creates something *imaginary*. So let us not think we *must* find a specific mental process, because the verb 'to understand' is there and because one says: Understanding is an activity of the mind.

In other words, the question as to whether, at least in the realm of mental phenomena, realists are victims of grammatical distortions or illusions generated by the nature of their own discourse, not only does not arise, but it *cannot* arise and be investigated within a realist methodology. (Indeed, a Wittgensteinian would want to add, that while beliefs may seem real if people believe they are real, that is not because believing is done by a special effort of will; it is because it is a special social practice, which is maintained by a particular pattern of social, political, economic, and linguistic relations; it is a matter of how one lives one's life.)

Furthermore, besides all these kinds of difficulties, there is a further difficulty to do with the implicit theory of human nature and action such a way of talking *commits* one to. Witness, for instance, how Manicas and Secord describe psychology's task:

> Chomsky's generative grammar is seen (rightly or wrongly) as a theoretical structure that enables persons to generate sentences, and thus provides a core explanation of linguistic competence.... We believe that psychology as an experimental science is best understood in analogous terms – as concerned with the structure of our competencies and not our realization of them in our everyday behaviour. (Manicas and Secord, 1983, p. 406)

But what is it that warrants the claim that a theoretical structure is, in itself, enabling? And what suggests the thought that once a 'competency' has been described in terms of its 'structure', a result of some psychological worth has been attained? From whence comes the complexly structured nature of Manicas and Secord's proposals. For surely, no one in psychology at the moment would claim to possess already a body of clearly organized empirical knowledge, or a set of generally effective experimental methods?

Again, a remark of Wittgenstein's (1953, no. 308) is, I think, appropriate here (and its application to Rom's (1970) formulation of powers will not escape notice either). In talking of how philosophical problems arise about mental processes and states, he says:

> The first step is the one that altogether escapes notice. We talk of processes and states and leave their nature undecided. Sometime perhaps we shall know more about them – we think. But that is just what commits us to a particular way of looking at the matter. For we have a definite concept of what it means to know a process better. (The decisive movement in the conjuring trick has been made, and it was the very one we thought quite innocent.)

In other words, the complexly structured nature of Manicas and Secord's proposals for the conduct of psychological research can be seen as issuing, not from an empirical knowledge of successful research projects in psychology, but from the nature of their *talk* about 'powers' and 'competencies'. It is the talk that generates the feeling as to what *must be* the case – talk which is in fact only formulated in this way, to make people's behaviour amenable to naturalistic methods of experimentation.

Conversational Realities

But, it might be arued, aren't what I am calling grammatical distortions, illusions and commitments just the kinds of thing realists think of as real anyway? Indeed, we all know W. I. Thomas's dictum 'If men define things as real, they are real in their consequences', and isn't this all that matters? Aren't the activities going on between people real, material activities with real material bodily *consequences* in how they actually live their lives? Don't they contain historically developed, reproduced stabilities which, while enabling certain activities, also place real constraints upon what can be said and done? And if we want to understand the determinants of people's actions, aren't these the structures we should attempt to describe? Yes ... but are there any such *structures*, really? And is that how the enablements and constraints clearly operating in our communicative activities are *best* characterized?

For what is in question here is not whether people can exert a material effect upon one another in their communications; nor whether they can create certain forms of order (and then submit themselves to their reproduction) in their activities – realists and social constructionists alike accept both these claims. The question is, in what do such orders consist? And the question arises because, as I see it, what is at issue is not just the proper characterization of the 'shape' or the structure of people's social activities, but the nature of their *moral* involvements with each other in the conduct of the formative processes concerned. In other words, do we require an ontology of things, or of morally significant activities? Rom has not answered this question, but has simply set his recent work in what he now sees as 'the primary human reality', i.e. that of 'persons in conversation'.

Some of the things Rom has argued (Harré, 1983, pp. 58–66) about the nature of our conversational involvements, and I think quite correctly and most importantly, are:

1. That a 'space', or a 'referential grid', or what one might call an *intralinguistic reality*, is constructed in such talk, which functions (among other things) to provide a set of 'locations' or 'places' structured by *moral and political* considerations.
2. That the use of such pronouns as 'I' (and 'you') are empirically non-referential, i.e. they do not refer to any empirically identifiable object, but work to index *momentary* status locations in such a space.
3. That other kind of indexical expressions, such as 'here', 'now', 'then', 'there', etc., function to locate, root, or anchor such an intralinguistic reality in a larger, more publicly accountable world.
4. That the actions or utterances occurring in such a space, can function both to refer to states or entities specified within the space, and, to change its nature, and in particular, to change the array and nature of status locations, i.e. the range, distribution, and interrelation of the conversational rights and duties momentarily available to those conversationally involved.
5. Finally, to add an important reminder, that while in such contexts, people are in a sense *simple* beings, i.e. they 'move' and are 'moved' by one another's immediate sayings and doings, they can also change from simple into complex beings, and 'move' from the immediately interpersonal realm into the realm of public affairs in an instant. It is when the interpersonal flow of activity between them breaks down and they must *account*, i.e. justify their conduct to one another, that

the 'situation' of such interpersonal exchanges in a larger social scheme of things becomes apparent. It is through the necessity for *accountability*, as Rom points out (Harré, 1983, p. 121), that the social enters the personal. For it is at a point when 'repairs' are necessary that a publicly agreed form of order can determine the nature of the repairs made. And it is this which ensures that personal affairs retain a 'rooting' or 'anchoring' in a public order of things. But in what does such an ability – to be publicly accountable – consist?

From Generative Mechanisms to Ethical Logistics

Although human beings who are already constituted as morally accountable, self-conscious human beings can go out and gather, in a wholly autonomous and individualistic way, what counts in their society as 'information' about the things and events around them, they cannot gain their knowledge of how *to be* such individuals in this way. Indeed, to an external, third-person observer, it is not all clear what would constitute the relevant 'information'. For it is not to do with what something 'is', but with how it *should* be judged. And, what Wittgenstein (1953, pp. 224–5) says about learning to judge people's motives –

> There is such a question as: 'Is this a reliable way of judging people's motives?' But in order to be able to ask this we must know what 'judging a motive' means; and we do not learn this by being told what '*motive*' is and what '*judging*' is.

or simply about determining the length of a rod:

> What 'determining the length' [of a rod] means is not learnt by learning what *length* and *determining* are; the meaning of the word "length" is learnt by learning, among other things, what it is to determine length

– applies here also. In other words, incorporated in all of what is accounted as human knowledge, is an evaluative or corrigible aspect. Thus, in acquiring any 'information' about one's circumstances, one must know how what one encounters *should* be accounted – for not *everything* one encounters in one's surroundings can be accounted as information by any means.

Hence, among many other things, what is involved in gaining one's autonomy and learning how to learn by acquiring 'information', is grasping the 'methods' of checking applied by other's to what are counted as claims to knowledge, and applying them in one's own attempts to learn. Hence, Rom's rejection of what he calls the 'Cartesian answer' to how such knowledge is acquired (Harré, 1986c, p. 288). An educative task of this kind cannot be accomplished simply by the transfer a subjectively known body of knowledge, through some communicative 'channel', into the subjective contents of another being – for, among other things, there would be no way of knowing that the transfer had been accomplished correctly. What must be involved, he says, is the appropriation by an individual of a *resource* made available (under the restraints, quite often, of a certain political economy to do with scarcities of access) in certain regions of public, social activity at large. But what is that character of that resource?

Actually, paradigms of its nature are not at all difficult to identify and articulate. Let us explore for a moment what happens as our linguistic competencies increase, and as adults we become more adept at constructing the whole network of *intralinguistic* references constituting a 'linguistic reality'. Now, instead of to an immediate, extralinguistic context, our utterances can refer to entities constructed within this intralinguistic context. But as we begin to talk more about entities and states of affairs not immediately present, there is a decrease of reference to what 'is', and an increase to what 'might be'. In other words, there is an increase of reference to an hermeneutically constructed, potentially fictitious (or theoretical) world. Such a way of talking, if it is to have any factual status, requires the development of *methods* for warranting in the course of such talk, one's claims about what 'might be' as actually being what 'is'.

In other words, morally responsible and autonomous people, if they want to be seen as talking factually, must incorporate in it procedures which establish, in addition to the structure of the state of affairs in question, that such facts are, for instance: (1) the same for everyone; (2) that they are independent of people's wishes and opinions; (3) that knowledge of them was based upon direct observation, etc. And if their talk is to pass as factual, they must make opportunities in it for their claims to be challenged, and to be able to meet such challenges, on the spot. It is by the use of such methods and procedures that adult forms of speech can function with a great degree of independence from their immediate linguistic context. In other words, as adults we have learnt to incorporate in our speech what might be called a 'rhetoric of reality', a way of talking which gives a sense, or a feel, for the reality we are taking about.

Here, then, is a paradigm which represents something of what is involved in talking with a sense of how what one is saying is going to be judged by others. But still more needs to be said, for we are still not yet wholly in the realm of the public: for the 'procedures' of warranting we include in our talk, only set out *accounts* of the ways in which our claims were supposedly checked. Yet more needs to be done if we are to have our claims *actually* 'rooted' (if not in the real world), at least in what counts for all of us as the real world. And *whose* task is it to do that work?

As Rom points out (Harré, 1983, pp. 58–66), the 'locations' created in a conversational reality specify a set of rights and duties, privileges and obligations, as to who may speak to whom and in what manner. In other words, among other activities, they can be seen as specifying or directing who should do what at what moment, in the processes involved in the social construction of meaning. This is what it means to say that meanings are socially negotiated; a kind of *ethical logistics* is required – a skill at *coordinating the management of meaning* (Pearce and Cronen, 1980). But it is most important to add here a another point Rom makes (Harré, 1983, p. 65) about the *unequal* distribution of such rights and duties.

In pointing out the need for our interpersonal exchanges to be located, not only in the larger public sphere, but also in 'the continuous space and time of physical reality', he goes on to say:

> The relation between the consequences of our joint location in both manifolds is mediated by the local moral order, particularly the unequal distribution of rights upon which I have already remarked. For example, one may be physically present with others in the same space and time of a meeting, but, in the position of secretary, may not have the right to contribute to the cognitive processes proceeding in the flow of conversation.

Or, by contrast, one may be involved in the flow of conversation, but have no right to ask a high-status speaker for clarifications, it being assumed that it is the duty of the listener. Indeed, it is precisely children's misunderstanding of what are the reciprocal (and possibly asymmetrical) rights and duties of speaker's and listener's, as to who should do what at what moment in making sense of a communication, that Rommetviet (1985) has been exploring to such brilliant effect recently. But much more is possible. In fact, such an analysis opens up a massive field of possible research topics to do with what one might call a political economy of communicative and developmental rights: to do with social identities in general, and gender identities in particular; to do with the unequal distribution of developmental opportunities; with rights of expression; with devices of accountability and warranting; with silences and the repair of misunderstandings; with closures, i.e. who has the right to define otherwise ambiguous expressions clearly, etc.; in short, to do with the psychological resources available to one in the public sphere, and one's rights of access to them.

Conclusions: Responsibilities of Communication

Before our final conclusions, there is still a little bit of work to do. As I said at the beginning of this paper, I wanted to explore some of the tensions between Harré the realist and Harré the social constructionist. The question we now face is: has he lost, by his turn to social constructionism, the very gains he sought by espousing realism, namely, the construction of some impersonal standards against which claims to knowledge could be judged? And finally the answer, I think, is 'no'. For, if it is the case that the world of all the differently morally managed ways of relating ourselves to one another – our different forms of social life – *is* socially constructed, then, as I maintained earlier, one *must* observe certain standards in one's conduct – or else one will destroy the very foundations upon which the intelligibility (and legitimacy) of one's actions rests. Indeed, others will hold one to them. Or to put it another way: if our forms of rationality are socially constructed, and if one knows this to be the case, then one cannot rationally deny in one's talk the (moral) grounds upon which one's rationality depends while still claiming, at the same time, that one's denials are rational. Although one's denial would not, perhaps, be logically self-defeating, it would certainly be, ultimately, rhetorically self-defeating.

For example, it makes no sense to offer, as a justification for the assertion that all people's actions must be caused by their external circumstances, the fact that it is possible to *doubt* their capacity to act freely. 'One simply tends to forget', says Wittgenstein (1980, vol. 2, no. 342), 'that even doubting belongs to a language game.' Thus even the expression of a doubt, if it is to be properly understood, involves one respecting what might be called, *the responsibilities of communication*. So, although we may, in a Cartesian sense, raise 'supposed' doubts about people's rights and capacities to act freely, we cannot in any practically effective sense deny them. Only a genuine doubt, a practical doubt that actually disturbed the 'ethical logistics' of the language games involved, would destroy the pattern of social activities which makes our opportunities for communication possible.

But what I have stated above is an ideal, a theoretical maxim; and furthermore, even as an ideal it claims that such denials will only *ultimately* prove self-defeating. In the meantime, it is perfectly possible for one to manage, like a Nero, to have all the rest of one's fellows burdened with the task of finding intelligibility and legitimacy in whatever one does. And while one waits for the self-destructive tendencies in this form of life to take their effect, and for boredom to supervene – for if everything we attempt is already permitted, nothing we do is an achievement – tendencies destructive of others are also at work. How can we know, ahead of time, whether such inequalities in responsibilities of communication will prove destructive or not? Furthermore, it is one thing to point to the responsibilities entailed in communication, and to say that one should not undermine the very relations upon which the force of one's own statements rests; it is quite another to find standards which allow one to judge *between* communicative practices. The answer to these two problems can only be found, I think, by situating the practices concerned in yet larger public contexts; and rather than a theoretical problem, it is a practical problem to construct them. In other words, genuinely political problems about actual practical social arrangements face us at every turn and cannot be solved in general theory ahead of time. But that does not mean that we cannot be more certain about particular things at a more local level.

Clearly, not only are rights of access to communication, rights of access to developmental opportunities, and rights to closure (of the openness making for ambiguities in meaning), all unequally distributed at the moment, but so also are the rights of accountability, the right to make or to call for 'repairs' which work to 'anchor' a discourse in a larger context, beyond its current 'reality'. Indeed, hidden in the current Thatcher/Reagan rhetoric of individualism is a destruction of the larger public sphere to which, as an otherwise powerless individual, one can address an appeal and expect to have the rational force of one's appeal felt. (Indeed, one can find in the *Observer* (1 November 1987) in 'Sayings of the Week' the following attributed to Margaret Thatcher: 'There is no such thing as Society. There are individual men and women and there are families.') But the tendency in science, no matter how much the degree of its backsliding in its more technological manifestatinos, is in the opposite direction: towards the enlargement of the sphere of public accountability. This also, I think, has been one of the effects of Rom Harré's work. As he put it in *Social Being* (Harré, 1979, p. 3), people have a deep sense of their own dignity, and a craving for recognition as beings of worth', and it has been Rom's project to show the worth of energy, tenacity, wit and intellectual and academic skill in helping to keep that sense of human dignity alive.

REFERENCES

Broadbent, D. E. (1970) In defence of empirical psychology, *Bulletin of the British Psychology Society* 23, pp. 87–96.
Broadbent, D. E. (1973) *In Defence of Empirical Psychology*, London: Methuen.
Harré, R. (1970a) *The Principles of Scientific Thinking*, London: Macmillan.
Harré, R. (1970b) 'Powers'. *British Journal of Philosophical Science* 21, pp. 81–101.
Harré, R. (1972) *Philosophies of Science*, Oxford: Oxford University Press.
Harré, R. (1979) *Social Being: a Theory for Social Psychology*, Oxford: Basil Blackwell.
Harré, R. (1983) *Personal Being: a Theory for Individual Psychology*, Oxford: Basil Blackwell.

Harré, R. (1986) Social sources of mental content and order. In J. Margolis, P. T. Manicas, R. Harré' and P. F. Secord (eds) *Psychology: Designing the Discipline*, Oxford: Basil Blackwell.

Harré, R. (1986) An outline of the social constructionist viewpoint. In R. Harré (ed.) *The Social Construction of Emotions*, Oxford: Basil Blackwell.

Harré, R. (1986) The step to social constructionism. In M. P. M. Richards and P. Light (eds) *Children of Social Worlds*, Oxford: Polity Press.

Harré, R. and Secord, P. F. (1972) *The Explanation of Social Behaviour*, Oxford: Basil Blackwell.

Harré, R. and Madden, E. H. (1975) *Causal Powers: a Theory of Natural Necessity*, Oxford: Basil Blackwell.

Harré, R., Clarke, D. and de Carlo, N. (1985) *Motives and Mechanisms: an Introduction to the Psychology of Action*, London: Methuen.

Macmurray, J. (1957) *The Self as Agent*, London: Faber & Faber.

Macmurray, J. (1961) *Persons in Relation*, London: Faber and Faber.

Manicas, P. T. and Secord, P. F. (1983) Implications for psychology of the new philosphy of science, *American Psychologist* 38, pp. 399–413.

Pearce, W. B. and Cronen, V. (1980) *Communication, Action and Meaning*, New York: Praeger.

Rommetveit, R. (1985) Language acquisition as increasing linguistic structuring of experience and symbolic behaviour control. In J. V. Wetsch (ed.) *Culture, Communication and Cognition: Vygotskian Perspectives*, London: Cambridge University Press.

Saussure, F. de (1960) *Course in General Lingistics* ed. C. Bally and A Sechehaye, London: Peter Owen.

Shotter, J. (1969) A note on a machine that 'learns' rules. *British Journal of Psychology* 59, pp. 173–7.

Shotter, J. (1974) The development of personal powers. In M. P. M. Richards (ed.) *The Integration of a Child into a Social World*, Cambridge: Cambridge University Press.

Vygotsky, L. S. (1962) *Thought and Language*, ed. and trans. E. Hanfmann and G. Vakar, Cambridge, Mass: MIT Press.

Vygotsky, L. S. (1966) Development of the higher mental functions. In *Psychological Research in the USSR*, ed. A. N. Leont'ev, A. R. Luria and A. Smirnov, Moscow: Progress Publishers.

Wittgenstein, L. (1953) *Philosophical Investigations*, Oxford: Basil Blackwell.

Wittgenstein, L. (1980) *Remarks on the Philosophy of Psychology*, vols 1 and 2, Oxford: Basil Blackwell.

Wittgenstein, L. (1981) *Zettel*, 2nd edn, ed. G. E. M. Anscombe and G. H. V. Wright, Oxford: Basil Blackwell.

14

The Realism of the Symbolic

Charles W. Smith

This essay could be considered in part an ethnography of an ethnography in so far as it relates some of the ways Rom Harré', both through his written work and daily life, has informed much of my own ethnographic work. I think that this is apt, since Rom's influence has generally been both professional and personal.

Rom Harré' snuck up on me. I wasn't expecting him and I really wasn't ready for him. As an American sociologist with a classical philosophical background, concerned with the philosophy of the social sciences, having a predilection for interpretive orientations, negatively disposed towards positivism, attracted if not seduced by Goffman, and evangelical when it came to George Herbert Mead, I first encountered Rom in the mid-seventies through Paul Secord, their book *The Explanation of Social Behaviour*, and the journal they jointly edited, *The Journal for the Theory of Social Behaviour*. A year in Oxford in 1979–80 coupled with a conference in Houston, which led to *Explaining Human Behavior*, further cross Atlantic travels on both of our parts, and my further involvement in the *Journal for the Theory of Social Behaviour* solidified what has become for me a most stimulating and rewarding personal and intellectual relationship.

I review these facts because they report some of the reality of Rom and his career, namely his ubiquitous 'causal powers', which support and reinforce his written work. Put slightly differently, Rom exhibits in his daily life many of the points that he has argued for in his theoretical writings. Moreover he has managed through his peripatetic activities as well as through his written works to induce others to recognize some of these same truths and to incorporate them within their own work, though, I should add, often not in the same way that he does. It is impossible for me in the limited space available to do little more than sketch some personal evidence in support of this proposition. I have elected to focus on two issues: the causal powers of agents and social structures and the relative importance of expressive rather than instrumental concerns in human affairs.

In the late seventies, I discovered that I had contacted, like nearly all sociologists trained in the early sixties, a case of incipient functionalism *à la* Parsons. I should note that there were benefits in this condition. For one thing, unlike many of my less fortunate colleagues in psychology and philosophy who had been seduced by positivism and behaviourism, I knew all about norms and rules. I even knew something about their inherent social nature. Unfortunately, like most sociologists I had a tendency to reify norms and rules to such a degree that not only had causal agents ceased to be of much relevance, but causality itself had become irrelevant as an explanatory concept. It really was not so much an issue of an over-socialized view of man, as it was an over-normatized view of everything. Rom was central in this new awareness.

Given that Rom has expended so much energy pointing out the degree to which human behaviour is governed by norms, rules, accounts, etc., it may seem strange that he should have sensitized me to this over-reliance on norms. The reason he was able to do this is that, like Goffman and unlike Parsons, Rom has always been highly sensitive to the role of agency in maintaining social orders. On the other hand, it must also be noted that although Rom has been one of the most forceful and articulate spokesmen for a realist conception of science, he seems subject to what I have elsewhere referred to as 'phenomenological drift' when it comes to the social sciences. That is, he tends to turn his back on his realism and accepts a highly phenomenological and interpretive view of human behaviour. In what follows, therefore, I would like to follow Rom in highlighting the importance of the expressive order in social life but to do so more within a realism context.

My research of auctions these last few years is in large measure a result of my newly awakened interest in the interplay among normative orders, human interests and capabilities, and social practices and structures. My fascination with various types of auctions has been and is due primarily to the fact that they so dramatically reflect the mutual causal influences of agency and social structures. It is all there: the social drama; the continual construction of both social beings and social structures; the exercise of various capabilities and powers. Would I have been able to see what I have seen without Rom Harré? I really do not know. Others, especially Bhaskar, Giddens and Manicas, have in recent years greatly influenced my work. Interestingly, many of these other persons have themselves been strongly influenced by Rom. What I do know is that Rom has served as one of the most persistent and irresistible gadflies.

The most common and classic view is to see auctions as embodying the best examples of 'rational economic man'. More specifically, from a conventional economist's perspective auctions are primarily exchange structures organized within a set of given parameters to match most efficiently preference sets of sellers and buyers. The goal is exchange with the determination of the selling price being the means. Most importantly, participants act in terms of their own known 'instrumental' interests with minimal external constraints. This is not to imply that environmental factors are ignored or that interest may not change through the auction process. Different studies have attempted to show how different conditions affect the decision-making of participants. What is not included in this perspective is a concern with the way the actual auctioning process serves to create/recreate both social definitions and social relationships. Participants are rather seen as participating in auctions as individuals with their own predetermined price expectations. Auctions are not conceived as processes whereby participants appropriate meanings which are concurrently being socially generated nor as means for generating and maintaining social relationships. As a consequence of the above, the critical expressive component of auctions is traditionally ignored.

In point of fact, this is exactly what most auctions are. Put slightly differently, they are processes not only of exchange, but also means for managing ambiguity by establishing social meanings and values. The sources of the ambiguity, however, vary from auction to auction. Sometimes the ambiguity revolves primarily around supply, at other times around demand, and at other times around 'inherent' value; in most cases there is also considerable ambiguity regarding the fungibility of the items in question. Finally, there is often a good deal of ambiguity regarding allocation which is quite separate from the issue of price. Each type of ambiguity requires slightly different methods of resolution. In nearly all auctions, therefore, it is not simply a question of matching the expectations of buyers and sellers, but of establishing these expectations. Equally important is the fact that the resolution of ambiguity occurs within a community of some sort. (Tensions among buyers and among sellers are often greater and more significant than those between buyers and sellers.) It is these communities that provide the context within which the resolutions are sought. Moreover and significantly, the auction process itself is constrained by the need to maintain these communities.

It is clearly beyond the scope of this paper to describe in detail how these various factors work in different types of auctions let alone present all the necessary supporting evidence.[1] I can perhaps suggest how my research findings support the dramaturgical view of social behaviour fostered by Rom Harré. More specifically, auctions are revealed to be highly expressive processes for defining ambiguous situations in which there is competition not only for goods, but also for personal power, status and honour.

What gives auctions their particular attraction is that they reveal in a clear way how the expressive/normative/dramaturgical aspect of human behaviour needs a grounding within a realist context.

I earlier (dogmatically) rejected the classical micro-economic view of auctions. This has important implications since the 'rational economic man' conception of auctions serves as the proto-type of economic exchanges in general. In rejecting the classical view of auctions, I in effect rejected the classical view of economic behaviour in general. This I am more than happy to do. In contrast to the classical view, I would argue that most economic behaviour, like other types of human behaviour, is rule-governed where the rules are embedded within shared worldviews. Where auctions differ from such other economic transactions is in that they are explicitly concerned with generating such interpretive frameworks.

The reason for this is that they emerge primarily in ambiguous situations, i.e. situations where values and allocation procedures are unclear. Such values and allocation procedures are, in turn, unclear because the normal methods for resolving such questions prove inadequate. This may be due to the fact that the goods can not be assigned meaningful cost/labour or replacement values because of artistic nature, age or use; uncertainty over supply and demand because of highly perishable and/or very unpredictable contingency factors; or because of variabilities in grading which generate fungibility problems. In short, the lack of interpretive clarity relates directly to the lack of structural consistency.[2]

That auctions exist in situations of structural and definitional uncertainty, explains in part why auctions tend to be used primarily with highly perishable goods, used goods, goods of questionable origin, and goods seen to posses certain artistic merit. In all of thes cases, there is a relatively high degree of value ambiguity because the goods cannot be related easily to a standard market of a standard/accepted formula for evaluation. The one other major category of auctions are those where, for fiduciary or other reasons, there is need to legitimate the price and/or allocation of a transaction. As in the other cases, this is also an instance of normal definitions and rules being seen as inadequate.

So defined, auctions clearly embody the various elements which Rom has stipulated as fundamental in human behaviour. Equally, if not more importantly, they also suggest why this should be the case. The emphasis, however, is somewhat different from that of Rom's.

For Rom, the driving force behind most social behaviour is the pursuit of honour and respect. As he argues in the beginning of *Social Being*, 'pursuit of reputation in the eyes of others is the overriding preoccupation of human life, though the means by which reputation is to be achieved are extraordinarily various' (1981, p. 3). There is much that goes on in auctions that would seem to support this view. Most auction participants are quite consciously engaged in making personal statements about themselves. 'Here I am!' they proclaim. 'Take me seriously!' In some cases, such as the premier art, antique and horse auctions where bids may reach into the millions of dollars, bidders often seem more concerned with their own 'presentation of self' than with the item being auctioned. In some situations, such presentations of selves by persons such as a major collector, museum curator, dealer or breeder may primarily be a case of maintaining one's position. In other situation, e.g. the new or aspiring dealer, racehorse owner or art collector, the emphasis seems to be upon acquiring status, prestige and honour. There are clearly other times, however, when this is not the case.

In many auction situations, some participants seem deliberately to avoid attention. The image of the major buyer sitting quietly and inconspicuously in the middle of the auditorium bidding with a raised eyebrow or a flick of his head is well known.[3] Other buyers rely on telephone bids or others to bid for them. Here it may be argued that this is just a case of particular buyers fearing that they will drive the price up if others know that they are bidding. In point of fact, however, aggressive bidding by a wealthy and knowledgeable buyer can and will keep the price down as well as drive it up. Some people are much more willing to bid against an unknown bidder than against a known power. In a similar vein, it is also true that though many auctions seem to be organized to enhance the social and expressive aspect of the auction, others seem organized deliberately to play down these facets.

The fact that auction participants do not always pursue honour and respect would indicate that honour and respect are not necessarily ends in themselves. They would rather seem to be means to some other ends. The question is what ends. The answer, I would suggest, has already been alluded to above, namely, 'a definition of the situation'.[4] Auctions flourish in situations of value and allocation ambiguity and uncertainty. They serve to resolve such ambiguities by establishing specific values for specific items at a specific time, though there are clearly broader implications for the definctions generated. In this respect, auction could be considered prototypes of many other types of social processes. The pursuit of honour and respect is a means for individuals to position themselves in this process. Honour and respect are not so much ends in themselves as resources that can be used in exerting influence in the collective enterprise of defining the situation. They are not, however, as auctions reveal, the only means. The situation is even more complex than the above might indicate since honour and prestige are not only resources to be used in defining the situation but also outcomes of such definitions. Here again it may be more common for individuals to work for definitions which convey on them honour and prestige, but there are individuals who may seek to avoid such definitions. The fact is that individual honour and prestige are only one element in any definition of the situation.

By refocusing on 'defining the situation', rather than the pursuit of respect and honour, we manage to recapture the basic social nature of the process in contrast to the more individualistic emphasis implicit in the search for honour and respect thesis. It also allows us to push our analysis of the process further toward its realist foundations. More specifically it allows us to ask the question 'Why this concern with generating, maintaining, and/or changing the definition of the situation?'

This question may appear to have already been answered. It was argued that the process of defining the situation, in auctions at least, is in response to the inherent ambiguity of the situations. Put slightly differently, the process of establishing some meaningful account is in response to the absence of such an account. This brings us to the crux of the matter. Why the need for such accounts? Rom would argue, and I would heartily agree, because that is the nature of human behaviour. It is reflexive and rule-governed. In order for there to be human behaviour as we know it consequently there must be a pertinent symbolic universe.

To ask further why this should be so, obviously takes us into evolutionary pre-history. Humans are minded creatures who live their lives within symbolic universes. How we got this way no one knows for sure. Nevertheless, there is a general tendency to attribute to meanings an ordering capacity, and to this ordering capacity, in turn, various instrumental advantages. The general view seems to be that human reasoning somehow allowed the species to better adapt and manage his environment. Rom fortunately does not seem to fall into this trap. The symbolic universe remains for him primarily a means for expressive and ritualistic behaviours of a highly social nature. Here he correctly gives much more emphasis to the social solidarity aspect of the symbolic than to its instrumental advantages. What is overlooked and what relates back to the pursuit of honour is the fact that meanings and symbols do not in and of themselves generate either solidarity or order. In fact, a good case could be made for just the opposite position, namely, that they are a source of disorder and dissension. This is one of the paradoxes of symbolic forms.

Although, as noted above, it is impossible to do more than to speculate on the origins of the symbolic capacity of the species, it seems reasonable, following in the footsteps of George Herbert Mead and others, to attribute this capacity to the species peculiar reflexive capabilities related to its reliance upon vocal gesturing, highly developed central nervous system and high sociability. As sight, sound and other sense of organisms increase awareness of environmental contexts, so this reflexive capacity allows humans to experience behavioural relationships symbolically thereby expanding qualitatively their awareness of their environment. Mind reveals behavioural connections, i.e. this act will normally result in this, which will normally result in that, etc., which are revealed through the other senses only through the behavioural process itself. There is nothing about these connections in and of themselves, however, which simplifies things. Just the reverse. A meaningful world, because it is that much more multifarious and complex, is inherently less ordered.

The process of generating a meaningful order requires work. Moreover, the maintenance of any symbolic order produced requires continual effort. To give an auction example, the fact that a number of individuals have placed a value on an object does not serve to resolve the question of the objects value. Since their assessments normally differ considerably, such definitions in and of themselves only serve to confuse matters. To resolve these differences it is necessary to establish fairly complex social mechanisms. In contrast, young children in a room filled with toys normally manage to allocate and exchange goods employing much simpler mechancisms, even if on occasion such mechanisms may include a yank, a scream or a smack.[5]

If there are apparently no immediate benefits to symbolic universes, one may question why they seem to have flourished. The fact is they have not. So far only one species, namely the human species, seems to have gone that particular route. In this particular case, the primary benefit appears to be the unique type of bonding associated with the mutuality of consciousness made possible by symbolic reasoning. To achieve such bonding, however, symbols must be shared. It is in this context that ordered worldviews acquire their appeal, since the more ordered a worldview the more easily it can be maintained and shared.[6] Put slightly differently, I am suggesting that fundamental appeal of the symbolic is its potential for bonding, but in order for this potential to be fully realized the symbolic must be organized into comparatively simply and order systems. This in turn required grounding the symbolic in collective behavioural processes. Ideational, i.e. normative/meaningful/symbolic, orders not only inform behavioural practices, they also emanate from such practices. The expressive order, in short, is not something which is merely projected unto behaviour by actors for individual self enhancement, but inherent in social structures.

This relationship is supported by a wide range of practices associated with auctions of varying sorts. It is perhaps most vividly reflected, however, in the different ways 'auctions' and 'markets' evolve. This same contrast between 'auctions' and 'markets' also sheds considerable light on both the dramaturgical/expressive aspect of social life and the pursuit of honor and respect.

Why is it that the New York Stock Exchange, which functions primarily as a double auction,[7] is commonly referred to as the 'stock market' while people refer to the auction of bonds as an auction? Why is it that people enquiring about what happened on a given morning at the Boston fish exchange will normally ask about the 'market' rather than the 'auction', while people enquiring about a particular horse sale at Kenneland's *will* ask about the 'auction'? Why will the sale of a crudely made footstool given to Rock Hudson by Elizabeth Taylor for $1200 cause hundreds of people at Doyle's to burst into applause while the sale of a diamond brooch for over $100,000 causes hardly a ripple?

The answer in all of these cases is tied to the degree of uncertainty and related creative opportunities associated with the evaluation process. As noted earlier, the most natural/normal method of economic exchange is not by auction, but rather through a fixed price system. Like other forms of social behaviour, most economic behaviour occurs within an ideational consensus of sorts which allows the participants to set prices according to certain standards. It is true that some participants may not be aware of how such fixed prices are determined but there is a general sense of trust that some 'legitimate' method was used. There are instances when there is sufficient uncertainty over the value of a particular item that negotiations over price occur. These exchanges are commonly referred to as private treaty or bargaining exchanges. What is interesting about these exchanges and consistent with points made earlier is that normally such negotiations occur within the context of some encompassing consensus. That is the disagreement is usually limited to the specific qualities of the given object not the more abstract principles of evaluation. Parties negotiate the price by pointing out specific qualities of the object and relating these qualities to various apparently shared criteria.

Auctions differ from both fixed price and private treaty system in that the degree of ambiguity is such that such negotiations are inadequate. There is usually the added problem of there being a number of interested buyers and/or sellers. The solution in these situations is to circumvent negotiations and simply have buyers and sellers state what they are willing to pay or accept. In short, the solution is to have an auction.[8] It is also worth emphasizing if only to counter the notion that auctions are natural, that despite instances of auctions in earlier societies, the great growth of auction markets has occurred in modern, complex societies lacking normative homogeneity.[9] Where everyone 'knows' everyone else and everyone 'knows' what everything is 'worth', there is no need for an auction. Exchange is a fairly straightforward matter.

How particular participants decide what they will bid will depend upon many factors. The rules and practices for resolving ambiguity of different types of auctions will moreover themselves vary. One fairly constant convention, however, is the tendency to seek guidelines in past practices. Given the high degree of ambiguity and uncertainty associated with the normal parameters used in determining price, e.g. original costs, replication costs, supply, demand, alternative, etc., great weight is given to recent past exchanges. Unfortunately, there are considerable differences when it comes to assessing the particulars of past transactions. In some cases it is comparatively easy to find a series of fairly recent similar transactions; in other cases, it is very difficult. Put in the more common vernacular, in some cases there is a fairly continuous market whereas in other cases there is not.

Differences in the relative influence of past sales, i.e. the market, on an auction is perhaps the most important single difference between auctions. It also reflects the process of structuration as well as anything I know. When people look to the 'market' to determine what they should do, they are not examining any set of expectations *per se*. They are looking at past practices. Obviously these behavioural practices were themselves informed by past expectations but the expectations were grounded in the behaviours. While these past behaviours constrain and influence present decisions, they do not completely determine these decisions. There is always some room for movement. Once these new decisions are taken they in turn become part of the market, i.e. the ongoing behavioural process, which impacts on future decision-making.

The more constant and visible the market, the more it tends to dominate the process. It tends to override not only individual preferences, but social expectations *per se*. That is, it is the meanings embedded in past practices that dominates. This explains the common usages noted above. The New York Stock Exchange is an auction, but the constant and visible character of past transactions is such that the 'market' dominates the 'auction'. Decisions are made within the limits set by the market. Individual investors may and do attempt to determine what they believe to be the correct value of a company by engaging in all sorts of research and cogitations. Such analysis may lead them to want to buy or sell a particular stock at various prices. At any given moment, however, what they will sell or buy the stock for will be determined primarily by the market at that moment. Much the same conditions hold for many commodities where there is a daily market. In contrast, there are other goods which may be sold according to a much more erratic schedule. Thoroughbred yearlings, for example, are sold primarily once a year. Certain bonds may initially come to market on a monthly basis. In these cases, especially when there have been subsequent transactions in different secondary markets, the previous market may not seem quite as significant.

In these latter cases, the 'auction' is more likely to be seen as dominating the 'market'. Similarly, given that each new decision is less determined but more determining, the role of individual buyers and sellers is apt to be seen as more significant. Where even very sizeable transactions in the stock market are seen as transactions in the market rather than as individual purchasers and sales – '200,000 telephone at the market' – a major yearling purchase is likely to be perceived in much more personal terms – 'Maktoum just paid two and a half million for the Windfields' Danzig colt'. Given the greater visibility of individual participants in the less market-controlled auctions, it follows that such auctions offer more opportunities for self-expression and aggrandisement. There are, however, subtle variations that deserve to be noted.

In some market situations such as the stock market, it is very difficult for an individual to enhance himself through the actual act of buying or selling. As noted above, attention is focused on the market, i.e. the ongoing transactions, rather than on the participants. Individuals can enhance themselves, however, if they prove highly successful. Even then, however, such glory and status normally requires a good deal of public relations including, and this is of utmost importance, the presentation of some philosophy which explains the success.[10] Often, good public relations accompanied by an attractive market 'philosophy/strategy', proves sufficient without the actual market success.

The situation is somewhat different in the more face-to-face markets such as occur in many commodity exchanges. Again the emphasis is upon the market and apparent past success, but in these situations people do know who is buying and selling. As a consequence, individual status can and often does play a more direct role in the ongoing transactions. In these situations, however, it is not so much a case of acquiring status and glory as it is a case of the influence of such status. In the stock market, participants do not follow the lead of their status leaders in the actual buying/selling of stocks, because they do not known at any given moment what they are doing. At best they can only attempt to do what these leaders claim they have done or will do, but there is no interplay here between 'thoughts and actions'.

In face to face commodity auctions in contrast, others will often act in direct response to the actions of such status figures. If the decisions prove profitable, the status leaders will continue to prosper and to maintain their positions of leadership.[11] If the decisions prove unprofitable, the status leaders should cease to prosper and consequently to lose their positions of leadership. In short, where status in the stock market is both generated by the market and impacts on the market indirectly, status in face-to-face market can have direct impact on the market, though it is normally generated indirectly. The fact that status can seldom be acquired in such auctions, coupled with the tendency of others to follow status leaders, explains why some 'leaders' seek anonymity.

The situation is quite different in what could be called non-market auctions. In these situations there is no market to serve as the guideline. As such, each winning bid sets new guidelines and each winning bidder by definition is the 'status' leader, in so far as status leaders are those who set communal standards for that moment.

It might appear from what was just asserted that with sufficient resources one can actually buy status in such non-market auctions. To a large extent this is true. Part of the reason for this is that a number of checks that operate in market auctions don't hold in non-market auctions. In the first place, items sold through market auction tend to be resold through the same auction or through some secondary market within a relatively short period of time. Unless the original buyer is willing and able to maintain the market, the price will not be maintained and our high bidder will not only cease to be the 'price-setter', he will also look fairly silly. In non-market auctions this is often not the case. Neither the particular item bought nor anything quite like it need be exchanged for a considerable period of time. Furthermore, when and if another similar item does come up for sale, our leader can always step in again.

There is a second difference. As noted above, most market auctions deal in high multiples of similar items. As a result there are normally many buyers and sellers at any given time. The status leader in market auctions, even if he has established himself as such indirectly, directly affects the fortunes of others. If he is wrong, i.e. if the future market does not conform to his expectations, others get hurt. In contrast, most non-market auctions deal with single items, be it a particular horse or a particular painting. Even if the price of that particular item in the future decreases, there will be few others hurt. It is consequently easier for a big spender in such non-market auctions to maintain his status even when proved wrong. There just aren't all those angry people waiting to knock him down a peg or two.

What, in effect, the above reflects is that the extent to which auctions are subject to an external 'reality' varies. It also indicates that there are different types of reality involved. In this regard, auctions of varying types are themselves part of a larger process. In all cases we confront an expressive order of some sort. These accounts differ, however, in terms of their individual versus collective status, the degree to which they are embedded in social practices, and the extent to which these social practices are themselves, constrained by 'natural', i.e. material processes.

In non-market auctions we encounter situations where what becomes the dominant account appears to be most free of external constraints of all sorts. Here individual interpretations tend to dominate especially given sufficient individual resources. The individual winning buyer sets the social price which in turn governs the exchange practices. In contrast, in fixed price systems the governing accounts tend to be social. That is, prices and allocation are governed by consensually accepted principles. Ongoing transactional practices and individual decision-making may modify such principles, but they are more often governed by them than vice versa. Individual accounts are consequently subject to external social constraints, but these constraints are themselves primarily ideational. In short, in both of these cases, transactional practices occupy a more secondary role.

The situation is just the reverse in what I have called market auctions. Here it is the past practices that dominate. Both individual and collective interpretations tend to be in response to past transactions. The stock market is, of course, a prime example of this process. Obviously, an individual with major resources may be able to influence such markets as will a collective judgment of some sort. There is clearly a sense, however, in which the major governing forces at work in such markets are past practices rather than either individual or collective interpretations *per se*. Somewhat ironically, this often generates more erratic markets than the other two cases.[12]

There is, however, another factor at work which can cross-cut the distinctions just made. I refer to the fact noted earlier, namely the impact of material processes. In some non-market auctions such as fine art auctions, for example, all that may be required to maintain a given definition of value is sufficient resources to support the market. In others, however, such as thoroughbred auctions, however, this is more difficult because the million dollar yearling is expected to race eventually. Even here, sufficient sums can delay, if not avoid, the day of reckoning. The horse, for example, can be retired directly to breeding. Correspondingly, it can legitimately be argued that even with a painting time will tell in the end. There remains a significant difference here, however, in that what will tell in the end with the painting is a social consensus influenced by patterns of social behaviour whereas in the case of the million dollar yearling we are dealing with a process which is to a large extent non-social.

Similar differences can be made among fixed price markets. Many markets seem to be highly respondent to social expectations. Others seem much more susceptible to natural processes. Commodity prices, for example, seem to be determined at least in part by such things as the weather where the value of other items seem to be determined almost exclusively by supply and demand where the supply and demand is itself socially generated. Again, such distinctions must be made with care as evidenced by the present price of oil and the demise of the hula hoop.[13] In all of these cases, of course, as in the cases discussed earlier, it is not only a question of social versus natural processes at work, but also often a question of overlapping and competing social processes.

It is perhaps market auctions, however, where the impact of competing social processes is most apparent. It is these markets consequently which I would suggest are most reflective of the constraints of social reality as compared to either social expectations *per se* or material reality. Such auctions are obviously not immune to either social expectations or material processes. What is distinctive about them, however, is the extent to which present practices are constrained by past practices which themselves are embedded within a complex of practices. It is as embedded in such practices, moreover, that the expressive order becomes part of social reality. One could, of course, argue that all social accounts, whether embedded in practices, collective worldviews or individual perspectives, are 'real'. I would suggest, however, that there are significant differences between an account which is held by a given individual from one which is accepted by a collectivity and even a greater difference between these two types of accounts and one embedded in an ongoing practice. These differences influence the degree to which the account is subject to a wide range of other powers and limitations.

Humans cannot fly no matter how much they, either individually or collectively, may wish to do so, nor matter how often they, either individually or collectively, imagine they can. This reflects the constraints of the natural world. Some individuals are afraid to fly in an aeroplane while orthodox Jews as a group will not ride in a car on their sabbath. These instances reflect individual and collective ideational constraints. When you miss your plane because you could not get a taxi in the rain and the trip to the airport took an extra hour because of the Friday traffic, you were constrained by social reality. The purpose of this brief exercise has been to indicate some of these differences as they apply to one area of social life with which I have some familiarity.

NOTES

1 For a more detailed account of these specifics, see my *Auctions: The Social Construction of Value*, New York: Free Press, 1989.
2 The fact that agency is less visible in fixed price markets does not mean, of

course, that it is absent. It is the greater ambiguity of auctions that reveals agency at work. In fixed price markets, it is less obvious because it is embedded in the onging reproduction of the norms and rules which serve to resolve the questions which generate ambiguity in auction settings.

3 Though such practices are quite common, it should be pointed out that the corollary, namely, having the auctioneer take a bid from a person who inadvertently scratches his nose, is false. The auctioneer knows either through past practices or prearranged signals when a bid is a bid and when a nose scratch is a nose scratch.

4 It may be argued that such 'definitions' may result but that they are not the 'objectives' of participants. I can only counter by asserting that my evidence indicates that most participants are quite consciously interested in resolving definitional ambiguities. In this particular case, I am in strong support of Rom Harré's view that actors generally do know what they are about even if they don't always know.

5 We are obviously dealing with different levels of meaning here and consequently different levels of social order. Any meaning is inherently social and shared. The application of a given meaning to a particular experience and the organization of meanings into an integrated meaning system, however, are quite distinct activities requiring social cooperation of a different kind.

6 This fact is recognized by any group of persons who have attempted to fabricate a story to which they can all stick. The secret is to keep it as simple and as internally consistent as possible.

7 A double auction is one in which different prices are being offered simultaneously by both buyers and sellers.

8 There are, in fact, many different types of auctions including the English ascending auction, the Dutch descending auction, various form of simultaneously auctions, various types of sealed bid auctions, etc. For a good review of the various types see Ralph Cassady Jr, *Auctions and Auctioneering* (University of California Press: 1967).

9 The best early examples of auctions, namely Babylonian wives and slave auctions and Roman war booty auctions are also notable in that they dealt with 'goods' which were not part of the normal economic market.

10 For a detailed analysis of the importance of such accounts, see my *Mind of the Market: A Study of Stock Market Philosophies, Their Uses and Their Implications.*

11 The close relationship between success of both leaders and followers in these situations is tied to the fact that these types of auctions deal in multiple goods. As such the same price tends to be paid by all for the same type of goods on a given day.

12 That market auctions should be more erratic than the other forms of transaction is not that surprising. What is reflects is the more 'open' character of behaviour system as contrasted to the symbolic systems of either individuals or collectivities.

13 The point here being that it does seem possible to maintain prices despite surpluses whereas social fads seem to run their own 'natural' course.

238   *Charles W. Smith*

REFERENCE

Appadurai, Arjun (ed.,) (1986) *The Social Life of Things: Commodities in Cultural Perspective*, New York: Cambridge University Press.

Benn, S. I. and G. W. Mortimore (1976) *Rationality and Social Sciences*, London: Routledge & Kegan Paul.

Berger, Peter L. and Thomas Luckmann (1966) *The Social Construction of Reality*, Garden City, New York: Doubleday.

Bhaskar, Roy (1979) *The Possibility of Naturalism*, Brighton: Harvester Press.

Cassady, Ralph, Jr (1967) *Auctions and Auctioneering*, Berkeley and Los Angeles: University of California Press.

Clark, Robert E. (1973) *On the Block: An Ethnography of Auctions*, University of Montana: Doctoral dissertation.

Clark, Robert E. and Larry J. Halford (1978) 'Going.... going.... gone: preliminary observations on "deals" at auctions'. *Urban Life*, Vol. 7: pp. 285–307.

Engelbrecht-Wiggans, Richard, Martin Shubik, Robert M. Stark (eds) (1983) *Auctions, Bidding and Contracting: Uses and Theory*, New York: New York University Press.

Giddens, Anthony (1976) *New Rules of Sociological Method*, New York: Basic Books.

Giddens, Anthony (1979) *Central Problems in Social Theory*, Berkeley and Los Angeles: University of California Press.

Giddens, Anthony (1981) *The Constitution of Society*, Berkeley and Los Angeles: University of California Press.

Goffman, Erving (1974) *Frame Analysis*, New York: Harper & Row.

Granovetter, Mark (1985) 'Economic action and social structure: a theory of embeddedness', *American Journal of Sociology* November.

Harré, Rom (1981) *Social Being*, Totowa: Rowman & Littlefield.

Harré, Rom and Paul Secord (1972) *The Explanation of Social Behaviour*, Oxford: Basil Blackwell.

Manicas, Peter T. (1987) *A History and Philosophy of the Social Sciences*, Oxford: Basil Blackwell.

Manicas, Peter T. and Alan Rosenberg (1985) 'Naturalism, epistemological individualism and "The Strong Programme" in the sociology of knowledge', *Journal for the Theory of Social Behaviour*, 15.

Margolis, Joseph, Peter T. Manicas, Rom Harré and Paul F. Secord (1987) *Psychology: Designing the Discipline*, Oxford: Basil Blackwell.

Mead, George Herbert (1934) *Mind, Self and Society*, Chicago: University of Chicago Press.

Milgrom, P and R. J. Weber (1982) 'A theory of auctions and competitive bidding', *Econometrica*, September 1982, 50, 1089–122.

Riley, J. G. and Samuelson, W. F. (1981) 'Optimal auctions', *American Economic Review*, June 1981, 71 381–92.

Reitlinger, Gerald (1961) *The Economics of Taste*, Vol. 1, London: Barrie & Jenkins.

Reitlinger, Gerald (1963) *The Economics of Taste*, Vol. 2, London: Barrie & Jenkins.

Reitlinger, Gerald (1970) *The Economics of Taste*, Vol. 3, London: Barrie & Jenkins.

Smith, Charles W. (1979) *A Critique of Sociological Reasoning*, Oxford: Basil Blackwell.

Smith, Charles W. (1981) *The Mind of the Market*, Totowa: Rowman Littlefield (paperback, 1983, Harper Colophon).

Smith, Charles W. (1982) 'On the sociology of mind', in *Explaining Human Behavior*, ed. Paul F. Secord, Los Angeles: Sage Publications.

Smith, Charles W. (1983) 'A case study of structuration: the pure bred beef business', *The Journal for the Theory of Social Behaviour*, Vol. 13, No. 1.

Smith, Charles W. (1989) *Auctions: The Social Construction of Value*, New York: Free Press.

Smith, Vernon L. (1967) 'Experimental studies of discrimination versus competition in sealed-bid auction markets', *Journal of Business*, January, 40(1), pp. 56–84.

Smith, Vernon L. (1982) 'Microeconomic systems as an experimental sciene', *American Economic Review*, December, 72(5) pp. 923–55.

Smith, Vernon L. (1986) 'Experimental methods in the political economy of exchange', *Science*, Vol. 234 pp. 167–73, 10 October.

Thurow, Lester C. (1983) *Dangerous Currents*, New York: Random House.

Turner, Ronny E. and Kenneth Stewart (1974) 'The negotiation of role conflict: a study of sales behavior at the auction', *Rocky Mountain Social Science Journal* 11: 85–96.

Vickrey, W. (1961) 'Counterspeculation, auctions and competitive sealed tenders', *Journal of Finance*, 16: 8–37.

Zukin, Sharon and Paul Dimaggio (1986) *Theory and Society* (15), special issue on Economy and Society.

15

Work in Organizations as Social Activity

Jose Luis Rodriguez Lopez

The purpose of this essay is to apply Rom Harré's conceptual framework to the social activity that is produced as work in organizations. Although Harré only has some reflections by way of an appendix to *Social Being* (1979) on this theme, we can certainly pick out various other fruitful ideas and concepts when he refers, in several chapters of the book, to institutions. We think, then, that this conceptual apparatus will allow us to achieve a useful job of clarification on the point at issue.

Harré states in *Social Being* that the expressive dimension dominates absolutely the process of material production in modern society; somewhere further on he adds that one can understand the way work is organized only by looking at the interactions between the expressive and practical systems.

The first statement, though, seems too strong, as it uses the term 'absolutely', whereas we cannot omit the structural point of view in any work organization if we are to have an adequate examination of the interaction between practical and expressive systems. Taking the latter, the expressive system, we shall look at informal institutions, the development of moral careers and the dramaturgical considerations that come into collective bargaining, ending with the study of the expressive aspects of value systems towards work.

We shall start with a short historical survey of work in industrial society to provide an introduction to the temporal dimension of work organization and to help to put work activity into context as it actually develops and future perspectives which appear.

Going back to the beginnings of industrial society, we can see that the commencement of factory work presupposes the removal of workers from their domestic workshops and even the expropriation of their working tools (Coriat, 1979). This process is carried out with much opposition on the part of the first proletarians, opposition which takes the form of being late for work (with the excuse of the scarcity and high price of watches), unjustified absences, and so on. Resistance to manufacturing work and the subsequent forms of organization it assumes will bring different reactions and create different informal institutions.

Getting closer to our time, at the beginning of the twentieth century, Taylorism arises as a way of work organization branded as scientific, and which we should characterize as purely instrumental, preventing the flourishing of the expressive dimension in workers. Stopwatches are constituted as refereees in measuring times used in task performance, at the same time alienating those who work from their professional abilities and skills and blocking their need to be able to display character and gain or lose reputation and dignity in their moral career. A career has to revolve around work, since this activity occupies the greater part of the worker's time, with working days that we would now judge excessive and exhausting. So far, economic exploitation and the consideration of man as a machine has led to several forms of resistance, from the trade unions' total confrontation to other forms such as turnover, absenteeism or cutting productivity, that is to say, the opposite of what Taylor proposed to achieve but which he nevertheless brought about to some extent.

Elton Mayo, who started with a scheme similar to that of Taylorism, broke away from it, in spite of the error in many of his conclusions and his dimension as publicist and ideologist of human relations (Rose, 1975). Mayo emphasized important aspects of working life. In attempting the social legitimization of industrial sociology and psychology, he provided a concept of the organization of work which makes room for expressive aspects of the worker. If, as was to be shown, productivity did not increase in direct relation to job satisfaction, nor were workers pathological beings, responsive to therapy when something went wrong at the job, Mayo demonstrated that, at least in the experimental field, the possibility of increased reputation exemplified by the Hawthorne effect, produced some increase in output which Taylor could have acquired with his method of scientific management. Nevertheless, Mayo's ideas fell on deaf ears in most organizations.

Mayo also stated another phenomenon of great important to the social psychology of organizations: the existence of informal groups outside the formal structure of an organization. Such groups were ruled by their own laws with respect to behaviour in the factory and standards of production, and are furnished with leaders very different from the powers designed by management to exercise control in the company. This topic attracted much attention and there were several attempts at bringing together formal and informal leadership in order to increase levels of efficiency by agreement with the workers. Informal groups also afforded their membership the ability to develop moral careers and the achievement of dignity and worth which was blocked or prevented by industry.

Nevertheless the bosses and employers' struggle against the loss of control over their enterprises continued. Taylorism gave way to Fordism, that is, to the assembly line, with a form of work organization that thwarted once more any possibility of realizing the expressive system. There were a new burgeoning of more or less concealed forms of rebellion which were reduced with the coming of World War II.

The postwar years, in Western industrial countries, initated a cycle of great prosperity reflected in the thesis of working-class bourgeoisification and full employment. It emphasized that at times of industrial crisis or recession, the main concern lies in the practical domain, because of the threat of unemployment. At times of economic development and low unemployment, there are attempts at attaining greater satisfaction for the workers. This was the case in the 1970s. Moreover, the working day also became shorter and shorter and workers' level of consumption increased all circumstances which led to the start of the discussion of leisure and the enjoyment of free time for community, family and recreational activities, opening up potentialities hitherto unrealized for the development of a moral career for workers for the most part within working organizations. At that time talk began of the cracking of the Calvinist work ethic and the appearance of a new ethic of leisure where work no longer holds the first place in the hierarchy of working-class values.

Concern with these topics contributed to American industrial sociology taking up Marx's concept of alienation, though with a different meaning. Alienation, according to Blauner (1964), does not refer so much to the worker's lack of control over the means of production and over the final product as to the feeling of lack of control produced by a particular work organization – a deficiency experienced above all at the assembly line. We could label Blauner's research as an attempt to restore the expressive aspects of work.

Another attempt in the same direction was made by a group of industrial psychologists, following Mayo, who emphasize the worker's psychological frustration, produced by an authoritarian style of leadership. The key for this group, labelled the Human Relations movement was participation.

A new path opened up in industrial social psychology has to do with the relation between technology and work organization. For many years it was postulated and today it still continues to be stated in different contexts, that there is a one-to-one correspondence between a particular technology and the subsequent work organization dictated by it, in such a way that job satisfaction cannot be improved while technology prevents it. There have been industrial sociologists who have demonstrated that there is no one-to-one correspondence and therefore a given technology does permit several forms of work organization. The conception of a one-to-one correspondence is still retained by management in its attempt to hold control over workers and, if possible, to increase it (Clegg and Dunkerly, 1980). Thus there arose round the Tavistock Institute a group of social scientists focusing on a socio-technical system where there is a close relationship between social and technical subsystems so that work organization in an enterprise is the result of interaction between both systems.

A whole series of new approaches, attempting to better working conditions and their intrinsic qualities through job enlargement, job enrichment, the redesigning of jobs, autonomous groups and so on, postulate a model of man which is not automatic, and replace the behaviouristic mechanical approach and other dominant trends in psychology (Harré, 1980). It is a model close to the one advocated by Harré in *Social Being* and *Personal Being* where man is endowed with the capacity for action and therefore can originate social activity, possessing autonomy and reflexivity alike. Thus, the worker must be able to exercise his autonomy and his responsibility and to take decisions about his work and the way it is organized, trying at the same time to develop his expressive dimension in his working life.

This conception of man, and certainly of the worker, involves a democratization of work, some of it far off, at any rate up to now. While political democracy is well established in Western countries as regards its more or less continual existence in the last two centuries, the same success is not found in those countries with respect to work organizations. None would be surprised that the governments of those countries are elected by the vote of all the citizens, something unthinkable in fact in organizations and enterprises of every kind, public or private, whether committed to profit-making or non-profit-making, such as hospitals, schools, universities and so on. Quite the contrary. A stage of greater concern about workers is succeeded by another stage when management tries, through new technology, to recover control over the workers: this is what is really happening today. We are on the threshold of a new technical revolution with a still uncertain future. In the area of work highly contradictory views are presented. On the one hand, computer science affords increased job automatization and the possibility of rigid control over the worker's activity as it can report in great detail to the management about the time employed in the execution of the job, the routines used and so on. Add to it that new technologies have given rise to structural unemployment on a large scale which frighten employees and workers, leading them to accept conditions unacceptable some years ago, since at least in Spain, a person who holds a stable and well-paid job is considered to be a fortunate and privileged person.

We should find, apparently, at one of these stages, as we said above, maximum control, where the dominant model would be that of the machine worker who only needs to push a button now and again. However, this is not the whole truth. Automatic systems require what today is known as the committed worker. Intelligent, active cooperation is needed for the good functioning of these systems, since a major break-down could cause the collapse of the whole range of activities they support. Moreover, the workers do not want to give up the improvements they have achieved and they put forward labour demands not only of a quantitative order, but also for the betterment of the quality of life at work. Thus, the dilemma arises between robot man and autonomous and reflective man. While the majority of managers still yearn for the former type of worker, work organization and workers' claims would demand the second type, who can also develop a moral career to a certain degree within the workplace. Though this is becoming increasingly difficult to acquire, the possibility of more leisure time and the existence of more civil liberties in other aspects of society would lead to a leisure ethic where work occupies a secondary place, resulting perhaps in a reduction in the efficiency of the productive system (and perhaps in better health for the workers).

The Emergence of Informal Institutions

No wonder that, besides what we have said so far, the inflexibility of the different forms of work organization since the beginning of industrial society, has favoured the emergence of informal institutions, at times hidden and on the fringe of the organization's formal structure. We have already mentioned Elton Mayo's findings about the existence of informal groups in the Hawthorne plant, groups which not only facilitate the development of the expressive system, of the members of the group, but also affected standards of production.

To continue, Goffman (1960) carried on with this task from a different point of view in his work *Asylums*, although he makes no explicit refer-ence to work institutions apart from those he labels total institutions. Harré, like Goffman, brings into *Social Being* the study of informal institutions bound up with the development of the moral careers of social agents, adding a greater theoretical refinement to the predominantly descriptive work of Goffman. Harré tells us about the Turkish ulemas, about the ways of achieving reputation in Japanese society and about the phenomenon of British football hooligans.

On the subject of work, Mars (1982) and Ditton (1977) have done interesting research on the theme under discussion. In Mars' opinion 'fiddling' is directly related to the features of the job along two basic dimensions: work performance on one's own or in a group, and the degree of control the worker is subjected to in his job. 'Fiddling' is in itself an informal, hidden institution which acts on the margin of the formal structure of the institutions in which it occurs. There is also a particular type of 'fiddling', that found in jobs submitted to greater control and needing group co-operation. This type is evidence of our proposition. Informal groups possess great cohesiveness and a very elaborate structure. The moral career can be developed from systematic risks which permit not only the increase or the loss of reputation apart from the different positions to be occupied that offer different opportunities for 'fiddling'. It is also carried out in such a way that none of the group members has exclusive access to that practice.

Collective Bargaining

Collective bargaining in a given organization cannot be just considered as the result of two parties with opposite interests (mainly economic), management and trade unions. This is the concept of a materialist dialectic which neglects, if not denies, the expressive dimension of social agents in confrontation in the bargaining process.

In fact, collective bargaining in Western societies comprises a situation where episodes of social action are structured in a format which is repeated at different times and where both parties put in motion a rethorical and ritual display which emphasizes the importance of the expressive system. We could say that an adequate system of collective bargaining might be undertaken with the use of a dramaturgical model, described by Goffman (1974) and developed by Harré in greater theoretical detail.

To illustrate it, we shall show the structure of collective bargaining which takes place in the Spanish Telephone Company (Compañia Telefónica Nacional de España) where the author has carried out research during the last decade. We shall employ three stages for the analysis.

The first act begins with the constitution of the Joint Negotiating Committee (composed of an equal number of members from management and trade unions with an independent President elected by both parties' mutual consent). The scene is set with the negotiating body occupying the front of the stage, the focus of the footlights. Trade union representatives put forward their claims for negotiation, including a wide range of topics such as salaries, working conditions, job security and so on. The apple of discord is usually economics. Claims in this instance, like others, tend to be far from what it is calculated that the management is ready to accept. There will always be time for reducing them.

The management representatives' answer is nevertheless laconic, paying attention to very few points in the claims of the trade union representatives. The economic counter-offer is very much lower than the claims put forward. All the conditions are there for the drama, which from its first act will be seen to be a violent one. During the first three or four weeks of negotiation, the deliberations resemble a discussion among deaf people. Each of the parties works out its discourse to play to the gallery, positions apparently toughen in such a way that bargaining may come to a standstill at any moment. At the end of this act the trade unions in their official releases to workers denounce the stand taken up by management and threaten to call for protest action.

In the second phase protest begins on a small scale (some of the employees concentrate on the Company's Head Office where the President works, trade union representatives lock themselves in their offices for two or three days, public demonstrations are held in the city centre), delaying more serious action (some hours' stoppage for two or three days or even for a whole working day). Protest actions are planned with an eye on public opinion and telephone users, in an attempt to discredit the company's public image. Nevertheless, trade unions try to avoid strikes of long duration, knowing from previous experience that the telephone service has achieved a high degree of automatization with few employees needed for software maintenance, so that a strike takes a long time in order to affect the service, time which the employees are not ready to support, with the consequent damage to their own unions.

During this phase, however, real bargaining takes place behind the scenes. Meanwhile at the official negotiating committee the demands and counter-demands continue, leading to the creation of parallel working committees where partial agreement is reached on matters to be brought up later in the Joint Committee.

The third phase, as in a play, corresponds to the *denouement* which unsually comes very quickly. Management, displaying a talent for negotiation and democratic behaviour, appears to make a great effort to approach the trade union's claims. The unions, for their part, have to make their audience understand that the management's offers are positive and that they have achieved success in the bargaining process, a success to be shared with the audience, and one which will provide them with a better public image.

The agreements made behind the scenes will come to the forefront and there is a move towards drafting the final text, in marathon sessions which may last many hours into the night. From this moment there remains only the signing, and the curtain falls. The negotiators congratulate each other and a ritual dinner firmly seals the agreement that has been achieved.

The usefulness of the dramaturgical model is evident since its distinctive elements are clearly identifiable: script, actors, performance played on stage and work behind the scenes, audience and the structure of the episodes. If any of the script is missing – for instance, the trade unions' ritual show of strength, management will make no concessions and, on the other hand, if management does not show itself to be tough at the outset, the audience may suspect that bargaining is pre-arranged between the two sides which appear as antagonists.

However, extreme situations should never be reached; excessive harshness from management would put trade unions in a difficult position, in which they would have to resort to serious measures such as a strike, and this would reflect negatively upon the company's image. Unions, for their part, will have to make concessions, retreating from some of their earlier demands, since there is prior knowledge that their first demands were very high, and there is no problem in cutting them down later on.

In those circumstances where collective bargaining brings about very conflicting situations, one has to look for new elements in its analysis, as follows.

Strikes

Harré makes some interesting remarks about strikes in his treatment of social change (Harré, 1979), taking as an example British coal strikes from two different periods. But we are going to look at the interaction between the expressive and practical systems, as we have been doing up to now. Strikes cannot be considered exclusively within the practical system, as we just have shown. In a strike, beside the demand for increase wages and the improvement of working conditions, there is an important claim for dignity on the part of workers and their representatives. The increasing importance of those expressive aspects can be exemplified more dramatically in the case of strikes we may call political. And for this we shall look at two recent cases in Spain.

In the first case we may mention the strikes that occurred in the last years of Franco's dictatorship and the first years of the transition to democracy. Demands and the reasons given by the workers for their strikes always went beyond economic considerations. In fact, during those years wage increases were higher than during the democratic era. The main reason was the attainment of trade union and deomcratic liberties – of expression, association and the right to demonstrate, and of course, the freedom to strike, something not permitted by the old regime. Democratic liberties provided above all a better chance of dignity and respect for workers and citizens, and even the achievement of a moral career.

Take another, even more recent, example. The Socialist government recently established an obligatory limit of 5 per cent for wage increases in all public companies (transport, ship building, ironworks, etc.). But the government's economic policy did not stop there. The huge industrial reconversion that has taken place, the rise in unemployment, the increased opportunities for redundancy, have driven the unions, including the socialist-inspired union of which all cabinet ministers are nominal members, to reject such an economic policy. The last straw that broke the camel's back came with derogatory comments towards trade unions from several ministers.

All this set off a wave of conflict and many strikes in the public sector, since private employers showed themselves more prepared to go beyond the wage limits. In fact the majority of agreements have gone beyond the limit fixed by the government, though in some cases the workers have received only a few hundred pesetas over the limit. But dignity has been restored, with a public demonstration that workers are not willing to bear the burden of the crisis, still less when they are publicly despised.

These examples are once again evidence that when the protagonists, in this case the workers, cannot achieve recognition of their dignity through official rhetoric, they turn to the building up and/or maintenance of informal institutions or to forms of rebellion that allow them, through a different rhetoric, to achieve recongition as autonomous and reflective beings, worthy of the respect which society denies them.

The Future of the World of Work: Organizational Culture and Organizational Change

We have already said that in recent years we have seen a speeding up of technical innovation, leading to what some writers have called a new technical and scientific revolution. This involves major transformations in work organization, of acute concern to employees and workers who will perform the new jobs. Thus, there is talk also of the need to change attitude towards work. However, the matter is not so simple as would seem from the conclusions of Kurt Lewin and his followers. It is not enough to apply group dynamics to the workers. There is something else. This is the reason why some of the those who study organizations have included the concept so much in fashion now – that of organizational culture.

The basis of organizational culture is not only constituted by workers' attitudes towards work. Organizational or institutional culture consists of many factors, including rules and regulations, codes of duties and rights, rewards and sanctions, instructions on the performance of tasks and so on.

There are other factors of equal or greater importance than these, which are not reflected in written documents. These are implicit rules, specific ways of carrying out the job, behaviour patterns, the attitude to authority, the image of the company held by members of the organization and members of the surrounding community and especially the values that emphasize involvement, such as tenure, faithfulness, loyalty to superiors or values which the organization discourages such as independence, the ability to criticize, solidarity, etc. Further, the origin and history of the organization assume an importance of their own since values and official rhetoric vary from time to time, changing in consequence conditions that make possible the development of the moral careers of organization's members. Thus attitudes towards work are one more component of more holistic factors.

There cannot be organizational change, then, without a change in organizational culture, and this change presupposes a phenomenon much more complex than a mere change of attitude. Even that, in some cases, is difficult to obtain.

The complexity of cultural change is rooted in the fact that values tend to be deeply emebedded. We said above that values are developed over a period of time and provide the means of development of the moral career of the organization's membership, the socially acceptable forms of attaining respect, dignity and worth. A profound organizational change alters social interaction and it is not suprising that it meets with some degree of resistance from the membership. This is what is happening with the present technological revolution, where not only are traditional ways of everyday work on the job challenged and threatened, but also the actual existence of the job of work is in serious danger. The reconversions in different productive sectors have thrown millions of workers in the developed countries of the Western world into unemployment., Once again we are seeing the practical dimension.

So in fact, in many organizations, there are attempts to change methods of work organization with a negative gain without taking into account the cultural starting-point, endangering the company's efficency and its workers' job satisfaction.

The 'Telephone Spirit'

In this connection, we shall report an experiment which illustrates our thesis. The research was carried out by the author in the Spanish Telephone Company. The firm's beginnings go back to the 1920s when it was founded by the American ITT. After the Spanish Civil War, the company was nationalized, enjoying the monopoly of telephone and related services in Spain. Although it is a private company, the state owns about half of the stock which gives it a majority on the Board of Directors. This accounts for the company's political loyalty, and in turn the President is appointed by the government. The political connection was also evident during the forty years of dictatorship.

Once political transition began, a profound organizational change was needed, a change accelerated by new technology in the communications area, where the technical revolution has brought about more profound, swift change. However, organizational change results in failure in various spheres, producing high quotes of worker dissatisfaction and a loss of efficiency in the telephone service rental and other services offered by the company, such as the data transmission network, maritime radio operations and so on.

We set up a study of some features of organizational culture and then interpretation, interviewing members of the organization (Rodriguez, 1986a, 1986b). As an explanation of the cause of the company's deterioration, many employees said that the 'telephone spirit' (*espíritu telefónico*) had been lost. This was a term introduced by the company and accepted by most of membership, especially by all those who had worked for the company for some years. Tenure was an important feature in the company, perhaps the most important and most valued by everyone, especially the management.

People joined the firm with very low educational qualifications; job competence was achieved over the years, promotion and salary increased gradually with tenure, independently of performance. The culmination of the professional career came with retirement, where economic conditions and social benefits were the best. So it was important to stay on, and the longer the better. In fact, most of the personnel completed their entire professional career in the company. It was their birthplace and their end in the world of work. It is not surprising that tenure was a variable of the first magnitude in respect of to the work values and attitudes of the members of the Company.

But the 'telephone spirit' assumed other characteristics, and that is why we decided upon further investigation of this term in organization during the last forty years, together with the resources deployed to achieve respect or contempt, since the greater the 'telephone spirit', the better were the possibilities of advancing the moral career.

In our research we found that the 'telephone spirit' was not something shared equally by all members of the organization. The subjects interviewed made a distinction between the company's employees and the *telefónicos*. The former maintained a merely instrumental relationship with the company, while the latter were those imbued with the 'telephone spirit'. In general, it could be seen that the 'telephone spirit' increased with age and tenure in the organization, and decreased with the rise in educational level. It was found too that this spirit had decreased with the growth of the company's size.

What are the main features of the 'telephone spirit'? First, though not of prime importance, we mention job involvement, where work is the main interest of the worker's life, over and above the rest of his activities, including family life. Job involvement was apparently unlimited and some of its effects would today be considered harmful to the worker's psychological and physical health. We might say that in this case the shaping of the work ethic was peculiar to the Spanish industrial process. However, we cannot speak, in Spain, of a Calvinist ethic because of the almost total predominance of Catholicism. It is this religion that has cast its own peculiar influence. Paramount in our conclusions was the observation in the interviews of the emergence of religious and ecclesiastical metaphors. The company was seen as a special entity providing an essential service for the community, the establishment of telephone communications, a service which appears invested with sacred overtones, for when these communications are blocked for any reason, there was no more binding obligation than their restoration. The Telephone Company, then, is like a church, where its personnel are endowed with a quasi-sacerdotal character and a sacred mission. The anonymous character of the society, with no known ownership, and where the workers play a large part in the action, confirms these qualities. On the other hand, management itself fostered this characteristic, and job-training programmes contained a great deal of explicit ideology, where workers were instilled with a sense of their mission and privilege. In fact, the workers' own image of themselves, like that of their fellow citizens is that telephone employees enjoy a privileged situation compared with that of other workers. The Telephone Company created its own schemes for retirement, health, culture and entertainment, something unprecedented in Spain at that time.

A second feature, perhaps the most specific of the ideology we are considering, is the conception of the company as a family. It is a commonplace to speak of 'one big telephone family', a phrase on the tip of the tongue when questions are put on the topic; so that even very different presidents, when addressing messages to their employees at Christmas or on other occasions, have always used the commonplace widely shared, making reference to 'one big family'.

The conception of the company as one big family means the existence of an authority of paternal characters, where solidarity must be the rule between members, since all are brothers in the family. Thus, the leadership style in the company has been paternalistic and authoritarian.

Improvements achieved through collective bargaining were concessions which the father made when his children were good. This was helped by the absence of democratic unions. Existing unions were called vertical, since they combined employers and workers together within the same union, with the former holding the presidency.

But as we have said, it was at the same time an authoritarian style, since all the authority flowed from the top without any possibility of opposition. Criticism was an abuse, leading inexorably to ostracism, and the impossibility of promotion to more skilled responsible or management jobs.

In this patriarchal family, the woman's role was secondary. Although their numbers were higher in proportion than nowadays, they occupied the organization's lower echelons, and their chances of promotion were clearly limited. Moreover, most on the woman's payroll were telephone operators, subject to strong control, greater than that found in the other departments.

The importance of the family meant that it was the most important source of recruitment for new members of the organization. So, we find that even today almost 50 per cent of those on the payroll have relatives also working or who have worked for the company, and it is not unusual to find fathers and sons, husbands and wives in the company. Moreover, an overwhelming majority of employees want their children to work for the Company, believing too that it has a certain moral duty towards them, as they have devoted all their working life to it.

On the other hand, all the specific institutions we have mentioned, made it possible for the *telefónicos* to relate to each other within and outside work, at the doctor's surgery, on holiday, in leisure time devoted to cultural, recreational or sporting activities. At this point symbiosis is such that it is difficult to say whether the organization extends into the family, or vice versa. As a consequence of this trend, which reveals a high dominance of the expressive system, the extinction of the Company might have been predicted, on Harré's analysis in *Social Being*.

It is not surprising that the only possible response from subordinates to this paternalistic and authoritarian leadership style was submission to authority, so that the majority did not protest or rebel against situations intrinsically unfair according to present criteria. The 'father's' commands could not be bad since a father always wants the best for his children, in the words of one of those interviewed.

A third important feature was the exercise of authority by means of an iron discipline, of a markedly military character. The term 'military' is not ours, but the interviewees themselves refer to the company as an army and to life in the organization as similar to life in a barracks. In the 'telephone war' the men joined battle at the front, laying cables and lines, with the women at the rear, establishing communications.

This disciplinary system was so strict that those interviewed could even speak of the loss or denial of personality, something which Goffman (1961) attributes to total institutions. This loss was expressed by employees with reference to the fact that on their arrival at work they had to take off their own clothes and put on a uniform; their names were replaced by numbers serving as identification.

We have already said that discipline was even stronger for women, especially among operators (all of whom were female). Before coming on the job they had to be lined up in military style, and entered their work room at the ringing of a bell. There was an inspection not only of their working tools, but also of their personal appearance, the cleanness of their uniform and the length of their hair. Some of those interviewed described their life at work as similar in some respects to prison life.

The Indoctrination of the 'Telephone Spirit'

The transmission of this work ethic would begin during the first stages of job-training and continued in informal talks on the job, in management communiqués, etc. However, the family appears to have played the most prominent role. Employees' sons say that from their early childhood this spirit was their mother's milk. Another factor which makes up the 'telefonitis' syndrome, i.e. the process through which employees come to be *telefónicos*, is tenure. (The term 'telefonitis' refers to innoculation of the telephone spirit as if it were a virus.) When a worker has completed several years (about ten) in the company, the case for staying on is better than for leaving. This trend was accentuated in those categories closely related to the telephone service, since because the company enjoys a monopoly in this service, these jobs have no equivalent in the outside labour market. In these positions telephone spirit penetrated more deeply, ensuring a better, though not always efficient, commitment to the organization.

The Evolution of the 'Telephone Spirit'

The work ethic in this company has undoubtedly undergone changes during the last forty years. In the early 1940s the telephone spirit appeared bound up with the institutions that supported Franco's dictatorship. We have seen the allusions to the family, the Church and the Army. The Army and the Church afforded coercion and ideology, while the family helped transmit what has been labelled sociological Francoism, i.e. those acts of submission to authority and fear of recourse to forbidden civil rights, *inter alia* which presupposes a certain implicit acceptance of the political regime.

Nevertheless, in the mid-1960s there was a noticeable evolution, with the introduction of a degree of economic liberalism into the country, leading to an opening up to the outside world, and a relaxation not only economic, but also cultural, social and ideological.

In the Telephone Company this was a time of great expansion with considerable automatization of the telephone network. This involved the addition of much new personnel, not recruited exclusively from workers' families. The new members were young people with a higher educational level then that of their elders, and an ideological openness which showed that they were, if not almost unanimously opposed to the political regime, reluctant to accept it. This personnel was to form the powerful secret democratic unions, one of the pillars of opposition to the dictatorship.

We have argued throughout that informal groups emerge in any organization when people cannot officially develop their expressive dimension. It was to be expected, then, that in the Telephone Company there would also emerge informal institutions for many people not wholly identified with the official ethic, the telephone spirit.

The underground unions became very powerful informal institutions which in addition to their political planning for the trade unions, opened up ways of developing a moral career for their members. (However, underground unions embodied a Marxist attitude towards work that was sometimes harmful to workers, as Anthony (1977) states.) Again, we see the usefulness of applying Harré theory to the analysis of organizations and work.

The final state of the company, that of today, coincides with the transition to democracy, accompanied at the economic level by a severe crisis, created by the obsolescence of the systems of production and the introduction of renovation accelerated by technology. Economic crisis has not yet affected workers' job security in this company, but it has profoundly affected their specifically social institutions, plagued with acute financial problems. The situation is leading to the collapse of the institution that financed retirement, so that employes will come under the system of social security, like their fellow workers. This has given rise to several strikes of varying length. Within a few years, the sense of privilege has been lost, the telephone spirit is crumbling, and the levels of job satisfaction, according to the latest surveys of the organizational climate are in steep decline, something very dangerous as the introduction of new technology requires an active and responsible attitude towards automatic systems. The loss of the telephone spirit at the same time facilitates and reinforces the search for new ways of satisfying the expressive dimension now that the hazards faced are new ones.

Thus we find that there has been a desire for rapid change in values and guide-lines of behaviour eschewing the telephone spirit and the symbolic and referential bonds of many of the workers with their company. The result has been very negative.

Organizational culture also involves the existence of unofficial institutions which help in the working out and development of a moral career. Culture and change means a more or less thorough reorganization of the ways of achieving social dignity and worth, assisting in the development of more and more autonomous, responsible and reflective agents. For this reason, the workers' rejection of new techniques is produced not only by the difficulties entailed in the use of their intelligence, abilities or skills. Resistance to change means, in many instances, the unwillingness to accept a new order requiring a reorganization of the social identity of the members of the organization.

REFERENCES

Anthony, P. D. (1977) *The Ideology of Work*, London: Tavistock.
Blauner, R. (1964) *Alienation and Freedom*, Chicago: Chicago University Press.
Clegg, S. and Dunkerley, D. (1980) *Organization Class and Control*, London: Routledge & Kegan Paul.
Coriat, B. (1979) *L'Atelier's et le chronometre. Essai sur le taylorisme, le fordisme et la production de masse*, Paris: Christian Bourgois Editeur.
Ditton, J. (1977) *Part-time Crime: An Ethnography of Fiddling and Pilferage*, London, Macmillan.
Goffman, E. (1959) *The Presentation of Self in Everyday Life*, New York: Doubleday.
Goffman, E. (1961) *Asylums*, New York: Doubleday.
Goffman, E. (1974) *Frame Analysis*, Cambridge, Mass.: Harvard University Press.
Harré, R. (1980) 'Man as Rhetorician', in A. J. Chapman and D. M. Jones, *Models of Man*, London: The British Psychological Society.
Harré, R. (1983) *Personal Being*, Oxford: Basil Blackwell.
Harré, R., Clarke, D. and de Carlo, N. (1985) *Motives and Mechanisms*, London and New York: Methuen.
Lippit, R., Watson, J. and Westley, B. (1959) *The Dynamics of Planned Change*, New York: Harcourt, Brace & World.
Mars, G. (1983) *Cheats at Work*, London: Unwin Paperbacks.
Rodriguez, J. L. (1986a) *El control y las actitudes hacia el trabajo en las organizaciones formales*, Madrid: Universidad Complutense de Madrid. PhD Dissertation.
Rodriguez, J. L. (1986b) 'En busca de nuevas metaforas para el estudio de las organizaciones', *Psicologia del Trabajo y de las Organizaciones*, 2 (3), pp. 5–9.
Rose, M. (1975) *Industrial Behaviour*, Harmondsworth and London: Penguin and Allen Lane.

16

Are Selves Real?

Uffe J. Jensen

I

Persons, particulars located in space and time, are real. Souls, conceived of as something over and above mental states and psychic processes, are not real. At least not according to the most widespread intuitions and philosophical positions of our age. But are selves real? It depends, many will claim, upon our ontology. As realism has become an influential, and almost dominant, philosophy of our time, 'selves' have become surrounded with respect, after having fallen into discredit after Cartesian ideas of selves as luminous substances were rejected.

Selves are apparently not particulars. But, it can be argued, they play a role. They have, or perhaps rather are, causal powers. For instance, I remember Bill as a lazy student. Having read some of his articles I ask surprised: '*Is* it really Bill who wrote these impressive papers?' 'Yes', the reply comes, 'he is not the same any more. He has changed completely.'

Of course Bill is the same person whom I met and came to know fifteen years ago. But he has changed *himself* and getting informed about that. I stop wondering if someone other than Bill really wrote the excellent papers. My puzzle is settled by a knind of causal explanation in which reference is made to Bill, not as a self-identical person but as a (changed) self.

It might be objected that selves are a strange kind of entity to be reckoned 'causes'. But in the climate of realism this sounds as a very old-fashioned objection. We often specify abstract objects making causal accounts. As pointed out by Dennett, we can answer the question 'Why doesn't that lamp tip over?' by replying, 'because its centre of gravity is so low'. Such an explanation can compete with other explanations which are clearly causal, as, for example, 'because it is nailed to the table'.

This leads to the hypothesis that selves are a kind of abstract object or theoretical entity; and that 'self' is a theoretical term rather than a name for the most luminous of all substances.

But if selves are theoretical entities, they are entities of a special kind, which in important respects differ from e.g. centres of gravity. And if 'self' is a theoretical term embedded in some 'self-theory', we are apparently dealing with a theoretical term and a kind of theory which play quite different roles from theories of the natural sciences.

In *Personal Being*[1], the most detailed study of selves as a theoretical entities, Rom Harré points out important differences between 'self-theories' and theories of the natural sciences. 'Unlike the natural sciences, in the human science,' Harré stresses 'the productive process, and in particular the beings involved in it, are themselves products of "educational processes" in which these very theoretical concepts play an indispensable part. These beings are what they are partly by virtue of holding this or that theory' (1983, p. 25).

The physical world is not what it is by virtue of our theories about that world. On the other hand, we human beings are partly products of theories and concepts (as aquired in educational processes). This says something about the difference between physical beings and human beings, and about the difference between theories of the natural sciences and theories of the human sciences. But it does not say very much, if anything, about the very special kind of theories in which 'the self' as a theoretical term is embedded. For such theories are, it seems, not at all theories of the *human sciences*. (Though they may come in the future, perhaps, to be respectable objects for the human sciences – thanks in part to Harrés work). The theory I am assumed to have as a self is not taught me as a student of the human sciences. And we have not grasped the special characteristics of 'self-theories' by being told that we are beings who are what we are, partly, by holding this or that theory. What psychological theories we hold (Freudian, Goffmanesque or others) may partly determine what kinds of being we are. But a theory of self is not a theory of that kind. Even if no one had formulated psychological theories (if it, let us say, was prohibited to do human science) we would, according to the self-as-theory view, still hold self-theories. Moreover, to differentiate these theories from theories of the human sciences in a future way, we are determined by our holding these theories in another way than we are determined by holding particular theories of the human sciences.

What then are the special characteristics of self-theories? How are these theories generated and in what way do they determine their object (the human self)?

Harré makes it clear that the 'theories of self' that create our personal being are theories of a very special kind. It is not just theories we learn

258 *Uffe J. Jensen*

from social scientists and psychologists. *I* appropriate such a theory from particular socio-linguistic practices in my society. Harré is thus not giving an account of the self-concept of psychologists, but of a more primitive concept which is *presupposed* by psychologists.

Harré presents, in *Personal Being*, a very detailed and complicated account of our acquiring self-theories. Another proponent of the theoretical-entity approach to selves. Daniel Dennett[2], has presented a much simpler theory. So to throw Harré's theory into relief let us consider Dennett's theory. It will be seen that Dennett's theory suffers from the serious deficiency that it cannot account for the distinction between being a self who is not a victim of self-deception and being one who is. Afterwards we shall have to investigate if Harré's more detailed theory fares any better.

II

Dennett presents a view of the self which seems to be very much in agreement with our intuitive conception of the growth of theoretical knowledge. As we develop our experimental practice and so make some parts of reality the objects of still more complicated tests, we develop our theoretical knowledge. 'Our selves', Dennett points out 'are constantly being made more determinate as we go along in response to the way the world impinges upon us' (Dennett, 1983, p. 13). But what does this really mean? That our selves are developing as a result of our interaction with the surrounding world, and that we as a consequence of that development can get still deeper theories about ourselves? If this was the point psychologists or other experts in interpreting and explaining human behaviour should furnish us laypersons with theories of our selves. But this is certainly not Dennett's point. On the contrary, what makes our selves still more determinate is not just our continuously developing new forms and styles of public activity (as the phrase 'as we go along in response to the world impinges upon us' might be interpreted), but rather the process of going back, thinking about one's past, and ones's memories, reflecting upon and rewriting them.

This can be understood in a quite straightforward manner: as I think about my own past I shall in all probability get knowledge about myself, knowledge I would not get if I was the kind of person who did not reflect upon my life and history. According to that understanding we might be selves all the time, but just not fully aware of ourselves, though capable of gradually acquiring greater awareness as we reflect on our past life. Dennett, however, wants to defend a much stronger thesis: namely that we create ourselves, we become selves through writing our own autobiography.

The process of making one self more determinate is construed in analogy with an author making one of his characters more determinate. If we ask John Updike to include in the *Rabbit* series a new novel about Rabbit's early days, we are not asking him to do research (as we might ask the author of biography of a real person). We would ask Updike 'to invent some more novel for us' (Dennett, 1983, p. 12). In doing that he is changing and developing the fictional character, making him determinate in ways he was never determinate before. According to Dennett, *we* are changing our 'fictional character' (ourself) similarly going back and thinking about our past.

But in what sense do we become more determinate by rethinking and rewriting our past? In reading through the volumes of Robert Musil's *The Man without Qualities*, the chief character Ulrich becomes more and more determinate to the reader in a very straightforward sense of determinate. All the time we get knowledge about the character, his actions and his reflections. It would, however, be strange to say that I, under all circumstances, become more and more determinate as a self by thinking and writing about my past. Let us say, that I just write a story about my past, not really intending to write a true account of my history. It might well be about my past, about my time in school, my life as a student, etc. I might write a chronicle of episodes, episodes which actually have been part of my life, but which espouses motives that I did not have and which presents my actions in a light that make them more admirable than they actually were. This is, of course, what many people actually *are* doing when writing their autobiography – either consciously trying to deceive the reader or being victims of their own self-deception in conceiving of their history in a more ideal light than can actually be justified.

Apparently, Dennett does not see any problems in this for his theory that the self is the chief character in our autobiography. We are engaged in all sorts of behaviour which is more or less unified. And, he says, we put always the 'best face' on it we can, 'we try to make all our material cohere into a single good story. And that story is our autobiography' (Dennett, 1983, p. 19).

Dennett's point, or postulate, that we are story-telling beings trying to make ourselves chief characters of coherent autobiographies, putting the best face on our life which we can, in some way reflects the Sartrean existentialist theory of man's inclination to live in *mauvaise foi*, to creep into some role, or character, to reduce himself to a thing, living *en-soi* instead of *pour-soi*. But while Sartre criticizes the self-deceived person in the light of his theory of the authentic responsible ego, Dennett's theory makes it impossible to distinguish between a self-deceived self and a self who has not been deceiving himself in making himself more determinate.

The theory of the autobiographical self (TAS) is a result of attempts to present an alternative to Cartesian and other substantialist conceptions of the self. If there is no 'inner self' to be *discovered* by reflection or introspection, the self must be our own *invention*, created in an ungoing proces of thinking about ourselves, writing our self-histories.

A concrete example may further illustrate the immediate plausibility of TAS, but it also indicates some serious shortcomings of the theory.

The German writer and journalist Günter Wallraff has in a number of books presented himself in various roles, as a journalist at a yellow paper, as a foreign (Turkish) worker in West Germany, etc. In his books Wallraff has revealed various kinds of corruption and incredible suppression in Germany today, and he has done it in a very moving way, not only writing documentary journalism but by presenting the stories in a fictional form. Wallraff has, however, not only been creating fictional characters. The series of books he has been writing in a way also constitutes his own autobiography. In a television interview Wallraff was asked how he had experienced this role-playing, constantly hoodwinking people into believing that he was a journalist sharing the attitudes of the colleagues at the newspaper, that he was a Turkish worker who had serious difficulties in expressing himself in the German language and so "Where is "*Günter Wallraff*" himself?', the interviewer asked him? Had he not experienced serious difficulties in maintaining his own self-identity during this long proces of living out changing disguises?

Wallraff did not choose a Cartesian move to resist the implication that he just had a chamaeleon-like existence. He did not claim that he had just been *himself* all the time. He answered the question in a way which at least apparently was very much in accordance with TAS. He had not, he stressed, just been playing roles. His characters were not just fictional character. They were at the same time characters in his own autobiolrgrahy. He had, to use Dennett's way of speaking, been making himself more and more determinate through writing the books.

But Wallraff had a particular motive for going through this process of personal development, or making himself more determinate. He quoted the famous Rimbaud phrase 'I am another'. This apparently paradoxical expression implies a rejection of any substantialist conception of the self. But, as interpreted by Wallraff, it also expresses a view on the self which is not contained in TAS. He has not made himself more determinate by *telling stories*, but by being involved in various kinds of *activities* and so by becoming parts of various kinds of human *communities*. Through these concrete processes, Wallraff had recognized what his *values* were, which people he had a feeling of solidarity with, and which people and attitudes and ways of living he was against and was willing to fight against.

Wallraff had, as he said, from his early youth been opposed to and critical of the petty-bourgois values which were embodied in his child milieu. His growing awareness of other values with which he could identify himself was captured in the phrase 'I am another'.

The Wallraff story suggest two dimensions of the theoretical concept of the self lacking in TAS. The self is in some way or other the function of *activities* as conducted in interpersonal relations, and a function of our realization of particular ideals and values in the light of which we can interpret our life-story, and in the light of which we can develop strategies for the future.

It is no accident that these practical and ethical aspects of our concept of the self are absent in Dennett's presentation of TAS. He finishes his paper by quoting Hume's famous dissolution of the self into a series of perceptions and memories:

> For my part, when I enter most intimately into what I call *myself*, I always stumble on some particular perception or other, of heat or cold, light or shade, love or hatred, pain or pleasure. I never can catch *my self* at any time without a perception, and never can observe any thing but the perception. . . . If any one, upon serious and unprejudiced reflection, thinks he has a different notion of *himself*, I must confess I can reason no longer with him. All I can allow him is, that he may be in the right as well as I, and that we are essentially different in this particular. He may, perhaps, perceive something simple and continued, which he calls *himself*; though I am certain there is no such principle in me. *(Treatise on Human Nature, I, IV, sec. 6)*

It is clear that Dennett has not taken into account the arguments that Kant and his followers developed against the Humean solution – arguments that paved the way for a new philosophical interpretaton of the concept of the self, incorporating it into practical philosophy and ethics.

Is it, however, not possible to elaborate TAS, keeping its basic assumption of the self as a theoretical concept, and then in the ethical and practical dimensions of the concept finding resources for drawing the distinction between adequate and inadequate self-theories, or between having a self theory and deceiving oneself?

Rejecting TAS in Dennett's version is certainly no reasom for dropping the theoretical entity approach to the self. The defects of Dennett's account are, on the contrary, a reflection of his rather superficial use of the notion 'theoretical entity'.

Theories, formulae, equations, etc. are not just verbal entities coming out the mouths of scientists. Theories are embodied in complex practices containing experimental equipment, experimental procedures and standards, Kuhnian 'exemplars'. It is not possible to individuate any theory or any theoretical entity if we ignore these complex contexts.[3]

Analogously, theories-of-self cannot be construed as merely verbal entities coming out of the person's mouth. The Cartesian ghost self seems to be haunting Dennett to such a degree that he imagines the self as arising *ex-nihi-lo*, just being emboided in the reports about myself coming out of my mouth, or silently being said to myself. A reminiscense of the Sartrean ego is also felt here. I am not a thing speaking through my own mouth. 'In the beginning was the world. And then through an apparantly inexplicable Virgin Birth I am present.'

But just as an understanding of the theoretical terms of scientific theories is only possible on the basis of account of the concrete context of which they are a part (call it paradigm, research tradition or whatever), so the self understood as a theoretical entity must be accounted for through an analysis of *the problems* to be illuminated through the introduction of the theoretical term, and through analysis of the *tools and procedures* used by me handling my interpersonal relationsships and my relations to the world in which I live, i.e. in particular ideals and values regulating my activities.

'I' does not reflect any ghostly substance. There is almost unanimous agreement about that. But as a concrete Strawsonian person acting among other persons, I am reflecting myself in these relations with others, in such a way that it is in my actions towards and together with others that I became able to account for my own actions and become able to express my values and to reflect upon them. It is through these relations and activities that I develop a concept of myself, that I acquire a concept, a theoretical concept, of I. Accordingly an anlysis of this concept requires an account of *the concrete conditions* under which the concept has been introduced.

III

It is exactly at this point that Harré's theory of the self as presented in *Personal Being* is superior to Dennett's. 'Autobiography is not just', Harré stresses, 'a chronicle of episodes, whether private or public. It has also to do with a growing grasp of capabilities and potentials. As such it involves the exploitation of the conditions for both consciousness and agency' (*Personal Being*, 1983, p. 214).

What, then, are the conditions for acquiring a theoretical concept of the self? We learn to think about ourselves as *selves* in the context of particular socio-linguistic practices. In some practices we acquire the capacity to direct attention to one thing from the standpoint of a point of view in an array of other things. In other practices the child is introduced to the idea of itself as an autonomous actor. And finally, in psychological symbiosis, one person's public display is supplemented by another person to satisfy the criteria of personhood with respect to psychological competences and attributes in day-to-day use in a particular society in this or that specific social milieu (*Personal Being*, 1983, p. 105).

The theoretical concept approach to the self (TCS) implies that we are not the lucky possessors of a luminous entity (selves); but that to have a self (a theory of the self) is rather to have *something*, namely particular capabilities and powers.

But can Harré with his theory of the self (TSS), which is distinctly different from and more complex than Dennett's TAS, answer the elementary question which Dennett could not answer in a satisfactory way: how do we distinguish between a person having an adequate self-theory and his having an inadequate self-theory? What counts as getting a self theory right? Or in the material mode of speech: When am I a real self?

Only at one point does Harré address himself directly to that question. Harré points to an important distinction between file selves and real selves. A file is a collection of documents unified by their common referent, a particular person A. On many occasions (e.g. as job applicants) we appear as just file selves, as assembled by a principle of selection or criterion of central relevance. And it is not the person, but the file-master (a professional or other specialist) who decides what is relevant and what should be embodied in the file.

What does the contrast between real selves and file selves tell us about real selves? Of course, file selves do not have the characteristics of selves (having neither consciousness nor agency). And further: self-knowledge and self-mastery, according to Harré, two essential characteristics of selves of Western culture, are limited by the existence of personal files to which one has no access.

Will it, however, not be unacceptable to conclude that real selves can only be characterized negatively – in contradistinction to file-selves? Do we not need a conception of persons having more or less real selves, persons who have got their self-theories more or less night? To show the importance of such a conception just imagine the following case.

I frequently consult health professionals and other professionals of modern society, complaining about all kinds of problems and deficiencies. I get a number of diagnoses. Then, in a Sartrean way, I become *en-soi*, I identify myself with my file story. Writing my autobiography I simply rewrite in my own language my various files.

An observer may pity me as a poor estranged person. Sartre would ridicule me for be a victim of *mauvaise-foi*. But am I not within the Harréan framework just as real as any other self?

I may well satisfy all Harré's criteria for having the theoretical concept of self (point of view, agency and the necessary social competences). I may at least have got sufficient competences for living in such limited, protected social milieux as institutions, therapeutic communities.

It seems that such cases show that we need a distinction between persons acting in the light of a life-history reconstructed by others, being unable to determine what their own values and ideals are, on the one hand; a and, on the other hand, persons who are *not* just embodiments of file-selves, but one in some sense real.

Perhaps Harre's three conditions are necessary for acquiring the theoretical concept of self. But they cannot be sufficient conditions. For, as suggested above, I may meet Harré's criteria but still be unable to access my own situation, determine my own values or recognize that my course of life really does not contribute to a realization of values with which I identify myself (but rather on the contrary undermines these very values through my own action).

In situations of this kind I am deceiving myself. A theory of learning to become a self should make it possible to describe and explain the difference between deceiving oneself and having an adequate understanding of one's own situation. Self-deception is not analysed by Harré in *Personal Being*. And this is not at all surprising if the account of the self presented in the book does not make it possible to distinguish between the self-deceived person and the person who has an adequate understanding of himself or herself.

IV

The considerations above do not imply a rejection of Harré's approach to the self as theory. A closer look at the symbiotic process will, however, reveal a complexity of structure not taken into account in Harré's theory. Extending the theory to encompass that structure and its contradictions will make it possible to draw and to explain the critical distinction just mentioned.

In the symbiotic process an individual who is in some respect weak and incomplete is supplemented by a stronger partner. But this process has a dual nature. The weaker partner does not only aquire some competence which he previously lacked. The process is also an embodiment of a moral ideal of ordinary human life.

In our everyday understanding there is a distinction between the legitimate, morally responsible, and the illegitimate, morally irresponsible, use of power. Our model for the morally responsible use of power can be summed up as folows. At a given time a person, B, is in the power of some other person, A, in the sense that A can cause B to do things he would not have done otherwise. Parents have this kind of power over their children, professionals over their clients and patients. When A causes B to do something which he would not have done otherwise, then A is acting morally responsible if his actions towards B aim at or contribute to making B independent of the power of A, or others having a similar power. To describe this activity in ordinary terms, we are acting morally responsibly towards other individuals or groups who in a particular context are weaker than us, if we try to act from their point of view and support them. This activity, which we assume to be the model activity of ordinary communal life, is not confined to priests or philosophers. It can be summed up as the basic moral principle of responsibility for the weak (Jensen, 1987).[4] Due to the existence of such model activity in our everyday life, ordinary people (and not just experts in theology, ethics or moral psychology) possess, and are able to use, a language of morals for commenting on, excusing and criticizing past and future actions, (in the last case, in so far as we recognize them as violating the basic moral principle).

The moral principle presecribing responsibility for the weaknesses of others is, as stressed above, to be explained by reference to a basic constraint on human communal life. We are involved in relationships characterized by dependency and power; we are not independent and self-sufficient individuals. The president, the managing director and the school master are three characters who quite consciously may violate the moral principle, believing that it cultivates weakness and so blocks the way for the freedom they experience and consider to be real moral ideal. Such Nietzschean characters deceive themselves; their present position is not simply a result of their own desire for power – they have been taught and influenced (by others), to behave in the way they do. We have no reasons to believe that humans could survive, let alone develop, if the principle of responsibility was removed from areas in which these basic aspects of human life are engendered. Even in their present positions such Nietz-schean characters are not omnipotent. In their relation to their families or friends, as in the case of threats to their health which even they cannot escape, they may suddenly be placed in the role of the weak, and so need to enjoy the protection of the moral principle.

The symbiotic process realizes an ideal of care or disinterested love, a basic principle of ordinary morality of responsibility for the weaker partner. Through the process the weaker partner is supported to make mutual relationship with the stronger partner possibile. So the process negates the initial power of the strong partner in the dyad. But here the contradictory aspects of this process appears. In the same process in which the strong and powerful negates power, acting in accordance with the principle of moral responsibility, he or she may, as a member of our culture, attempt to complement the weak not only by supplying him with required competences but also with ideals of individual power and perfection. Such ideals of power which make a fetish out of particular human qualities (physical strength, or succes in social competition or just personal image) are turned into criteria of human worth. This teaching of ideals of power, for instance in attempting to make children meet these ideals, is, of course, not just a result of parents being ambitious on behalf of their children. The contradictions in the symbiotic process between the moral principle and ideals of power reflects a contradiction within our culture.

When used as a yardstick for personal quality, ideals of power will in general give the individual a distorted and unrealistic assessment of himself and his situation which will contribute to strategies of action undermining the ideals implied by the moral principle. In this way ideals of power will promote self-deception understood as a conflict between the moral principle taught in personal relations and the agents' actual action strategies. Local moral orders encompass ideals of power (in our present Western culture typically embodied in such powerful idols as Rambo or the yuppie character), that are perversions of the idea of 'an active self-conscious being' which is, according to Harré, central to *our* theory of personal being.

But why call such idols perversions? By reference to which standards can such a claim be justified? If we had only recourse to the, so to speak, manifest norms of moral orders, norms which prescribe what the individual needs to manage in a competitive society, having personal success and strength as its basic values, then the idols embodying omnipotence could not be morally assessed as being perversions. Having recourse, however, to the dual character of the symbiotic process and to the principle of interpersonal responsibility implicit in the process, we can adopt a moral stance to the ideals of power and their various embodiments.

It is, however, not only possible to evaluate and criticize ideals of power from the standpoint of the moral principle claiming that such ideals are unethical relative to *that* principle. This critique would not bring us very far, presumably being met with Nietzschean counter-attacks on the moral principle from the standpoint of the omnipotent idol. A really devastating critique of ideals of power should make it clear that personal being and personal development unconstrained by the chains of self-deception has as its primary condition the appropriation of the moral principle of interpersonal responsibility, and actual training in acting in accordance with this principle.

Clinical psychology, psychotherapy and psychiatry have amassed huge amouts of material telling us what happens to the individual who becomes a victim of the contradictions in the symbiotic process, the individual who internalizes ideals of power and who becomes unable to identify himself or herself as a being of *human* stature, i.e. as a being with strengths and weaknesses to be balanced in a communal life governed by the moral principle of interpersonal responsibility. Measuring myself, my worth and human quality by the yardstick of omnipotent idols I may follow two equally dangerous routes. Identifying myself with the ideal of power I may, at least temporarily, conceive of myself as just or almost as almighty as the idol. This counteracts, however, the process set going in the symbiosis towards aquiring a self-theory, a conception of myself as a unity. If I cannot separate myself from my idol (say, Rambo), this prevents my acting in accordance with the moral principle. Acting as if I have and conceiving myself as having, ominpotent capacities blocks my entering into interpersonal relationships of mutual support. If I, following the other dangerous route, find myself extremely small as measured by the yardstick of omnipotence, my self-esteem will be undermined and not even the most sympathetic and warm support in a symbiotic dyad may be sufficient for repairing the damage to my sense of identity caused by having adopted unrealistic yardsticks or standards of human worth and moral quality.[5]

The importance of the moral principle (and of the individual being trained in using the principle) for our aquiring a self-theory in a Harréan sense has also been shown by at least one psychological study. This is a study inspired by Vygotsky to whom Harré credits one of the basic ideas in *Personal Being* namely that the private and subjective should be understood as an appropriation of something social and collective.

Vygotsky suggested to Luria that he should carry out a large-scale psychological experiment to that or illustrate the thesis that the basic forms of human cognitive activity are determined by socio-historical conditions. Such a project was carried out in Uzbekistan in the beginning of the 1930s.[6] The project included research on the development of various cognitive functions (perception, abstraction etc.) and also on the development of our ability to engage in self-analysis and self-assessment.

Those who took part in the research on self-analysis were asked to assess their own character and to describe what they conceived of as positive and negative features.

Members of a selected group of old, illiterate peasants who had been living under feudal conditions reacted in a typical way to these questions by describing material conditions in their life. Asked about personal shortcomings a peasant would answer 'I have bad neighbours.' When they did not transfer the features in question to other people, they would perhaps characterize themselves by using judgements which neighbours had given of them, and typically it would be judgements about concrete activities.

Luria tried to show that only at a later stage of development, and influenced by another form of social life, will individuals aquire the ability to judge themselves. In a group of youngsters with some experience of active participation in community life and some education, Luria's request for self-analysis was well understood. Typically, the judgements had direct recourse to the norms and demands of the local moral order.

Self-analysis in our meaning was, however, only found in a group of people who, during the experiment, had acquired the opportunity not only to take part in communal activities, but to be responsible for running and managing in a farm. Through such communal activities ideals for social collaboration are developed (and as Luria says: ideas of an ideal 'I' is developed as a yardstick for self-analysis).

Luria's research shows, among other things the importance of *inter-personal responsibility* (what above I called *the moral principle*) and the training in developing it in practice for acquiring capacities for self-analysis, and hence for aquiring a theory-of-self.

If it is true, as suggested above, that the moral principle is a principle of ordinary human practice, a principle not just embodied in modern communities, then even the old peasants who had been living under feudal conditions should have had this principle. But in their concrete life they had got no training in using the principle, in so far as they remained members of a feudal order embodying ideals of power according to which the peasants had no *right* to take part in the management of communal life. As the member of a modern society may become very small and insignificant, of no *worth*, compared with the dominant idols of power of the age, so the feudal peasant was not conceived as a worthy participant in the administration of society. Hence in social practice the moral principle was superseded by ideals of power; and under these circumstances the moral principle could not be a principle of action.

V

The account of the dual character of the symbiotic process implies a revision of the Harréan theory of the self as a theoretical concept. Aquiring a personal point of view, an idea of agency and the capacities demanded by the local moral order are not sufficient conditions for getting a self-theory, for becoming an autonomous agent characterized by self-mastery and self-knowledge. The moral principle implicitly procured in the symbiotic process is crucial. As self-conscious persons we are not only playing out the roles of the local moral order, but we are reflecting on and judging our activities *ethically*, for example, by reflecting upon how we are using the power associated with our role in relation to other and relation to ourselves.

One of Sartre's examples of *mauvaise-foi* illustrates what it is *not* to have aquired a theory-of-self. Sartre describes a servant who is over-zealous and too careful. Being a servant is not just a job, it has become a vocation or mission in life. He moves around among the tables not as an individual person but as a *thing*.[7]

To Sartre this servant lives in self-deception because he does not take responsibility for his own life. Seing my role as a mission, my actions cease to be something I could choose to do or choose not to do. But, Sartre stresses, he *could* choose to stay at home in the morning instead of going to his job.

Sartre cannot, however, explain to us why the servant should be criticized for being completely absorbed in the role. Why is it wrong to be self-sacrifising?

According to Sartre, the individual creates his own values. Therefore *my* way of living cannot be criticized or morally blamed from the outside. But Sartre is criticizing the servant, and for more than forty years readers have read, understood and in many cases agreed with his criticism. Why? Because Sartre's own value-relativism is wrong. Because we actually share – in our own and in other human communities – a basic model of interpersonal responsibility. We become acquainted with this model in ordinary human intercourse (in the first place in the symbiotic relation-ship between parents and child), as we enter into interpersonal relations. But the conception of responsibility acquired in this way (namely that power should be used to emancipate and not to suppress the weak) can, of course, be used on an individual person, to judge his or her relationship to himself or herself. This is exactly what Sartre does in the case of the servant. The servant has surrendered himself to the role as a servant. He crushes himself as a self. Therefore he is, in accordance with our ordinary concepton of responsibility, acting irresponsibly towards himself.

The Sartrean story becomes comprehensible in the light of our ordinary model of responsibility. But more than that. Having illuminated the role of this model in our acquiring a theory-of-self we can explain why the servant acts as he does: he has not acquired a theory-of-self.

Of course he has grown up, he had been part of symbiotic processes, so according to the account given of the symbiotic process above the Sartrean servant must also have became acquainted with the moral principle. Having a theory is, however, more than being acquainted with some principles. A person can only be said to have a theory (a theory of the natural sciences, a theory of the human sciences or a self-theory) if he has got routines and procedures for using the principles, laws, etc., applying it to the relevant problem-situation. In the servant's life the moral principle has been superseded by an ideal of power, the ideal of the *perfect* servant.

VI

In recent years several philosophers have brought together pieces of a picture of the person as a moral evaluator. Besides Harré, Charles Taylor and David Hamlyn have in important ways contributed to this new orientation in our philosophical understanding of personal being.

As selves, as moral agents, we articulate values. We reflect, as stressed by Taylor (*Philosophical Papers*, 1983 vol. 1, p. 27) 'in a struggle of self-interpretations.' The question at issue being 'which is the truer, more authentic, more illusion-free interpretation, and which on the other hand involves a distortion of the meanings things have for me'. So, 'our identity is defined by certain evaluations which are inseparable from ourselves as agents' (ibid., p. 34).[8]

Taylor and others have in this way contributed to illuminating what kind of problems we face as selves, and how we become selves by handling particular kinds of problems. Their analyses do not, however, contain or imply any explanation of *how* we become able to act out of certain particular evaluations or how moral articulation is possible. The self-theory account of the human self satisfies such a condition. I become an evaluator by appropriating certain principles and procedures for using these principles. When Wallraff accounts for his life-history by using the phrase 'I am another', he implies that he has carried out continous self-interpretations during various kinds of communal activities from a moral stance, in the light of the principle of interpersonal responsibility. He became himself by acting in accordance with that principle in various social contexts.

But when do we become real selves? When did Wallraff become a self? When he could first *express* his determination to change himself by saying to himself and others 'I am another', implying another than the person governed by the ideals of power dominating his original social milieu? or will Wallraff not become a self before he truly can say 'I *have* become another'?

There are no clear-cut answers to these questions. All selves, i.e. all beings who have appropriated the principles of point-of-view, agency and interpersonal responsibility and who in symbiotic processes have been supplied with necessary social capacities, are real. But some selves are more real than others. According to the arguments presented in this paper, our training in acting in accordance with the principle of interpersonal responsibility and training in judging ourselves and making self-interpretations in that light and developing our communal activities correspondingly will make us more real selves and so reduce the risk of self-deception, which in its extreme forms means not having a self-theory but instead of that identifying oneself with omnipotent idols or destroying oneself by submission to them.

NOTES

1 Basil Blackwell, Oxford, 1983.
2 'The Self as a centre of Narrative Gravity'. The Houston Sumposium 1983.
3 I have argued for that in 'Preconditions for evolutionary thinking' in U. J. Jensen and R. Harré (eds) *The Philosophy of Evolution*, Harvester Press Brighton, 1981.
4 Uffe Juul Jensen, *Practice and progress. A theory for the modern health-care system*. Blackwell Scientific Publications, Oxford, 1987.
5 I have argued in detail for this view in *Selverkendelse og selvbedrag* (Self-knowledge and self-deception). Reitzel, Copenhagen, 1987.
6 Alexander Luria: *Ob istoritschenskom raswitii posnawatelnych prozessow* (On the historical development of cognitive processes). Moscow, 1974.
7 *L'être et le néant*, Gallimard, Paris, 1943.
8 *Human Agency and Language, Philosophical Papers*, vol. 1, Cambridge University Press, Cambridge, 1985.

17

Hysteria, Belief and Magic

David Taylor

We cannot command nature except by obeying her.

Bacon

First, four stories in crescendo.

A courageous GP refers a boy aged eight who has 'gone off his legs' that morning. The GP says he knows it's hysterical but that he cannot stop it. The boy is brought by car. A kind psychiatrist negotiates through the window the need for the boy to mount the steps to come and talk. The boy comes. He talks about how his estranged father had promised first a trip to the Cup Final and then to the replay and had twice let him down. The anger and love and disappointment and the humiliation in front of his friends took his legs from under him; turned him weak at the knees; turned his legs to jelly. He walked out of the consultation and remained well.

A fourteen-year-old boy has a fixed flexion deformity of the right hand. Sudek's atrophy is beginning. The psychiatrist is the eleventh sort of specialist to be consulted. A sudden painful inexplicable bruise on the back of the hand has been casually dealt with by a locum GP; after a sleepless night mother and child waited in Casualty for hours, finally to be told that spontaneous bruises were not treated there. The Casualty Department of an orthopaedic hospital, however, provided a plaster, an appointment to review in two days' time then admitted him because of pain in plaster, an admission which had lasted for eight weeks before the psychiatrist was called. Several persuasive chats and devices were needed before the hand was able to recover fully.

A very mature thirteen-year-old girl has twice been admitted for abdominal pain. Following the removal of a normal appendix, anaesthesia develops round the wound and gradually spreads. When encouraged to be upstanding she shows marked astasia abasia. The psychiatrist is called synchronously with a surgeon who, 'not going to be caught out', orders a myelogram and a scintillation scan. The family meeting is angrily supportive of the child's right to be ill. Mother works in the medical field, father is affable but largely absent on business and is said to have a chronic illness, a brother is described as having had an accident in which 'he left most of his blood in the road but was otherwise all right', another brother's school and university careers were ruined by 'lymphoma' which turned out to be spastic colon. Over the ensuing years, despite treatment, the girl works her way through a variety of illnesses including one from which she emerges with the sort of scar she might otherwise have derived from wrist-slashing.

A girl of nine vomited her lunch when her sister and boyfriend started to punch one another. The fighting stopped and she was 'rushed to hospital'. Later, a recurrence of vomiting led to another admission and then one lasting six weeks, requiring intravenous fluids. The psychiatrist met her gently mewing into the steel bowl provided. Her trick of deliberate vomiting continued inexorably. Her mother had died of an overdose of drugs and alcohol, her father was a recidivist jail-bird. Both her brothers were in jail for serious offences. No negotiation with her about her facility to vomit proved possible over eighteen months in psychiatric care nor a subsequent stay at another hospital. There she suffered a rupture of the oesophagus from the stomach and, following an heroic repair, she requested orange juice by mouth. When refused this she made to vomit, reopened her wound, and exanguinated fatally.

A number of young people are being presented to doctors, with sicknesses of great morbidity and occasional mortality, which ape illnesses or suggest serious diseases, but which are attributed to either unknown or to arcane physical processes by the sick person or his supporters. Doctors, acting on their ordinary assumptions about physical illness exert themselves and may exhaust themselves in their search for aetiology. In the absence of classical signs, pathognomic illness or conventional pathological changes, the doctors may then attempt to exit from their engagement via reassurance of the patient that all is well, despite the apparent sickness. This offer may be accepted but it may be blocked by the patient or his family if they are deeply committed to the sickness in its structural sense (Taylor, 1986; Goodyer, 1986). Even worse, diagnostic frustration or the physician's personal needs might ensnare him into formulations on which reputation is staked and so are not easily relinquished. While it is unarguable that there are yet undiscovered diseases (Slater, 1965), it has also been true throughout the recorded history of medicine that people, transiently or chronically, and for a variety of motives, lay claim to physical ailments, impairments and disorders which they do not have and for which they are prepared at times to manufacture the evidence. As I see it, such people have a belief about how they are, and they are prepared to go to great lengths to make the world congruent with that belief (Robins and O'Neal, 1953; Maloney, 1980; Flechet et al., 1983). In children's medicine it is usual for the beliefs to be held by the family, or some part of it, or by some other system which can include doctors (Goodyer, 1985; Byng-Hall, 1986). Doctors who are not caught up in the system have called these sicknesses deceits (Naish 1979; Bayliss, 1984) or, more dispassionately or compassionately, hysteria.

There is nothing unreal or imaginary about these sicknesses even though they are of the imagination, just as the novel or the play are not imaginary though they were imagined. I shall argue that they are an aspect of a defence mechanism, a mechanism which from one perspective we call hysteria but from another perspective we understand as belief, and from another, as magic. The dramas of which I gave examples above are mostly chronic socialized medical versions of the hysterical mechanism which is normally of very rapid onset and offset. I see these dramas as mobilizing every bit as powerful reactions as the more dramatic situations to which I shall later refer.

Belief

I want to draw attention to the fundamental part played in these scenarios by beliefs. Doctors' training is more directed towards what people say and how they act and too little concerned with what they believe. In a largely godless society, there are few people who experience the power of a benign conviction with which it is easy to empathize. But the mental action of believing, of 'accepting propositions as true on the grounds of the testimony of others or on the basis of facts beyond observation', while it clearly has survival value, is also subject to abuse. Thus, while it is necessary to have a mental mechanism which allows judgements to be made and action initiated on the basis of incomplete information, such a mechanism does allow false convictions to be arrived at either spontaneously or by the contrivance of others (Taylor, 1987). Included in the definition of beliefs are 'propositions accepted on the grounds of evidence', but I do not think really that one can be said to believe in the moon, though one might believe it spherical or to be made of green cheese. Words like 'trust' and 'persuasion' come into belief. Unlike other animals, we can believe what we are told or be persuaded even by that which has not yet been seen and has not yet been directly experienced. We can entertain the notion of terror. Indeed such a split can be produced within us that, provided we do not believe it, we seek terror for fun. This split between experiential and propositional knowledge, what is true for us against truths of a more empirical sort in the outside world – like 'the most beautiful girl in the world' as compared with the 'height of St Paul's', may be an important component in the sense of conviction where the individual experiences as propositional, empirical, what is actually experiential.

Belief is very carefully treated in psychiatry partly for these reasons and partly because it is essential to respect beliefs, albeit they might seem alien and odd, otherwise psychiatry could claim immense and improper power. Perhaps because of this, the source, impact and dissemination of beliefs are little studied (but see Jaspers, 1962). People can develop, sometimes quite suddenly, powerful and subsequently incorrigible beliefs (Sargant, 1973). The Christian paradigm is St Paul. These beliefs are not regarded as delusional if they are sanctioned within a relevant social network (Goldberg et al; 1987), but they can be damaging to health. Beliefs and normal convictions are the powerful basis of much human behaviour, including illness behaviour.

I shall argue that hysteria, as it presents clinically, arises from deep convictions, avowals, about abnormal states of health or of functioning which are maintained within a small social system about casually selected, if not entirely random, victims who are presented as sick. The characteristics of the victims and the nature of their disorder are the subject of a long debate in medicine (Roy, 1982). But the characteristics of the victim and the physiology of the disorder may be less crucial to our understanding if we are simply dealing with a medical perspective on an aspect of normal human behaviour which might be differently interpreted from other perspectives and at other times (Rabkin, 1964; Mayou, 1975; Hurst, 1983).

In 1961 I was house officer to William Sargant. One Saturday he admitted to our ward a teenage girl diagnosed schizophrenic on the evidence of her terrifying sensation of being the victim of systematic persecution by 'dark forces' and the fact that an older sister had already been institutionalised for some years with a similar illness so diagnosed. Starting treatment seemed unwise until contact could be made with her parents. Initially she resisted this, explaining that contact could only be made via intermediaries. As her terror diminished and her confidence grew she agreed by late afternoon to initiate the contact. Within an hour I was telephoned by her father. He took the view that his daughter had been abducted into hospital by a witches' coven and that he would proceed through public pressure to secure her release. Her fiancé appeared. He was induced, against what he regarded as his better judgement, to reveal to me that the family were extremely

276 *David Taylor*

secretive because they were in great danger. He instanced occasions when his future father-in-law had explained to him the ominous significance of a coil of string in a gutter, a dab of paint on a wall, an ostensibly courteous remark by a waiter. Each was evidence of the malign plot. Armed with this key a further interview with the patient revealed stories of black rays striking out of clear skies where her father 'might have been' and of a Jaguar car hurled to destruction across the M1 which father 'could have been driving' had he not, cunningly, been in a small Ford in Devon at the time. Father meanwhile had alerted most of the national press to the incident and telephoned so incessantly that the GPO had to protect the hospital number. Finally, on Monday morning, he appeared with his wife each carrying several large baskets of food and bottled water. To my civil greeting he replied, 'You! You are obviously a warlock!' Fortunately by then I had contacted other agencies who revealed to me that he suffered from schizophrenia so there were only five and not six participants in this 'folie' whose beliefs ranged from the delusional through the overvalued to the intense.

The construction we place upon this incident in a psychiatric ward in England, in the late twentieth century, is not of a family bewitched but of a small confined group powerfully influenced, to believe and act upon the basis of a belief, held by a schizophrenic, a man suffering a serious chronic disorder of brain function. The rest were in thrall to the power of his conviction. It is a clinical example but there are abundant political and religious examples that readily come to mind in the world today and we have the recent history of madmen like Mr Jones, 900 of whose believers were readily persuaded to a synchronous suicide in Guyana.

Hysteria

In its most general sense in medicine, hysteria implies laying claim to, or making an avowal of, bodily dysfunction for which the typical causes are not apparent and in a manner which somehow parodies the sorts of distress produced by organ pathology (Head, 1922; Walshe, 1965). It is dangerous ground for everyone; hysteria might entail pretending by the patient on the one hand and yet it will also subsume ignorance and error by doctors on the other (Slater, 1965). It has a long history in medicine which encourages doctors to believe that it is a disease, (Guze et al; 1986), tangible in some sense (Flor-Henry et al; 1981; 1985;, that they are diagnosing rather than a description of how things stand between a doctor and his patient, and the patient and his world (Mayou, 1984). Some descriptions of hysteria continue, on the conceit of requiring longstanding claims for sickness in many systems, to portray a syndrome, but hysteria had also to encompass the transient sickness of schoolchildren on a day out. Confusion between hysteria, as that which is being experienced, and hysterics, as those who are experiencing it, has increased the problems in the discourse. Is hysteria something that only hysterics can do? A further problem concerns possible differences between the mechanisms that enable the hysterical response and those that maintain it to a clinical presentation. A conviction might be suddenly arrived at but be abandoned or become incorrigible according to circumstances. The circumstances include the intra-psychic life.

What constitutes hysteria to different doctors is determined by their personal perspective and by their locus in the health care organization. Psychiatrists mostly see and have written about long-established cases, neurologists have been preoccupied with not allowing themselves to be deceived nor yet overlook organ pathology; both have hankered after running the great neurosis to earth in the neurone. Physicians have leant towards seeing hysteria as a moral flaw or a deceit. Paediatricians, well used to deflecting children's and parents' offers of sickness, are nevertheless sporadically overwhelmed by bravura performances and then sometimes feel so shy they do not like to let on (Dubowitz and Hersov, 1976; Goodyer, 1981). Almost all doctors, almost all the time, participate in the sexist plot to regard hysteria as a sickness of women despite the efforts of physicians from as long ago as Briquet and Charcot to the contrary (Owen, 1971), while largely ignoring the massive issue of wartime hysterias.

Very important insights into the probable basis of the hysterical mechanism have come to attention through wartime casualties and through the epidemic hysterias. It is because these occasions recruit so readily from otherwise ordinary human beings that they provide us with a glimpse of possible mechanisms. The arguments about hysteria will continue until the mechanism is clarified. To separate off epidemic and war hysterias from clinical cases is simply to evade the issue and at the expense of learning a useful lesson.

The literature on hysteria during and after the Great Wars reveals the scale of the problem (Sargant and Slater, 1940; 1941). Thousands of men were affected and, while battle casualties were an important core of the group, much of the hysteria was contributed by non-combatants. Despite an attentive and relatively humane method of dealing with the casualties they were subsequently largely useless for combat (Slater et al., 1941). Considering the extremely detailed persistent work of the St Louis school and its finding that the male relatives of females with Briquet's syndrome are psychopathic, it is worth noting that many hysterical men were regarded by the military doctors as having been neuraesthenic, psychopathic and shiftless in their pre-military careers. The language of these reports is derogatory in style and condescending, patronizing, in flavour.

Particular attention was drawn to the model provided for Pavlov by the drowning and near-drowning of his experimental dogs in the Leningrad laboratory flood. The dogs that succumbed to the terror by losing their conditioned reflexes and becoming subsequently untrainable (which must have been annoying to Pavlov), were regarded as having what he called 'weak' or 'strong excitatory' central nervous systems. 'Transmarginal inhibition' was the ambiguous term he applied to the state of brain into which they more easily lapsed than those Pavlov called 'lively' or 'calm imperturbable' types. Similarly the war casualties were graded in personality traits, background and history with epithets so that groups of men, similar in character to the dogs, could be shown to have behaved similarly under varying degrees of stress. Obviously, invaliding out on psychiatric grounds had to be controlled and the disparaging language reflects negative military attitude to the faint of heart. But it suggests too that, for men at least, the option of going transmarginal will be associated with severe loss of esteem whatever the scale of the precipitating event (Sargant, 1973).

In war, men came to accept the proposition that they might well die, often on the evidence of their own eyes, but also on the testimony of others they had, as soldiers, accepted the possibility of death as a fact beyond observation. In other words, they came, at varying degrees of remove from the evidence, to believe they might die. The transmarginal inhibition was a defence. Pavlov believed that ultimately every human being had the capacity for it. T. A. Ross (1941), in his interesting short book on war neuroses, quotes from an earlier book by Babinski and Froment in which is a report written by a French medical officer. His report is astonishing.

When *La Provence* was torpedoed we were able to study the manifestations of emotion close at hand apart from any commotional state.

We found that the pithiatic (hysterical) phenomena did not occur until later when the survivors were in safety. These phenomena yielded to an energetic treatment which was immediately applied, and did not recur during the week which followed the accident. Our experience was divided into four periods.

1st period. On board the boat seventeen minutes between the explosion and the complete disappearance of the boat – period of pure emotion. The crew were anxious and dumb. No cries. Many were in a state of agitation. Later an officer shot himself through the head. This was followed by a small epidemic of suicide. There were however no fits, convulsions or paralyses. In seventeen minutes there was nothing left on the water but wreckage, swimmers and drowned.

2nd period. In the sea for eighteen hours. Seventeen of us clung to a raft during this period. At first there were some expressions of despair but a cheerful fellow pulled them together by saying he had often been in a much worse hole and was sure he would get out this time. One man began a religious lament which began to upset others, but the officer told thim if he did not keep quiet he would throw him in the water. None of the men died.

3rd period. After eighteen hours we were picked up by a torpedo boat and when all were on deck I inspected them. Several now showed neuropathic phenomena: quadraplegia, paraplegia, mutism snarling, weeping, barking, shaking amounting to spasmodic movements of the upper limbs. I sent them down to the engine-room close to the engine where the temperature was very high. The number of my patients increased as new survivors arrived so that out of six hundred picked up there were about forty showing nervous disturbances.

The treatment was simple. They were stripped naked in an overheated room and engergetically rubbed by two vigorous sailors with a hair glove soaked in alcohol. As soon as they had been warmed externally and internally with rum, I took each one separately and smacked him harder and harder until the disturbances disappeared, all the time speaking kindly to them and expressing my delight at the rapidity of their recovery. No one resisted more than ten minutes: many were cured of contagion on witnessing the treatment of the others. The majority expressed to me their gratitutde on witnessing the treatment of the others.

4th period. I was able to see my patients for a week and there were no relapses.

The report describes the traumatic event leading to pervasive stunned shock or a self-destructive altenative. Then, while peril remains but before rescue, a long period of apparent calm. Then, as seen from a medical perspective, some of the phenomena of relief from trauma and peril. Silent tears, congratulatory embraces, gales of laughter are not mentioned; only those men whose 'symptoms' might have some medical connotation however various they may be. It is honest about the aggressive nature of the brainwashing treatment. The difference between these symptoms and clinically presented hysterias is that they were experienced by people from a group known to be well only a while before and there are no supporters of their sick condition. Once these circumstances change, the belief, the hysteria, could take a more chronic hold.

Ross's other contribution is to note the paradox of how differently the civilian population, who had ostensibly had the cream of their manhood withdrawn from them, react to the devastation of civilian bombing from which they can neither escape nor make reprisals with relatively low rates of hysteria as compared with the troops. Ross wonders whether the deliberate training of military personnel to states of near mindlessness contributes at all to their subsequent breakdown. Of course, the terror and horror and appalling revulsion experienced as a ship is blown up or while under fire in the trenches can only be imagined, but there are accounts of reliving them under abreaction described by Grinker and Spiegel (quoted by Sargant in *Battle for the Mind*, 1957). This is as near to the moment of the manifestation of the hysterical mechanism as we can get descriptively:

> The terror exhibited . . . is electrifying to watch. The body becomes increasingly tense and rigid; the eyes widen and the pupils dilate, while the skin becomes covered with a fine perspiration. The hands move convulsively. . . . Breathing becomes incredibly rapid or shallow. The intensity of the emotion sometimes becomes more than they can bear, and frequently at the height of the reaction, there is collapse and the patient falls back in the bed and remains quiet for a few minutes . . .

Abreaction does not require the reliving of the traumatic event which seemingly precipitated the hysterical symptoms (Shorvon and Sargant, 1947). Its therapeutic value lay in the intensity of an emotional catharsis. It seems to offer a close approximation to the physiology and psychology of the overwhelming event. Sargant (1957) sets this description against one of Wesley's congregation reacting to his hellfire preaching, and coming to believe through crisis; truly a convert.

> Friday, June 15th, 1739 (Wesley's Journal)
> Some sunk down, and there remained no strength in them; others exceedingly trembled and quaked; some were torn with a kind of convulsive motion in every part of their bodies, and that so violently that often four or five persons could not hold one of them. I have seen many hysterical and many epileptic fits; but none of them were like these in many respects.

For Wesley this process, which he called 'sanctification', was instantaneous work. It is crucial to my thesis that such depth of conviction is achieved in a moment. Indeed it is recognized for what it is by its being the work of a moment.

Now consider the mechanism which enables the hysterical response. What would be the biological and evolutionary value of such a mechanism with instantaneous onset and offset? While the response to threat in human beings through flight or fighting back is amply described in student textbooks of physiology and psychology, little is said about responses to events in which these options are both precluded. What options remain? Consider the condition of stunned shock in the bird or the mouse which the cat has caught. They are close to death and maybe, in stupor or even by self-induced death, at least avoid further pain. But there may be a fine margin of profit in playing possum. Several species feign death to deflect potential predators or mimic injury to draw predators away from helpless young. Even the alternative, the frantic, non-congnitive, headless chicken, 'violent motor reaction' just *might* secure escape. These two responses were described by Kretschmer (1961) in casualties of World War I and have been confirmed by others since in wars and disasters. They are seen, albeit at lesser states of intensity, in the classic epidemic hysterias.

The settings of epidemic hysterias, the trigger event and the symptoms are important to understanding hysteria (Moss and McEvedy, 1966; Alexander and Fedoruk, 1986). So too are the nature, quality and the stridency of the alternative explanations which are always insisted upon by a section of the community (usually relatives of victims) which assist in the promotion and maintenance of symptoms (Watson, 1982; Small and Borus, 1983). In these dramas the actors and the audience are equal partners. When the sick are presented to doctors the doctors are compelled to act from their perspective just as the parents or the crowd acted from theirs. In this way the medical procedures tend to validate the sickness to the relatives in the same process which invalidates it to the doctors. Epidemic hysterias arise couched in social settings which enhance emotionality and promote the rapid 'mental acceptance of propositions as true even if beyond observation'. The sorts of events that recruit these responses are unavoidable apparent threats which have emerged through some form of ultra rapid group consensus. Removal of the affected individuals from the group normally allows them a rapid return to normality since the so-called threat exists much more as a function of corporate than of personal belief. The parallels in animal behaviour are in the extraordinary rapidity of communication in herd and flock behaviour. A recent epidemic of hysteria on the Israel/Arab border, however, was politically exploited and by precluding appropriate treatment of young people the epidemic persisted longer and spread wider than usual (Hefez, 1985).

> Thirty-four students . . . were suddenly afflicted by an attack of blindness, headache and stomachache, as well as cyanosis of the . . . limbs . . . The doctors noticed that two girls had developed complete blindness with respiratory complications and transferred them by ambulance to Affula Central Hospital where they were admitted to the intensive care unit.

Within the affected group in the hysterical epidemic there will be some who are at that moment so placed that, for them, the hysteria is psychologically opportune. This leads to recidivism, as it did in that report, especially if non-symptomatic contacts are keen to exploit the occasion to air their beliefs about aetiology. Currently non-validatable high-technology credos are favoured as bases for these epidemics; viruses, allergens, crop sprays, nuclear fallout etc. Sadly and tragically, these credos also affect sick children presenting individually whose sicknesses, because they are sporadic, are easily initially misperceived and become even more deeply established as a result of the interventions and investigations required to invalidate medical diagnoses once they have been entertained. In order to make an investigation ethically, the doctor must entertain the same possibility as the complainant and this reinforces the possibility and it is the possibility which is the important element in the belief.

Magic

The most trivial meaning of magic is prestidigitation by which people are induced to believe what they did not see. Jakob Bronowski (1978) in his *Magic Science and Civilisation Lectures* traces the change in our interpretation of nature from magic to science to the period between 1500 and 1700. He defines magic as 'that logic which is separate from the logic of everyday life but which, given the secret key, could command nature'. Only the initiates would have this power. Of all the situations where people might wish to command nature such as fire or drought; sickness, especially in their children, must be the most pervasive and seductive. Since medicine has been largely technologically powerless for most of its history, it is not surprising to find its alliance with magic (Maple, 1968). Magical precepts fail, according to Bronowski, as compared to science, in that magic formulae never produce alterations in things at a distance from the magician, except seemingly through the credulity of people. (Hence the peculiar fascination of Uri Geller.) Where magic formulae succeed they become technology, for example cinchona bark. According to W. Lehman (quoted by Mauss in *The Theory of Magic*, p. 130), 'magic derives from errors of perception, illusions and hallucinations, as well as acute, emotive and subconscious states of expectation, prepossession and excitability' and according to Mauss (1950, p. 142), 'The magician ... puts to work collective forces and ideas to help the individual imagination in its belief.' Magical cures, then, simply reverse the process of hysterical sickness.

The 'forces' to which Mauss refers are to my view originally in the individual and derive from primitive animism, that historical, but also and more persistently, developmental phase to which we variably readily regress, and about which we are variably embarrassed when we do. Primitive animism implies that all objects are imbued with their own spirits which have motives and their behaviour is regulated by the interaction of these spirits, leaving man a hapless bystander, unless he can command them. It is an almost universal experience especially when we have been let down by a machine. There is thus ample scope for deceit, prior conviction and delusion to comingle and interact in manipulating these moments of disorted conviction. If the magical convictions are powerful enough man can be persuaded to give up life itself (Beecher, 1962; Milton, 1973):

> the expression on his face becomes horribly distorted. . . . He attempts to shriek, but the sound chokes in his throat, and all that one might see is froth at his mouth. His body begins to tremble and the muscles twist involuntarily. He sways backwards and falls to the ground, and after a short time appears to be in swoon; but soon after he writhes as if in mortal agony, and, covering his face with his hands, begins to moan. *(Basedow, 1925, quoted by Cannon, 1942)*

This description of death through conviction, through 'pointing of bones' is compellingly similar to the sequence of events in sudden religious conversion, abreaction, war hysteria and epidemic hysteria given above. Like the 'stunned shock' and 'possum' reactions, recovery is immediate if the curse is lifted by the person who imposed it, even when seemingly profound physiological changes have supervened.

More common than such executions are the living deaths or the temporary deaths to which I initially referred. Some of these sicknesses are very long, troublesome and costly; they deserve our attention. They differ from serious diseases by being lived with almost triumphantly, though protestingly, while still maintaining a belief system which conventional medicine does not hold.

> In 1985 a 12-year-old boy was referred for a further opinion on management. His parents' view was that he suffered numerous life-long somatic complaints and, increasingly, behavioural problems which were due to multiple allergies. His allergy to rain had made the national press but he was also said to be allergic to North Sea Gas and a wide variety of other substances, not often thought of as allergens. Initially he could not be brought into the building where I work because his mother could see that was the type of building in which potential allergens abound. But 'neutralising drops' available in phials costing £25 each were used. The touch of these under the tongue instantly enabled him to enter. Nevertheless his 'allergic' response was judged by his mother to be evidenced by his pathetic foul-mouthed observation that she might now leave. He was born, nine years after his only sibling, to an elderly mother. Termination was considered. She suffered from high blood pressure and many 'allergies' that limited her diet. Her husband was a bizarre man of extraordinary social behaviour who had been subject to psychosis from the age of 21. He was still in regular psychiatric care. He also claimed migraine due to potato allergy. Their implacable beliefs were that their son exhibited life-long allergy as evi-

denced by his having had episodes of sickness and of diarrhoea as a baby and developing stomach pains, weak feelings, muzzy headedness and his own parody of 'aggression' from his first days at school. They could no longer afford private allergy treatment. They hoped he could be placed in a 'bubble' so that he could recover while protected from the alien world.

The boy, when separated from his parents, was just an obese, dull, unhappy child who reiterated the family beliefs. The parents initially rejected psychiatric treatment and admission to hospital but reluctantly conformed when the question of school avoidance and its legal consequence was raised. He lived for four months in hospital taking ordinary hospital diet and going swimming with the school. No evidence of any form of 'attack' was witnesses except those involving his parents and consisting of childish rudeness and slaps. They were always interpreted by them in terms of reactions to allergens. A consultant paediatrician expert in allergy found only minor traces of evidence of marginal relevance. Initially, the boy began to settle to the fuller life and improve his impoverished education and social skills. But as pressure to remove him from home more permanently increased, he regressed in his general behaviour and became firmer in his beliefs about his allergic state. At the same time father's psychosis decompensated and mother's beliefs became more fervent and frantic. It became clear that the local authorities felt unable to act on behalf of the child on the basis of the available evidence of abuse, and the parents removed the child from hospital. A year later his 'unique problem' made the Sunday newspapers. He was pictured at home, indoors on a rainy summer day. He is the real prisoner of their imaginations. Lévi-Strauss (1967) recognized these sicknesses now being variously labelled by the technologists, he called them 'Piteous sicknesses, the total surrender of existence in a last ditch defence of the self by total capitulation.'

This capitulation by the organism, often partial sometimes total, is being hypostatized, made into yet another illness. In hysteria there exists an alternative defence mechanism to fight or flight. It is widespread in animal species. It has an aspect of stupor and an aspect of frantic mindless activity which is not organized flight. In animals these mechanisms are accessed through extreme terror, usually in situations which imply potential imminent demise. It is crucial that these physiological defence mechanisms unlock instantly if the situation improves. In man the mechanisms are readily accessed in situations of terror, horror or revulsion, experienced from outside. But in man these states can also be accessed from within as a result of beliefs. Beliefs are generated by information which is accessed within a feeling tone. Beliefs differ from certain knowledge in that they are generally arrived at on the basis of partial information and can derive from experiential rather than empirical knowledge. This is not necessarily verbally encoded in memory and is hence inaccessible to verbal approaches. This has survival value but allows of error. Belief and false belief are thus tied into the third defence mechanism. In groups it is in the nature of belief to be contagious. Magic plays its tricks through the mechanism of belief.

Sickness evokes aspirations to command nature. In man, through belief, through magic, a mechanism of potentially lethal power can be manipulated. But there are more chronic terrors, more persistent states of being where neither flight nor fighting back are available. One possible diversion lies in a mechanism which is perceived as sickness and this at times will be opportune and give rise to lengthy dramas. Unfortunately doctors cannot guess at that before they become embroiled in them. But they can beware.

REFERENCES

Alexander, R. W. and Fedoruk, M. J. (1986) Epidemic psychogenic illness in a telephone operators' building, *Journal of Occupational Medicine* 28, 42–5.
Bayliss, R. I. S. (1984) The deceivers, *British Medical Journal* 288, 583–4.
Beecher, H. K. (1962) Nonspecific forces surrounding disease and the treatment of disease, *Journal of the American Medical Association* 179, 437–40.
Bronowski, J. (1978) *Magic, Science, and Civilization*, New York: Columbia University Press.
Byng-Hall, J. (1986) Family scripts: A concept which can bridge child psychotherapy and family therapy thinking, *Journal of Child Psychotherapy* 12, 3–13.
Cannon, W. B. (1942) 'Voodoo' death, *American Anthropologist* 44, 169–81.
Creak, M. (1938) Hysteria in childhood, *The British Journal of Children's Diseases* 35, 85–95.
Dubowitz, V. and Hersov, L. (1976) Management of children with non-organic (hysterical) disorders of motor function, *Developmental Medicine & Child Neurology* 18, 358–68.
Durkheim, E. and Mauss, M. (1963) *Primitive Classification*, trans. and ed. Rodney Needham, London: Cohen & West.
Epstein, S. (1967) A sociological analysis of witch beliefs in a Mysore village. In *Magic, Witchcraft, and Curing*, ed. J. Middleton, London: University of Texas Press.
Ernst, A. R., Routh, D. K. and Harper, D. C. (1984) Abdominal pain in children and symptoms of somatization disorder, *Journal of Pediatric Psychology* 9, 77–86.
Flechet, M. L., Priollet, P., Consoli, S., Vayssairat, M. and Housset, E. (1983) L'oedème bleu de Charcot, *Ann. Med. Interne* 134, 35–7.
Flor-Henry, P. (1985) Hysteria. In *Handbook of Clinical Neurology* Vol. 2 (46), ed.

P. J. Vinken, G. W. Bruyn and H. L. Klawans, Amsterdam: Elsevier Science Publishers.

Flor-Henry, P., Fromm-Auch, D., Tapper, M. and Schopflocher, D. (1981) A neuropsychological study of the stable syndrome of hysteria, *Biological Psychiatry* 16, 601–26.

Goldberg, D., Benjamin, S. and Creed, F. (1987) *Psychiatry in Medical Practice*, London: Tavistock Publications.

Goodyer, I. (1981) Hysterical conversion reactions in childhood, *Journal of Child Psychology & Psychiatry* 22, 179–88.

Goodyer, I. M. (1985) Epileptic and pseudoepileptic seizures in childhood and adolescence, *Journal of the American Academy of Child Psychiatry* 24, 3–9.

Goodyer, I. M. (1986) (Monosymptomatic) hysteria in childhood family and professional systems involvement, *Journal of Family Therapy* 8, 1–12.

Guze, S. B., Cloninger, C. R., Martin, R. L. and Clayton, P. J. (1986) A follow-up and family study of Briquet's syndrome, *British Journal of Psychiatry* 149, 17–23.

Head, H. (1922) The diagnosis of hysteria, *British Medical Journal* 1, 827–9.

Hefez, A. (1985) The role of the press and the medical community in the epidemic of "mysterious gas poisoning" in the Jordan West Bank, *American Journal of Psychiatry* 142, 833–7.

Hurst, L. C. (1983) Freud and the great neurosis: discussion paper, *Journal of the Royal Society of Medicine* 76, 57–61.

Jaspers, K. (1962) *General psychopathology*, trans. J. Hoenig and M. W. Hamilton, Manchester: Manchester University Press.

Kretschmer, E. (1961) *Hysteria, Reflex and Instinct*, trans. V. & W. Baskin, London: Peter Owen.

Kriechman, A. M. (1987) Siblings with somatoform disorders in childhood and adolescence, *Journal of the American Academy of Child and Adolescent Psychiatry* 26, 226–31.

Lévi-Strauss, C. (1967) The sorcerer and his magic. In *Magic, Witchcraft, and Curing*, ed. J. Middleton, London: University of Texas Press.

Maloney, M. J. (1980) Diagnosing hysterical conversion reactions in children, *The Journal of Pediatrics* 97, 1016–20.

Maple, E. (1968) *Magic, Medicine & Quackery*, London: Robert Hale.

Mauss, M. (1950) *A General Theory of Magic*, trans. Robert Brain, London: Routledge & Kegan Paul.

Mauss, M. (1979) A definition of the collective suggestion of the idea of death. In *Sociology and Psychology*, trans. Ben Brewster, London: Routledge & Kegan Paul.

Mayou, R. (1975) The social setting of hysteria, *British Journal of Psychiatry* 127, 466–9.

Mayou, R. (1984) Sick role, illness behaviour and coping, *British Journal of Psychiatry* 144, 320–2.

McEvedy, C. P., Griffith, A. and Hall, T. (1966) Two school epidemics, *British Medical Journal* 2, 1300–2.

Meadow, R. (1984) Fictitious epilepsy, *The Lancet* ii, 25–8.

Milner, A. D. (1985) Psychogenic cough in childhood, *British Medical Journal* 290,

1847–8.

Milton, G. W. (1973) Self-willed death or the bone-pointing syndrome, *The Lancet* i, 1435–6.

Moritz, A. R. and Zamcheck, n. (1946) Sudden and unexpected deaths of young soldiers, *Archives of Pathology* 42, 459–94.

Moss, P. D. and McEvedy, C. (1966) An epidemic of overbreathing among school-girls, *British Medical Journal* 2, 1295–300.

Naish, J. M. (1979) Problems of deception in medical practice, *The Lancet* ii, 139–42.

Owen, A. R. G. (1971) *Hysteria, Hypnosis and Healing: The Work of Jean-Martin Charcot*, London: Dobson Books.

Precope, J. (1954) *Medicine Magic and Mythology*, London: Heinemann.

Rabkin, R. (1964) Conversion hysteria as social maladaptation, *Psychiatry* 27, 349–63.

Robins, E. and O'Neal, P. (1953) Clinical features of hysteria in children, with a note on prognosis. A two to seventeen year follow-up study of 41 patients, *Quarterly Journal of Psychopathology* 10, 246–71.

Ross, T. A. (1941) *Lectures on War Neuroses*, London: Edward Arnold.

Roy, A. (ed.) (1982) *Hysteria*, Chichester: John Wiley & Sons.

Sachdev, P. S. (1985) Koro epidemic in north-east India, *Australian and New Zealand Journal of Psychiatry* 19, 433–8.

Sargant, W. (1940) The hyperventilation syndrome, *The Lancet* i, 314–16.

Sargant, W. (1957) *Battle for the Mind*, London: Heinemann.

Sargant, W. (1973) *The Mind Possessed*, London: Heinemann.

Sargant, W. and Slater, E. (1940) Acute war neuroses, *The Lancet* ii, 1–2.

Sargant, W. and Slater, E. (1941) Amnesic syndromes in war, *Proceedings of the Royal Society of Medicine* 34, 757–64.

Shorvon, H. J. and Sargant, W. (1947) Excitatory abreaction: with special reference to its mechanism and the use of ether, *The Journal of Mental Science* 93, 709–32.

Slater, E. (1965) Diagnosis of 'hysteria' *British Medical Journal* 1, 1395–9.

Slater, E., Debenham, G., Hill, D. and Sargant, W. (1941) Treatment of war neurosis, *The Lancet* i, 107–9.

Small, G. W. and Borus, J. F. (1983) Outbreak of illness in a school chorus, *The New England Journal of Medicine* 308, 632–5.

Stanley, A. and Freed, R. S. (1967) Spirit possession as illness in a north Indian village. In *Magic, Witchcraft, and Curing*, ed. J. Middleton. London: University of Texas Press.

Taylor, D. C. (1986) Hysteria, play-acting and courage, *British Journal of Psychiatry* 149, 37–41.

Taylor, D. C. (1987) Epilepsy and prejudice, *Archives of Disease in Childhood* 62, 209–11.

Walshe, F. (1965) Diagnosis of hysteria, *British Medical Journal* 2, 1451–4.

Watson, N. (1982) An outbreak of hysterical paraplegia, *Paraplegia* 20, 154–7.

Zoccolillo, M. and Cloninger, C. R. (1985) Parental breakdown associated with somatisation disorder (hysteria), *British Journal of Psychiatry* 147, 443–6.

18

Ordinary Animals, Language Animals and Verbal Tradition

Vernon Reynolds

Rom Harré's view of man, expounded in his talks and books, shows us man as a teller of stories, a language user. And not just a language user, he is also the creator of a world of linguistic images and conventions, a re-creator of the entire perceived world, re-modelling his own being into a new fabric that is quite separate from the world of animals and inanimate things. Separate in that, although wholly material in its basic components (the neurones of the human brain, which in the end, are 'all there is') it comes alive, gets reified, for us as the world of 'reality' we live in, with its man-made cultural history, and its ever-present sanctions in the here and now. This fabric is largely built out of language, which pervades all our actions. Where social behaviour in other species evolves as a consequence of natural selection, in humans other, cultural conventions are paramount in determining the forms our social actions take.

Take a simple action: wearing a tie. Why do it? Some people don't. But others do. Why bother? It's hard to do up, shirts have a top button anyway so it's nothing to do with keeping warm (a sweater would be better). In England, men at hot, humid board meetings nearly always wear ties. So do bank clerks. It's something to do with being 'properly dressed', 'formal'. What is formality? We seem to be talking about self-presentation as a recognizable agent in a bureaucratic structure. What an extraordinary and rather elusive thing wearing a tie turns out to be! Of course, there are ties and ties. There are so-called loud ties that film-stars are expected to wear. The loud tie says: 'I have so much money I am free of convention.' We expect to see a loud tie on a rather fat, ugly man in a shiny jacket with a smiling young lady close by. Not on a lord out grouse-shooting, heavens, no. Nor, really, on a bank clerk.

All the subtle meanings and conventions that melt and flow into each other and that form the cultural world we live in are represented verbally in our minds and we somehow manage to steer ourselves through real social situations, either passively adapting and adjusting or, more boisterously, rocking the boat, modifying the very conventions that hold us in place.

But where does the demonstration of the complexly verbal social world get us? We started by saying that man's uniqueness was puzzling because he seemed to be operating according to a different principle from that of the rest of the animal world. Did the example given bear this out? Or could other explanations for tie-wearing be found, not involving the kinds of complex explanations put forward? Certainly animals do adjust their appearance according to circumstances. Colours of males get brighter in the breeding season, new colours, plumes and other devices appear. But there are two ways in which these displays are quite different from tie-wearing and its social meanings.

First, with regard to mechanism, animal displays are hormonally mediated, or mediated by some other change in physiology. A few animals adorn themselves or their surroundings with objects but that too is a part of a hormonally mediated display. Second, the function differs. Colour, shape and size changes in animals serve three functions: intra-sexual competitive display, display to potential mates, and camouflage. For an organism to show such displays, there must have been selective advantages to them in the past. Badges of office – things like ties – are not hormonally mediated. Arguably it may work the other way round: putting on the regalia of high office may change a person's hormonal state, but not vice versa.

The second difference may look at first like a similarity, but it is not. Does not a tie serve as an intra-male competitive display? Even if this sometimes happens, the parallel is not close. For in the animal case it has to be reproductive advantage that leads to the transmission of the displayed character. In the human one there are at least two further ifs: even if the be-tied boy succeeds in seducing the girl, either or both of them may wear contraceptives. Yet ties go on. And second, even if be-tied boys always really did have more children than open-necked ones, generation after generation, a flip of fashion could change this, as we know from history. Ties can end suddenly, without the disappearance of humans. Peacocks feathers cannot end suddenly unless peacocks go extinct; they could, if selected against, go into a gradual decline but ties do not gradually get smaller before they disappear! Animals and their display characteristics are intimately allied, all part of a single epigenetic porcess; humans and their display characteristics are not.

So there, at last, we have it; there are no genes for the rules governing the wearing of ties, so humans are unique. Untrue! Ties and their use can be seen as part of the range of variation found in human phenotypes. Just as a hare's coat goes brown in summer to give camouflage, so soldiers in battle wear khaki and daub their faces with soot. Genes provide an insufficient account in both cases. What genes do is make proteins. All that follows is organized higher up the scale of causation of behaviour, where intricate systems, still poorly understood, combine their effects, using inputs from the environment arriving through the sense organs. These systems are controlled by complex checks and balances. For instance, the system that makes the male red grouse strut about his lek may be inhibited in which case he opts out of the competitive scene and makes for the edge of the moor, losing his chance of mating for the season (he may make up for this the next year). Genes make certain things possible, that's all. Epigenesis does the rest. And why should we draw the line at organic epigenesis? Why exclude cultural features of the epigenetic process? Epigenesis can't be left out. Without epigenesis we could not wear ties. Not just epigenesis for hands and necks, but for learning culturally accepted patterns of behaviour, for assimilating a self-concept, for learning the rules of the game, and learning them through language. In other words epigenesis for a certain kind of psychology, of which language is very much a part.

Man is a very psychological species, if the expression can be allowed. This fact is deeply present in all Rom Harré's work. He would say 'Yes, and a social-psychological one at that.' I agree. The extent to which we are products of our social psychology is remarkable. Animals also have their social psychology. A chimpanzee, accepted by the other members of its group, becomes a lively, interactive individual; placed in a group where it is rejected there can even be recourse to suicide. Nothing needs to differ but the social context, or to be precise, the reactions of the other group members. Man, like his primate cousins, is a species that is very much, psychologically, a product of the reactions of his fellows, and whose particular genome allows him, thanks to the linguistic community in which he lives, to model and re-model his thoughts and actions on the norms he perceives around him. He tries things on and he tries things out. Today a tie, tomorrow an open neck. This evening a noisy vulgar session in the pub, tomorrow the school carol service; next day feet up in front of the television. Different audiences, different selves to match. Because of the different social worlds in which he moves he has, compared with other primates, a wider range of selves than they do. And if forced to spend time in a group that is verbally rejecting or hostile, he too can be reduced to depression and suicide.

Chimps also have more than one self. Over long periods chimpanzee behaviour changes – witness the outbreak of violent behaviour by Goodall's Kasakela males after years of (relative) peace. Those males showed themselves capable of changing from normally aggressive, fundamentally peaceable apes to vicious brutes bent on killing others of their kind. It is not yet clear what brought about the change, but something changed the rules of behaviour: instead of avoiding males from the neighbouring group they went out and killed them.

Thus woodland chimpanzees, like humans, have their history; groups wax and wane in numbers and in the area they control. Memories are doubtless long, resentments may linger, attitudes be transmitted from mothers to offspring. But none of this is verbalized, it is a silent tradition. Perhaps it is this matter of a verbal tradition that should be our point of departure in thinking about where we most differ from other species. It is within this verbal tradition possessed by all human societies that the rules of comportment, the reified social structures, the sanctions and rewards of normal life are contained. Lacking a verbal tradition other species cannot develop a detailed social self based on historical continuity. The self-concept of apes lacks time-depth; in humans it is time-dimensioned. In both it is volatile, changing with time and circumstance. But the penetration of tradition into the self cannot be great in the complete absence of words.

So I would agree with Harré when he singles out language use, not just as an aspect of human achievement, but as the formative element in man's social psychology. In this respect too we can see that 'language use' by apes, whatever it really is, cannot compare with the human case. Without in any way challenging man's animal status, and without denying all we have in common with other primates (more and more of which we are discovering as the years go by) there is a difference. But I would want to add to the concept of language use the time dimension and call it 'language tradition'. This is, of course, implicit anyway, since we do not re-invent language in each generation (except in a very specialised sense in child development). But it could perhaps be made more explicit: man differs because he builds himself out of the materials provided by verbal traditions. This does not set him above the animals, but it marks him off from them; it is his extreme specialisation (as sonar is for bats) and it has proved, so far, a highly effective way of building vigorous, long-lasting social systems.

Having established man as the language-using animal, and as the species that constructs its self-concept out of the materials supplied by the verbal tradition, I want next to move on to a topic that is again near to Harré's heart: intentionality. I want to discuss the topic itself briefly, and then move on to integrate it with the inheritance of verbal tradition.

In recent years, studies of primate social behaviour have forced many ethologists, psychologists, zoologists and others to conclude that there are lively cognitive minds in the heads of our close relatives in the animal world. Monkeys and apes are thoughtful creatures rather than thoughtless ones. They are not 'driven' by instincts or other drives so much as careful planners with complex strategies aimed at solving particular problems.

Take for instance the process of status determination in rhesus macaques. We have known since the 1950s that such monkeys form coherent matrilines, with the offspring in the female line of an old female sitting together, grooming each other and supporting each other in conflicts with the offspring of other females. Datta has recently made a close study of how young rhesus monkeys establish their social status.

The matrilines are not equally ranked. The offspring of a senior old female all rank above those of a junior one. This is achieved in the following way. When a juvenile in a senior lineage gets into conflict with an adult in a junior lineage, the juvenile is supported by its (senior) relatives (especially its mother) and so, with this support, it comes to dominate the older monkey. But that is not all. Close study shows that young monkeys of high-ranking lineages take into account the presence or absence of relatives before threatening an older monkey in a low-ranking lineage. If no relatives are present, the youngster makes no effort to dominate. Only if relatives are to hand does it produce a show-down. And when it does, it may use very dirty tricks to do so – for instance, it may give a fear screech, out of the blue, looking directly at the monkey to be defeated, who will then be threatened, chased or even attacked by its relatives.

In all this we can see social scheming of a high order, involving knowledge of the rank relations of others (gleaned by careful observation) together with careful timing and spatial positioning at the time the move is made. Let it not be said that such a monkey lacks intentions: in monkeys and apes intentions are complex and their realization is a persistent and devious process, in which a lot of thinking and planning is involved.

Here, in the social world of primates, we can perhaps discern the outlines of the world of neckties and other cultural paraphernalia with which we started. Maybe in man the status-game goes on just as it does in monkeys, though at a more refined level. Harré would, I feel sure, subscribe to the idea that human life is very largely a status game. And if monkeys can be as subtle as we know they can, then how much more subtle can we humans be? Gamesmanship, one-upmanship, all are ingrained, perhaps since millions of years, in the human psyche.

And in all this, we intelligent, intention-ridden language users make full use of cultural traditions. Having learned, through language, what the status symbols are and how to manipulate them we start to assemble them around us and to embellish our social selves. We reconstruct our physical appearance to cultivate an air of effortless superiority. We drive cars to match, or in wondrous inverted snobbery, do not drive cars to match.

Something like inverted snobbery also occurs in primates. In a study of baboons living in Amboseli National Park, the primatologist Glenn Hausfater noticed that whereas dominant males would not engage in ritualized greeting behaviours with those close beneath them in rank, they would do so with very low-ranking males.

Tradition, in human society, is not just what is handed on, in the sense that an old grandfather clock passes down the generations. Tradition also embodies values. In our Christian society and many non-Christian ones values of honesty and trust are transmitted. Thus we must engage in status games bearing the weight of this honesty ethic. Here, in the world of values, we are perhaps once again, as with language, in a world apart from the animals. Status manoeuvring, for a baboon, may present complex dilemmas but it does not involve debates about fairness, only about whether the place, circumstances and time are opportune. If a young baboon does not take a morsel of tasty food from an old crippled female it will be because of either kinship, or more likely because of the close presence of a more dominant supporter of the female; it will not be because of a sense of injustice.

People, by contrast, have to labour under all these extra burdens – having worked out that the time is right for a move in the status game there may yet be moral considerations causing hesitation. Thus do our intentions get thwarted: not by the social milieu but by inner considerations arising from early moral conditioning. We have this extra layer of inhibition to add to all the ancestral primate layers. It is surprising, in fact, that we can do anything at all. Yet we can and do. The actors on Harré's stage are nothing if not lively. They strut about, exchanging brilliant verbal displays. If we take a long view of them, without prejudice, they appear bustling with vanity and life, dressing and powdering themselves like players in a Molière comedy.

When we look at monkeys we see them as God no doubt sees us. How eagerly they engage with each other, quarreling and making up, grooming and copulating with each other. Each monkey is totally *engagé*, caught up in a world it cannot understand, swept along by the rush of life. And so, exactly, it is with ourselves. The person who stops to think soon feels the chill and gets back into the warm comfort of society.

Perhaps that fact, the comfort of friendly social life, is as much a driving force behind the social life of primates as the more tangible benefits (de-lousing, sex and protection from predators). It has been said that a lone chimpanzee is no chimpanzee. So too perhaps of ourselves. In the end, however we differ from apes in our use of language and tradition, and our cultural self-construction, we probably have more in common with them than we care to admit. And if, one day, monkeys start to study us, they may well have less difficulty than we do in ackowledging the extent of our common kinship.

REFERENCES

Berger, P. and T. Luckmann (1967) *The Social Construction of Reality*, Harmondsworth: Penguin.

Datta, S. B. (1986) The role of alliances in the acquisition of rank. In J. B. Else and P. C. Lee (eds) *Primate Ontogeny, Cognition and Social Behaviour*, Cambridge: Cambridge University Press.

Goodall, J. (1987) *The Gombe Chimpanzees*, Cambridge, Mass.: Harvard University Press.

Harré, R. (1979) *Social Being*, Oxford: Basil Blackwell.

Lock, A. (1980) *The Guided Reinvention of Language*, London: Academic Press.

Reynolds, V. (1980) *The Biology of Human Action*, New York: Freeman.

Terrace, H. (1979) *Nim*, New York: Knopf.

Part IV
Commentary by Rom Harré

Exploring the Human Umwelt

Rom Harré

The essays in this volume deal with three major philosophical topics that have long been among my preoccupations. The defence of scientific realism has proved a perennially absorbing interest for me as new forms of anti-realism have been invented, each calling for its own rebuttal or refutation. Why there is the perennial urge to devalue the status of scientific knowledge is a question of great importance, but I make no pretence to tackle it in this commentary. The special sciences each has its own bouquet of philosophical problems and I have found myself over the years drawn back and forth between the fascinations of physics and the frustrations of the human sciences. I propose to organize my comments around the corresponding three groups of contributions.

I Realism

In recent years we have all come to see that 'realism' is not the name of one philosophical position, even within the philosophy of science. Nor is there just one range of arguments for and against a realist position. Nevertheless, 'realism' and 'anti-realism' are generic terms for clusters or families of doctrines for each of which there are loosely related ensembles of arguments. Part of my purpose in writing *Varieties of Realism* was to demonstrate that there was a significant polarity in the cluster of realisms. Realist doctrines differed not only in their metaphysical underpinnings, but also in their relative vulnerability to fairly traditional anti-realist arguments. At the time I wrote that book I thought that no one realist doctrine could be successfully defended for the physical sciences at every stage of their development. I now see that there are ways in which the two main varieties of realism I want to defend – viz. a strong 'policy realism' and a weak 'convergent realism' – are inter-related, though they are not, I believe, either mutually reducible or simultaneously applicable.

The first step in clearing one's mind on the nature of realism should be an attempt to catalogue the most obvious varieties. For the purposes of this commentary I want to highlight a major division into epistemic approaches and pragmatic approaches.

1. The epistemic approach uses concepts like 'truth', 'falsity' 'verisimilitude' and so on to characterize its variety of realism. The most conspicuous modern form of the epistemic approach is 'convergent realism'. According to this approach the greater predictive success (empirical adequacy) of a theory, the more truly it depicts the world (the greater its verisimilitude). By varying one's conception of empirical adequacy, say by taking it as persistent survival in the face of vigorous attempts at falsification, one can arrive at a cluster of 'realisms' that includes the doctrines of both Newton-Smith and Popper.

In common to all versions of the epistemic approach there is the *Principle of Bivalence*. According to this principle the statements of a theory are true or false by virtue of the way the world is whether we know it or not. To apply the principle of bivalence to sceintific reasearch we need another principle to support claims for verisimilitude for as yet untested statements. Of equal prominence then in recent discussions of realism has been the *argument to the best explanation*. This argument has a mundane use in which we say that the best explanation of the predictive success of this or that theory is that it is true. And it has a transcendental use in which we say that the best explanation of the long-run success of the physical sciences is that science, as a whole, is getting nearer the truth. There are, it is not hard to show, alternative explanations of this success, that are not so good – for instance, that the success is the result of a vast, long-running coincidence. Of course, much of the force of the argument hinges on the criteria for 'best'. Lipton (1985) has shown that there is an essential ambiguity in the criteria for 'best' which greatly weakens the argument.

The other pole is occupied by a family of positions based on pragmatic notions like 'intervention', 'manipulation', 'material practice', and so on. The concepts of truth and falsity give way to notions like reference and denotation. Science is seen as a practical rather than as a cognitive activity and its products as material things rather than propositions. I shall be developing this pole further in commenting on the essays of Marjorie Grene, Peter Manicas, John Lucas, Jerry Aronson and Roy Harris.

I have presented the two main families of realisms as polarities rather than antitheses. They interpenetrate one another to some extent. By treating the establishment of reference in terms of the satisfaction of certain propositional functions, the relation of reference is transformed from a phsyical link between an embodied scientist and a material being into a semantic indication determined by a set of true and false propositions. On the other hand, polar oppositions germane to practice, such as success or failure, seem to mimic the polarity between truth and falsity.

Realists of the epistemic persuasion seem to take for granted that the aim of sicence is the enunciation and testing of laws. If the truth of laws eludes us by virtue of traditional objections to inductive universalizations, then perhaps we can be sure of the falsity of some conjectured laws. The tendency to focus on laws in this way is closely correlated, not surprisingly, with a tendency to take theories simply in their discursive form, as sets of propositions ordered by the deducibility relation. However different their epistemologies may have been, this conception of theory is shared by both Hempel and Popper, and it accounts in part for the disparities between their philosophies of science and scientific practice.

For those of the 'pragmatic' persuasion the role of laws is secondary to that of interlocking structures of analogies, models and metaphors in the organization of scientific knowledge. The Hempel–Popper deductivist conception of theory is seen as the realization of a rhetorical convention for scientific writing rather than as the necessary basis for an account of scientific cognition and of the genesis and development of scientific theories in the thought collectives of real science. Theories, as philosophers have tended to analyse them, are momentary abstractions from evolving theory-families. The theory-family idea has appeared from time to time in different guises. Whewell wrote of 'the development of an idea'; Ludwig Fleck used the expression 'thought-collectives'; Thomas Kuhn called such entities 'paradigms' and Lakatos described them as 'research programmes'.

Given the vulnerability of the epistemic variety of realism to quite simple sceptical arguments can we find a better line of defence for the pragmatic variety? If we can, how can at least some of the valuable aspects of the epistemic variety of realism be reconstituted? I have in mind such concepts as 'scientific progress', 'increasing verisimilitude', and so on.

The historical pageant of science has been presented as if it were a linear progress from the verifying or corroborating of the laws of the observed to those of the unobserved to those of the unobservable. At each stage greater hazards to fortune are offered in that subsequent work stands a greater chance of revealing inadequacies in what has gone before. But there were richly elaborated accounts of the transcendental realm as integral parts of physics long before the present era. A case can be made for saying that the overall pattern of thought in the physical sciences has changed very little, despite huge changes in content and in the sophistication of the experimental equipment and of the mathematical tools. A methodological insight of Archimedes or of Robert Boyle ought to hold good for today's physics. The physics of the past ought to be as good a test object for efforts to make judgements about it intelligible under our alternative realisms as contemporary physics.

Be that as it may, any variety of realism needs a platform in perception relative to which the status of beings described by theory, but which are currently unobserved or even unobservable, can be assessed. If the apparatus I see before me is a subjective phenomenon, hazardously projected into interpersonal 'space', all further discussion about the rights and wrongs of realism is pre-empted. To escape the traditional shackles of phenomenalism I turn first to the contributions by Marjorie Grene and Peter Manicas.

I share with Marjorie Grene an admiration for the psychological work of J. J. Gibson, not only for its technical sophistication and its remarkable experimental programme, but also for the depth of the new conceptual system he proposed. In sharp contrast to the traditional picture of the perceiver as the passive recipient of stimuli-producing sensations, integrated thereafter into perceptual structures, Gibson presented his vision of the human perceiver as an active being exploring his or her environment. The longest-running threat to a realist reading of natural science has been the idea that perception is, at bottom, subjective. Locke's ideas and Hume's impressions are modes of the consciousness of individual people, strictly incomparable with the ideas and expressions experienced by anyone else. It is an easy step forward into Machian sensationalism or back into Plato's cave. How can it be known that there is a common world which scientists collectively study by experimentally exploring it and theorizing about it in a way that is indirectly disciplined by the results of these explorations? At best the existence of this world is a hazardous assumption. In response to this, it could be claimed that we have little idea what it would be like to discover that our hypothesis of a common world and of a community of scientists like ourselves was false. But this kind of move, however nicely elaborated, is not as good as a positive demonstration of the psychological plausibility of the common-sense view that there is a common world and that we jointly explore it.

The traditional view took it for granted that perception is the result of a synthesis of atomistic sensations which are presented subjectively. Gibson held that sensations had little importance as such in the perceptual process. He believed that our senses were integral parts of perceptual systems, which had evolved to explore the ambient flux of energy in which we ourselves cast a shadow, so to speak, and to detect certain higher-order invariants in that flux. These invariants were the effects of physical objects. Gibson called this 'pick up' and the whole process 'direct perception'. There was no synthesis and nothing mediated in any sensory way between things and people. This robust account was supported by a huge range of ingenious experimental evidence. Marjorie Grene is right to point out the rather peculiar sense in which Gibson uses his vocabulary and to the wide range of misunderstandings to which it has been susceptible.

As she herself remarks, Marjorie Grene's exposition of Gibson's ecological psychology of perception is but a sketch. I want to elaborate her account in two ways to strengthen its appeal as a support for the platform in perception that realism seems to need. General ecology is in debt to von Uexkull (1909) for a number of refinements of the idea of an environment. He introduced his distinctions to try to differentiate the various ways that animals and plants are integrated into the physical world. For the purposes of this discussion his most important contribution was the concept of Umwelt. The Umwelt of a species of organism is that part of the material world that is available as a living space to the members of the species by virtue of their specific modes of adaptation, such as distinctive perceptual and manipulative capacities. The same 'total' world contains any number of possible Umwelten. I want to say that Gibsonian ecological psychology encourages us to think of the physical world we share as human beings, as an Umwelt. It is the living space made available to people through their perceptual and manipulative capacities. If Gibson is right it is the human Umwelt which is the object of study of the physical sciences. I propose to treat experimental apparatus and the advancing techniques of observation as prosthetic extensions of or as 'organs' added to our perceptual systems e.g. telescopes, as Gibson saw them. It would follow that the human Umwelt is changing historically. It would be in the spirit of Gibson's psychology of perception to say that scientists are enlarging or diminishing the human Umwelt, rather than that they are revealing more of a universe which was, neutrally, there. Of course, the universe is richer than the current Umwelt, and I am the last to deny that there is scientific progress.

Marjorie Grene leaves her admirably clear exposition of Gibson's concepts short of his other notable contribution: the idea of an affordance. According to Gibson the most important properties observable in the Umwelt, that is, available to us by the use of our perceptual systems actively to explore the ambient flux, are such attributes as durability, solidity and so on. These are properties of the Umwelt but affordances of the 'total' world, the universe. Why 'affordances'? Because they are material dispositions relative to human activities and practices. 'Using' is the activity correlative to 'durability'. A paved patio affords walking and a particle accelerator affords the photographing of tracks. I do not think it is doing too much violence to Gibsonian ideas to go a step further and take the tracks so photographed as affordances of the apparatus. In the advanced sciences the apparatus with which we manipulate the material world also delimits it as an Umwelt.

According to convergent realism, successive theories are better and better approximations to a perfect representation of a fixed and given but partially unknown world. But in the Gibson–von Uexkull framework I have been putting together there is an enlarging human Umwelt which is that aspect of the 'total' world that our perceptual systems and the apparatus by which we have extended and enlarged them, makes available to us. In one version or another this is an old idea. For Vico and for Kant it was the root of the intelligibility of society and of empirical experience respectively.

The world will not always afford what we expect (the thin ice that does not, after all, afford walking; the gold that was to be the outcome of alchemical manipulations). This seems a natural way of expressing an insight but ultimately it is an unsatisfactory way of talking. We should not say that the world does not afford these activities or products. There would be no walkability to afford or not to afford were the vertebrates to be wholly avian or aquatic. We now know that the world does afford gold under another manipulative procedure. This is the kind of relativism which I believe Niels Bohr was trying to express in his 'correspondence' principle. The occurrent properties of the world, the 'total' world, which ground the dispositions we ascribe as affordances, can never become available to us independently of the apparatus that we have the ingenuity and technical skill to construct. 'The limitations of my equipment are the limits of my world!'

The remarkable way in which both James and Spencer, in their different ways, anticipated certain Gibsonian themes comes through strongly in Manicas's remarks. According to Manicas, James and Spencer agree on the organic origin of some kind of prior organization of the human organism which predetermines some structural and invariant properties of perceptions. I am not sure whether, in interpreting this as a cognitive phenomenon, Manicas is quoting James himself. As Manicas reads James' position it is for an evolutionary origin of the Kantian categories. James (1911, p. 58) says, 'concepts and percepts are consubstantial'. 'Concepts are like evaporations out of the bosom of perception, into which they condense again whenever practical service summons them.' If we try to match this with Kant's account of the role of the synthetic *a priori* in perception we find some, but not all, of the ingredients of the Kantian 'machinery'. Concepts and categories are not distinguished; and, instead of the schematisms, we have the metaphors of condensation and evaporation – charming but imprecise. How should we take James' denial of Spencer's apparently very similar conceit, 'the equilibration of thought and things'? According to Manicas, James thought that there could not be an evolutionary guarantee of perceptual judgements because there are a multitude of 'laws' in the mind as bases for diverse kinds of such judgements. For instance, there are norms of aesthetic and moral assessment as well as those involved in the making of perceptual judgements as to the material furniture of the world. It is highly implausible to single out just one from this broad set of bases for judgement as that which has its origin in the organic evolution of mankind. On the face of it this seems a particularly feeble argument. One could argue *a priori* that perceptual and aesthetic judgements were radically different, both in their criteria and in the practical consequences that followed from them, only the former having biological survival value. And one could argue *a posteriori* that there is both historical and cultural diversity in moral and aesthetic judegements that contrasts with the universality of the basic repertoire of perceptual distinctions among substances (say solid and liquid), among shapes (say long and broad, rectangular and circular), and so on. James seems to me to be proposing a culturally relativized Kantianism, the 'Pragmatism' in which I find it hard to discern. In discussing what corresponds for him to the Kantian schematisms he says (James, 1911, p. 38): 'In obeying this [the pragmatic] rule we neglect the substantive content of the concept, and follow its function only . . .' What then is its function? To guide action? Not so. On p. 37 of the same work we find: 'The pragmatic rule is that the meaning of a concept may always always be found, if not in some sensible particular which it directly designates, then in some particular difference in the course of human experience which its being true will make.' I must confess that I cannot see the difference between this and the verificationism we have all learned to abhor. For James, the 'practical service' of concepts seems to be the distinguishing of perceptions, not the guidance of action. Pragmatism is not philosophy of praxis.

A main thrust of my own point of view is against the assumption that the prime product of science and the main instrument of its creation of knowledge is the statement (or proposition). Before the proposition is the 'scientific act' (cf. Bachelard, 1934, p. 11), a purposeful intervention into a natural system, guided by theory and assessed by reference to criteria of practical success or failure. Of course, theories are cognitive entities. My point is that it is not their truth or falsity that is of importance but their role as guides for action. The significance of such acts was seen clearly by Robert Boyle and exploited by him in his attempts to provide a firm empirical grounding for the 'corpuscularian philosophy'. A 'scientific act' has the following structures: a person acts on something, X, by the use of a certain manipulative technique, T. The point of the action is to manipulate something else, Y, through the medium of X. (A person heats a gas-filled tube so as to increase the mean kinetic energy of the molecules of the gas.) Our actor conceives this aim by virtue of tentatively holding a theory about X in which the concept 'Y' figures. Changes in Y, that which has been indirectly manipulated, have effects Z, which a suitably alert and well-equipped person can observe or detect. (The increase in mean kinetic energy of the molecules of the gas results in an increase in pressure which changes the observable state of a manometer.)

What can now be said about the gas? The pragmatic claim is that we now know that X has a certain disposition, a Gibsonian affordance, that is, it affords Z on condition of manipulation T. As an affordance this disposition cannot be reduced to Z, its overt display, since the human act, T, and perhaps a humanly devised detector, is required for the display. By performing scientific acts we can explore the boundaries of the human Umwelt. But we must bear in mind that the boundaries are jointly determined by the nature of the material world, whatever it is, and the range of manipulative techniques we have invented with which to explore it. For me scientific knowledge is not a collection of true beliefs (or if you prefer so far unfalsified conjectures) *about* X, Y and Z. It is the totality of scientific acts we know how to perform in an environment bounded by X, Y and Z.

The remarks above already foreshadow the ontological claim that a policy realist will make on the basis of successful scientific acts. The indirect target of the human manipulations, Y, must also be included in the human Umwelt. This needs argument and I propose to provide it in what follows. It was plainly assumed by Boyle and I hope to show that this was not without some reason. The theoretical sciences gain credit with us only in totalities of such acts, because our concepts of what we are manipulating occur intelligibly only within evolving theory-families. The view I have called 'policy realism' requires that we read theories not as sets of true or false statements but as guides to possible scientific acts. Manipulative practices can be successful or unsuccessful. Theoretical concept denote states, structures, individuals, properties and processes which tentatively enter the Umwelt as manipulables. The metaphysical categories just listed are conservative. This is partly a consequence of the origins of most theoretical concepts in displacements of existing concepts, and partly a consequence of the role of apparatus in fixing affordances. The states of apparatus must, as Bohr pointed out, be perceptible. Once all this is in place programmes for developing techniques for extending the human Umwelt, through its manipulable contents, can be set in motion. The Boylian idea that I have labelled 'scientific act' lets us shift from the epistemological dichotomy between the observable and unobservable to the pragmatic dichotomy between the manipulable and the non-manipulable, with a consequential shift of criteria of adequacy for theories and of the demarcation of the boundaries of the knowable.

Why, asks Manicas, do I need Gibson? On the classical Gregory account every perception is a kind of judgement, a hypothesis subject to all the troubles of the underdetermination of theory by data, and other forms of inductive scepticism. But for Gibsonians, perception is a practice, an exploration of the Umwelt not a conjecture about it. On the conjectures (Gregory) account the gap between the observable point of application of my efforts and the ultimate target of my interventions (to borrow Hacking's (1983) term) is a yawning chasm. On the neo-pragmatist view this gap does not exist. Both the point of application and the target of our manipulations are material beings. ('If you can spray them they are real': Hacking.) Basing ourselves on Gibsonian 'direct perception' and 'affordances' we have a shared platform from which ontologically secure inductions can extend the compass of reality, the human Umwelt, in all sorts of directions.

But this cannot be the end of the matter. What of 'galactic jets', 'continental drift', and so on, to which the idea of a scientific act as direct or indirect manipulation can hardly apply?

Of course, a jet of matter several lights years in length, moving under the influence of powerful fields, is not a manipulable as such. But I would argue that a study of how it is accommodated within our systematic physics shows that the concept is such that it has its root in manipulability. From whence comes the conceptual cluster which I used above to characterize the phenomenon? Clearly the origin is in some laboratory manipulation in which plasmas are guided, constrained and so on. Just as the familiar explanation of the auroras is rooted in the experimental manipulations by Ramsay and Rayleigh, so too is the sketch above of galactic jets.

Read sympathetically, James' objections to Spencer's optimistic evolutionism (as reported by Manicas) seem to me to be a species of a familiar genus of arguments against causal theories of perception. Whatever kind of perceptual judgement we are considering, be it scientific or even of the states of our own bodies, there are historical, cultural and conventional aspects of the total repertoire of reasons for making the judgement. Philosophers have tended to take for granted that that aspect of scientific judgements can be cauterized to leave a crystalline statement of fact. For instance, in an otherwise excellent study of Wittgenstein's philosophy, Robert Ackermann (1988) seems to rest content with the account of language in the *Tractatus*, provided it is taken as the topography of only one of the suburbs of Wittgenstein's city, that district we could call 'Science'.

However, if we take a closer look at the way scientific communities use even simple, singular declarative statements, the *Tractatus* model begins to lose its plausibility. Sociologists of science have collected a corpus of material that illustrates how far the situated discourse of scientists is from that picture. We cannot assume that their utterances are adequately understood if we treat them as attempts to describe the natural world; nor is their linguistic significance exhausted by displaying their logical form say in terms of the predicate calculus. We should look at the larger context of scientific discourse that spreads far beyond the confines of the written scientific paper. In generalizing Boyle's argument. I have portrayed the statements of a theory as guides to action, rather than as hypotheses to be tested for truth or faslity. As such, they appear as parts of a network of fiduciary acts fully intelligible only in the light of our knowledge of the structure and history of those scientific communities within the moral orders of which they have their place. This is a very far cry from the picture theory of the *Tractatus* or any other account of truth as correspondence.

How much of the traditional conception of science can be salvaged once we start to study science as a human phenomenon? John Lucas argues for a diversity of 'rationalities' to match the diversity of modes of reasoning found in scientific communities. His remarks can serve as a brake on the headlong slide into sociologism. There is something of great importance to be learned from studies of scientists at work, but it is not wholly clear just what it is. Recourse to logic by scientists themselves seems to be best seen as a socially motivated strategy of defence of one's own competence or as an attack on the competence of one's rivals, rather than as a standard technique of knowledge production or criticism. It is very difficult to find unambiguous cases from the history of science in which the demonstration of an internal contradiction has led to a theory being dropped or dismissed. Provisional remedies are attempted and case studies show (Gilbert and Mulkay, 1983) that these proceed only so far as to end controversy. The mid-eighteenth-century demonstrations that Newton's version of 'Newtonian physics' was internally contradictory led to a proliferation of remedial innovations, motivated, it seems, more by metaphysical predilections than by the aim of restoring any purely logical coherence. The history of a theory-family is a story that perhaps would best be told in the framework of dialectics. I know of no serious attempts at such analyses. Most philosophers of science are heirs of Russell and share his distaste for the German tradition. I believe that, in abstracting the logical form of finished scientific writings, philosophers of the logicist persuasion have not revealed the true skeleton which endows the discourse with its epistemological, ontological and pragmatic qualities as science. Rather, they have picked out a relatively superficial stylistic convention whose investigation belongs to study of scientific rhetoric.

Lucas provides a neat and instructive taxonomy of what I should like to call 'attitudes'.

1. Adopting the attitude of objectivity we present ourselves as considering things as they are, while under the attitude of subjectivity we present ourselves as considering things as they seem to be.
2. Under the attitude of subjectivity, things can be believed to be more than they seem to be or to be just as they seem.

Scientific realism needs to take account of the standing of these attitudes. Brute objectivity is unattainable. But, as Lucas points out, there is a kind of objectivity which is not opposed to the attitude of subjectivity. By taking objectivity as the totality of views from everywhere we reach a kind of Gibsonian position *a priori*. Science is a set of techniques, both cognitive and practical, for arriving at beliefs about what is invariant for all views. But there is nothing which is independent of any view. In this way the slide from the realization that there are no brute facts to anti-realism is halted.

Lucas comes at the problem of the assessment of scientific progress from a different angle from my sociological-cum-pragmatic approach. But the upshot is the same. He distinguishes between aspirations and their realizations. In time we learn to tailor our aspirations to what we know succeeds. There are boundary conditions which are not rationally groundable and which we can modify in experimental set-ups. Then there are natural laws which both reflect what is intransigent in nature and can be grounded, at least relatively, in some reasoned discourse. Perhaps Lucas and I differ in our sense of what it is that we refer to by 'reason'. For me, the rational threads that run through the cognitive aspects of scientific activity are judgements of similarity and difference, underpinned by chains of displaced concepts. The structure of these chains can be expressed in a number of ways, through models, analogies and metaphors. For Lucas, I suspect, the formal patterns of abstract reason still have hegemony.

In the penultimate chapter of my *Varieties of Realism* I tried to show that the relation of the subject matter of a scientific discourse to human experience and human techniques of manipulation and detection profoundly influenced the way the typical modal auxiliaries of scientific discourses would be interpreted. By drawing on Kripke's useful fantasy of 'possible worlds', one could associate a different formal syntax of modal expressions with different levels of subject matter, as defined by my Realms 1, 2 and 3. I must admit that I had not thought of taking this analysis one step further to associate different styles of rationality with each modal syntax. Lucas has persuaded me that the step is worth taking.

In Realm 1 discourse it is taxonomic principles and definitions of species, genera, etc. that seem to be apodeictic. The choice of classificatory criteria is, at bottom, arbitrary in the absence of any theory of empirical real essences. Here the style of rationality is set by the way the community chooses to deal with marginal cases. The laws of classical kinematics are strict derivatives from the apodeictic principle of uniform acceleration as the second derivative of space with respect to time. This is what uniform acceleration *is* in kinematics. Marginal cases do not provoke revision of the laws of kinematics, but the introduction of dynamic corrections such as friction and viscosity which themselves are accomodated in further laws. The second generation of laws are empirical and inductive.

The point of creating a discourse with terms that denote beings which have so far not been observed by reason of some merely contingent difficulty is to ground the principles that appear as laws in Realm 1 discourse by referring to mechanisms that would bring about the regularities they describe. While the apodeictic principles of Realm 1 discourse are true in all possible worlds, those of Realm 2 discourse are true only in those worlds in which mechanisms of the required kinds exist. With the help of the Kripke models a syntax for the modal expressions of this discourse can be chosen from among the modal grammars. A different style of rationality must prevail for Realm 2 discourses. The development of a theory-family within which the mechanisms of Realm 2 are to be conceived depends on those displacements of concepts I briefly alluded to above.

The modal qualifications of hypotheses about Realm 3 beings obey yet another 'grammar'. Classifications of such beings into kinds are internally related to the dispositions they display in experimental manipulations. But unlike Realm 1 dispositions which are, in principle, groundable, the attribution of a cluster of these dispositions to some being is the end of the matter, so to speak. Further study of Realm 3 discourse shows that this picture is too simple as it stands. Realm 3 discourse is hierarchical, and is full of attempts to ground the dispositions taken to be fundamental by one generation of scientists in hypotheses of structure thought up by the next. For instance, the proton is no longer a basic being characterized by a certain charge and mass. It can now be thought of as a triad of quarks, which are themselves further differentiated by ungrounded dispositional properties.

Despite these instabilities it does seem right to follow Lucas in the thought that just as there are varieties of realism appropriate to each realm so there are varieties of rationality. What counts as 'good thinking' will not be the same throughout the domains of physics; nor should we expect the modal 'grammars' to be uniform.

The position I have called 'policy realism' is epistemologically modest. Under certain conditions it is reasonable to read the terms of a theory as denoting as yet unobserved phenomena. By 'phenomena' I mean Niels

Bohr's sense of that notion, that is, the products of the interaction between a noumenal reality and the apparatus and techniques of observation devised by human beings. In such a reading a tentative extension of the human Umwelt is proposed. The connotations of theoretical terms are then taken as the basis of a programme of exploration designed to bring to light the right kind of Bohrian phenomena, if any such are to be found. Taken as moments in the development of a theory-family, individual theories can be shown to differ in respect of a cluster of properties I have summarily called their relative 'plausibility'. An assessment of plausibility is based, so it seems from historical studies, on a history of growing empirical adequacy, that is growing power to predict and retrodict the results of experiments and observations accurately, while metaphysical propriety is maintained. Giving the molecules 'volume' improves the empirical adequacy of the kinetic theory, while maintaining the meta-physical status of molecules as material things. According to policy realism it is reasonable to read a theory that meets these conditions as if its terms denoted real things, and to use the sense of those terms as guides to setting up practical procedures for attempts to manipulate or perhaps actually to disclose their putative referents. Plausibility assessments do not license prior inferences to the correctness or incorrectness of the picture the theory offers of a part of the human Umwelt, before we know the outcome of the use of the exploratory procedures. The view that plausible theories are *a priori* more likely to be found to depict reality accurately is a much stronger form of realism than the policy realism I have been advocating. The stronger view is sometimes called 'convergent realism'. Both Aronson and Harris raise the question of whether the modest policy realist position may not be able to be elaborated to give support to some form of convergent realism. In short, the advocate of convergent realism hopes to show that, by and large, the scientists of one generation are not only better at manipulating the material things of the world than their predecessors, but also are able to tell more true stories about it.

Before turning to examine the suggestion in detail I shall briefly review the original arguments for policy realism. The argument proceeds by two steps.

1. There are model cases which demonstrate the wisdom of taking a theory in the policy realist manner. In these cases both the original field of phenomena in which the empirical adequacy of the theory has been tested and the metaphysical propriety of the kind terms in the theory have instantiations which are objects of ordinary unaided perception. In these model cases it is clear that the theory used in this way is plausible in the sense referred to above. Plausibility is not a sign of the verisimilitude of

the theory but of the rationality of testing it for referential adequacy. Verisimilitude on this account of realism is always a matter to be assessed *a posteriori.* Scientific progress is conceived ontologically, not epistemically – not an accumulation of truths but of things disclosed in practices.

2. Many scientific theories denote (that is, are used by scientists to refer to) beings that are currently unobservable. With suitable technical developments, beings of such kinds could appear as part of the human Umwelt. There are huge numbers of cases like this: extra-solar planets, bacteria and viruses, geographical features of the sea bed, 'subterranean' Martian water, and so on. The distinction between the extensions of denoting expressions in theories whose domain is Realm 1 from the extensions of those whose domain is Realm 2 is historically contingent because it is relative to the state of technology which sets bounds to the human Umwelt.

The conclusion of this argument is the rationality of making policy realist readings of plausible Realm 2 theories. The objects to which scientists can refer using these theories are of kinds familiar from Realm 1. So the procedures for searching for instances and what counts as their finding are also familiar. This is achieved automatically in the formation process for Realm 2 concepts, since they are created by displacement of Realm 1 concepts, under the constraint that ontological kind be preserved during the displacement. Thus natural selection is the displaced version of domestic selection, and both denote processes in which only certain plants and animals of a given generation breed.

3. A final step to incorporate theories the extensions of whose denoting expressions are in Realm 3, the domain of beings doomed to lie beyond the bounds of possible experience, cannot be made without severe qualifications. The point is this: the role of theory in our first two realms is, among other things, to sketch the properties of underlying objects and processes that ground the dispositions we assign to things on the basis of the Bohrian phenomena which they afford to a human observer or manipulator. The rationale for taking such theories in this common-sense way is that by virtue of the arguments employed in steps 1 and 2 above we stand some chance of checking out claims about those groundings. But there is no chance whatever of undertaking a similar programme for a theory whose domain of reference is Realm 3. The properties we can confidently ascribe to that domain are never more than affordances.

Of course, there is an element of contingency even in the boundary we currently think separates the domains of the unobserved and the unobservable. But the general argument that no extension of the human Umwelt could encompass the whole of Realm 3 remains unaffected by that consideration. Yet the structrue of theorizing, even given the restriction to affordances, is more or less the same for all three Realms. So there is sense in the idea that we should read theories in all three realms alike. The difference lies in what can be revealed by theory-guided experimental programmes in each realm. As I have argued elsewhere with regard to quantum field theory, a realist reading is enlightening just in so far as we maintain a restriction of properties assigned to the beings of Realm 3 to affordances, relative to the kind of apparatus we can construct. But more about that in later discussion of the contributions of Weingard and Redhead. This is more or less the same point as Aronson makes with his Principle of Epistemological Invariance.

By there is more to it. Realms 2 and 3 can be tied together more strongly by the manipulation argument of Boyle and Hacking.

The first step in enhancing the plausibility of a theory abstracted from a theory-family denoting beings in Realm 2 would surely be successful manipulations. The theory would seem more implausible if the manipulations for which it is being used as a guide persistently failed. Davy became more enamoured of the 'ionic' hypothesis the more success he had in manipulating unobservable electrically-charged particles by electrical techniques, for instance his success in the decomposition of the alkaline earths.

In many cases theories that passed the 'manipulation test' became available for a 'perceptual test' when technical advances promoted their denotata from Realm 2 to Realm 1. This was what happened when Pasteur's 'manipulative' success with anthrax bacilli was perceptually confirmed by Toissant's microscopic examination of the contents of the gut of earthworms living near buried victims of the disease.

But we have clear cases of manipulative success and failure for theories whose denotata are in Realm 3. Sub-atomic physics provides a very rich trawl of examples. For instance the Stern-Garlach apparatus is a device for manipulating particles distinguished by their catalogue of quantum numbers to yield an observable effect. It fits the manipulation schema perfectly.

Scientist performs operation A which manipulates an unobservable of type B. (The A–B manipulation has an observable counterpart from which the concept for it was displaced in the construction of the relevant theory.) Changes in B have observable consequences C.

The inductive argument now runs as follows:

In Realm 2 manipulative success has been correlated with ontological success, after a technical advance has moved the contingently located boundary between Realms 1 and 2.

The location of the Realm 2/Realm 3 boundary is also contingent (but resting on a different contingency – the limits of the human Umwelt).

Therefore (inductively) manipulative success with Realm 3 beings is a good ground for a (revisable) ontological claim on their behalf.

Those philosophers who have favoured a defence of realism by the use of the argument to the best explanation as well as those who, like van Fraassen, have revived a Berkeleyesque anti-realism, must accept the rationality of inductive reasoning on pain of undermining a necessary condition for the cogency of their own positions. (So far as I can see, the 'critical empiricism' of van Fraassen is exactly the doctrine Berkeley lays out in *Siris*; cf. Moked's (1971) exegesis.) Aronson's attempt to take policy realism as a ground or starting point for an enlargement of the argument to support a form of convergent realism depends on an induction. For the policy realist, the plausibility and implausibility of theories are indications of whether a research programme based on the theory is likely to be worthwhile, that is to come up with a Yea or a Nay to the question of whether the terms used by the community to refer to so far unobserved beings do actually denote something. Plausibility is not an inductive support for the conclusion that the outcome of a search programme based on that theory will be favourable. The original argument for policy realism does not support an extension to verisimilitude, since it is just as much a worthwhile outcome to a theory-guided search programme if the terms in question are found not to denote anything remotely like what they had been expected to denote. The polarity supported by the original policy realist argument is between worthwhile and worthless projects. It is not a polarity between successful and unsuccessful outcomes. Can it be extended to favour the 'successful' pole of the polarity?

Aronson's argument runs as follows:

1. We do find, as a matter of fact, that plausibility is inductively correlated with verisimilitude, that is, with the likelihood that the terms used referringly in 'good' theories do indeed denote real things, for those theories whose empirical basis and theoretical domain both lie in Realm 1. For instance, car mechanics and other service engineers use plausibility criteria in diagnosing faults and in setting up the procedures to correct them. When both the phenomena and the explaining mechanisms are in Realm 1 predictive success, at the phenomenal level, that is, empirical adequacy, is in fact correlated with verisimilitude, success at the level of existence claims for causal mechanisms. As a diagnostic session proceeds, the hypotheses of the mechanic do get nearer to the truth as he tests this or that part of the mechanism, so that finally when he dismantles it, there indeed is the worn gudgeon pin.

2. The second stage of Aronson's argument is familiar from the above exposition of policy realism. Realms 1, 2 and 3 do not differ in a way which is essential for the relationship between predictive success and verisimili-

tude. For instance, the fact that the explaining mechanisms denoted by the referring expression in many theories are in the domain of Realm 2 is historically contingent, and, again inductively, the history of science shows a supportive correlation developing between predictive and denotational success as technical advances push back the Realm 1/Realm 2 frontier. One might go on to use the Gibsonian point about the confinement of our world to a human Umwelt. In effect that point weakens the distinction between Realms 2 and 3. The distinction is our distinction, not something absolute. It is not independent of any point of view whatever. If we could assemble the totality of Umwelten (subhuman, human and superhuman) into a Lucasian objectivity, would there still be a Realm 3? Kant seems to have thought that his account of experience was universal so that there would always be something noumenal relative to any experience whatever, whether human or alien.

Aronson concludes that 1 and 2 taken together support a general extension of the empirically verified correlation between empirical adequacy and verismilitude in Realms 1 and 2 to Realm 3 and so to science in general. This is a kind of argument to the best explanation since it uses the empirical adequacy of the policy realist thesis to inductively support an explanation of that fact by reference to verisimilitude.

Attractive though this argument seems to be at first sight, there are difficulties. They emerge when one turns to examine in detail what is actually achieved by an experimental procedure. It looks as if Aronson must take for granted that it is true or false propositions that emerge from the empirical part of science. If he holds this position in an unqualified way, then the traditional, two-level, sceptical attack looks devastating. There is no guarantee that what we thought was true (or false) of a certain class of beings may not have to be revised. But more radically, we can never know that the world may not change so as to display a character so radically different that our hard-won knowledge is rendered worthless. In other words, the laws of nature are not logically necessary, nor are there any necessary beings. (It has long been realized that Popper's claim to have solved the problem of induction is rendered empty by his failure to distinguish the two levels of inductive scepticism.)

The policy realist thinks that scientists progress in their projects by achieving a better sample of what there is in the world. The convergent realist thinks they progress by achieving a better description of the world. The policy realist stocks a museum. The convergent realist stocks a library. Can we convene a dialogue between 'curators' and 'librarians'?

Finally, for Aronson's approach there is the problem that becomes clear only when we reflect carefully on the nature of Realm 3 beings. They are not like the break in the circuit observable by the television engineer after he has dismantled the set. Nor are they like the HIV virus. The former is available to the unaided senses, the latter to the senses technologically enhanced. The structure of the 'infolded' dimensions of the Kalusa–Klein treatment of subatomic physics can never be presented to an observer *in either way*. At best such beings are susceptible to the Boyle–Hacking type of intervention defence, vulnerable to acts of indirect manipulation.

Notions like 'a better picture of the world' and other perceptual metaphors tend to figure in attempts to make out a useful sense for the vague notion of verisimilitude, as well as familiar epistemic notions like 'truth', 'correspondence', etc. Popper had no luck at all with his idea of reducing relative verisimilitude to a relational property of two theories based on a measure of the balance of their respective true and false consequences. By examining the most recent version of this idea, Oddie (1986) has shown it to be *generally* misconceived. A closer look at what experimental programmes actually accomplish may help to sharpen ideas about what a theory-led development in a scientific field actually accomplishes. It is a commonplace of scientific research that things very rarely turn out to be just as one expected. Sociologists of science (Knorr-Cetina, 1981) have shown how research programmes are rewritten to present the actual results as programme-relevant. A great many research programmes involve technical developments that enable scientists to scrutinize beings that exemplify the theoretical categories in question. Success for the theory that controls the search for exemplars usually consists in the successful demonstration that this or that kind of being exists. Idiosyncratic properties of exemplars are discounted. A theory is counted as a failure if it appears that no such exemplar can be found and the kind must be dismissed. In the course of the successful procedure reference has been established. For me, reference is a physical relation between an embodied scientist as a user of the theory and an exemplar of the right sort of entity within an extended human Umwelt. Manipulative success is one of the signs that one has established that kind of relation. Observational success (disclosure) is another.

The problem for Aronson's style of argument has been on the books, so to say, for some time. It has appeared recently in the guise of the idea of 'epistemic access' adumbrated by Boyd (1979). Can we use demonstration of the existence of a being of the right sort to be a referent for our theories to claim epistemic success, the production of knowledge? At best we can say we now have epistemic access to a researchable domain. A bridging principle is needed because it is quite possible successfully to establish a referential relation with the help of descriptive statements that are or that turn out to be false. It is *characteristic* of scientific development that there are three stages to the enlargement of our knowledge, In the first a new vocabulary is devised by displacement of concepts. With the help of this vocabulary the community of scientists can discuss their next step. Embedded in the 'grammar' of that vocabulary is sufficient content to abstract a set of instructions for engaging in a search for exemplars of the kind of beings in question, and for establishing physical contact with one or more of them. The third stage lacks the glamour of the initial discovery of such a being, but should be of the greatest interest to philosophers. For during this stage further, often tedious, research leads to massive changes in the content of the original speculative theory, as more and more is learned about the beings now disclosed. In the course of these changes most of what we first claimed about the being of the kind in question turns out to have been false. There is no such thing as an unrevisable discovery.

But the question is – unrevisable to what level? 'So the dinosaurs where not cold-blooded, but they were organisms!' (and not strange petrous deposits). 'So the craters on the moon were not volcanoes but they are geological features!' (and not visual illusions like the canals on Mars). The second phase of research usually, if not always, involves 'backing up a revisability hierarchy', through species to genera and ultimately to ontological kind. Is that where we stick? If so the librarian can permanently catalogue some of his materials, and the curator need not fear too drastic a reorganization of his exhibits. In short, the librarian can now at least name the exhibition halls of the museum in some permanent way that will satisfy the curator.

Whether we can 'stick', that is expect no further revisions, depends on two matters.

1. How good is the double-inductive argument sketched above? It links Realm 1 to Realm 2 theorizing by the citation of historical examples of a preponderance of successful perceptual investigations guided by plausible theories. The argument links Realm 2 to Realm 3 theorizing by citation of historical examples of preponderance of successful manipulative investigations guided by plausible theories. The whole scheme is welded together by the citation of historical examples of successful manipulative investigations guided by Realm 2 theories which have also been perceptually successful. If this argument is good, then ontological attributions are empirically defensible for Realm 3 beings.

2. But historical examples also show that claims to scientific truth and knowledge are apparently indefinitely revisable. However, even a cursory examination of these revisions shows that they are hierarchically ordered. Accidental attributes are revised first, natural kind classifications next, and finally, *in extremis*, ontological classifications may be revised. For instance, the question of whether neutrinos perhaps have a very small rest mass has been raised – a revision of the first order. The suggestion that light

propagators are not distributed wave fronts but localized photons is a revision of the third order, a revision of category or ontological kind. This revision occurred despite the enormous manipulative success of the wave theory.

Our conclusion must be that while global scepticism (at the lower level of the two levels of inductive scepticism) is rebutted by the double-inductive argument (1) above, the evidence of revisability, right up to ontological kind, demonstrated in argument (2) above, shows that there is no support for global antiscepticism either.

To the question 'Is it really true that light is propagated by photons and really false that it is propagated by waves?' we still have to say, 'Wait and see.'

In the discussion so far I have been presenting what I take to be the strongest inductive *argument* for a variety of realism since it recruits both the successes and the failures of past scientific research projects to its evidential basis. But a price has to be paid. The variety of realism which this argument supports is weaker than one would hope ideally to establish. To see this one can juxtapose the varieties of anti-realism to the argument.

We can classify anti-realisms by reference to the verificationist principle of meaning. Logical positivism and Machian sensationalism are anti-realisms of the first kind. Policy realism, as defended so far in these comments, is strong enough to defeat anti-realisms of this variety. But there are weaker anti-realisms which may escape. The oddly named 'critical empiricism' of van Fraassen is a case in point. In many ways it seems to be a revival of sixteenth-century fictionalism, say as advocated by Ursus, together with the late Berkeley of *Siris*. According to this view theories mean what realists take them to mean. But a rigid distinction between observables and unobservables is imported to control the interpretation of the kind of success now customarily called 'empirical adequacy'. Only observables denote the empirically real. The fact that a policy realist must believe that the entities denoted by theory probably exist for the setting up of a project to hunt for them to be rational, could be sloughed off by adherents of this view as a mere psychological condition. *Until* the unobservable becomes an observable no claims for truth or falsity, denotation, etc. can legitimately be made.

This position is fraught with internal difficulties. The most serious concerns the mismatch between prospective and retrospective inferences from the success or failure of research projects. A theory cannot be said to denote anything the nominal term for which is currently an unobservable. So in 1600 the term 'magnetic desmesne' which was used to refer to the elementary magnets that were supposed to have been oriented in the magnetization of a magnetic material, does not denote anything in the world. Nor do the capillaries required by Harvey's circulation theory.

Improvements in microscopy disclose both elementary magnets and capillary vessels. What can we say retrospectively? If van Fraassen concedes that we now know that the terms denoted real entities all along, realism is also conceded retrospectively. Those who took plausibility to be a good ground for a realist reading were right and those who did not were wrong. Prospectively, it must now be the case that some of us are right and others are wrong about our readings of theories, though we will not *know* which are which until some future time. Nevertheless, we do have pretty good inductive grounds for judging who are right and who are wrong, namely the relative plausibility of the theories. Those who have refused to give a realist reading to a relatively plausible theory in the past have usually turned out to be wrong. Since this is an inductive argument we can accommodate those few cases when they turned out to be right. One might also press the critical empiricist on how he thinks existence is related to observability. If he denies that there can be retrospective *validation* of ontological hypotheses (and there will be retrospective invalidations too) it looks as if he has to hold the absurd view that whole categories of beings are brought into existence by the validation procedure itself.

We can now assess our two inductive arguments in the light of this discussion. Realm 1 and Realm 2 were linked through the 'moving boundary argument'. We were inductively justified in believing that terms used to refer to Realm 2 beings did indeed denote something real provided that the theory in which they were embedded conserved natural kinds from Realm 1 and was empirically adequate. The second argument was used to link Realm 2 and Realm 3 theories through the manipulation argument. A technique of manipulation in which manipulative act, target of manipulation and subsequent qualitative change were all in Realms 1/2 can be applied in the context of a Realm 3 theory. But in that context the target is necessarily unobservable. Successful manipulation is a good inductive ground for making a claim about the terms in the Realm 3 theory which are used to refer to the unobserved targets as actually denoting beings of that natural kind, say the charged ions in a Stern–Gerlach apparatus.

Policy realism is obviously strongly supported by these arguments. It is clearly rational to read plausible theories as if they denoted real beings, and tailor our research efforts in the light of that reading. The question is how much further can we go? Is there support for convergent realism too? Of course, the support will be weaker. It is one thing to expect a determinate answer to a question about whether a certain class of beings exists or is possessed of this or that property, another to expect the answer 'yes, it is!' Nevertheless there are two further arguments that point in that direction.

Let us argue it out in terms of beliefs about existence. The point to be established is that it is not only rational to give a realist reading to plausible theories in the expectation of some determinate answer to the question as to whether one was right in one's reading, but that it is rational to believe prior to the determinate answer that the terms in the plausible theory denote what they seem to denote.

The first argument depends on a generalization of Strawson's presupposition theory. A statement can be assessed for truth and falsity only if we are willing to accept the existential presupposition of its terms. Likewise the implementation of a policy realist reading is only rational if we are willing to believe in the existence of the beings apparently denoted. Of course, if we are thinking in terms of there being a Nay answer as well as a Yea answer to the *existential* question this argument cannot be exactly Strawson's argument for existential presuppositions. But our argument is for the rationality of belief, not certainty. One would surely be irrational to spend huge sums of money and invest a great deal of time in looking for something one did not belief probably did exist. So to proceed with a policy realist project if one had in mind only the even-handed possibility of getting either determinate answer would be irrational. Looking for something as a project has the pragmatic presupposition that one is more likely than not to find it. But one can go further. It is not just a matter of there being an even chance of being right or wrong. The realist reading is rational because there is a much greater payoff if we are right or wrong about the existence of the beings we refer to by means of a theory, than if we adopt any of the anti-realist readings and do not pursue the relevant research programme, except by accident.

The second argument comes from Aronson, a point he has urged repeatedly. Provided we understand verisimilitude aright (and that means not in the way it is taken by those who build their realism on bivalence, such as Popper or Newton-Smith) the inductive argument from greater plausibility to greater verisimilitude does go through. The key to rebutting the arguments of such as Laudan lies in how one handles the fact that all our empirical claims seem to be revisable. My own response to this argument, as used by the anti-realists, was to point out that there is a revisability hierarchy. I owe to Aronson the further observation that revisability hierarchies are not indefinitely open.

To argue that the 'realist' induction is invalid because all subsequent empirical disclosures and manipulations cannot protect a result against revision embodies a serious philosophical error. Revision of results is always hierarchical. That is, when a hypothesis is revised the revision follows the following pattern. First the specific attributions are revised (it is not a sheep, it's a goat). Then the more generic (it is not an animal, it is a bush). Finally the metaphysical category or ontological kind may go (it is not a material thing, but an optical effect). We have seen just this kind of hierarchical revision applied to the tales of UFOs for instance. Now Aronson's point is that revision does not *and cannot* extend beyond a supertype or ontological kind, because that is the Realm 1 footing on which the hierarchy rests. I proposed a similar argument in *Varieties of Realism* in using Gibsonian psychology of perception to defend Realm 1 realism. If we admit the Realm 1 to 2 to 3 induction, via disclosure and manipulation links, then we must also admit that the boundaries of observability shift outwards from Realm 1, and this at least is shared by the anti-realists of the second van Fraassen kind (see p. 316 above). There is a limit to revision, and it is set at just the point that allows the inductive argument beyond strong policy realism to weak convergent realism. It must be *weak* convergent realism because it would be hopeless to try to argue that plausible theories give us unrevisable access to the world. That we do not need. All that is necessary to save a realism which preserves a measure of verisimilitude is to show that the revisability of results is not indefinitly open. A somewhat similar line of argument is pursued by Devitt (1984) in which he emphasizes the weakness of the revisability argument or 'pessimistic meta-induction' when it is spelled out in detail.

Finally, it is worth pointing out that disputes with anti-realists of the second kind do not involve the whole of Hume's version of the 'revisability' argument. Hume's scepticism comes at two levels. At the first the argument goes like this: no scientific reasonings are fully rational because our knowledge of a stable world is unproveable. That is the form of the revisability argument with which I have been dealing. Neither Aronson nor I have to deal with the argument at the second level of inductive scepticism, namely that no reasoning whatever about nature is rational because we can have no surety that the world will not so change that whatever we did know about its current state is worthless as a guide in the new conditions. Madden and I (1975) called this the 'neurotic problem of induction' and it is clearly irrelevant to our debates.

In Roy Harris's paper we confront the problem that underlies much of our discussion so far: how are we to account for the way language is used by scientists when they are pursuing their trade? According to Harris, the traditional distinction between pure science and Baconian science has linguistic implications. Those who hold the 'pure' attitude to their researches will tend to assume that there is a semantic discontinuity between the language of science and everyday language. Baconians, on the other hand, should favour semantic continuity. The result of scientific research could hardly be applied to everyday life if there were no phenomena in common, and so no genuine synonyms. According to Harris, Baconianism requires an easy 'transition' between the professional and lay dialects of science. Statements in the one must be transalatable into statements in the other. 'Myalgic encephalomyelitis' is the same condition as 'Yuppie flu'. I am surprised that Harris does not pause to castigate those who talk of two *languages* in this context. The fact that the professional conversations of scientists are now largely conducted in English, though with other Indo-European languages in the historical background, is a fact of some importance. The 'language of science' is surely a dialect of the root language, English itself.

I think Harris has two possible ways in mind in which an account of the dialect of physical science could be given. A global reductionist would treat the science of language in which such an account would be given as a branch of physics. In the spirit of Rutherford's famous aphorism – that what is not physics is stamp collecting – science becomes a completely self-contained enterprise, accounting for its methods and its linguistic tools by the same techniques and theories as it accounts for natural phenomena. Whatever may be the long-term prospects for a global reduction of all the special sciences to physics, it is hardly an immediate threat. We must turn to Harris's other idea for current enlightenment. We could try to show how, by a continuous semantic transition, the dialects of physics, chemistry and microbiology, etc. have arisen out of ordinary language and its quotidian uses. If linguistics is a science, and we are not sure just what that means, it is ontologically independent of physics for all practical purposes. The implausibility of global reductionism leaves open the possibility of many other less dramatic projects for embedding linguistics in other sciences, for instance in evolutionary biology or ethology. But the attempt to tailor a 'science of language' has been influenced by specific philosophical positions, and not for the better. Positivism not only distorted the philosophy of science but had an equally disastrous effect on the attempt to inaugurate a science of language. In Bloomfieldian linguistics we reach the nadir with the thesis that in every dialect a term denotes (and so via verificationism is taken to mean) what physical science says its putative referent is. This is an extreme form of the surrogationalist thesis Harris finds anathema.

Surrogationalism incorporates two main principles:

1.   Words *stand for* entities.
2.   These entities are *given independently* of the words.

The combination of strong policy realism with qualified convergent realism that I have been advocating over the years is a version of referential realism, namely that terms in theories denote real beings, even though what we think we know about them may have to be revised. This would seem to require a surrogationalist view of the way language is used by scientists. It seems that scientists use terms to denote beings that exist independently of acts of reference. How far do Harris's criticisms of the basic surrogationalist theses tell against referential realism?

It is important to admit that entities are never *given* independently of words, concepts, procedures and practices, though they may exist independently of the activities of the scientific community. Policy realism as a species of referential realism is not committed to the second surrogationalist thesis and so is unaffected by its abandonment. However, all varieties of realism must incorporate the first surrogationalist thesis. Each of the three root ideas in this thesis, 'word', 'entity' and 'stand for' are ripe for critical philosophical examination. There is no one surrogationalist doctrine to which realism must conform. As I shall try to show, the Harris criticisms serve to refine rather than to undermine the policy realism I am defending.

Harris seems to have two main objections to surrogationalism. The most telling is that it is prescriptive. There is something that words mean all along and physical scientists will, with luck, find out what it is. But he also objects that the 'standing for' relation is contrary to the fundamental Saussurean principle of the arbitrariness of the linguistic sign.

Harris's second objection seems to me not to be well taken. For instance, surely our growing understanding of what we call 'electricity', which is incorporated in the elaboration of its semantic field, could equally well have been a growing elaboration of the semantic field of the *word* 'luz', had Phillip II been a bit more successful with his Armada. The English might have taken their scientific vocabulary from Spanish.

Dealing with the other objection that Harris makes to surrogationalism calls for a very careful examination of the role of words in acts of reference. These are practices in the course of which, if all goes well, a physical relation is established between an embodied scientist and beings which could be within the human Umwelt. Understanding a word used referentially is not a passive appreciation of the fact that it denotes or might denote some being. That idea enshrines the baptismal model for the acquisition of meaning. But we are enabled, somehow, to grasp the meaning of many words, that is to know how to use them, before any baptismal act has linked them to an already given entity. In scientific contexts this prior understanding of community norms usually derives from a displacement of concepts from a familiar context to another, less familiar one. But does this not require that there be an original context? And how is meaning established there? I think it right to treat this question as at least partly a matter of the psychology of development. Bruner believes that his studies show that there are no primitive baptismal ceremonies in which words are tied to things carried out in the presence of and with the understanding of an infant. Instead there is a growing mastery of the use of sounds in manipulations. Just as 'pain' in Wittgenstein's account is intelligible only because it is used in ways that take over the role of groaning, so 'Gimme ball!' takes over the role of pointing and reaching (Bruner, 1979).

Given this innocuous way of understanding the 'stand for' relation, can we go on to rescue realism from the taint of prescriptivism? The variety of realism I have been advocating involves holding the following linguistic theses.

1. Novel uses of words appear in theoretical contexts. In most cases these uses are intelligible because they have come about through displacement of concepts from existing contexts in which they already have a use. Metaphors are among several tropes of this kind. There are some cases of almost pure contextual determination where one has had to learn a new language game by participation, but they are rare. As I tried to show in my contribution to Brown and Harré (1988), even in the most recondite branches of physics meaning is created by displacement of concepts from one context to another.

2. In certain contexts, namely those in which an extension of the human Umwelt has taken place, the new uses turn out to be descriptive. 'Virus' is introduced into microbiology from a general medical context to enable scientists to refer to an unknown vector of disease. Improvements in microscopy have made these beings visible. Now the word has accumulated a descriptive content, even for the lay public.

3. Words are usually used in science in a double context, that of experimental procedures and that of theoretical reflection. A downmarket version of the too tightly defined and metaphysically antiquated distinction between nominal and real essence can be used to expound the history of the uses of a word-sign, a 'term', as a dialectical interaction between uses in each of these contexts. Put this way we are clearly on the verge of prescriptivism.

Much depends on how we take linguistic sameness in the history of the uses of a word. If it is supposed to be a history of the very same term, that is, some linguistic entity at some level of abstraction that is semantically identical throughout the period being described, then we are required to assume:

(a)   that those who used it at all times prior to the present did not use it correctly; and

(b)   that scientists have now revealed what the world really meant, though its users did not know it.

Harris suggests that the attempt that Madden and I made to sketch the history of the word 'copper' falls into just that trap. And he takes our exposition of this history as the focus of his criticism of pernicious surrogationalism. Can prescriptivism be avoided and yet the main outlines of such a 'semantic history' as our account of 'copper' be preserved?

To find our way through these geniune difficulties some distinctions and some observations are needed. One must clearly distinguish between linguistic essentialism, the thesis that there is something which a word *really* means, and 'material essentialism', the thesis that each kind of material being has a constituent structure, whose particular manifestation in this or that instance of the kind is causally responsible for the manifest properties of its sample realizations. I take it that linguistic essentialism is false and that material essentialism is true, at least in some restricted domains such as inorganic chemistry. To give a full account of material essentialism requires a number of qualifications such as the observation that how properties are assigned between 'essence' and 'proprium' will depend on the context and purpose of an enquiry.

Realism is problematic on linguistic grounds only if it is taken to be an investigation of a world independent of human activity and thought. But the only world we can investigate is the Umwelt, the world we can reach with our perceptual systems and instrumentation guided and interpreted by our language and other symbolic resources. All we can ever *say* about the world beyond all possible experience is confined to what we know it affords to our exploratory efforts and techniques. What these are is usually determined by the kind of equipment our technology allows us to build and our theories allow us to understand.

The obvious rejoinder to Harris's criticism is to draw attention to the multiple identity conditions for lexical items, and the many ways that 'a word' might be held to be self-identical over time. Provided we think of the thread of continuity as no more than the qualitative identity of instances of a word-sign type we can hold on to material essentialism and at the same time give a historical description of the ways instances of the word-sign type were used at different periods which reveals that at any two adjacent times the sets of rules of use overlapped. 'Only now have we found out what poliomyelitis *really* is' is compatible with there having been a long history of uses of instances of the word-sign 'poliomyelitis' which do not conform to our latest discovery of what we now take to be the real essence of the condition. Nevertheless there is historical continuity in use in the sense just sketched.

Are there any grounds for claiming that these changes of use have been improvements? And if so, to what? Let us continue with the case of names for metals. Taking the multiple dialect view of language, each of which is characteristic of one of the suburbs of Wittgenstein's city, there seems to me to be no reason why we should not have it linguistically, both ways. In the dialect of chemical metallurgy the current ways of using the word-sign 'copper' are tied in with a wider Umwelt and with improved techniques in handling ores, castings and what not by a complex cluster of interlocking criteria, than are the ways the word-sign is used among the proprietors of hardware stores. When I go to Gills for a few copper nails neither Mr Apsley-Penny nor I need be using the dialect of metallurgy. Nevertheless, we pick out items made of a material stuff that is the same stuff as that of which metallurgists are so vastly knowledgeable. There is a discernible historical continuity between their dialect and ours. But there are significant differences. 'How can I be sure that this is copper?' calls for one kind of comment in Gills and quite another in the metallurgical laboratory. Compare 'How can we be sure this [Turin] shroud was used to wrap the body of Christ?'

I have shown that induction from the evidence of scientific practice supports two conclusions. Policy realism is strongly supported while there is also support for convergent realism provided there is an adequate account of revisability. These linguistic observations point in the same direction. What we are talking about is an Umwelt, that which the noumenal world affords to our perceptual systems and empirical techniques. The old vulnerable form of convergent realism could be expressed in the image of scientists as miners digging deeper in search of the gold that was there independently of their nature and activities. Our new robuster, because more subtle pair of realisms can be expressed in another image, that of engineers reclaiming the polders. The result is indeed more land, but it comes into being through human efforts to drain the estuaries.

Harris might have gone further in his condemnation of a certain attitude to language manifested by many philosophers of science, namely that the vocabulary of science is not only surrogational in the sense Harris condemns, but intelligible independently of the material practices of the scientific community. Experiment is not an afterthought, indulged in to accumulate a repertoire of singular propositions with which to play *modus tollens or modus ponens* or engage in enumerative induction, etc. It is the very stuff of the scientific enterprise. To get our account of science right we must describe the language games of a community and show how they fit within its form of life. And this is a very different matter from studying the formal properties of written scientific discourses.

II Philosophy of Physics

The realist controversies that I have been discussing have surfaced over the last 500 years in a fairly regular cycle. Each turn has seen the revival, often unconscious without explicit acknowledgement, of well-worn arguments and conceptions. For instance there has been the revival of Clavius' paradox of 1600 in the observation that considered as deductive structures, theories are underdetermined for truth or falsity by the data to which they are relevant. I am well aware that much of the general position for which I have argued in recent years has already been adumbrated by C. S. Peirce. Generally, arguments for and against this or that variety of realism have drawn on examples from the physical sciences.

Of all the physical sciences, physics itself, which we now see as the foundation of all the other sciences of material stuff, has been at the focus of intense philosophical discussion since Osiander tacked on his famous preface to the *De Revolutionibus* of Copernicus. For the most part this discussion has not only been retrospective. The active role of philosophical though in promoting and disciplining developments in physics itself has been prominent feature of the subject since the fifteenth century. Contemporary philosophy of physics is no exception. While there has been some passing attention to the problems of thermodynamics, most work has been directed to the conceptual foundations of quantum theory and of the relativities.

I have long believed that the science of physics, in both its experimental and its theoretical 'wings', should be admired as *one of* the greatest of all human achievements. Nevertheless a celebratory aspect in the philosophy of physics does not preclude the critical exposure of confused thought, even among its greatest practitioners. But, on the other hand, the technical difficulty of physical theories and the effort needed to abstract their physical and conceptual content from the mathematical expression that is essential to their formulation means that philosophers of physics can never be wholly confident that their analyses are directed to the right target. The recent reappraisal of Wittgenstein's philosophical work on the nature and foundations of mathematics, has made it abundantly clear that the greatest practitioners were often guilty of their share of nonsense, and even of misunderstanding their own technical innovations. I derived great pleasure from reading Stuart Shanker's recent (1987) study of Wittgenstein's philosophy of mathematics, bringing back vividly the classes given by Waismann in the early fifties. I believe we should take Wittgenstein's methods in his remarks on the foundations of mathematics as our model for the philosophy of physics. Unexamined grammatical analogies and unnoticed assumptions, built in to the very language that is being used by physcisists and philosophers of physics, will be the focus of my attention.

Physics, as a discourse situated within a context of experimental and observational practices, grows at the boundaries of existing linguistic conventions, ever pressing up against what Ackermann (1988) has nicely called the 'horizons' of language games. So the intelligibility of the latest pronouncements of physicists is usually in question. But physics has always grown through transcending the horizons of earlier linguistic practices. So the history of physical thought and experimental practice is – or ought to be – as much a part of its philosophical exploration as the study of the latest fashion. Could it be that profound misunderstandings of the roots of contemporary concepts have actually survived into the thinking of the existing community of physical scientists? I shall return to that heretical thought.

Though the distinction does not run very deep we can usefully distinguish in the philosophy of physics between two main clusters of topics.

1. There is the identification and critical analysis of the patterns of reasoning used by physicists. For example, there is Newton's 'esteeming' move by which he described the relation between the physical properties of unobservable material corpuscles and observable material things. Or there is the double reversed analogy between virtual and real species of genera of particles by which quantum field theory both grows conceptually and engenders experimental programmes – a pattern of reasoning I have tried to analyse in both *Varieties of Realism* (1986) and in my contribution in Brown and Harré (1988).

2. Then there is the analysis of physical concepts, by a study of the way certain words are used, and certain mathematical devices developed. There are concepts peculiar to physics, such as 'electromagnetic potential', 'isospin', and so on; and in the mathematical expression of physical thought there is the use of constraints such as covariance, the real line, and so on. But there are also concepts which are carried by idioms with a much wider range of applications, such as 'space', 'time', 'instant', 'causality', etc. Here Wittgenstein's revelations of the power of existing grammatical models to constrain the way words are used (and the mathematical analogue of that constraint) bear thinking about very carefully. The problematic aspects of the former are bound up with their history, of the latter with their continued role in quite humdrum contexts. Even as smart a fellow as Robert Weingard can fall into a bewitchment of the intelligence in just that way, as I hope to show.

3. These targets of study can be pursued by the analysis of written scientific texts, indeed they usually are. The deconstruction of those texts is also a task for philosophers of physics. Much greater attention must be

paid in future to rhetorical aspects of the presentation of scientific ideas.

4. But there is another neglected aspect of real physics. I believe that far too little attention has been paid to the role of experimental techniques, and the engineering of the apparatus they depend upon, in the formation of concepts and in the development of patterns of reasoning. As I have tried to show elsewhere the double reversed analogy of quantum field theory is strongly influenced by the availability of certain kinds of experimental techniques which produce certain quite characteristic artefacts.

John Roche makes the very interesting point that the study of the concepts and patterns of reasoning of classical physics is not strictly speaking an historical undertaking because classical physics has never been superseded by the glamorous specialities currently absorbing the attentions of philosophers of physics. Quantum theory and relativity are rooted in classical concepts and theories. It follows that the study of nineteenth-century physics is not an antiquarian interest, which we could say of the efforts that have produced the vast literature devoted to the physics of the seventeenth century.

Roche reminds us that there is a great catalogue of concepts, still in use, that have never been clarified. His own studies of the concepts and theories of classical electromagnetism illustrate this point abundantly. Misconceived concepts become mere counters in a formalistic game. It seems to me that his listings of philosophical work to be done are of the greatest interest. Let us hope they can be realized in cooperative projects. But for me, the most interesting of all his suggestions is the reminder that mathematics has appeared in several different and distinctive roles. Physics includes both *auxiliary* and *representational* mathematics, and each interacts differently with the pure mathematics from which its techniques and conceptual resources are drawn. In a representational use of a mathematical technique every concept employed in the mathematical analysis of a natural phenomenon has physical meaning. So statistical mechanics, as a treatment of the classical physics of gases, employs concepts each of which can be given a meaning in terms of the assumption that gases are aggregates of moving molecules. An auxiliary use of mathematics is strictly heuristic and concepts other than those which are defined immediately in the phenomena have no physical meaning. It is of the greatest importance to make the distinction between these two main ways in which mathematics is used. Neglect of it is the source of much misunderstanding and illusion.

However there are several different cases of auxiliary uses.

1. In classical physics there are instances where there is a 'natural' reading of the mathematics as a description of a possible mechanism for generating the phenomena. The use of the auxiliary circle in the mathema-

tical treatment of simple harmonic motion is a perfect illustration of this. There could be a mechanism of wheels and sliding cranks that realized the geometry of rotation and projection. It is a simple matter of observation as to whether there is any such mechanism at work when a weight is bobbing up and down on the end of a spring. We should note that statistical mechanics as a treatment of thermodynamics could be made to look auxiliary. How we take it depends on whether we have a commitment to an ontology of molecules or not.

2. There are other cases where no such 'natural' reading is available. The Hilbert space treatment of quantum mechanics strikes me as a near perfect example of this sort.

3. Finally, there are cases in which the mathematics seems to have a natural reading, but closer analysis shows that this is an error. Contemporary physics provides a good example in the oscillator plenum invoked in vacuum physics to account for zero-point fluctuations, the Lamb shift, and so on. As Aitchison (1985) made clear in his excellent review paper, the oscillator plenum is not and could not be a picture of some medium filling the whole of physical space. It is more like Hilbert space than it is like an auxiliary circle. And it is not at all like the molecular plenum that is coextensive with a sample of gas because that is what the sample actually is.

Robert Weingard's debate with me over the status of global space–time is particularly instructive by reason of the issues it raises in philosophical method. He presents our disagreement as if it were a straightforward, if sophisticated, debate as to the epistemic status of claims about possible existents, the usual menu of linked ontological and epistemic problems which has been the traditional subject matter of discussions about realism. But I hope to show that the matter is not at all as Weingard thinks it is. It is not an ontological issue, but a *grammatical* one that divides us. I shall use this discussion not only to try to clarify what is at issue in discussions of global space–times, but also to illustrate the power of Wittgenstein's innovations in philosophical technique.

The first point to notice is that Weingard presents the issue as if it were a matter of whether certain global space–times, cylinders, 'strips' or whatever were real, that is, whether such space–times existed or could exist independently of any system of material bodies. If they did or could, then it might be right to say that the material system existed 'in' that space–time. And it would certainly be right to ask what properties the space–time had independently of its encapsulating the material world.

My first question is this: is the mathematics of the relativity family of 'theories' auxiliary or representational? Weingard does not address this as a prior question but takes it for granted that the mathematics is representational. In this he is not exceptional. It is a characteristic assumption of many contemporary philosophers of physics. The difference that one's attitude to the mathematics would make is profound.

1. If the mathematics – particularly in this case, the Minkowski geometrical presentation of relativity – is read representationally, then not only does it present a certain class of relational properties among material things, the set of world lines, but the manifold within which these world lines extend has the same status as the material system itself. A world line is just one among an indefinite set of trajectories that are well defined within the geometry. A moving and persisting body simply occupies one.
2. But, as auxiliary mathematics, the Minkowski presentation is just a neat way of expressing certain relations (both actual and possible) between material beings. The geometrical manifold has no more claim to reality than does the grid of longitude and latitude.

Weignard's space–time realism is an example of the kind of illusion to which otherwise cautious thinkers are subject when they take the whole of the mathematical apparatus representationally. It would be as if there were a ghostly circular motion accompanying every simple harmonic oscillator. How can we make progress in deciding between the available readings? A 'use-question' can help. What is the mathematical device used for? To what is Minkowski space–time analogous? This is the question that Wittgenstein frequently used to open one's mind to alternative possibilities.

Let us return to think about the grid of latitude and longitude. It is used to relate places on the surface of the earth to one another and to navigate surely on that surface. There is not the surface of the earth *and* the manifold. I put it to the reader that the Minkowski space–time is more like cartography than it is like anything else to which geometry is applied. It enables one to locate material events relative to one another and to navigate surely in the electromagnetic flux. There is not the electromagnetic flux *and* the manifold of Minkowski space–time. One way of expressing this insight, namely the superiority of the cartographical analogue, is to argue an anti-realist case for global space–times. And in its turn this is one device for bringing out the conclusion that the right way to read the mathematics, in all its elegance and beauty, is as auxiliary.

The next step in my exorcism of the spell to which my old friend has been subject is to turn to examine very closely what the properties are which space–time cartographers are presenting. Through such a scrutiny we shall be able to see how it is that the problem of the status of global space–times is not ontological but grammatical.

I would like to begin this analysis with a quotation from a work of John Gardner, only too briefly a colleague at SUNY Binghamton before his tragic death. The quotation comes from Book 3, section V of *The King's Indian*.

> Onward forever the dead come, soundless and staring. In me they exist, not 'back there in the past' because there is no past, there is nothing in all this universe but the razor's edge between my memory and imagination, the instant's perception between things dead, unlimbed for ever, and yet to be born . . . or yet to be borne. My very existence one second ago is banished out of life eternally. Second by second the world falls shut like a coffin-lid.

Of course, Weingard and I must surely share the view that space–time geometries enable us to present to ourselves certain relations between things and events. The point on which we differ is whether one can go on from that to construct a manifold out of the positions and locations which seem to be denoted ad lib by particular sets of numbers taken as co-ordinates. But what properties are they?

For space they are exclusion relations between things – and this is presented in principles like 'no two things, under certain ontological restrictions, can be in the same place at the same moment' as if this were some kind of pervasive fact. It is, of course, a grammatical proposition, in the sense of Wittgenstein, since it delimits the sense of the expressions 'thing', 'place' and 'moment'.

For time there are exclusion relations between events, typically presented in principles like 'two events at the same place, under certain ontological restrictions such as the realization of different determinates under the same determinable, cannot occur at the same time.' Again it should be clear that principles like this are 'grammatical'.

At this stage of the analysis 'thing' and 'event' seem to obey norms of sense that are remarkably similar. It can come to seem as if the grammars of *Thing/place* and *event/moment* are in essentials indistinguishable.

Let us now turn back to reflect on how Weingard might set about 'building' his space–times. Not only must he detach the manifold from the system of material bodies and material events certain of whose interrelations it describes, but he must assume that the grammars of 'thing', 'event' and their counterparts, 'place' and 'moment', in the representational manifold are more or less similar. (The expression 35N/2E must behave like the expression Palma de Mallorca, and both must behave like 2100 hours.)

But the similarities in grammars are superficial. In the aspect most relevant to the question of whether it makes sense to assemble global space–times in addition to the material beings of the universe, the grammars of the key expresions are quite different. The difference emerges when we reflect on the kind of totalities that can be forged out of places and out of moments. Their relation to existence gives the clue to how radically they differ.

Space is a conjunctive totality of places. 'Here' and 'exists' are not tied together conceptually. The quantifier by which a totality expression for places is created is an 'all '. 'All xs exist and all pairs of xs coexist'.

Time is a disjunctive totality of moments. 'Now' is conceptually tied to 'exists'. 'An event can only happen *now*' is a grammatical remark. Hence its apodeictic character. No advance in physics could make us give it up. Of course, physics may so develop that the grammer that is expressed in this idiom is inelegant, clumsy or misleading. But one must be quite clear that in shifting to another dialect a new notion of 'event' is introduced without rendering the previous one obsolete. Calling space vehicles 'ships' is a grammatical innovation which leaves the use of that lexical word sign for boats untouched.

The question then sharpens. Does Weingard have good grounds for proposing a new dialect in which the radical differences in the totality concepts for each component of the space–time pair is washed out? Notice that this question is only relevant if the mathematics of the Minkowski geometry, for instance, is taken as representational rather than auxiliary. If it is merely auxiliary then the only parts of a Minkowski manifold or any other global space–time that come under the kind of grammatical constraints at issue here are the world-lines. On the 'nothing can exist except now' principle they are disjunctive totalities of events. Global space–time is a fiction, a mode of discourse. And each world-line is ontologically a human *story*, not a pantemporal being. The argument that is needed to block the introduction of the new place and moment concepts with their new grammar as physical concepts, in contrast to features of the auxiliary mathematics, turns on what emerges when we reflect on what happens in experiments. I do not mean what is said to have happened when the goings on in the laboratory or the observatory have been described in the terminology of the auxiliary mathematics, but as it all happens. On this score it seems to me that Niels Bohr was absolutely right in insisting that the results we get *must* be expressed in the vocabulary of classical physics. In that dialect the grammar of expressions like 'track', 'place', 'event' and so on is just what was once misleadingly set out as traditional metaphysics. There is no conceivable way in which a dialect with expressions that obey the grammars of the key terms of relativity theories could be used to any effect in laboratories or for the reporting of results.

The family of relativity theories is one of the very greatest intellectual achievements of mankind, but we do it a disservice by reading it as anything other than auxiliary mathematics. In its time the ghost circle was as ingenious a device for handling simple harmonic motion mathematically.

My conclusion is that the Minkowski way of presenting special relativity is auxiliary rather than representional. It is the simplest 'global space–time' after the Euclidean. But so far I have been discussing it as if it were a kind of picture or model just as the *grid* of longitude and latitude is a visual image that could be presented alongside a picture of the earth. This is still to misunderstand the point of such mathematical innovations as the global space–times. Turning back to Wittgenstein's way of thinking about such matters, ought we not to treat the principles of special relativity, for instance, as a grammar; as rules for the use of a cluster of concepts bearing certain family resemblances to our everyday concepts of relative spatial position, before and after, and so on? Since, as I have argued above, attention to the way experiments are carried out precludes the substitution of this new grammar as a preferred representational dialect, there has to be some other explanation as to why the expressions whose norms of use it presents have the family resemblances that they do. It is important to see that there are two parts to an answer. One is the obvious historical story drawn from the history of attempts to formulate rules for the mathematical treatment of moving bodies. There is also the requirement that the auxiliary mathematics should be readily intelligible. The treatment of simple harmonic motion as the projection of uniform circular motion on to a diameter is intelligible to a child. The presentation of this treatment as an exercise in Cartesian geometry is not.

The phenomenon of an auxiliary mathematical treatment of some laboratory results taking on the mantle of an ontology is widespread in physics. I believe we should be very cautious in the way we read mathematical treatments. To take the general relativity notion of the 'curvature of space' ontologically undoubtedly gives one a frisson. But, in the cold light of day, what is it but a geometrical metaphor for a certain kind of causation? To argue this point out in detail one would need to look very closely into two species of argument. One is represented by Nerlich's book *The Shape of Space* (1976). I think that his discussion is in effect a gigantic non sequitur since his argument requires that there be non-Euclidean space through which his malleable test object drifts. But if non-Euclidean spaces are mere presentations of non-uniform causation by material bodies then the argument fails to gel. The other tack is to argue – and Weingard favours this move – that there are solutions to the equations of certain plausible cosmological theories for space–time devoid of matter, which require a non-Euclidean structure. To which the reply is as above – odd consequences of a bit of auxiliary mathematics cut no ice.

But the vice of promiscuous geometrization is not confined to philosophers of mathematical cosmology. An equal thrill can be brought on by contemplating the Kalusa–Klein equation in the same sort of way. The excess variables above the minimum needed for the presentation of spatio-temporal aspects of sub-atomic phenomena can be taken as 'compacted spatial dimensions'. So at any point in old-fashioned space – time there is a kind of closed cell of scrunched up spatial dimensions whose structure takes on an explanatory role in dealing with the experimental results. This sort of thing really does need the full Wittgenstein treatment. First of all one must go back to the laboratory and just *look* at what happened there when the apparatus was switched on. Then one must return again to follow through the mathematical treatment, now seen as a language game in which the uses of word signs are tied in with the material practices of the experimentalists. Now the deep question of whether the mathematics is representational or auxiliary can be tackled. One must look out for a step I would like to call 'remodelling'. Take the Kalusa–Klein equation.

The additional dimensions represent the following physical phenomena, as revealed by apparatus which works in a certain way. Now comes the remodelling. These parameters are now read as a spatial structure. But analogous to what? Not to the old Newtonian container, for that would put material stuff back into the world. These cells are analogous to the ontologized space–time whose equivocal status began the argument. But in the laboratory experimental scientists need not only the heuristic power of the auxiliary mathematics, but the everyday grammar of the word-signs for spatial and temporal exclusions, domestic space and time. And now we are back again with Bohr's correspondence principle.

I have attempted a fuller treatment of world-lines as histories, indexically tied to speakers, in my *Varieties of Realism*. In that scheme 'now' and 'exists' are grammatically tied together but there is no way that a collective 'now' can be constructed out of the totality of strict first person indexicals. What does this tell us about the possibility of a cosmological 'now', a plane orthogonal to all world-lines? Nothing is easier than to provide a specification for a cosmological 'now'. It is the set of events distributed over the whole material system which would be correlated by the use of an infinite signalling velocity. What exactly prohibits the inclusion of this concept in contemporary physics? Is it ruled out by some matter of fact, say the result of the Michelson–Morley experiment? Reading the special theory of relativity as a grammar sets up a horizon of sense for that language game. It follows that inertial frame multiple 'nows' do not preclude cosmological 'nows'. These two notions do not stand in contradiction to one another.

That would be to suppose that they were embedded in one super language game. The stand outside one another. A rough way of putting this would have been to say that they belong in incommensurable paradigms. But that idea has turned out to be fraught with all kinds of difficulties, not least because transitions from one paradigm to another have looked, at least from a distance, to be irrational. The language-game idea, which ties clusters of linguistico-material practices together by relations of similarity and difference, gets nearer the intuitions about how the dialects of our language work and how they are related one to another.

I would like to use the occasion of Michael Redhead's elegant exposition of the shortest ever proof of the Bell inequality to reflect again on the mesmeric quality of the Einstein–Padovksy–Rosen paradox – EPR for short. I want to try to diagnose the particular way that the intelligence of the physics community continues to be bewitched by this very deep puzzle. Not so long ago the two-slit experiment served as the focus of discussion of the significance of quantum mechanics, and the collapse of the wave packet was the tantalizingly bizarre concept with which the conceptual difficulties of the theory were more often than not presented.

It seems to me that the shorter the 'proofs' of the Bell inequality the clearer become the deep and pervasive conceptual muddles through the persistence of which EPR seems to be so outageously puzzling. Redhead's treatment is so transparent that it enables us to get very close to the heart of the matter.

Let us begin by reminding ourselves that EPR consists of two phenomena. (Again, as always, I shall be using that expression in the sense of Niels Bohr, that is to refer to events within an indissoluble totality of man-made instrument and independent world, that is to a feature of the human Umwelt.)

1. Certain paired states of 'distant' objects are found to be correlated.
2. The correlations are preserved in the course of routine manipulations of a sort which, in the classical framework, ought not to permit their preservation.

Given the classical/common-sense meanings of all the concepts involved in detailing the above, the phenomena 1 and 2 together are so strongly counterintuitive as to present an air of paradox.

Let us now turn to Redhead's model. There is a black box which initially at least has two slots out of which pop counters, so engraved and coloured that ready comparisons can be made and a statistical survey undertaken without ambiguity. The Bell inequality emerges very rapidly from some elementary assumptions. Its violation occurs as swiftly when the engravings on successive pairs of contemporaneous counters follow the pattern of correlations of any version of a real EPR experiment.

Redhead's characteristically ingenious move in this paper is the construction of a probabilistic model for goings-on inside the black box that will lead to the counters manifesting satisfactory Bell violating behaviour. There are some very enlightening presuppositions in Redhead's development of his model, the examination of which will throw some light on why it is that EPR seems worrisome.

In the model the probability concepts are applied twice, once to the phenomena and again to the putative causes of the phenomena via the lambda state. What are the conditions for the application of probability concepts to anything? To apply probability concepts classically we need to assume that the phenomena whose patterns they describe are independent of one another. That is just what violations of Bell's inequality tell us is not true of the events that are characteristic of any version of EPR. The events are not independent of one another.

What is the matter with Redhead's model? He assumes that probability concepts are applied classically inside the black box. But can he not assume what he likes provided that he gets the right answer? No. Because that assumption goes along with another. That the counters *come out of* the box, that is, that they pre-exist the human acts of picking them up, reading off their markings and colours, and so on. This is a simple and very clear display of the unexamined assumption that lies behind the usual puzzle-enhancing treatment of EPR: that the correlation pre-exist the human efforts to detect them.

These features of the model, in particular the pre-existence assumption, which might be more rightly seen as part of the grammar of 'counter' rather than as a free-standing assumption, has two preconditions. The properties that are assigned to the counters by those who read them are always occurrent properties. The counters would have these properties, if, *per impossibile*, the inside of the box were open to view. Secondly, Redhead's treatment assumes that the probabilistic structure of the sequences of counter-readings reflects a corresponding structure within the box. This is of course, the basic assumption of classical range theory – that if red and black come up equal numbers of times in a large trial then the wheel must have equal numbers of red and black slots. Given an equipossibility assumption then it is enough just to count the slots. But in the case of the sealed box we cannot count the slots but must content ourselves with a probabilistic estimate of their distribution – Redhead's *lambda*.

It is the assumption of the *pre-existence* of each counter that imposes a conservative grammar on the discourse available to one who tries to describe the magician's game with the slots and the participating members of the audience. Let us now turn back to EPR to see that it is correspondingly conservative in the raw physics. How does EPR come to appear as a *puzzle*? At the heart of the impression that the EPR correlations signal something out of the ordinary is the application of what I shall call the 'separation assumption' to events engendered in a special way, the way described in the generic EPR apparatus, say with spin components as the measured properties. It is clearly an error to talk of spin states – say, spin-up or spin-down – since this is already to prejudge the kind of the measured properties. They are assumed to be occurrent rather than dispositional. The separation assumption looks pretty innocuous. It is that events are individuated, in part, by the places at which they occur. By virtue of the spatial separation of the correlated events (the fact that the counters are examined by two stooges) it follows that EPR must describe correlations between *separate events*. But this separation assumption is obviously grammatical, in Wittgenstein's sense. Let us now examine the consequences of looking at the matter this way.

1. The event concept whose grammer is partially expressed in the separation assumption is our everyday concept, not far removed from a happening in everyday life. But the language game of happenings in the experimental contexts of the EPR type may bear only a family resemblance to the language games of the historically ancestral common-sense/classical concepts.
2. The persistence of violations of the Bell inequality could point to the dubiousness of the above assumption, just as the persistent failure to achieve a surface both red and green all over has more to do with the grammar of 'red' and 'green' than with the physics and physiology of light.
3. The usual treatment of EPR doubles up the error by adding a causation assumption also drawn from common sense, that is, that correlations between distant events must be brought about by some intermediary process. For instance it might be e1 $\rightarrow$ e2 or it might be $e3\langle^{e_1}_{e_2}$.

   There is a number of other possibilities, as Michael Redhead himself has sketched out. But like the separation condition of which this could be seen as a corollary, it too assumes the common-sense grammar of 'event'. And at this point the clash with relativity is usually evoked.

Correlations can appear in the running of experimental apparatus either (i) because two events are causally linked or (ii) because one event manifests itself to human observers under two aspects, initiating causal chains in two media – for example, as in the correlation between the lightning flash and the roll of thunder. Only if we slip into treating the separation conditions as inviolate, as part of the grammar of 'event' are we driven towards (i) as our exegetical principle. But this is just the principle whose ruthless application leads to all the trouble.

It is my view that the phenomena typified by the generic EPR experiment call for a new grammar, a development in which the separation condition for the individuation of events, of what are to be called 'events' with all that that denomination implies, is replaced. Redhead toys with such an idea in his fascinating paper 'Passion at a Distance' (1988) in which among the schemata he offers is one that, if taken seriously, would have the radical consequence I propose. But there is more to the underlying linguistic structure than just the pressure on the grammar of 'event'. There are also assumptions about 'property' at work in the argument. Part of what makes it hard to abandon the idea that in EPR set-ups there are separate events is the analysis of the phenomena in terms of occurrent properties. This is just the assumption that we saw above to be built in to the idea that the stooges are deciphering the inscriptions on counters which pre-existed engraved and coloured just as they pop out of the slots in the infernal machine. I shall call this the *assumption of the uniformity of property grammars*.

Redhead offers us two ways of embedding the Bell inequality into our reasoning, and in effect two ways of resolving the apparently bizarre consequences of the steady accumulation of EPR-type phenomena. Each way of embedding Bell is related to a different assumption.

1. The assumption built in to the derivation of the Bell inequality is that the choice of a particular act of looking at a counter by observer D does not affect the result of observer L's act of looking. Call this assumption I. Then the argument goes as follows:

I entails the Bell inequality
Bell is violated by experiment so I is false.

The resolution of the EPR type of problem is that there is some form of *interaction* between the observers.

2. Redhead's 'lambda' is introduced as a schematic representation of a stochastic process by which the statistical results of D's and L's observations are determined. Expressed as an assumption this runs as follows: there is some randomly changing property determinative of what is seen by observers. Call this assumption II. The argument tying this assumption to Bell is then:

II entails the falsity of Bell

II is given by plausible theory and the falsity of Bell by experiment.

These are two quite different argumentative strategies. In the former the experimental result is effective through modus tollens; in the latter by the kind of induction that Gassendi called the 'natural instrument', that is, by the formally invalid pattern of affirmation of the consequent. According to Gassendi's treatment of this version of the underdetermination of theory by data, the force of the argument pattern depends on the plausibility of the theory. Is the introduction of a randomized hidden variable a plausible way of proceeding?

My treatment of these alternatives requires a stepping back from the arguments themselves to ask first of all what sort of statements the assumptions I and II actually are. How do they function in the discourses considered as language games? Only when this question has been answered can we make an informed choice between the alternative strategies.

Choosing the second strategy would require one to make two noxious commitments. One would be required to assume that the conditions for applying the probability calculus, with the help of which Redhead works out the consequences of introducing the 'lambda' property, are universally satisfied. Secondly, one is committed to the belief that the counters pre-exist their examination. But this latter commitment involves the enshrining of a pre-Bohrian, and I must say naive, conception of phenomena.

Choosing the first strategy requires a shift in a language game. It requires a novel grammar for a concept only analogous to the old concept of event, the concept incorporated in the strategy whose commitments I have outlined above. The change in grammar is such as to drop from among the rules of normative use for the new concept 'B-event' (that is, Bohr-type event) the requirement that spatial separation entails independent individuation. In short, there is only *one* event, that of D-and-L-looking-at-two-counters. As a Bohr-type phenomenon, this event has certain characteristics, namely those revealed in the experiments. Now we can see why the elegant derivation of Bell via the magician's infernal machine model is so very misleading. It enshrines the grammar of the common-sense and everyday concept of 'event'. In the picture invoked of magicians, stages, stooges and quite large plastic counters (perhaps something like tiddlywinks only bigger) with engraved symbols, etc., anything other than the received grammar for talking about what is going on seems utterly quirkish. But in Aspect's laboratory, surrounded by another class of infernal machine, the bonds of everyday language games are loosened and a new language game in which the sibling concept of B-event has a different horizon of sense can seem quite a comfortable option.

But behind this way of opting for alternative I without the causation assumption − let us call it option Ia−lies something deeper. How could

Michael Redhead be so bewitched by a grammatical model as to carry the metaphysics of, say tennis, into physics? (The new balls are in the refrigerator before the players begin to use them.) One answer can be found by examining another central concept of EPR-type experiments and their models. What sort of property concept is incorporated in the two treatments? In both, the counters are assumed to have the properties that they reveal to D and L before they are deciphered, and indeed in alternative II to have them before they pop out of the slots. (We might call Redhead's model the 'two-slot experiment'!) But suppose we treat what happens in the physics laboratory as the manifestation of affordances, in the Gibsonian manner. An affordance is a dispositional property of some generic substrate which manifests itself in some particular form of human manipulation. It is real, since unless the substrate does afford spin-up and spin-down particles in the right relations the result of operating on the substrate with, say, Aspect-type apparatus, would not be the way it is. But we are not entitled to say that, prior to that set of operations, the substrate possessed just that property. It is a property of the human Umwelt, but we can ascribe to the Welt itself only the affordance. Looked at in this way Redhead's magician's box example is wildly misleading, since it makes it virtually impossible to treat the properties of the pairs of counters with their observers as affordances. According to the affordance way of looking at phenomena, EPR-type experiments have revealed a new kind of event which occurs over a spatial distribution. It is more like a sunset than it is like a pair of lightning flashes.

Redhead himself has often spoken with enthusiasm of the philosophy of physics as the source of new metaphysical insights and puzzles. Properly interpreted, the EPR class of results is an occasion for a pair of metaphysically innovative moves, leading to developments of new concepts of property and of event.

The essays by Weingard and by Redhead illustrate complementary ways of getting into trouble by tying oneself to grammar. In my terms, Weingard seems to be advocating a new grammar for the concepts of space and time, namely to allow them to be used to speak of joint manifolds of places and moments which could exist independently of there being any things and events to ground them. To him I offer the reminder that in any cartographic use of mathematical manifolds the mathematics is necessarily auxiliary and the conceptual basis of its application/interpretation must needs be conservative. But to Michael Readhead I offer the complementary reminder. Sometimes the experiments which exploit a new range of *equipment* present to our startled eyes kinds of phenomena for the description of which our existing grammars are inadequate. By slipping into taking the grammatical rules of our old concepts as metaphysical principles it is easy to slide into bewitchment in these circumstances. The way out looks easy, but in detailed fact often proves the most difficult option of all. For it requires not only the mastery of a new discourse, but also a careful exploration of its horizons of sense and of its relations to what passed as the deepest way of talking before.

III The Study of People and Their Ways of Life

How to present what is distinctive about the approach to psychology advocated by myself and my friends? I owe to B. Davies the suggestion that one might usefully start with a sociological distinction, used for instance in feminist writings, to put across the difference with the traditional approach.

Feminist writers have drawn attention to the socio-linguistic processes by which people are *constituted* as 'subjects' or as 'objects'. Dubious concepts like 'modes of subjectivity' can be avoided in expounding the distinction by favouring such notions as 'point of view', 'rights to express an opinion in this company on that subject-matter', etc. When a person is constituted as an object their point of view, opinions etc. are downgraded to the status of mere data. They do not enter into the discourse of which they are the subject-matter or the practices of which they are targets as contributors, that is, as complementing, supplementing or disagreeing with the views of those who are taking the active role in the social activities in point. It may even happen that those constituted as objects accept this ascribed status as their natural role. A number of sociological metaphors such as 'domination' and 'false consciousness' are closely related to the idea of the polarized ways in which people can be constituted.

Fully committed 'new' psychologists are concerned to ensure that, even in the psychology laboratory, people are constituted as subjects, that is, taken seriously as contributors to the laboratory discourse as members in good standing of the scientific community that is producing the alleged scientific knowledge supposed to emanate from this or that piece of research. As Shotter and others have long pointed out, this issue is not just a matter of methodology (do you or do you not take accounts seriously?), but also a matter of social morality (are you or are you not treating your fellow human beings with contempt?). It is important to realize that the intentions of a social actor and the upshot of the practices in which he or she willingly engages may be quite disparate, and this is particularly the case in the matter of the moral and intellectual quality of psychological research; the fact that some psychologists' practices can be displayed as downgrading their subjects from true human status does not demonstrate that the perpetrators are villains. Trapped within a paradigm neither psychologist nor subjects have any room for manoeuvre.

I prefer to head this third section of discussion without including either the word 'science' or the traditional terms 'psychology' and 'sociology'. I have to confess that I view them both with considerable scepticism. Since the first attempts to extend what were taken to be the methods of the physical sciences to the study of human affairs, which I suppose really dates from the beginning of the nineteenth century, it seems to me that these and most subsequent versions of the 'human sciences' have been shot through with sophistry and illusion. There has been one notable exception to this generalization, namely most of what has gone under the heading of anthropology, both physical and cultural.

The essays that my friends have so generously contributed to this volume fall into two main groups, and I shall structure my comments around that manner of organization.

1. Methodological matters: Argyle explores the question of the proper technique to adopt in studying social interactions between people. Crowle provides a very deep analysis of what it is reasonable to regard as the subject matter of a psychological investigation. Secord's contribution turns on the distinctions that are needed in the underlying metaphysical framework of human studies to avoid many of the traditional failings to which they have fallen prey. Finally, de Waele explores the main alternative 'rationality' to the syllogistic mode of reasoning and its descendents, a mode more appropriate to following through the threads of human lives and the histories of social orders.

2. Substantive studies: Out of the struggles of the last couple of decades, to see clearly into the heart of human affairs, has finally come a clear enough overall position to merit the claim to be the focus of a movement. This is social constructionism. Minds are social products, though not all individual action arises from social causes. Shotter's essay roams largely over that position. I see the essays of Jensen, Smith, Reynolds, Rodriguez and Taylor as tackling particular topics of interest by reference to that way of thinking. The social constructionist view of the human social umwelt is tied up with the idea that the primary human reality is conversation, in some extended sense. It is not that speaking is a kind of surrogate for wordless actions, but that all human action should be thought of in terms of its contribution to the developing discourse. This idea has recently been extended to the analysis of emotions as human acts, with great fruitfulness (Armon-Jones, 1986). In discussing the symbolic and linguistic universe Smith and Reynolds are, in my terms, exploring the horizons of the human social Umwelt. But at the centre of the ripples of action that pass through that environment are individual people. Jensen develops the idea that the

selves, which are naively taken to be free-standing psychological units, are the result of processes of social production. The essays of Rodriguez and Taylor can also be looked at in terms of the idea of an Umwelt. For Rodriguez it is the mundane world of work which turns out to be double-sided, being an arena of both practical and social activity. Taylor takes us into the penumbra of fictional and imaginary Umwelten with which human beings surround themselves both creatively and pathologically.

When I first began attending classes in social psychology and reading the standard material I must confess to having had a feeling of incredulity. That a field of academic specialism should exist so shot through with conceptual confusions. unexamined assumptions from antique philosophical positions long since demolished, and propounding theories of such gross implausibility seemed to me quite shocking. And this not least because social psychology was presenting, if nothing else, a picture of mankind to itself. If anything was a moral science, it should have been social psychology. Michael Argyle's paper shows how far we have come from those days. In his usual clear way he gives a nice diagnosis of the successive steps back from the morass towards the shore. But though one illusion about people has been dispelled I am struck by the fact that the new wave of social psychologists seems to be backing rapidly into another. Gone are the mindless automata, but they have been replaced by more sophisticated mechanisms whose reactions are the result of even more mysterious inner workings: the flux of 'information processing'. It seems that the academic study of social interaction is still reluctant to close with the actualities of social life, of the social world as discourse. It is still unwilling to ditch the trans-Atlantic connection and abandon the individualism which has set the standard for methodology. (I should emphasize that many North Americans are well aware of the illusion of individualism, but only there is what is essentially a political doctrine entrenched in methodology.) And there is still a confusion between norms and causes. For example, in the social constructionist view, owing a good deal to Wittgenstein, rules are not potent entities driving behaviour but expressions of those normative systems by means of which: (a) whatever happens is interpreted by those involved (and sometimes by the bystanders too); and (b) character is sustained or undermined. Not rules using people to become instantiated, but people using rules to make sense.

I propose to examine closely only three of Michael Argyle's neat little models for exhibiting the form of the successive cognitive social psychologies. In his round-up of research, Argyle argues that each of the models has an application, in that there are different classes of social phenomena to each of which one of his 'models' can be applied. It is worth noticing in passing that the use of the word 'model' to characterize these schemata bears not even a family resemblance to the use made of this term by physical scientists, where it mostly denotes an explanatory analogue of an unknown causal mechanism. In Argyle's use it picks out a schematic theory.

Argyle's Model 1 is the schema S → R, an old friend from the awful past. If there are cases of something perceived being regularly followed by an intelligible reaction then this could be a psychological schema. In real science correlations are signs of causation and hypotheses of causation require informed guesses at causal mechanisms. Psychologically speaking, the only mechanisms that can be invoked in cases where the Model 1 schema is of use must be physiological or a flux of unintended consequences in some social circle to which the actor belongs. The latter possibility never occurred to any psychologist so far as I know when the 'individualist' assumption held sway.

In Model 2 *cog* for 'cognition' enters the story. We immediately come up against a problem. What does 'cog' stand for? 'Cog' also appears in Models 3 and 4 but not, at least on the face of it, in Model 5. To try to get a grip on the meaning of 'cog', and so of what 'cognitive social psychology' might be, one will have to work from the examples cited by Argyle – since he does not give an independent characterization of the central concept. From Model 2 we get 'attribution' (meaning the assigning of responsibility to someone) and 'intention' (meaning the prefigurement of an action or act). Both are, at least in the examples cited, conversational acts. After training in the skills of public discourse people learn to talk to themselves in these and other fashions. In Model 3 'cog' includes beliefs. Some 'S', a catchall sign for all the myriad ways people are impinged upon by their environment, leads both to a reaction and to a cognition. In the cited example the cognition is said to be a belief, e.g. that of a paranoid patient. Unfortunately, the concept of 'belief' is itself troublesome. There has been a tendency to suppose that there are entities, 'beliefs', which lie behind declarations of belief and explain them in much the same way as the kinetic energy of molecules lies behind and explains manifestations of temperature. But in the example of the application of this schema there were only declarations of belief, that is, contributions to a (one-sided?) conversation with a psychologist.

There is a problem too in that the work cited is Zajonc (1980). The conceptual confusions it embodies ought to alert one to the superficiality of the model, and to the problem with 'cog'. In so far as Zajonc reports 'results' they are not psychological. Affective *reactions* are certainly not emotions, though they often play a role in the construction of emotions. It would be quite extraordinary if there were not a range of affective reactions built in to the human organism as the result of organic evolution. Why should one suppose that these were cognitively mediated if ' 'cognitively' means, as it seems to mean in these social psychological contexts, mediated by public or *sotto voce* conversation? But if it were the general information processing theory of brain function that was being invoked by the use of 'cog', it would be another matter. When embedded in very complex social and conversational practices, some reactions become emotions. Some do not.

Model 4 confirms the hypothesis that Argyle is using 'cog' as a synonym for 'conversation'. In that model some presumably physiological process in the brain and central nervous system has resulted in some action, or in some of the cases cited, a social event has placed certain exigencies in the way of the embedded actors, who have politely fallen in with the conventions under which events of this kind usually occur. When the unfortunate victims of some of these procedures are confronted with what they have done, now described in another and antithetical rhetoric, they talk their way into a restoration of their own social standing. Argyle quite brutally breaks down the subtlety of many of these techniques of speaking by the use of the catchall phrase 'cognition is a reaction to behaviour'. One also notes with dismay that the work cited is from the most dubious period of trans-Atlantic 'experimentalism'.

Whichever of the models one turns to there emerges the strong impression that 'cog' refers to the occurrence of some kind of discourse. My final step in deconstructing the latest phase of social psychology will be to look at Argyle's Model 5, that for the joint production of a fragment of social life, CIM or the 'coordinated interaction model'. I shall take CIM as a kind of template for the future.

Apart from the theories (= models) progressively introducing cognitivism into social psychology, Michael Argyle's paper surveys a vast amount of material. I would like to concentrate the rest of my remarks on two matters only, which will, I hope, bring out some of the unease I feel at the way things seem to be going. We have already seen that the theoretical concept 'cog' is not univocal in the five models. In a way it is 'present' in Model 1 by virtue of the glaring fact of its absence. In cognitive science proper Model 1 is just the occasion for proposing computer analogues and information processing as the hidden mechanism. But in the other models 'cog' appears mainly as a synonym for acts of speaking, for discourse. But sometimes it seems to be referring to a pre-Wittgensteinian universe of fictitious mental entities such as beliefs and motives. As we have seen, these can be parsed out and all that needs to be said can be expressed in terms of the concept of conversation. In the old social psychology there was not enough mind. In the new there threatens to be far too much.

But now conversation cannot itself be something to be understood under the coordinated interaction model (CIM) because it *is* that model. By that I mean that so far as anyone has ever been able to ascertain, there are only two human realities: physiology and discourse (conversation) – the former an individual phenomenon, the latter collective. If 'cog' boils down to a synonym for conversation, then individual bits of cognition are secondary phenomena, detached and perhaps abstracted from the basic reality which is collective. We can see this vividly if we try to lay down the conditions for the existence of a simple speech act, say a declaration of love. These speech acts occur only in those societies whose cultures recognize the phenomenon. It has no serious role in Islam, for instance. A speaker utters his phrases but unless they are taken up by the target of his ardour they have no existence as speech acts. An insult is hardly that unless the victim is aware that the phrase is derogatory. The logical subjects of speech acts are *always* multiple. When individual people learn the game of speaking for an audience of one the multiplicity is, of course, notional. But we need a complex grammar as exemplified in such expressions as 'I chided myself', since the speech act of chiding is completed only if the intentions of the speaker are matched by the uptake of the hearer. In general, these intentions and uptakes are not hidden subjective states but are themselves conversational acts within the public world.

But my second set of reflections takes me much deeper into the metaphysical background of Michael Argyle's programme, and comes very close to the source of my unease. First consider the 'application test' for the viability of any piece of research. This is laid out in causal terms, as if there were an end-state to be achieved and the research revealed the causes of states of that type. Applications consist in so acting as to activate the causes, and then – hey presto – the desired states will follow. This is a very odd way of glossing the matter and its oddness comes through very clearly when we find that in applying these 'results' we do such things as teaching someone a new concept, inaugurating them into a new conversational practice, a new style of self-presentation and so on. The result is a smoother-running social world, that is, a world of conversations which do not lead into knots, blind alleys, repetitious circles, and so on. But this is not an *effect* of the training, in any but a highly metaphorical sense. It is the actual performance of that which the person has been trained to do. This is not the sense in which the cause–effect relation might be found exemplified in a chemical synthesis or in the behaviour of an electrical circuit. 'By not smashing your racket into the ground Mr McEnroe you will have the effect of winning your game.' Enough said!

Generally, throughout the 'new' social psychology there runs a thread of confusion, continuous with a similar muddle to be found in the old. It is a confusion between causal necessity and moral obligation. Was it because the good Samaritan caught a glimpse of himself in some wayside pool about twenty seconds before he came across the wounded traveller that caused him to cross the road? (If Mother Teresa had ever heard of Duval and Wicklund and their extraordinary account of 'helping behaviour' I am sure she would have boxed their ears!) The point of the story has remained the same for a couple of thousand years. There is a moral obligation to help the injured. It is no excuse to plead that one had not received that jolt of self-awareness that seems to be needed among the students of such and such university to take action. I must say that whenever I come across this washing out of the demands of a moral order I feel a sense of moral outrage. Social psychology of that sort strikes me as a profoundly immoral enterprise. The social world is structured as a moral order. Or better – since the displacement of moral issues by techniques of management would lead to a unified moral universe – one should say that there are many social worlds structured by very diverse moral orders.

At last to the research on happiness. The first point to make is that 'happiness' is a concept embedded in a very complex semantic field along with 'contentment', 'satisfaction', 'gloating', 'relief', 'amusement', 'ecstasy', 'fun', 'joy' and lots of unpleasant feelings, emotions and moods as well. I do not find a thorough exploration of this semantic field in the writings on happiness. Is it a generic concept comprising some of the above list? Or is it one among them? Or does it function in both ways?

Let us go one stage deeper. The whole array of concepts under or cognate with 'happiness' are one and all loaded with moral weight, and differently loaded at different times and in different social conditions. ('Happiness is a warm gun' . . .?) The principle 'Have technique; willing to apply it' simply ignores the 150 years of profound discussion around the merits of the varieties of utilitarianism and of all those opposed to deontological positions. J. S. Mill realized that there is a profound paradox at the heart of a 'happiness' morality, that implicit in Argyle's warmhearted efforts to cheer everyone up by pressing the causal buttons that will bring a smile to every face. Isn't it better to be Socrates dissatisfied than a pig satisfied? Or is pushpin as good as Pushkin?

Quite apart from the perennial confusion between causal and moral necessity, there is another long-revealed but still ignored flaw in much of the work Argyle cites, for instance that of Rubin (1970). Someone who did not look more warmly on the good of others would not count as being in love. This is a conceptual, not a causal necessity. There are many cases of semantic tautologies masquerading as substantive results and indeed that particular muddle has been pointed out as long ago as 1966 by A. R. Louch.

One final worry – many of the alleged 'facts' cited by Argyle are drawn from the published writings of authors like Bem (and, as I have already mentioned, Zajonc). Many of these writings have been deconstructed (for instance, I have myself had a close look into the inner workings of the Duval and Wicklund corpus). When taken apart, it becomes quite clear that they are not reports of discoveries of scientific laws or even empirical generalities. They are often reflections of local cultural norms, perhaps so local as to be indexical of the very 'laboratory' in which these strange occasions were enacted. Too much must not be made of such writings. Even in the physical sciences, as Latour and Woolgar (1979) have shown, there is a degree of indexicality that is deeply covered over by the rhetorical devices characteristic of scientific discourse.

If, as one might say, Argyle's 'models' represent the ultimate stretching of the old methodology and metaphysics, the papers of Crowle, Secord and de Waele represent the first stirrings of something radically new. Once the concept of 'person' replaces that of 'subject', with all the connotations so comprehensively spelled out by Secord, two radical changes in procedure are inevitable. Persons are individuals in the radical sense that they are Leibnizian monads, obeying the principle of the identity of indiscernibles. Numerical difference entails qualitative difference. In so far as social psychologists are studying persons then some measure of idiography *must* be introduced. The question is, how much and relative to what matters? De Waele and I in our 1979 paper simply took for granted a domain of idiography and then drew the methodological consequences. The beauty of Crowle's paper is that he has identified some main patterns of idiography. But the introduction of the concept of 'person' has another profound effect on methodology. Persons are not automata but moral beings and, as Secord shows, their actions are tied in with conceptions of moral responsibility. From this it follows that human actions, as the actions of persons, are defined only within some or other moral order. In short, we cannot even begin to say what the phenomena of social life are unless we have a clear conception of the local moral order in terms of which they are defined as having this or that moral quality.

Though Crowle begins his paper by citing the utterance of 'IDKWIDI' by deviants, it is of course a remark very widely used by everyone. Sometimes it *is* used to escape from a predicament, but more often it is a mark of just that problem that Crowle's deviants find themselves facing. Crowle's first move is to suggest that his characters do not 'know the formula that links [their] actions with [their] circumstances', but this interim hypothesis is quickly discarded because there may be no such formula. As he points out, the ANOVA [analysis of variance design] pattern of experimental manipulation may be inapplicable not just for moral reasons but because the degree of idiographic diversity among people is usually too great. A nice touch in the paper is to think of the social and material circumstances of someone's life as replete with 'attack' variables, while he or she is protected by attributes Crowle calls 'defence' variables, which are all the time tending to be undermined. We recognize a very old schema here, the traditional Christian conception of the moral life: the world, the flesh and the Devil, on the one side, with prayer and the Church resisting, on the other. It is the plot of the medieval morality play. This for me is the strongest possible recommendation, since I have little doubt that medieval Christianity gave us as powerful a social psychology of deviance for its time as anything currently on offer does for ours. A person's actions are intelligible only in terms of the pattern of attack and defence which has unfolded in his or her actual life. Some level of generality is possible. For instance, Crowle sketches six possible large-scale patterns. It would be very interesting if these patterns could be tested out against the assisted autobiographies created by de Waele and his team in Brussels.

Among the very many insights and suggestions with which Secord's paper is richly endowed the most poignant is a description and diagnosis of the struggle that has been put up by the old guard to preserve the implausible psychology of 'subjects', while each refinement to the old methods and assumptions lets in more and more of the conceptual consequences of a fully 'person'-oriented human science. The extensive revision and elaboration of cognitive dissonance research has not only transformed the concept by the 'death of a thousand qualifications'. It has also introduced considerations that would have been unthinkable in the old paradigm, in particular contextuality. The subject as isolated auto-maton has virtually disappeared from this research. I admire Secord's restraint in forebearing to say 'I told you so!'

Among the many changes that go along with taking persons and their actions as the subject-matter of social psychology, one of the most im-portant is the shift from attempting to study abstract entities like 'disson-ance' or 'bystander effect' or 'the risky shift' to a methodology that focuses on situated human action, concrete activities.

But the change of most profound consequence is the seeping in of the admission that people are moral beings, and that issues of moral responsi-bility are usually paramount in what they do. Thus all actions are embed-ded in moral orders, local systems of obligation and duty with associated valuation criteria, all tied in with conceptions of the propriety and virtue of one's self and one's associates as persons.

All this shows that merely reforming one's method – for instance, taking the participant's accounts into consideration as contributions to the analy-sis of the results of some contrived or real-life social event – is not enough.

As Secord points out, the misunderstandings of our advocacy of account analysis have been both frequent and instructive. There must also be a reform of the metaphysics. And this is just what has been happening with the intrusion of the person concept into recent social psychology.

But there is more to it, and I would like to highlight another of Secord's important observations. Once one starts on this kind of reform the concept of 'action' is also modified. How are actions to be described? It is not enough to include the intentions of the actor and the complementary understandings of the other people involved. The moral quality of actions must also be included, since the persons who engage in them are, as has been amply demonstrated, deeply engaged in issues of personal responsibility. This was the dimension that was so plainly lacking in Milgram's 'experiments'. Neither he nor his assistants paid any serious attention to the moral order of the events that he was actually creating, only to a fictitious moral order presupposed by certain prior conceptions as to what the people were doing – namely, that they were obeying.

One last point: it is very pleasing to see Secord warning our colleagues that our proposals, first formulated in 1972, and refined and extended over the intervening years, are radically different from any form of phenomenology. Our hermeneutics is a system of interpretative practices for a public world, and we see the subjectivity of individuals as a detached and partially fenced-off abstraction from that world. This insight is commensurate with the positions of both Wittgenstein and Vygotsky. It is not at all close to the conception of subjectivity of Husserl.

In many of the contributions to this volume antitheses and antagonisms are described that are important parts of the dynamics of social life. For instance, in Crowle's development of the consequences of taking a declaration of 'IDKWIDI' seriously, the life structures he sketches come alive through the dialectic between attacking 'variables', defensive 'variables' and underminings. There is no way in which a linear conception of causality could be applied to his six generic life-forms. We must be grateful to de Waele and Gorren for their attempt at a thorough analysis of the grammar of the dialectic relation. The ubiquity of the 'action and reaction' dynamics is perhaps underemphasized in their paper. A moving electron produces a field with which it 'dialectically' interacts. The attack 'variables' that impinge on someone are transformed by the growth or decline of his or her defence 'variables', and these in turn are transformed by those promptings of the Devil that Crowle calls 'underminings'. Again in the context of a general 'constructionist' social psychology the Crowlian 'variables' can be mapped on to the collective/individual polarity, since what are for this or that individual defensive capabilities are, in their origin for him or her, appropriations from the social matrix. The most general form that this polarity has taken can be found in the writings of Giddens and Bhaskar in which it appears as the thesis of structuration (duality of structure). In becoming people, human beings appropriate structure from the social Umwelt and, so structured, produce an Umwelt that realizes structures akin to those from which the individual's organization arose in the first place.

As with all logics, conceived as the grammars of specialist discourses, only time will tell. But the point is not, so I hope, to provide us with a kind of algorithm for 'doing dialectics'; but rather to create a means of presenting very clearly the underlying skeleton of a kind of discourse. Whatever may be the defects of logicism as a *theory* of language or of mathematics or of the conditions of meaning, a logicist approach to grammar does bring out those aspects of the structures of discourses that may never have been specifically attended to before. This is particularly evident in de Waele and Gorren's demonstration that the negation of the contrary of the thesis appears in every step of a dialectical development.

Turning now to substantive approaches to the problems of understanding social life, I want to comment first on Shotter's very thorough discussion. This sets the scene for the kinds of studies that would be counted as legitimate from our point of view. I want to use his presentation and resolution of the tension that he discerns between realism in the two contexts of physics and psychology to state my own point of view more clearly. This is the proper place to undertake that task since I do not think that my ontology differs in essentials from that which John Shotter has been evolving over the last twenty years or so.

As I now see it, the only sustainable variety of realism for the physical sciences can be characterized in the following way:

1. There is a world, which exists independently of human beings. It is at best partially available to us as an object for portrayal and manipulation, that is, as an Umwelt.
2. In the ultimate stages of the hierarchical development of the physical sciences we have passed beyond what is available to us via Gibsonian 'direct perception' to the affordances of that World.
3. We know that these are the affordances of an independent reality because the objects in our human umwelten are only so far malleable to human manipulation.

The cognate realist stance with respect to social and psychological studies can be expressed in the following way:

1. There is a species-wide and history-long Conversation, only partially available to individual human beings, as their social Umwelten. But

• these Umwelten are structured for each of us by local moral orders, that is, by tacitly accepted systems of rights, duties and obligations, fixing the roles of contributors to this or that conversation.

2. In the ultimate stage of the development of the reflexive study of human life we pass beyond the investigation of those language games which are transparent to any one of us, to the open set of possibilities that are the affordances of the Conversation.

3. The Conversation is only *so far* amenable to the influence of individual speakers.

And we must add that the physical *sciences* which, moment by moment, fix the horizon of our language games (including, of course, those directed to the modifications of matter), that is, set limits to our Umwelten, are themselves part of the Conversation. As such its community of speakers and writers carry on their activities within a moral order.

Not only are these characterizations isomorphic to one another, but, as I tried to show in *Varieties of Realism*, the former is comprehended under the latter.

Shotter was right to worry about the consequences of adopting the concept of 'rule' as the main explanatory device for a psychology in which the social dimension was to be fully incorporated. I too began with the feeling that in that concept we had found something which could function to pick out the 'powerful particulars' of the human world. But very early on in my reflections on the use of this concept I ran into a debate with my then pupil, the late Michael Brenner. He soon wanted to reject the use of the concept of a rule because, for him, it carried the implication of a rigid and fixed control of reality. But Secord and I had never intended the concept to be taken in that way.

Returning to Wittgenstein's writings, it soon became clear to me that rules fixed what was to count as an X, and not as causal agents in the production of Xs. Rules were formal causes, not efficient causes. The role of a rule is like this: A wants to do something that is to *count as*, say, a congratulation. His resources for doing this – (which I then came to call a social cognitive matrix) consisting of rule-clusters and situational definitions – are available as a repertoire of means for fixing on the appropriate move, or for correcting and bringing into order what has already been done. The question of what causes movements and noises to occur and what endows them with this or that significance are separate questions. Rules do not use people; it is people who use rules. But that was still not quite right. Again Shotter and I moved along paths that were both parallel and converging (non-Euclidean, of course) to the position that I think we now both hold. We hope we have a way of bringing out the cash value, so to say, of the rather vague and global exposition of realism in psychology with which I began this section.

We share the view that ontologically the Conversation is the primary human reality. The potent 'things' in the human world are not people but the things they say, the component speech-acts of the conversations that are the tesserae of the mosaic of human converse. People are secondary constructions. Their powers are both given to them and delimited by the range of speech-acts (and other potent social displays) available to them, not as unique individual people, but by virtue of their locations in this or that moral order or orders. In our book of 1972 Secord and I were still thinking in terms of the traditional metaphysics, in which the ontology of human studies is grounded in human beings. But I have come to see, in a way similar to Shotter, that the analogy with the ontology of the physical universe ties people to places as locations, and ties speech-acts to things. People, as agents, are secondary existents. What X, Y or Z can do effectively is fixed (loosely) by their locations in moral orders. Human life is lived with respect to two intransigent, imperfectly knowable 'realities'. As embodied beings we are located in physical space-time and have such powers as our material embodiment endows us with. But as psychological and social beings we are locations in another world. Potent things exist at each of us. Reduction of one of these worlds to another is impossible for a much deeper reason than those Secord gives. The ontologies do not mesh, since what are things (the basic particulars) in A are punctiform locations in B, while what are basic particulars in B are at best attributes in A. I say 'at best' because it is not so much the acts that are properties of persons considered as organisms as the actions that carry those acts. Actions become acts only when standing in this or that relation to other acts, and are thus essentially part of a social world.

The radical diversity of our point of view does show up sharply against the well intentioned but limited 'realism' advocated by Manicas and Secord in their important paper of 1983. Their realism is grounded in an array of persons as the basic particulars and hence there is a touch of that closet individualism that Shotter is rightly wary of. Nevertheless Manicas and Secord are, contrary to the way Shotter presents their views, right to insist that the object of research ought to be the resources, the 'grammars' in Wittgenstein's way of expressing these matters, that are any individual's means for action. These resources are available to someone only with respect to how that person is located at that moment in a relevant moral order. This actually fits very well with an important observation of Shotter's, that in becoming persons human beings have to learn not what is the case but what should be so. In my Wittgensteinian terms, they must acquire grammars of action, that is, a grasp of what counts as this or that social act and the proper means of performing it. Learning to be a natural scientist is also learning a set of just such grammars.

In underlining John Shotter's final remarks on the turn to ethical logistics, one can recall Lucas's comments on the proper concept of objectivity. A conversational matrix with its associated moral order, is the same from all points of view, that is, from whatever location within it one views the practice. Both chairman and secretary speak according to the rules that determine what counts as a contribution to the discussion. Knowing one's way about the social Umwelten is to know both the geography and to what areas, as a person of this or that sort, one has right of access. All this is rather abstract, but there have been many successful applications of something like this way of looking at things human. I turn now to some examples.

The conceptual framework developed by Shotter, Secord, myself and others, was, so to say, crying out to be applied. One had to show how adopting that framework would facilitate the understanding of human life. It seemed to me that there were, in principle, three ways in which one lived as a human being. One had a *social mode of being* defined through one's relations to others in all sorts of joint activities. Then one had a *personal mode of being* defined by one's relation to oneself, through which one existed for oneself as an individual. Finally, one had a *physical or material mode of being* defined by one's relationship, as embodied, to the material world and to others as embodied beings. The thesis of social constructionism requires that the two latter modes of being be demonstrable as subtypes of the former. In brief, the concept of oneself and the concept of one's body are both social constructions. The final set of essays on which I wish to comment, those by Rodriguez, Smith, Jensen, Taylor and Reynolds, are constributions, or can be read as contributions, to the elaboration of each of these applications.

For a human individual to exist as a social being it is necessary for that individual to have acquired a certain corpus of knowledge in the sense of skill or 'know how'. Some of this knowledge can be expressly formulated as rules (or the equivalent), through which norms are displayed and by citation of which those norms are maintained. But as O'Neil, Morgan and I showed in our 1977 study of nicknames there are many norm-maintaining practices other than explicit citation of rules. Social beings can lead a social life, that is can be competent contributors to ordered and structured collective episodes of social acts, only if they are, so to say, reasonably well informed. The emphasis in trying to construct explanations of the genesis of such episodes in which social being is realized must be on formal causes, the structural templates of subsequent order, rather than on efficient causation. I remain sceptical of the project of finding any significant regularities in the efficient causes of social action, and Crowle's demonstration of the ubiquity of the propriety of crying 'IDKWIDI' further substantiates that feeling. But that is not enough. We need some general hypothesis of a motivational system through which people are bound into the various projects that constitute social and collective action. A wide-ranging course of reading ethnographies and histories suggested to me that it was at least worth trying out the idea that the one consistent theme to be picked out of a huge mass of descriptive material was the search for honour and reputation, and the ritual means by which, in various societies and moieties of societies, this was achieved. From Goffman I got the idea of a moral career, the life-course of a human being seen against the background of the 'honour' system of his or her cultural milieu.

This idea seemed to clash sharply with Marxism, the most powerful general theory of history, with its emphasis on the dominance in human social arrangements of the social system of the production of the material means of life, and the dialectical processes of its development. Certainly as a theoretical account of human motivation, as a social psychology, Marxism was extremely implausible. Yet one would be unwise to deny the enormous influence on human life of the way we scratch a living. (Ironically, the 'New Right' are as devoted adherents of the idea of the economic determination of social order as are the 'Old Left'!)

Goffman's depiction of the micro-world of small-scale human institutions struck me as entirely convincing, yet it was not embedded in a larger point of view. It was the work of an observational genius. But without the beady eye of the man himself how could the Goffmanesque revelations of moral careers be made to crystallize out of the complex and often incompletely specific and indeterminate flux of human social life? The final step for me was the discovery of the sociology of Thorstein Veblen, the sociology of emulation. Social being, it occurred to me, was defined by the location of an individual human being within *two* evolving and interacting social structures. I called these the 'expressive order', that cluster of social arrangements in which honour and reputation are created, lost and maintained; and the 'practical order', those social arrangements by which the means of material existence are generated. It seems to me that every human action has to be considered as having two aspects. There is its contribution to the moral career of the actor (and, in strongly collectivist societies, that of his or her relevant group). This is the expressive aspect. But there is also its contribution to the maintenance of life itself. This is the practical aspect. There is a dialectic, but not of the sort Marx supposed. The dialectic is between the sometimes contradictory demands that the expressive and practical orders place on historically situated actors. The essays of Smith and Rodriguez are further applications of this dichotomous distinction to some institutions of modern life, institutions that are not the usual fodder for sociological study.

There are a number of refinements of the idea of the duality of orders sketched above to be found in Smith's paper. In my way of expounding the distinction I had assumed that what Thomas (1918–20) called 'the situation' could be taken as a prior given. But in Smith's accounts of auctions the very point of the institution is to resolve ambiguities, not only as to what something is worth, but as to what its 'station' is in some symbolic universe. And that of course has to do with who is seen to take part in the auction and what effect on his or her location in the expressive order the act of bidding has.

The duality of social orders is nicely illustrated by Smith in his analysis of what is achieved by an art auction. We succeed in doing something in the practical order, namely moving a painting from a stately home to a museum, and we also succeed in enhancing or diminishing every participant's standing *vis-à-vis* some pre-existing status structure. Smith might have gone one step further at this point. Seen as a status maintaining or transforming activity, an auction has the same social force as more overt ceremonials, say those in which outstanding scholars are given honorary degrees. Looked at in this light, the *ceremonial* aspects of the auction as a formal episode with an act-action structure would be well worth studying.

I was very interested in Smith's distinction between the 'market' and the 'auction'. The market counts as a pre-existing practical order into which the 'thing' in question, be it a consignment of fish or the cocoa futures, are inserted. The anonymity of the traders reflects the fact that in the market the practical order dominates the expressive. In the world of art auctions the dominance is reversed. In another study of an apparently practical activity, the pure-bred beef business, Smith (1983) has shown that almost none of the actions performed by those engaged in that business, which looks on the surface like 'farming', could be explained without recourse to assumptions about expressive motivations, and without the interpretation of all the material things involved as symbolic entities having their meaning only as they have a role within the processes by which honour and respect are claimed, assessed and confirmed or disconfirmed in that tightly closed world.

Rodriguez's researches add two other dimensions to the study of the interaction of the expressive and practical orders. There are the transformations of an institution under external forces and there are the consequences of realizing the collective nature of the honour system. The '*expíritu telefónico*' is a phenomenon in which the honour of every individual is bound up with the honour of the institution itself. This appears in the rhetoric which draws on the three *collective* pillars of pre-democratic Spanish society, the Church, the Army and the family, as familiar exemplars with which to express the inner meaning of being a true *'telefónista'*. The attitude of 'the show must go on' reminds one forcefully of the mythology of the stage where some of the rhetoric, namely the constant references to the family and the figures of the family, is the same. In reading Rodriguez's summary of his massive study I was very struck by the extent to which the expressive order created by being a 'telephone person' was consciously attended to by the rank and file of employees when coping with the expansion and technical transformation of the company. Again, as in Smith's study, I missed any reference to the ceremonial devices by which position in the practical order is expressed. My hypothesis on reading through the research summary is that the mode of expression is by translation of the status acquired by service, etc. back into the practical order, so that that order is seen by the employees themselves as the expression of their *honor y dignidad*. In this respect the *'espíritu telefónico'* is very different from the moral order obtaining among the various moieties of the scientific community, at least in Western Europe. To translate one's standing as a scientist into commercial terms has been, since the scientific establishment looked askance at Lord Kelvin, continuously disparaged in the history of recent science. It would be very interesting to know if other state monopolies, such as the postal and the telephone systems of some other member states of the European Community, were revealed as such clearly defined worlds within worlds. Perhaps it was the unique social and political history of Spain in the twentieth century that had to be the breeding ground for so interesting an institution.

The central topic of the study of personal being must be how one exists for oneself and how that mode of existence is possible. Placing the emphasis on discourse allows us to refine the question to this: how can one be a subject of predication for oneself when it is that very self that is performing the acts of self attribution? It cannot be because one discovers oneself. Philosophers have long been aware that there can be no introspective route to self-awareness in that sense. I can become more self-aware in the sense of knowing more of my attributes, my strengths and weaknesses, but that is not at all to become more aware of that which has these attributes. Of course, there may be nothing which has these attributes except the public person. But that intuition, sound as it may be, does not capture the ground of the practices of self-commentary and self-awareness. From a social constructionist viewpoint the nub of the matter must lie in exploring the hypothesis that one learns reflexive practices of self-commentary on the model of the way others comment upon one as a public person. But while my public person is a readily available entity, empirically given to those others, its subjective analogue, the self, is not so given. For me, my self must be a theoretical entity which is *given* only as a theoretical concept. This is the view shared by Jensen and myself, and it has a certain similarity with the account of the self offered by D. C. Dennett. At least one major difference is that Dennett does not include an account of the origin of the concept of self in his treatment, its origin in a collective practice. He has no idea of psychological symbiosis.

Jensen is concerned to develop a deeper explanation of the origin of the concept of self and an enrichment of what that concept might be. He begins with a critical commentary on Dennett's position and uses that as a springboard to bring out certain deficiencies in my more complex account. In effect Jensen argues that my use of the concept of psychological symbiosis to point to the role of social practices in the manufacture of selves is too simplistic; and that it actually requires a further step which elaborates the account in an important way, namely in drawing attention to an overlooked moral dimension. Via this route we come back to something like Shotter's 'ethical logistics'.

Of the three main roles for a 'transcendental unity of apperception' in the organization of an individual's sense of themselves, namely as centre of conscious awareness, as source of action and as subject of autobiography, Dennett concentrates only on the latter. Though he makes no refence to the pioneering work of De Waele on the empirical study of autobiographical practices, he reaches the same conclusion. As my story of and for myself unfolds, so my self becmes more determinate. In my terms, my roles as actor and as spectator become more clearly identified. Furthermore Dennett rightly seems to be keeping in mind the difference, usually ignored by academic psychologists, between answers to two questions. 'What attributes do I have?' defines the cluster of reflexive beliefs that are my self-concept. Answers to the question 'What *am* I to be able to have such attributes and such beliefs about them?' defines the logical subject of those beliefs, the self. My answer to the latter question is more complex than Dennett's. It is that which is conscious, that which is capable of action and that which accumulates a history of itself. It is not an object to be discovered, but a concept to be acquired, in the (growing) possession of which I, as a person, acquire the capacity to structure my experience according to a hierarchy of personal unities. The differences from Dennett are thus far two-fold. For me there is a triple unity of unities and for both Jensen and myself there is the aetiological priority of the public person over the private self.

It is in the aetiological aspect that I differ most strongly from Dennett. Before I go on to comment on Jensen's criticisms of Dennett's views and his proposals for remedying their shortcomings I propose to elaborate a little further on my own misgivings. There are three aspects to the importance of psychological symbiosis as the aetiological antecedent of selfhood.

1. It is in being treated as a person, in public practices, that a nascent human being acquires the concept of personal unity that we have called the 'self'. The point is that the apprentice person learns to construct him or herself analogously to the way they are constructed as persons by their relevant community. For instance, the particular way that responsibility for actions is taken by a fully determinate person will reflect, according to this view, the way responsibility is assigned in the community. It may be predominantly individual or predominantly collective. In the latter mode responsibility is assigned to the family of the actor, or even to his or her ancestors.
2. The growth of the powers to do these things as an autonomous individual, of the power to deploy effectively the local concept of self, emerges out of psychological symbiosis in which others do these things (for instance, recalling a personal history) for the neonate and novice human being. These others deploy the local concept of person.
3. The main medium for the symbiotic relationship and its transformation into a set of individual and autonomous capacities, are the language games of attribution and their local grammars.

My differences with Dennett amount really to a complaint that his treatment is overly simplistic, and my remedy is supplementation. But Jensen's criticism goes deeper. He points out that Dennett's account leaves no room for the phenomenon of self-deception. Whatever tale the individual tells him or herself is the source of that level of determinateness of self. This means that in Dennett's scheme there is no place for any qualitative distinction between selves, particularly when the quality in question is moral worth. This is not just a matter of telling a tale in which an empirically false concept is deployed. I may disclose that I have a multitude of false beliefs about my levels of comprehension, power and autonomy, the self-deceptions of a Sartrean victim of *mauvaise foi*. But I may also disclose a defective concept of self, for instance as passive, unreflective, dependent, etc. This too is capable of expression in Sartrean terms, but now as a normative judgement. There are better or worse selves according to some standard. This criticism is just as telling against my more complex account of the self-as-a-theoretical-concept as it is against Dennett's oversimplified one.

However, Jensen's remedy can, I think, only be applied to an account at my level of complexity. Jensen emphasizes that the relationships summed up in a relation of psychological symbiosis provide a further model or ideal which could (or should) be the source of the extra element in the account that will sustain the distinction between better and worse selves. Willy-nilly, the senior member of the dyad takes responsibility for the junior member, and necessarily abdicates some of his or her initial power in the face of the display of acquired person presentational skills by the junior member, in particular demonstrations of mastery of the local self concept. Does the responsibility of the senior extend so far as to sustain the final autonomy of the junior member as a fully-fledged person? Clearly, Jensen holds that the clash between power over and responsibility for the development of the autonomy of the junior member *ought* to be resolved in favour of the latter.

This is not a naturalistic ethical principle, that is, it will not take effect automatically as a consequence of the given natures of the beings involved. For instance, it is not uncommon that the sense of responsibility that someone may have for certain others is so great that he or she hangs on to the symbiotic relation tenaciously. Notoriously, this leads to a pathology of self in the junior member. Translated into political terms, the pretensions of an overweening bureaucracy can lead to a pathology of the citizenship of the members of such a state. Of course it is well recognized that the tendency to prolong the dependence of symbionts is itself a mark of a pathological personality in the senior member.

Thus Jensen is right to point out that despite the greater – dare I say it – sophistication of my account over Dennett's, we both fall into the same error, namely a failure to take account of the need to find a location for the normative concept of better and worse selves. I think that there is one aspect of the argument in the fourth part of my *Social being* that comes close to addressing the issue, albeit in another context. There I argued that in a social world in which the primary social and psychological reality was conversation there was necessarily one inalienable right that must accrue to any creature that purports to be a human being, a member of some society or other. That right is the right to be heard as a contributor to the conversation that defines the social moiety to which that putative social actor belongs. The pathological condition of a psychologically symbiotic dyad occurs when the senior member persistently talks for the junior member, performing all the necessary psychological acts to sustain an appearance of personhood vicariously. On our view this is a kind of ultimate evil.

Our third mode of being is physical or material. Philosophers have used a variety of conceptual models to demonstrate that the concept of personal identity, at least as it is incorporated in *our* conceptual system, necessitates the assumption of bodily continuity. Just as personal being is tied in with social practices in which a human being is treated as a transcendental unity with respect to experience, action and belief, so too that physical mode of being is tied in with bodily individuality and continuity. As personal beings we exist both as ourselves and in relation to ourselves. So too as embodied beings we exist both as our bodies and in relation to our bodies. It is I who looses weight, but it is my body which I subject to the discipline of a regime.

In discussions of the mind–body problem, both ancient and modern, and independently of the way a philosopher resolves this ancient duality, it is the 'mind' side that usually goes on to receive the lion's share of philosophical attention. The human body may be set aside as just another corporeal being, a kind of thing. I am very far from taking that line with the concept of the human body. There are at least four contexts in which human embodiment offers problems of great philosophical interest. First, there is a range of ethical problems concerning how our bodies should be treated and disposed of, which are now comprehended in medical ethics and in the philosophy of feminism. Closely tied in with these questions is the larger issue of whether there are different kinds of human bodies, differently located in moral orders. Should the possession of one kind of body rather than another determine one's fate as a social being, for instance? Then, there are questions about the evaluation and treatment of bodily states, the boundaries of concepts like health and illness, in which the body is the central concept of concern. Thirdly, there is a range of problems that arise when we consider the practices of those who treat their bodies as art objects to be refined, remoulded and competitively displayed. Finally, there is the way in which the body and its parts are both symbolic and conceptual entities and attract their own peculiar symbolic codes. These matters are in the end tied back to questions of the evaluation of the body and its parts.

The issues raised by David Taylor and Vernon Reynolds bring to the fore two questions: how far is what we are and what we undergo bodily, socially constructed? There are evidently two levels at which there are likely to be influences of social definitions on that which we take naively to be an objectively given physical state or process. Since the science of biology is the creation of a social order with its own internal structure and imperatives, biological 'facts' like all other matters of the natural sciences are partially socially constructed. It was an important aspect of my recent attempt to get realism right that this insight into science should be incorporated and its influence felt and properly assessed. Indeed, the great Ludwig Fleck initiated the critical social analysis of scientific work with a study of the history of a disease, syphilis. But syphilis exists as an objective physical condition, albeit embedded in complex social processes. As

Taylor reminds us, there are bodily conditions that have no other existence except as social constructions. This not quite right, because there are natural phenomena incorporated in the constructions, but, in the course of this incorporation, their nature is wholly transformed. I would like briefly to summarize Taylor's paper to highlight the *social* nature of the construction processes he describes so vividly. Not only are they social in the sense of pertaining to collectives. They are also particularly striking examples of psychological symbiosis.

Step 1 in Taylor's analysis ('belief') involves drawing our attention to a pure case of psychological symbiosis. The belief in persecution is not individual, though it emanates from one man. It is a collective cognitive state engendered and sustained within a closed social group by symbiosis, in which the father of the family thinks the paranoic thoughts for everyone.

Step 2 in Taylor's analysis ('hysteria') is the point at which he proposes a biological Darwinian model for the existence in human beings of a tendency towards a particular kind of response to situations of great danger. The argument is of a familiar kind in which analogy is used to support homology. In battle hysteria stunned stupor and frantic and disorderly behaviour are juxtaposed. The evolutionary advantages of the former are used to account for the continued presence in embodied human beings of the biological basis of the latter. But, argues Taylor, in the human case alternative hypotheses to explain this response multiply. We have had demonic possession, and not always as an alternative, some form of sickness, and now we have allergies. But the trick is this: even seeking medical hypotheses and conducting tests to invalidate these claims involves taking them seriously, this confirming the fantasists in their fantasies.

Step 3 in Taylor's analysis ('magic') is to draw our attention to the continuation in the resources of our culture of the animistic idea that there is a proper nature to everything. With the right moves, this nature is controllable. Of course, pan-allergism is just such an animistic belief. But again in the sad, indeed tragic case that he describes for us, it is evident that there is a strongly symbiotic relationship between the various members of the victim's family. In this case it seems to have been the mother who defined the beliefs that were assigned to all the other members of the family.

Taylor's hypothesis is that the 'stupor' reaction can be accessed both from without, in the context of a battle, and from within via a system of beliefs. In both the detailed examples he gives us, the second mode of access is also from without. It is a collectively defined and symbiotically sustained belief system. Perhaps all forms of hysteria are like that.

In Reynolds' paper the direction of the organic analogy is reversed.

Taylor draws on ethology to make determinate a certain range of human phenomena, while Reynolds draws on the corpus of human concepts to make the behaviour of primates intelligible as a way of life. This is a biological use of anthropomorphism we have jointly defended elsewhere. It does allow a biologist to build up an evidential basis for the thesis that there is a continuity between the life-forms of all primates including man. Using the human conceptual system enables one to identify those forms of behaviour which, relative to the characteristics that they take in human life, can be seen as rudimentary. This is no more a case of circular reasoning than is the use of 'particle' concepts in developing a mechanics for electrons. But how does all this bear on the thesis that the human body is largely socially constructed out of much simpler biological materials?

One way of putting that thesis is to extend Reynolds' point that the possession of language as a symbolic system allows human beings to create representations of states of affairs that do not now currently exist, thus having pasts and futures, autobiographies and intentions and plans. But it also facilitates the reconstruction of material entities to accord with and fit into conceptual frameworks. Perhaps the chimpanzee and the other primates are in a certain sense social constructions too. Once again we can advert to Ludwig Fleck. Syphilis as such and such a condition, testable for by such and such a procedure, is not brought into being by the activities of a thought collective, but it is made epistemically determinate thereby. In a similar way it would be absurd to say that the hairy little friends of Jane van Lawick-Goodall were brought into existence by primatology, but their determinateness as chimpanzees, as we know them now, is surely a social construction, to which she herself, as a member of the relevant thought collective, has been a major contributor. But there is more to this. I was most interested in a recent contribution to the narratological analysis of theorizing in the natural sciences, in which the evolutionary account of the descent of man (and the ascent of woman) was deconstructed to reveal an age old story line, the heroine transcending and overcoming all kinds of difficulties to emerge triumphant in the end. Seeing prefigurements of human life forms in the lives of chimpanzees is a part of that story line. No doubt we did get our bodies from the organic stream of Darwinian evolution, but even in presenting that insight to ourselves we must develop the story in a dramatic form worthy of the subject-matter him/herself!

REFERENCES

Ackermann, R. (1988) *Wittgenstein's City*, Amherst: University of Massachussetts Press.

Aitchison, I. (1985) 'Nothing's plenty: the vacuum in modern quantum theory', *Contemporary Physics* 26, pp. 333–91.

Armon-Jones, C. (1986) 'The social function of emotions'. In R. Harré (ed.) *The Social Construction of Emotions*, Oxford: Basil Blackwell.

Bachelard, G. (1934) *Le Nouvel esprit scientifique*, Paris.

Boyd, R. (1979), 'Metaphor and theory change: what is 'metaphor' a metaphor for?' In A. Ortony (ed.) *Metaphor and Thought*, Cambridge: Cambridge University Press, pp. 365–408.

Brown, H. and Harré, R. (1988) *Philosophical Foundations of Quantum Field Theory*, Oxford: Clarendon Press.

Dennet, D. C. (1978) *Brainstorms*, Hassocks: Harvester Press.

Devitt, M. (1984) *Realism and Truth*, Oxford: Basil Blackwell.

Hacking, I. (1983) *Representing and Intervening*, Cambridge: Cambridge University Press, 1983.

Harré, R. (1979) *Social Being*, Oxford: Basil Blackwell.

Harré, R. (1986) *Varieties of Realism*, Oxford: Basil Blackwell.

Harré, R. and E. Madden (1975), *Causal Powers*, Oxford: Basil Blackwell.

Harré, R. Morgan, J. and O'Neill, C. (1977) London: *Nichnemes* Routledge & Kegen Paul.

Harré, R. and Reynolds, V. (1983) *The Meaning of Primate Signals*, Cambridge: Cambridge University Press.

Harré, R. and Secord, P. (1972), *The Explanation of Social Behaviour*, Oxford: Basil Blackwell.

Harré, R. and de Waele, J. -P. (1979) 'Autobiography as a research method'. In G. P. Ginsberg (ed.) *Emerging Strategies in Social Scientific Research*, Chichester: John Wiley & Sons.

James, W. (1911) *Some Problems of Philosophy*, New York.

Knorr-Cetina, K. (1981) *The Manufacture of Knowledge*, Oxford: Pergamon Press.

Latour, B. and Woolgar, S. (1979) *Laboratory Life*, Los Angeles: Sage.

Lipton, P. (1985) *Explanation and Evidence*, Oxford: Doctoral Dissertation.

Louch, A. R. (1966) *Explanation and Human Action*, Oxford: Basil Blackwell.

Manicas, P. and Secord, P. (1983) 'The implications for psychology of the new philosophy of science', *American Psychologist* 38, pp. 399–413.

Moked, G. (1971), 'A note on Berkeley's corpuscularian theories in *Siris*', *Studies in the History and Philosophy of Science* 2, pp. 257–71.

Nerlich, G. (1976) *The Shape of Space*, Cambridge: Cambridge University Press.

Oddie, B. (1986), 'The poverty of the Popperian programme for truth-Likeness', *Philosophy of Science* 53, pp. 163–78.

Redhead, M. (1988) 'Passion at a distance', ed. J. Cushing, forthcoming.

Rubin, A. (1970) 'Measurement of romantic love', *Journal of Personality and Social Psychology* 16, pp. 265–83.

Shanker, S. (1987), *Wittgenstein and the Turning-Point in the Philosophy of Mathematics*, London: Croom Helm.

Smith, C. S. (1983), 'A case study of structuration: the pure-bred beef business', *Journal for the Theory of Social Behaviour* 30 (1), pp. 3–18.

Thomas, W. I. and Znaniecki, F. (1918–20), *The Polish Peasant in Europe and*

America, New York: Dover.
von Uexküll, J. (1909), *Umwelt und Innenwelt der Tiere*, Springer: Berlin.
Zajonc, R. (1980), 'Feeling and thinking: preferences need no inferences', *American Psychologist* 35, pp. 151–75.

Index